New Frontiers in Asia

THE FAR EAST:

❀ PARADOX ISLE, *by Carol Bache*

❀ GOVERNMENT BY ASSASSINATION,
by Hugh Byas

❀ THE JAPANESE ENEMY: His Power
and His Vulnerability, *by Hugh Byas*

❀ PEOPLES OF SOUTHEAST ASIA,
by Bruno Lasker

❀ JAPANESE MILITARISM: Its Cause
and Cure, *by John M. Maki*

❀ CHINA'S CRISIS, *by Lawrence K. Rosinger*

❀ BATTLE HYMN OF CHINA,
by Agnes Smedley

ALFRED A. KNOPF, Publisher, New York

NEW FRONTIERS IN ASIA

A Challenge to the West

BY

PHILIP JAFFE

NEW YORK : ALFRED A. KNOPF

1945

FIRST EDITION

(((v)))

CONTENTS

New Frontiers in Asia

CHALLENGE TO AMERICA

❁

ONE OF the most striking facts about the American economy during the war years following Pearl Harbor was the attainment of unprecedented prosperity without the adverse features of previous boom periods. On the one hand, there occurred the greatest production era in American history. Unemployment disappeared almost completely; the national income rose to phenomenal heights; and the financial structure of business in general was strengthened, with corporate resources larger than at any time in their history. On the other hand, no runaway inflation developed; the national debt was kept within manageable bounds, subject only to the maintenance of full employment; and the American people accumulated more than sufficient savings to purchase all their requirements when civilian production was resumed.

Thus, during the greatest national crisis in our history, we not only experienced an era of unparalleled prosperity, but at the same time acquired a strong economic base from which to go forward to new heights. Two factors made this possible. One was the physical destruction, in the process of waging war, of more than half our national production. In terms of economics, the war plowed under not only the ever-accumulating surpluses that had plagued our economy in recent years, but so much more than these surpluses that widespread shortages developed. The second factor responsible for our particular era of war prosperity was the active participation of our Government in the planning and controlling of every condition under which our war economy operated. Although wartime controls were not successful in siphoning off all the excess profits and earnings, they did succeed in keeping inflation within bounds and did enable the American people as a whole to accumulate enormous savings for postwar use.

There is as yet no clear picture of what role the American Government will play in economic planning for the future, but the American people are keenly interested in the possibilities suggested by the experience of the war years. They like prosperity; they like full employment; they will even tolerate shortages and inconveniences to obtain these results, provided it does not take a war to make them possible; and they will accept governmental controls if essential to the fulfillment of their hopes. All sections of the American people — industrialists, bankers, managers, workers, farmers, and professionals — share the common hope that our economy in the postwar period will operate at full capacity. Toward the attainment of this goal, innumerable plans have been proposed by both private and governmental agencies. The vast majority of these plans, however, particularly those advanced by private business groups, do not take sufficient cognizance of the basic needs of our economy.

These groups are too easily content with plans for the immediate future only, and are inclined to rely upon individual ingenuity to solve later problems as they arise. They are highly optimistic concerning the possibility of capacity or near-capacity production and employment in the postwar years. But, unfortunately, this optimism is based mainly on three factors that, at best, can provide only a temporary period of prosperity: (1) the domestic demand for a long list of commodities that were not available during the war; (2) the American share in the reconstruction of war-devastated areas, particularly in Europe; and (3) the export of goods to satisfy the large credit balances built up in this country by foreign nations, particularly those of Latin America, because of our inability to export to these countries an amount sufficient to balance our extraordinarily large wartime imports. Undoubtedly, the satisfaction of these three types of demand could, after a short period of reconversion adjustments, produce a period of industrial activity that might take on the characteristics of a boom. But it is equally certain that this period will be relatively short unless long-range plans are made to create a permanent demand for the products of the American economy.

There are those who, for a variety of motives, contend that our domestic market can be expanded sufficiently to maintain a permanent program of full employment by internal measures alone. They propose to increase the earning power of the American people to such a point that its purchasing capacity would equal the value of the national production. But that could be a solution only if the American people were prepared to abolish the profit motive in their economic structure. So long as this motive remains dominant, the simple act of raising wages without regard to prices, profits, and interest rates cannot prevent the inevitable accumulation of surpluses out of profits. Increases in wages must, of course, follow upon increased productive efficiency, if we are to avoid more serious consequences than we have already suffered. The struggle of American labor for higher wages and shorter hours has played the decisive part not only in raising the living standards of organized workers but also in narrowing the gap between production and consumption. But so long as America remains a capitalist economy, that gap cannot be closed entirely even though investors are forced to accept ever lower rates of net profit.

It is true that in the United States there are still some backward and undeveloped areas, notably in the South and Southwest, which could provide limited opportunities for economic expansion. But when one considers that our national income rose from $40 billion in 1932 to $160 billion in 1944, and that we have emerged from the war as a colossal creditor power with huge commodity and capital surpluses, it becomes clear that the development of these backward areas in our own country can provide only a fractional solution of our major problem.

This study, therefore, is based on the premise that, although the United States has emerged from the war with the most developed internal market of any country in the world, this internal market cannot possibly absorb the enormously increased productive capacity of American industry and agriculture. Furthermore, the United States has become so decisively the chief world source of capital goods and investment funds that our domestic market cannot alone absorb this great accumulation of wealth. Nor can the domestic market of any other highly industrialized nation play more than a minor role. Only the exploitation of new and hitherto undeveloped and under-developed external outlets for capital and industrial goods, can be effective in maintaining the high levels of employment and national income attained during the war.

These "new economic frontiers" can be found in the economically retarded areas of the world whose consuming power has hitherto been severely restricted by poverty and industrial backwardness. These areas possess vast, untapped natural resources and over one-half the population of the world. They constitute huge potential markets for all forms of American goods, provided that they can be helped to develop democratic, modernized, and expanding economies that will raise the living standards and purchasing power of their people. It is a well-known fact that the United States, after the American Revolution, became an ever-expanding and highly profitable market for foreign capital investment. Huge quantities of foreign funds poured into the phenomenal economic growth of our country, and yielded a handsome return to their investors. Furthermore, the development of American resources with the aid of foreign capital served as a powerful stimulus to the concomitant economic growth of Europe. The countries of Asia, Latin America, and Africa can play a similar role for both America and Europe, but on a much wider scale.

The process of developing these countries to the point at which they could become large-scale purchasers of industrial and consumer products would serve to bring about that expansion of world trade which is so essential for the prosperity of the United States and the countries of Europe. For America, the task of supplying the material needs of these backward areas would offer a vitally needed substitute for the war demands that raised our exports to the record level of $1.5 billion a month and enabled us to achieve a national income of $160 billion a year. For the war-torn countries of Europe, the development of such new markets would serve a far more permanently useful purpose than would direct rehabilitation loans, since it would give them new opportunities to sell, and thus increase their ability to buy and pay for the things they need to rebuild their shattered industrial and agricultural systems.

Furthermore, such a program would do more than anything else to free the world from the fetters of exchange controls and other trade restrictions that invariably persist in a contracting or stagnant world economy. It would serve, in fact, as the best possible answer to the difficult and controversial problem of cartels. Cartels, or giant aggregations of monopoly capital, developed historically at a time when the world economy entered a period of contraction and there was no further room for the expansion of free enterprise. They were organized to divide the world into spheres of interest and to control production and prices in order to prevent suicidal competition. Behind them were the most reactionary and oppressive exploiters of our society, who not only utilized the backward feudal and comprador interests in the colonial countries to maintain their power, but also established close alliances with the cartels of Nazi Germany and militarist Japan that helped build up the power of the fascist states.

It must be recognized, however, that it was only because the cartels functioned in an ever-contracting world system of production and distribution that they developed their reactionary and oppressive characteristics. It is therefore not trust-busting or anti-cartel legislation that will effectively eliminate the old-style system of international cartels, but rather the removal of those factors in the world economic order that made cartels a logical development. Certainly, large industrial firms would rather buy and sell in an expanding though competitive market than in a contracting one, even though the latter assured them a higher rate of profit on a limited scale. Faced, for example, with the alternative of doing a fixed billion-dollar annual business at 10% profit or a two-billion-dollar business at 6%, there is little doubt which the average business firm would choose, particularly when the two-billion dollar business has room to grow still bigger.

Some months ago, Mr. Alfred P. Sloan, Jr., of General Motors, told a convention of the National Association of Manufacturers that General Motors was making its postwar plans on the predication of a peacetime national income of $100 billion and that on this basis General Motors was prepared to invest half a billion dollars in new plant and equipment. It may be assumed that Mr. Sloan, having been for so long the successful pilot of the affairs of General Motors, has every reason to believe that his company can make a profit given a national income of $100 billion. However, aside from the question of whether Mr. Sloan is correct in this assumption, his statement is a sad commentary on the unwillingness or inability of some American business leaders to learn the lessons of history. Mr. Sloan and other leaders of the National Association of Manufacturers continue to think of the postwar world as an opportunity to start from scratch and continue what they term a system of "free enterprise" without regard for the events of the past twenty-five years. They maintain unshakable faith in the principles of laissez faire and believe that the future of America can safely be left in the hands of private business and unregulated free enterprise. It seems incredible that Mr. Sloan should not even be prepared to explore the possibilities of maintaining our wartime high levels of production in peacetime, especially since the majority of American economists are unanimous in their belief that a national income of $100 billion a year cannot possibly maintain full employment. The explanation for the narrow outlook of Mr. Sloan and his colleagues is that they are cartel-minded in the old-fashioned sense.

Even for cartel-minded business and financial interests, the opening up of new economic frontiers and the expansion of world trade is a better way out of their difficulties than fighting to retain monopoly control over ever-contracting markets. The elimination of feudalism and colonialism in the backward areas of the world can release the forces of economic progress and open the world anew to genuine and honest free enterprise that will automatically remove the reasons for the existence of the old type of cartel. Under such conditions international cartels can take on a modern and progressive character in which their function will be to rationalize production, organize a more equitable distribution of raw materials and patent rights, and provide the mechanism for international coöperation in the investment of capital in backward areas. In such a world, Mr. Sloan and his colleagues would not need to limit their outlook to a national income of $100 billion or even $150 billion. If, however, they insist on pushing the clock of history back, they will be rewarded with world-wide opposition that can lead only to more wars and their own certain extinction.

The primary purpose of this book is to examine in some detail the economic and political problems affecting the development of India and China, which, by virtue of their extensive natural resources and vast populations, easily rank first among the potential new economic frontiers for the United States. So important is the welfare of these two countries — which together contain almost half the population of the world — that, unless they are enabled to increase substantially their productive capacity and purchasing power, America and the other industrial nations may not be able to maintain for long even their prewar levels of production, much less to expand them. Undeniably, there are serious obstacles to be overcome and difficult political problems to be solved before we can hope to establish mutually beneficial economic relations with India and China. But the overcoming of these obstacles and the solution of these problems constitute a challenge to America that must be met if we are to ensure our own future peace and prosperity.

The potentials of the China market have long been one of the dominant influences on our Far Eastern policy. But the golden dreams of supplying the virtually limitless demands of 450 million customers never became a reality because of China's semi-colonial status, her economic backwardness, and the extreme poverty of her people. Today, however, the picture in China has changed in one important respect. China has won her political independence as a result of the cancellation by Britain and America of the unequal treaties and extraterritorial rights. Consequently, China is in a position to undertake a program of economic development free from foreign pressure and restrictions. Furthermore, she will soon be in possession of the rich industrial resources of Manchuria as well as those of China Proper. Under these circumstances, there is no reason why China could not embark on a nation-wide program of economic development and industrial expansion that would create an enormous demand for all types of capital goods and construction materials, as well as provide profitable opportunities for capital investment.

During the years 1939–45, however, the picture in China had its dark and discouraging aspects. The extreme right wing clique of the Kuomintang — China's only legal political party — steadily tightened its control, not only over the Party machinery, but also over the Government bureaucracy. This clique derived its power from the feudal-minded landed gentry and old-time war lords who were chiefly interested in preserving intact China's oppressive and outmoded agrarian system. They and their spokesmen in the Government opposed political democracy and industrial progress because it would inevitably undermine their own power. Instead, they sought to persuade the Chinese people to retain the "virtues" and social structure of ancient feudal China in a world in which that social structure could mean only economic stagnation and certain subjection to more powerful countries.

This ruling clique resisted all demands for a more democratic system of government and for agrarian reforms, and resorted to Gestapo-like methods of "thought control" and police surveillance to suppress civil liberties and the political rights of minority parties. And because of its fear of the social and economic reforms introduced in the guerrilla areas (the Border Regions) of China, it maintained a strict military blockade against these areas from 1939 onwards, thereby weakening China's unity and powers of resistance. On the economic front, the ruling clique failed to take effective measures to check the hoarding, speculation, and profiteering indulged in by its supporters among the landlords, merchants, and militarists, and thus served to weaken still further China's precarious economic position. Clearly, if the philosophy of this ruling group should continue to be dominant in postwar China, there would be little hope of a sound program of economic development and the creation of a prosperous and expanding internal market.

Another disturbing feature in the situation in China was the fact that Chiang Kai-shek appeared unwilling or unable to challenge the entrenched forces of reaction. There was cumulative evidence that he was losing contact with the people and was showing much less of that flexibility in dealing with opposing political forces that had been the source of his great power. More and more he appeared to be leaving the tasks of government to the bureaucratic clique, while he himself indulged in abstract political and economic theorizing of a dangerously reactionary character, as in his recent book, *China's Destiny*. Furthermore, he had developed an implacable hatred of the Soviet Union and also of the Chinese Communists, which made it impossible for him to deal calmly and constructively with questions concerning them.

On the other hand, the period from 1939 to 1945 was not without important encouraging features. There developed an increasingly strong demand from all sections of the people in Free China for greater political and economic democracy. Conservative, liberal, and radical groups alike opposed a monopoly of power by the small, bureaucratic clique that had failed to tackle any of China's basic problems. It is true that the demoralization suffered by China while in the grip of the feudal-minded bureaucracy will leave deep wounds requiring a long period of healing, even though the restoration of the industrial centers along the coast and in Manchuria will mean a revival of the political power and influence of the industrial and banking groups whose more progressive attitude toward industrialization has been overshadowed by the reactionary outlook of the landed gentry. Fortunately, the beginnings of a democratic political and economic system have already been introduced in the areas controlled by the guerrilla forces, with results that may become more apparent after the war. Certainly the political awakening of millions of Chinese as a result of their participation in guerrilla resistance will be a potent force for progress in the postwar period.

The continuous struggle between the democratic and the reactionary forces in China has precipitated many crises that on occasion have threatened to develop into civil war. Often there have been seemingly good reasons to believe that a successful compromise between the two was in the making. But, such hopes have invariably proved illusory, not necessarily because there was not good will on both sides, but primarily because their differences were too deep-rooted — as deep-rooted as the conflicts between feudalism and industrialism in Europe during the eighteenth and nineteenth centuries. The main question, as far as the United States is concerned, is what kind of American policy can best help the Chinese people to free themselves from the paralyzing grip of a landed bureaucracy, without at the same time promoting violent internal conflict or necessitating any external military intervention. For, as we shall see when we come to examine the Chinese situation in more detail, only a democratically constituted government can ensure political unity and stability in China, and only such a government can undertake the development of the kind of economic program that will create a prosperous and expanding market for American goods and capital.

In India a different set of obstacles and problems confronts the United States. As a potential new economic frontier, India offers even more advantages than China because of her greater wealth of natural resources. But, unlike China, India is an economic and political colony of Great Britain and is therefore not free to undertake the development of these resources or to deal with other countries on an equal basis. It is, of course, true that even if India were given her freedom tomorrow, there would still remain a host of complex problems and conflicts within the country. For, though many of these problems have been aggravated by the operation of foreign rule, they would not be wholly removed on the morning of the attainment of political freedom. As in the case of China, however, only a democratically constituted government can hope to solve these internal Indian problems and undertake a sound program of economic reform and development. And so long as India remains a colony she cannot achieve this essential democracy. For the United States, therefore, the major question concerning India is this: Under what circumstances will Great Britain relinquish the substantial advantage she now enjoys by virtue of her control over Indian industry, finance, and trade, and remove the restrictions hitherto imposed on Indian political and economic development — in short, give India complete freedom to be the mistress of her own destiny?

There is widespread anxiety in Great Britain over the prospects for British trade in the postwar years. Britain's financial position has been greatly weakened as a result of the loss of much of her overseas investments and the curtailment of her income from financial and shipping services. Furthermore, she will be confronted by an enormously powerful America as a competitor in world markets. Britain does not possess anything comparable to the American domestic market or to American domestic sources of food and raw materials. For her, foreign trade is an even more vital necessity than it is for the United States. Under these circumstances, can Britain be expected to grant to the United States and other nations free access to trade and investment opportunities in India, even though she herself would unquestionably benefit in the long run from the development of an expanding economy and a consequent rise in Indian purchasing power? Is it not more probable that Britain will attach greater importance than ever to maintaining a privileged trade and investment position in her empire and particularly in India, which has served for so long as a source of raw materials for British industry and as an outlet for British capital and manufactured goods?

Despite the decisive defeat of the Churchill government in the July 1945 elections, the clue to Britain's intentions must be sought in recent British policy toward India, which, as we shall see, does not indicate a desire to facilitate India's progress toward either political or economic independence. One reason for that reluctance is unquestionably a sincere fear of American economic competition and a desire to conserve all available resources to combat the enormous economic and financial power of the United States. A major problem confronting the United States is, therefore, how to allay that fear by showing Britain that she need not depend upon a closed imperial bloc and colonial exploitation for her continued existence as a great industrial and trading nation. India's economic future and her ability to serve as a complementary economic area for the United States are thus involved in this wider problem of Anglo-American relations, and will be determined, in large measure, by the degree to which England and America can establish a basis for economic coöperation rather than cutthroat competition in the postwar world.

The general problem of Anglo-American economic rivalry also has a direct bearing on the question of China's future development as an economic frontier for the United States and other industrialized nations. Britain's reluctance to renounce monopolistic control of colonial areas is not limited to India — as witness, for example, the official British attitude concerning Hong Kong. Here again, fear of American competition is a powerful contributory factor in Britain's desire to retain all possible points of advantage in the China market.

Nor is the question of Anglo-American relations the only problem that may affect the course of American economic relations with China and India. At least two other major problems must be considered: the future treatment of Japan and the role of the Soviet Union in Eastern Asia. It is obvious that the development of China and of other Far Eastern countries will be vitally affected by the kind of political and economic structure that prevails in postwar Japan — i.e., whether that structure is geared for peace or for a renewal of aggressive expansionism at some future date. There are powerful forces in the world that are striving to preserve Japan as a politically "reliable" power to serve as a counterbalance to the aspirations of the colonial nations for national freedom. Yet it is clear that the existence of a revengeful, power-hungry Japanese ruling oligarchy would make it impossible for China to emerge from poverty and backwardness into economic and political maturity.

It is equally clear that the Soviet Union cannot be regarded as other than a major Pacific power and that the future course of American-Soviet, Chinese-Soviet, Anglo-Soviet, and Japanese-Soviet relations will have a profound bearing on the political stability and economic progress of Eastern Asia. Certainly there will be little prospect for such stability if the natural differences in approach between the Soviet Union and the other powers are intensified and distorted by the professional promoters of anti-Soviet sentiment, who miss no opportunity to foment unwarranted suspicion and distrust of Soviet policy. A calm and unbiased appraisal of Soviet policy in Asia will go a long way toward removing the obstacles to effective coöperation among the "Big Four."

Thus the future development of China and India as economic frontiers for the United States involves many complex and difficult tasks. It necessitates the overcoming of serious internal obstacles in both India and China, and, in addition, it necessitates the construction of a general framework of security and economic coöperation that includes not only China, India, and America, but also Russia, England, Japan, and other countries. Both these aspects of the problem call for constructive thought and leadership on the part of the United States.

As far as the American people themselves are concerned, the new position of the United States as by far the strongest financial and industrial power in the world involves new responsibilities and a wholly new outlook with regard to international economic relations. Although America has for a long time been a powerful financial and industrial nation, we have devoted little attention to the development of external markets or outlets for capital investment commensurate with our strength. Furthermore, although we have been inevitably affected by economic depression and political conflict in any other part of the world, we have until very recently sought to avoid participation in world politics or collective security arrangements in the erroneous belief that we could isolate ourselves from the outside world. At times we have criticized the imperialist policies followed by other industrial nations in their struggle for monopoly control of markets and sources of raw materials, but we have taken no constructive lead in suggesting an alternative system whereby colonial exploitation could be eliminated. Instead, since the First World War we have made the position of other trading nations more difficult by refusing to adopt a policy suited to our position as a creditor nation.

It was customary to explain these apparent anomalies by references to the American aversion to "entangling alliances" and the desire to escape involvement in foreign wars. A more accurate explanation, however, is that the chief characteristic of American economy has been the combination of rich natural resources and a huge internal market — a characteristic which, until the First World War, made it possible for the United States to give pre-eminence to the internal market as compared with the development of foreign trade. This feature of the American economy explains in large measure the strong provincialism or isolationism that has characterized the political thinking of dominant sections of American society. So long as there were seemingly inexhaustible economic opportunities to be had at home, why concern ourselves with the rest of the world except to see that our internal market and our standards of living were adequately protected from foreign competition?

This provincialism is obviously incompatible with America's present world position. Leadership in the rebuilding of the world economy must of necessity devolve upon the United States as the primary source of capital goods and international investment funds. Furthermore, the costly experiences of the years between the two World Wars have taught America that she herself is more dependent than ever before on the prosperity of other nations and on an expanding international trade. She can no longer rely primarily on her internal market to maintain full employment, absorb the production of her vast industrial machine, or provide profitable investment opportunities for all her surplus capital. And just as America needs new export outlets, so she also needs increased imports to satisfy the demands of American producers and consumers, and to provide other nations with the means with which to pay for American exports as well as service their international financial obligations.

In a general way, the American people recognize the necessity for the expansion of a two-way foreign trade and the importance of developing the backward areas of the world. The people of the United States, however, have for so long been conditioned by economic provincialism and political isolationism that, despite their recent experiences in world affairs, they still find it difficult to think in terms of international economic coöperation. There is as yet no clear recognition of what such coöperation involves in terms of our domestic economy and our foreign trade and investment policies. In the first place, the development of the backward areas will require not only the export of enormous quantities of industrial goods of all kinds, but also the investment of huge sums of capital in the form of long-term loans to finance these exports and to pay for the initial development of mines, railways, factories, public utilities, etc., in the receiving countries. It may even be necessary, for a long time, to convert the sums resulting from favorable trade balances into additional capital investment. This point — particularly applicable to a country like China — is discussed in greater detail in the chapter dealing with the future economic relations between China and the United States. Some business and political leaders in this country have sought to ridicule and discredit the idea of any such large-scale financial expenditure on the grounds that the United States cannot afford to "play Santa Claus" to the world and should keep its money and natural resources at home. But the United States cannot hope to find profitable employment for all its capital and all its vast productive system at home. Furthermore, the American people willingly spent over $90 billion a year to win the war. Is it ridiculous, visionary, and impractical to suggest that they should be equally willing to lend large sums to win the peace and secure their own future prosperity, particularly as they have seen what the full utilization of their resources can mean in terms of national income and employment?

A second point to be recognized is that if such financial and material aid is to accomplish the desired purpose of creating sound and expanding economies in the receiving countries, thus ensuring a profitable return on our investment in the form of expanding foreign trade, these loans cannot follow the old pattern of imperialist exploitation that sought only a quick and high profit without regard for the welfare of the countries concerned. Loans of this character, as past history proves, would defeat their own ends by keeping the receiving countries impoverished and their consuming power low. The countries of Asia and Latin America are eager for foreign capital investment and willing that such investment should yield reasonable profits. But they are also determined that it shall not lead to foreign domination and that the use of both foreign and native capital shall be decided in the light of mutual national interests.

Some critics argue that such loans would be likely to suffer the same fate as American capital investments in Latin America, where from one-half to two-thirds of American loans made to governments and corporations were in default prior to the Second World War. The answer to such criticism is that the history of the past hundred and fifty years proves that the financial and economic position of a growing and progressive country is fundamentally sound. It is only when the economy of a country begins to contract that the country is unable to pay debts and interest charges. If the proposed loans are made on favorable terms and utilized for constructive purposes that will raise the living standards of the countries concerned, these countries will have no difficulty in meeting their obligations.

To take the case of Latin America. Foreign capital investment did much to develop Latin America. It built railways in Mexico and packing plants in Argentina; it developed silver, gold, copper, and tin mines in Mexico, Peru, Chile, and Bolivia, and coffee, sugar, and banana plantations in Cuba, Brazil, Ecuador, and Central America. But many of these foreign loans were made to autocratic governments on stiff terms and for wasteful purposes, and neither these governments nor the foreign corporations that operated most of the mines and plantations took any interest in the welfare of the people as a whole. Furthermore, the economic development produced by these foreign investments was extremely one-sided, with no effort to promote industrialization. The emphasis was placed on the development of a few export commodities such as coffee, sugar, minerals, etc., which suffered from wide price fluctuations because of their complete dependence on the world market. Then, too, only a small group in each country shared in the new wealth created by foreign investments, while the workers on the plantations and in the mines remained sunk in miserable poverty. Government revenues fluctuated greatly, and when depressions set in, as after 1929, governments as well as private firms found it impossible to service their foreign debts.

The lesson of this experience is not that we should refrain from investing in Latin America and other backward areas, but that we should make certain that such investments are used only by democratic governments for developing more rounded economies that will raise the living standards of the people. The combined national incomes of all twenty Latin American countries, with a total population of about 120 million, is estimated at approximately $15 billion. More than half the Latin American population lives on family incomes of about $100 a year, while only a very small percentage has as much as $1,000 a year. So long as these conditions persist, it is futile to expect Latin America to become a large-scale purchaser of American goods, or a safe credit risk. If, however, the living standards of these peoples can be raised and the revenues of their governments correspondingly increased by a sound and balanced program of economic development, Americans can count on a reasonable profit from their investments and on a steady expansion of foreign trade with the countries of Latin America. To illustrate this conclusion, we need only note that the modern industrialized economy of Canada, with a population of less than 12 million people, bought almost as much from us before the war as we sold to the more than 120 million people of Latin America, eight times more than we sold to the 450 million people of China, and fourteen times more than our sales to India with a population of 390 million.

As far as the United States is concerned, a third essential condition for the success of such a development program is the active participation of the American Government. The political problems involved are too intricate, the amounts of capital required too vast, for private industry alone to undertake the task. Individual firms will be unable to supply the funds required and unwilling to extend the necessarily long-term credits. But what individual firms cannot do by themselves they can do collectively — in other words, by government action. Furthermore, the investment of surplus capital for the development of increased economic activity and consuming power in the backward areas will effectively keep Americans off the public pay rolls. It will create an increasing demand for American products that will keep American industrial capacity fully utilized and thus enable private industry to provide the employment opportunities necessary to maintain a high level of domestic prosperity. Once the process has been set in motion by Government-sponsored loans and begins to show results in the form of increased prosperity and purchasing power in the backward countries, private firms and individuals will be able and ready to risk additional investments that can supplement, and perhaps in time replace, financial aid through Government channels.

There remains the question of what methods can be used to promote the large-scale export of American goods and capital to the backward areas of the world, and what the United States must do to facilitate the repayment of such investments. These questions will not be considered in detail because the main purpose of this study is not to propose precise mechanisms but rather to demonstrate the need for such a program and to explore the factors, both favorable and adverse, that will affect its implementation in India and China — the two major undeveloped areas of the world. Besides, if the will exists, ways will be found to carry out the program. The recent activities of the Export-Import Bank suggest one possible procedure. The functions of this bank have been extended far beyond its 1944 limit, when in August 1945 its lending authority was increased from $700 million to $3,500 million. Another possibility is the continuance of Lend-Lease in a different form — such as Rehabilitation Lend-Lease — during the early years of the postwar period, pending the time when such newly proposed institutions as the International Monetary Fund and the World Bank could begin to provide loans for reconstruction and development purposes. The continuance of some form of lending program after the war is essential if we would prevent a sudden and drastic drop in American exports. During most of 1944, exports were moving at the rate of approximately $1.5 billion a month; but, of this total, Lend-Lease accounted for nearly $1.2 billion. By continuing a lending program, the United States could bridge the difficult reconversion period and also pave the way for an expansion of exports through normal commercial channels.

Whatever methods may be chosen to stimulate industrial development in the economically backward areas, one condition remains constant, namely that the United States make it possible for these countries to pay on such loans. In other words, we must ultimately be willing to accept a greatly increased volume of imports. The importance of a prosperous American market to world economy as a whole can hardly be over-estimated. It is virtually impossible to imagine any considerable volume of world trade if the American economy is depressed. Much of the current discussion regarding the expansion of our foreign trade seems to be concentrated entirely on the question of finding bigger and better markets for our exports, without recognition of the fact that foreign trade is a two-way process — that, if the United States wishes to sell, it must also be prepared to buy. This means that an essential feature of any external development program is that America should maintain a prosperous domestic market and a high level of buying power through ever higher wages, shorter hours, large-scale public and private construction and reconstruction developments, advanced social legislation, and a high level of prosperity for agriculture, as well as an adjustment of tariff policies to suit our position as a creditor nation.

The question of tariff adjustment is undeniably one involving great difficulties. America has traditionally been a high tariff country, and a common criticism of the idea of aiding backward countries to industrialize is that our own products would be forced to meet much greater competition from those produced by low-paid workers in foreign lands, with the result that even higher tariffs would be necessary to protect our standards of living. The fact is, however, that the workers in unindustrialized countries, or in those where industry is less mechanized than our own, receive low wages chiefly because of their low productivity. The introduction of modern industrial equipment in those countries would inevitably serve to increase labor productivity and therefore wages, just as it did in the United States. Obviously, however, approximate equalization of wages on a world-wide scale cannot be achieved overnight. For that reason, our tariff schedules will have to be flexible and adjustable so that they can give reasonable protection to our living-standard and wage levels, and at the same time encourage a steadily expanding two-way trade with the rest of the world.

That our government is aware of the relationship between exports and imports is evidenced by the fact that, in addition to its traditional function of seeking markets for American exports, the Department of Commerce plans to make a determined effort to stimulate American buying of foreign products. During the pre-war years, 1930–39, American exports averaged $3,096,266,000 annually, as compared with imports averaging $2,623,623,000. This excess of exports over imports was met chiefly by the shipment of gold to this country, a process that helped the United States only to add to its already huge and disproportionate stocks of gold. Treasury experts admit that without an ultimate balance between American imports and exports, our foreign trade will suffer. It is therefore a hopeful sign that the Department of Commerce plans to have foreign service experts abroad searching for products that can be exported to the United States, while experts at home seek buyers and markets for these products. If a similar policy were adopted for the investigation of specific opportunities for capital investment in the backward areas that are ready for industrialization, we could achieve not only the balancing of our imports and exports, but also a large-scale increase in both categories.

A final question to be considered is what countries should be the main beneficiaries of any program of American capital investment. As stated earlier, the contention of this study is that the industrially backward countries are best suited to provide new economic frontiers for the United States. This does not, of course, preclude an expanding trade with Great Britain, the Soviet Union, the British Dominions, and the countries of Europe. But because these countries are for the most part already highly industrialized, they do not offer the same opportunities for either continuous large-scale export of capital and capital goods or the substantial increase in purchasing power that are offered to capital investment in the backward areas. It is clear, too, that the industrial nations of Europe and elsewhere would also gain substantially from the development of the backward areas, and that the profits obtained by them from an expanding trade with

Latin America, Africa, and Asia would make them better customers for the United States. The new markets resulting from the industrialization of areas with a total population of more than one billion people would obviously provide ample opportunities for every industrial nation. Such a vast world-wide program in its fullest sense is far too great an undertaking for any one or two nations. In fact, it is certain that not even the total industrial plant of the world today would be sufficient to supply the demands of such an industrialization program.

For American purposes the most logical countries to be considered are those of Latin America, Africa, and Asia. In each case, a properly administered program of capital investment could serve to develop hitherto unexploited resources, stimulate the growth of domestic industries, raise the purchasing power of the people from its present excessively low level, and create a new and expanding market for American goods. In the case of Latin America, moreover, geographic proximity and the trade relations already established provide a logical base for increased economic coöperation on the part of both governments and private firms.

However, of all the economically backward countries, India and China stand out as of preëminent importance by virtue of their wealth of natural resources, their vast population, and their great potential importance as the leading countries of Eastern Asia. In contrast to a combined Chinese and Indian population of nearly 900 million, Latin America has a population of only 120 million, divided among 20 republics each with differing resources and at different levels of political and economic development. Africa, though vast in area, is relatively poor in natural resources and has a population of only 130 million. Furthermore, it is divided into so many different colonial segments that any large-scale program of economic development would necessitate political arrangements of an exceedingly complex nature. It would also have to be of a long-range character and therefore could not be expected to meet the needs of the American economy in the immediate future.

The investment of American capital in both Latin America and Africa under favorable political conditions would unquestionably produce beneficial results and should form part of American postwar economic policy. But it is in India and China that we find the really great potential markets of the future. Moreover, the development of India and China as stable and expanding economies would constitute the surest guarantee of peace and progress in Asia and the world as a whole. For unless these two great countries are able to become free, strong, and prosperous, there can be little hope for an expanding world economy or for the elimination of colonialism and fierce economic rivalries that must lead inevitably to future wars.

To some readers, this insistence on the importance of an international approach to the economic problems of the United States may appear exaggerated or even wholly false. For, though most Americans have learned that politically the United States can no longer hope to isolate itself from the rest of the world, they have yet to grasp the fact that unless we root out economic provincialism in all its manifestations, political isolationism will reëmerge in due course and set the stage for a third world conflict. America is unquestionably the most powerful single nation in the world today, but even she is not strong enough to play a lone hand in either the political or the economic sphere. Neither those who preach the doctrine of national "self-sufficiency" nor those who dream of an American drive to dominate the markets of the world without regard for the needs of other nations can possibly achieve security and prosperity for the United States. It is easy to be lulled into a feeling of security when day after day the newspapers, periodicals, and radio pour forth an endless stream of soothing postwar plans, all chanting the magic phrase of "free enterprise." There is nothing wrong with free enterprise if its meaning is not frozen to an unrecallable past; but the principles of a bygone era cannot be transferred artificially into our lives of today without producing violent distortions. What unregulated free enterprise and economic isolationism were unable to accomplish in the thirties, they will be still less able to accomplish in the forties and fifties.

It is natural for a people weary from the effects of an all-consuming war to be impatient with long-term planning and to ignore the need for an advanced international outlook, especially when the immediate future promises to be prosperous. This is particularly true of the American people, who have never been accustomed to think of their domestic needs and interests in relation to the outside world. But just for this reason it is all the more important that Americans should understand that economic and political isolationism can no longer serve America's economic needs, and that it must be replaced by a policy of constructive international coöperation in the economic as well as the political sphere, if the "boom" following the conclusion of the war is not to prove as illusory as that of the twenties.

It is of equal importance that the people of America should be informed as to conditions in both India and China. For without such knowledge we cannot adopt constructive policies to overcome the serious obstacles that now block the way to the development of mutually beneficial relations between them and the United States. In both countries revolutions are in progress that involve complex political issues and problems over and above the serious economic crisis that has resulted from the war. Obviously, the people of the United States are vitally concerned with the development and outcome of the internal conflicts now raging in both India and China. For unless these struggles end in victory for those groups that wish to see their countries advance rapidly in the construction of a modern and democratic political and economic system, there is little hope that either India or China can become anything but a liability in the postwar world. Yet the American people have been kept largely in the dark or actually misinformed as to the developments in both India and China by the policy of strict news censorship and active propaganda that has been followed by the British and Chinese authorities respectively in an effort to win American support for the existing regimes and to discredit the aims and achievements of the opposition forces.

So long as Americans continue to harbor carefully fostered but erroneous illusions about conditions in India and China, they will not be able to formulate practical and constructive policies for aiding in the postwar economic development of either country. There is also the danger that this problem will be approached in too narrow a setting if the relation of British, Japanese, and Soviet policy to the question of postwar economic development in Eastern Asia is not taken fully into account. The next two sections of this book are therefore devoted to a detailed analysis of the background and present situation in India and in China. This analysis is followed by a discussion of the other factors that will inevitably affect America's future relations with these two countries — i.e., the aims of British policy in Asia and the problem of Anglo-American economic relations; the postwar treatment of Japan; and the role of the Soviet Union in Eastern Asia. Only in the light of all these factors is it possible to evaluate the prospects for the future development of India and China as new economic frontiers for the United States and the other industrial nations of the world.

New Frontiers in Asia

PART ONE

PROSPECTS AND PITFALLS

IN INDIA

❋

CHAPTER I

THE INDIAN CHALLENGE TO AMERICA

❀

THE INDIAN people are bitterly disappointed that America has not taken a deeper interest in the Indian problem, or at least has not expressed official concern over it. They have seen the reports on Indian affairs written by such high-ranking American representatives as Henry Grady, Louis Johnson, and William Phillips buried in the files at Washington. During the months following the failure of the Cripps Mission, they suffered brutal repression at the hands of the British, with America standing passively on the side lines. A famine of such proportions that five million died and fifty million more were physically incapacitated by malnutrition and disease occurred in 1943 without a single official American effort being made to relieve it.

The Indian people have witnessed the mishandling of the Burma campaign of 1942, the brushing aside of legitimate Indian interests at the UNRRA and Bretton Woods conferences, and many other injustices that they were helpless to combat without outside support. It is no wonder that they sought anxiously for American intervention and were deeply disappointed when it was not forthcoming. The British authorities, by a strict censorship on news from India and by deliberate propaganda efforts, have encouraged American apathy toward the Indian situation. They have also fanned the flames of Indian indignation against the United States until there is considerable disillusionment in India with regard to America's alleged sympathy with the oppressed peoples of the world. In fact, many Indians express the belief that there exists a tacit alliance between Britain and America to keep India in subjection.

But it is an open secret that the conclusions reached by those Americans who have been able to study the Indian situation at first hand have been extremely critical of British policy. Only the close friendship existing between England and America as allies prevented this resentment and disapproval from becoming an open issue. Perhaps the most severe observations made on the Anglo-Indian problem were those of William Phillips, former American Ambassador to Italy, who visited India as President Roosevelt's personal representative during the eventful months following the arrest of Gandhi and the other Congress Party leaders in August 1942. After his return to this country in the spring of 1943, Mr. Phillips reported his impressions of the Indian situation to the President. One of his letters was first published in Drew Pearson's column on July 25, 1944, and was eventually released to the press by Senator Chandler and published by the *New York Times* on September 3, 1944. Although this belated disclosure was apparently unintentional as far as the Administration was concerned, Mr. Phillips's ideas are so essential to an understanding of the Indian situation that they are worth quoting in full:

May 14, 1943

Dear Mr. President:

May I add a few words to what I said to you on Thursday afternoon when I had the pleasure of giving you an oral report on my impressions of the Indian situation.

Assuming that India is known to be an important base for our future operations against Burma and Japan, it would seem to be of highest importance that we should have around us a sympathetic India rather than an indifferent and possibly a hostile India. It would appear that we will have the prime responsibility in the conduct of the war against Japan. There is no evidence that the British intend to do more than give token assistance. If that is so, then the conditions surrounding our base in India become of vital importance.

At present, the Indian people are at war only in a legal sense, as for various reasons the British Government declared India in the conflict without the formality of consulting Indian leaders or even the Indian Legislature. Indians feel they have no voice in the Government and therefore no responsibility in the conduct of the war. They feel that they have nothing to fight for, as they are convinced that the professed war aims of the United Nations do not apply to them.

The British Prime Minister, in fact, has stated that the provisions of the Atlantic Charter are not applicable to India, and it is not unnatural therefore that Indian leaders are beginning to wonder whether the charter is only for the benefit of white races. The present Indian army is purely mercenary and only that part of it which is drawn from the martial races has been tried in actual warfare and these martial soldiers represent only 33 per cent of the army.

General Stilwell has expressed his concern over the situation and in particular in regard to the poor morale of the Indian officers. The attitude of the general public toward the war is even worse. Lassitude and indifference and bitterness have increased as a result of the famine conditions, the growing high cost of living, and continued political deadlock. While India is broken politically into various parties and groups, all have one object in common — eventual freedom and independence from British domination.

There would seem to be only one remedy to this highly unsatisfactory situation in which we are unfortunately but nevertheless seriously involved, and that is to change the attitude of the people of India toward the war, make them feel that we want them to assume responsibilities to the United Nations and are prepared to give them facilities for doing so, and that the voice of India will play an important part in the reconstruction of the world. The present political conditions do not permit of any improvement in this respect.

Even though the British should fail again, it is high time that they should make an effort to improve conditions and re-establish confidence among the Indian people that their future independence is to be granted. Words are of no avail. They only aggravate the present situation. It is time for the British to act. This they can do by a solemn declaration from the king emperor that India will achieve her independence at a specific date after the war, and, as a guarantee of good faith in this respect, a provisional representative coalition government will be re-established at the center and limited powers transferred to it.

I feel strongly, Mr. President, that in view of our military position in India, we should have a voice in these matters. It is not right for the British to say this is none of your business when we alone presumably will have the major part to play in the struggle with Japan. If we do nothing and merely accept the British point of view that conditions in India are none of our business, then we must be prepared for various serious consequences in the internal situation in India which may develop as a result of the despair and misery and anti-white sentiments of hundreds of millions of subject people.

The peoples of Asia — and I am supported in the opinion by other diplomatic and military observers — cynically regard this war as one between fascist and imperialist powers. A generous British gesture

*to India would change this undesirable political atmosphere. India
itself might then be expected more positively to support our war effort
against Japan. China, which regards the Anglo-American bloc with
misgivings and mistrust, might then be assured that we are in truth
fighting for a better world. And the colonial people conquered by the
Japanese might hopefully feel that they have something better to look
forward to than simply a return to their old masters.*

*Such a gesture, Mr. President, will produce not only a tremendous
psychological stimulus to flagging morale throughout Asia and facilitate our military operations in that theater, but it will also be proof
positive to all peoples — our own and the British included — that this is
not a war of power politics, but a war for all we say it is.*

Sincerely yours,
(*signed*) WILLIAM PHILLIPS

It may be that the official and nonofficial critics of British
policy have judged the Anglo-Indian problem without sufficient
understanding of the background of the struggle within India
and without giving due consideration to that problem in the
context of world affairs. But the facts are undeniable that India
is the innocent victim of an extremely complicated world situation, that she has emerged from this war as a liability to the world
rather than an asset, and that this is a matter of direct concern
to the United States.

As a nation of nearly 400 million people and the third richest
country in the world with respect to natural resources, India
is preëminently suited to serve as a new and expanding economic
frontier for the American economy in the postwar period. Yet,
though India has all the potentialities for developing a prosperous and expanding economy, she has emerged from the war seriously weakened economically. Millions of Indians have died of
famine and disease. Millions more have been permanently weakened by malnutrition. Nothing has been done to modernize
India's primitive agricultural methods, reform the present oppressive system of land tenure, or ease the tremendous burden
of peasant indebtedness. Nor has there been any important expansion of Indian industrial facilities, and the total volume of
industrial production appears to have actually declined as compared with prewar years.

Furthermore, India's long struggle to win genuine political independence appears no nearer success. The British Government

has steadfastly maintained that the Cripps offer of 1942 constitutes an honest offer of independence to India and that it is now
up to Indian leaders to take advantage of that offer. But, as we
shall see, the Cripps proposals were not in fact an unrestricted
offer of independence. The British also contend that India has
made great economic progress during the war because she has
paid off her sterling debt and accumulated large sterling balances
in London. Those balances, however, represent a bookkeeping
transaction in which the ledger is controlled by the Bank of England, with India having no power to determine how they are to be
utilized.

India's immediate future is, to say the least, not bright. All
signs point to her remaining a British colony weakened by the
war and poorer than ever. The British Government insists that
India is none of our affair. Yet, as Mr. Phillips points out, our
silent acquiescence in British policy in India is winning for us
only the distrust and suspicion of all Asiatic peoples. Moreover,
if anything has been learned during the past quarter of a century, it is the close relationship, both economic and political,
that exists between any one country and the rest of the world.
It is more than a poetic phrase to say that the world cannot live
in peace, half-slave and half-free. What happens to an Indian,
or a Rumanian, or an Englishman, or a Russian has a direct
bearing on what happens to an American. It is inconceivable
that a nation of 390 million people, producing commodities on
the basis of the low living standards of the Indian people, would
not be a major obstacle to the freedom and economic prosperity
of other countries in Asia — notably China. An economically
backward and colonial India would be a direct menace to the
future stability and prosperity of Eastern Asia and thus to American interests in that part of the world. For this reason, if for
no other, the Indian problem and its solution are of vital concern
to the United States, and cannot be ignored simply because of
the recognized need to maintain Anglo-American unity.

WHAT AN INDUSTRIALIZED INDIA WOULD MEAN

IN ANY appraisal of India's importance as a potential market for
American industry, many political and economic factors must be
considered. Disregarding for the moment the political aspects of
the question and considering only India's economic qualifications,
there is no doubt that India has the capacity for extensive in-

dustrial expansion. And it is equally certain that a large-scale program of industrial development and the modernization of Indian agricultural methods would create a huge market for all types of capital and consumer goods — many of which the United States by virtue of its great industrial plant and experience in mass production is peculiarly well fitted to supply.

In the first place, India's natural resources, as far as they are known at present,[1] are exceeded in variety and size only by those of the United States and the Soviet Union. Her mineral resources include one of the largest high-grade iron-ore fields in the world, with an estimated reserve of three billion tons averaging 64% iron content.[2] She possesses the world's second largest reserves of manganese, 49% of the world's bauxite, and rich deposits of chrome, magnesite, sulphur, graphite, and other minerals. She also leads the world in the production of mica and ilmenite. Estimates of Indian coal reserves range from 36 to 60 billion tons, although the quantity of coking coal is reported to be comparatively small. This deficiency is more than offset, however, by immense potential hydroelectric power resources, which are estimated to total more than 30 million horse power — second only to those of the United States.

Like the United States, India is also capable of providing a strong agricultural base to support her industrial structure. Even under the present backward and oppressive agrarian system, she ranks among the world's greatest agricultural nations. She is the second largest producer of cotton, rice, and tea, and is among the leading producers of wheat, barley, hemp, rubber, lac, and silk. Jute production is a virtual Indian monopoly, and before the war India headed the list of the world's producers of tobacco, sugar, and oil seeds. She is also the largest producer and exporter of hides and skins.

Thus India is potentially capable of supporting both light and

---

[1] Only one-fourth of India's total area of 1,581,410 sq. miles has so far been properly surveyed by geologists.

[2] Dr. Cyril Fox, retired director general of the Indian Geological Survey, in a memorandum on mineral resources submitted to the Grady Mission, stated that as far as he has been able to ascertain, the reserves of high-grade iron ore in India were the largest in the world and certainly far larger than the official figures here given. On the question of coal, too, Dr. Fox stated that the figures for coal reserves are out of date and that they are much larger though deficient in quality. These corrected estimates are supported by D. N. Wardia, the leading geologist in India.

heavy industries on the basis of her own natural resources, as well as of maintaining an ample volume of agricultural production to feed her people and to supply raw materials for industry and export. Furthermore, India possesses a vast supply of labor power with a heritage of skilled craftsmanship dating back to the days when India was one of the leading manufacturing countries in the world. It should not be forgotten that it was the lure of India's wealth in manufactured goods — not raw materials — that first attracted European traders to her shores. For centuries before the British conquest of the country, India's silks, cotton textiles, metal manufactures, and woodwork were known and prized throughout the world. Because of the backwardness of Indian industry in our own period, comparatively few Indians have had the opportunity to learn the mechanical skills needed to operate modern machinery. But American engineers and factory workers who have coöperated in the development of the few modern Indian industries, such as the Tata iron and steel plant, attest to the fact that Indians respond quickly to technical training and that not only the workers but the engineers, chemists, and technicians are the equal of any in the world. The American Technical Mission (the Grady Mission) also stated in its preliminary report: "The Mission has been impressed with the good quality and excellent potentiality of Indian labor. The Indian is skillful with his hands, and, given satisfactory working conditions and security of employment, is dependable and industrious."

Thus India possesses the natural endowment for extensive industrial expansion. The thing that most forcibly strikes the observer of Indian economic conditions is the tremendous gap between the potential resources and the actual level of economic development. Fewer than 1% of the Indian people are supported by modern industries. The annual coal production was less than 30 million tons before the war, while steel production had not reached 1 million tons annually. Only 3½% of the vast hydroelectric power resources had been developed. The only industries employing more than 100,000 workers were cotton mills, jute mills, and railway workshops. A few light industries, such as sugar, soap, and matches, had expanded somewhat in the two decades following the First World War, but India possessed virtually none of the basic heavy industries and was dependent on foreign sources for most types of steel manufactures, all forms of machine tools, industrial chemicals, nonferrous metals, etc. "So backward still is Indian industry," wrote H. N. Brailsford in 1943, "that no plant exists capable of manufacturing a tractor . . . or an internal-combustion engine of any kind."[1]

This failure to develop modern industries as an alternative source of employment is primarily responsible for the severe overpressure on India's primitive agricultural system. Nearly 70% of the population subsists on agriculture, and about 90% is directly or indirectly dependent on the land. This overpressure on an agricultural system that — because of the conditions of land ownership and taxation, primitive methods of cultivation, and lack of an adequate system of rural credit — is peculiarly ill fitted to withstand it, explains the extreme poverty of the Indian internal market. India's gross national income, of which 20% is derived from industry and 80% from agriculture, amounts to barely $19 per capita per year or five cents a day. For 60% of her population of 390 million, the average per capita gross income is not more than 2 cents a day. Not until this basic agrarian problem is solved can India hope to create an expanding domestic market for her own and foreign industries.

This basic problem of poverty must be tackled through a large-scale program of industrial development and agricultural modernization accompanied by the expansion of mining industries, road-building, irrigation works, and hydroelectric power projects. By furnishing employment, increasing agricultural output, and thus raising the purchasing power of the Indian people, such a program would create an expanding market not only for all types of capital goods but also for all types of consumer goods that are now far beyond the reach of the average Indian peasant.

Some idea of the nature and extent of Indian requirements for capital goods may be obtained from the *Plan of Economic Development for India* drawn up by a group of eight leading Indian industrialists, chiefly associated with the Tata and Birla interests, and commonly known as the "Bombay Plan." The first part of this Plan, issued in January 1944, called for a trebling of India's present national income in three successive five-year plans at a total cost of some $30 billion. Priority would be given to the development of basic industries, including power, mining, metallurgy, chemicals, automobiles, and armaments. Of the total capi-

---

[1] H. N. Brailsford: *Subject India* (New York, 1943), p. 3.

tal cost, 44% would be allotted to industrial expansion, 12% to increasing agricultural production by expanding irrigation facilities, improving methods of cultivation, etc., 10% to extending communications, 10% to education and public health, and 22% to housing. The aim of the plan was to raise the net output of agriculture to a little over twice the present figure, and that of industry, both large and small, to approximately six times the present output.

In addition to the Bombay Plan, a voluminous report edited by Jawaharlal Nehru, and published in 1939 and 1940 by the National Planning Committee of the Indian National Congress Party, outlines a far more rounded and all-inclusive program of economic development. As of 1945 these two plans constitute the chief proposals put forward by important Indian groups, and it is interesting to examine their differences, since these illuminate some of the most urgent problems involved in a solution of the Indian problem.

The major differences between the two plans are as follows: First, the authors of the Bombay Plan are satisfied with a National Government vested with full freedom in economic matters and enjoying what is described as "fiscal autonomy." They propose to acquire full political sovereignty only after this economic transition period. Nehru, on the other hand, declared on June 4, 1939, on behalf of the National Planning Committee that: "It is clear that the drawing up of a comprehensive national plan becomes merely an academic exercise, with no relation to reality, unless the planning authority is in a position to give effect to that plan. . . . An essential prerequisite of planning is thus complete freedom and independence for the country and the removal of all external control." The supporters of the National Committee Plan contend that the Bombay Plan puts the cart before the horse and thus makes progress difficult.

Second, the Bombay Plan defers discussion of the vital question of "distribution" to a future date; while the National Planning Committee, adhering to the Congress Party Bill of Rights adopted in 1931, seeks to regulate distribution. As one critic of the Bombay Plan pointed out: "Without an equitable distribution of wealth through minimum living wages, social security, etc., an all-around increase in the standard of living is not possible; . . . a plan which defers distribution or ignores it . . . cannot

be called a 'plan' for economic development; it will only assume
the character of the prospectus of a new Company." [1]

Third, the two plans adopt different approaches to the question of ownership of industry. The majority of the National Planning Committee favor public ownership of defense and key industries as well as public utilities, together with government
regulation of others, which they consider as essential features
of an orderly development of industry in the twentieth century.
A minority of the National Planning Committee contends that
State ownership is not necessary and that only State regulation
of key industries is required. The Bombay Plan, on the other
hand, ignores this aspect of planned development entirely.

Fourth, on the question of financing national economic development, the Bombay Plan estimates that a large part of the
capital required, amounting to at least $10 billion, would have
to consist of "created money" in the form of borrowing against
ad hoc securities issued by the Reserve Bank of India. The authors of the plan also admit that "during the greater part of the
planning period, financing of economic development by means
of created money on this scale is likely to lead to a gap between
the volume of purchasing power in the hands of the people and
the volume of goods available." After thus acknowledging that
what they propose would produce large-scale inflation, they
suggest only that "in order to prevent the inequitable distribution of the burden between different classes which this method
of financing will involve, practically every aspect of economic
life will have to be so rigorously controlled by government that
individual liberty and freedom of enterprise will suffer a temporary eclipse." The supporters of the National Planning Committee's program, on the other hand, would avoid such inflationary
policies. In their view, a more equitable method of financing an
economic development program would consist in "cutting down
profits, doing away with luxuries, fat salaries, and commissions,
strict rationing of necessities, etc."

Of all the features of the Bombay Plan, however, the most
severely criticized by supporters of the Congress economic program is its treatment of the agrarian problem. It places its main
emphasis on the expansion of industrial production, and —
though it calls for improvements in agricultural methods, pro-

---

[1] B. T. Ranadive: *The Tata-Birla Plan* (Bombay, 1944), p. 11.

tection against soil erosion, better varieties of seeds, irrigation projects, and consolidation of land holdings — it avoids all mention of the need for fundamental reforms in the system of land ownership, taxation, and rural credit, in order that the vast Indian peasant population may become sufficiently prosperous to support an extensive industrial structure. This ignoring of one of the basic causes of Indian poverty evoked sharp criticism. The previously quoted commentator, for example, declares bluntly that "India's agriculture has no future, India's peasant has no future, unless the present landlord-ridden, scattered, antiquated agriculture is replaced by a thoroughgoing agrarian revolution with scientific and large-scale coöperative farming. . . . The Indian peasant is the customer, client, and the ultimate market for the industrial goods that will be produced. In the last resort, it is he who will determine whether heavy industry will continue to work or not. . . . Keep him landlord-ridden and rack-rented and he is a poor customer and has no purchasing power. He holds back industrial progress."

But although the Bombay Plan, as issued in 1944, is not so far-reaching as the program advocated by the Congress Party, and is open to criticism on the grounds that its authors appear more concerned with their immediate industrial interests than with the welfare of the Indian people as a whole, it nevertheless constitutes a significant example of the scale on which Indian business leaders are thinking in respect to their country's future economic progress. Regardless of which program is adopted — whether the Bombay Plan, or the National Planning Committee's proposals, or some compromise plan — it is clear that if India were free to undertake a program of economic development, she would be in the market for huge quantities of capital goods, and that the United States would be in a position to meet such demands on comparatively favorable terms. It also seems likely that India would turn to America for technical aid, in view of American experience in connection with large-scale development projects. Two of India's most important industries — steel and hydroelectric power — already owe their existence to American machinery and engineering skill. Furthermore, as a result of the war many Indians have become familiar with the products of American manufacturers and with American machinery and manufacturing methods; and this too, should serve to increase the demand for American products.

CHAPTER II

A STUDY IN COLONIAL ECONOMICS

❋

T HAT INDIA possesses all the necessary qualifications for developing a prosperous expanding economy that could provide important outlets for American surplus production needs no further elaboration. The important question is: what has prevented India from developing such an economy in the past, and is it likely that these obstacles will continue to exist in the postwar period? The answer to that question is, in brief, that for 150 years India has been a British colony with an economy suited to the needs of British industry and finance, and that there is as yet no evidence that she will be able to free herself from that colonial relationship in the immediate future.

The conditions under which Great Britain might be expected to give up her preferential position in the Indian market and the special advantages that she enjoys by virtue of her control over Indian finance, industry, and trade, will form the subject of a later chapter. Here we are concerned with the background of India's present economic situation — namely her development as the colony of a highly industrialized power.

Dr. Vera Anstey, a noted British authority on Indian economics, has aptly described India as a case of "arrested economic development." Prior to the British conquest, India's economy was based on small-scale agriculture combined with a highly developed system of handicraft industries, and the country enjoyed a large measure of economic self-sufficiency. Following the establishment of British rule and the completion of the industrial revolution in England, however, British economic policy toward India was designed to satisfy the needs of the new British manufacturing class for raw materials and markets. Indian handicrafts, unable to compete with the flood of British machine-made goods, declined in importance or were completely ruined. The basis of the traditional village economy was thus destroyed and, in the absence of a compensating development of modern factory industries, Indian artisans and craftsmen by the millions were forced back to the land, thereby creating the terrific overcrowding of agriculture that has remained one of the critical problems of India up to the present time.

The nineteenth century witnessed India's transformation into an agricultural colony of British industry, and by 1900 India had become a large exporter of rice, wheat, cotton, jute, tea, oilseeds, etc., and an importer of British manufactured goods, especially cotton textiles, iron and steel products, and machinery. The construction of an extensive network of railways during the latter part of the century was one of the most important factors in this transformation because it facilitated the commercial penetration of the country and the large-scale production and export of raw materials, and also led to the investment of British capital not only in the railways themselves but in plantations, mines, and factories in order to increase the production of essential raw materials. The achieving of British economic aims in India also necessitated the development of roads and ports, the establishment of postal and telegraph systems, renewed attention to irrigation projects, and the inauguration of a Western-style banking system through which India's finances, commerce, and industry were controlled by Government and private foreign banks.

By linking India with world markets, giving her a modern system of communications and transport, establishing and maintaining internal law and order, opening up iron and coal mines, and training administrative and technical personnel, the British unquestionably performed a great and constructive service in breaking down the static and isolated village economy of India and in laying the material foundations for the development of a modern industrial economy. But it is equally true that this development was artificially arrested at a low level and that the greater part of India's resources remained undeveloped because of the necessity of protecting British industrial, commercial, and financial interests. Regardless of the efficiency of British administration or the material benefits bestowed on India in the early days of British rule, the fact remains that British interests in India are not and have never been organized for the purpose of aiding Indian industrialization, for increasing the inadequate food supply for internal consumption, or for developing India's domestic market.

Prior to the First World War, British capital investment in

India was confined almost entirely to enterprises related to the production and export of raw materials — e.g., railways, coal mines, jute mills, and tea, coffee, and sugar plantations — while the development of Indian-controlled industries was officially discouraged. The war, however, gave a powerful impetus to Indian industrial expansion, and existing industries operated at full capacity and made enormous profits. The war also served to call attention to India's serious industrial deficiencies and for a variety of reasons caused a temporary shift in the official British attitude toward Indian industrialization. For one thing, the British strategic position in the Middle East was weakened by the lack of heavy industrial bases in India. For another, foreign competition, especially from Japan, was threatening to break down the British monopoly of the Indian market — an eventuality even more repugnant to British interests than the growth of industry within India, which could always be subjected to a substantial degree of British control. Finally, there was the need to secure the support and coöperation of Indian business interests.

Thus, in 1915 the Viceroy, Lord Hardinge, in a despatch to the Secretary of State for India, declared that "it is becoming increasingly clear that a definite and self-conscious policy of improving the industrial capacity of India will have to be pursued after the war, unless she is to become the dumping ground of foreign nations. . . . After the war India will consider herself entitled to demand the utmost help which her Government can afford to enable her to take her place, as far as circumstances permit, as a manufacturing country." A similar view was expressed in the Montagu-Chelmsford Report of 1918, which stated that "on all grounds a forward policy in industrial development is urgently called for, not merely to give India economic stability, but in order to satisfy the aspirations of her people. . . . Both on economic and military grounds, Imperial interests also demand that the natural resources of India should henceforth be better utilized. We cannot measure the access of strength which an industrialized India will bring to the power of the Empire."

This war-inspired interest in Indian industrialization continued during the brief postwar boom period, and large amounts of British capital were invested in India. The vision of extraordinarily high returns was irresistible. The average dividend paid by leading cotton mills in Bombay in 1920 was 120%, and in some cases was as high as 250%. Dividends of jute mills averaged 140%, and 41 British-controlled jute mills showed a profit of £22.9 million during the four year period 1918–1921, in addition to £19 million added to reserves. British investors were naturally eager to have a share in these tremendous profits, and consequently the annual export of British capital to India increased from £14.7 million during the period 1908–10, to £29 million for 1921 and £36 million for 1922.

Officially, the changed attitude toward Indian industry was reflected in the inauguration of a protective tariff system. In 1921, the Indian tariff duty on cotton textiles was raised to 11%, and in 1922 the general import duty was raised to 15%. In 1924, the Indian iron-and-steel industry was granted the protection of a 33⅓% import duty plus a system of government subsidies. By this time, however, British interest in Indian industrialization had begun to cool. The brief postwar boom of 1920–21 was soon followed by a disastrous crash in which many of the Indian firms formed during the boom went bankrupt, and the flow of new British capital investment to India dropped abruptly to £2.6 million for 1924 and to less than £1 million for 1927. A similar change was apparent in official policy concerning the protection of Indian industry after 1924. Following the granting of protection to the iron-and-steel industry, a series of further applications from other industries were for the most part refused, and when the iron-and-steel protective system came up for renewal in 1927, the basic duties were lowered, the subsidies abolished, and the principle of Imperial preference was introduced.

Thus the short-lived period of Indian tariff "autonomy" came to an end. By the "Fiscal Convention" of 1921, it was understood that the Government of India, in framing its tariff policy, should regard itself as the guardian of Indian interests, and that, if the Government and the Central Legislature were agreed, the Secretary of State for India would not exercise his overriding power on behalf of any British interest. This agreement has been frequently cited by British spokesmen to show that India enjoys complete tariff autonomy, and they point to the ruin of the Lancashire cotton-textile trade with India as concrete proof of the fact that the protection of Indian interests was paramount in the minds of the British authorities in India. It must be noted, however, that the Fiscal Convention leaves the power to determine Indian tariff policy in the hands of the "Government" (i.e., the British Viceroy and his appointed Executive Council), which can override — and on various occasions has overridden — the vote of the Indian Legislature on trade and tariff policies, notably in the case of the Anglo-Indian trade agreements of 1935 and 1939. Furthermore, the protective tariff on cotton textiles was necessitated primarily by the British trade war with Japan and by the desire to keep Japanese textiles out of the Indian market, even at the cost of ruining the Lancashire interests.

The keynote of the Indian tariff system from 1927 to the outbreak of the Second World War was Imperial preference, by which British manufactures gained a competitive advantage over both non-Empire and Indian products in the Indian market, while India in return received favored rates for the sale of her raw materials in the British market. This system was welcomed by British industry, which wanted to protect the Indian market against invasion by foreign competitors, particularly Japan. But it was strongly opposed by Indian industrialists, who wanted protection primarily against their British competitors. Under these conditions Indian industry suffered severely — particularly during the world economic depression. The value of India's production of raw materials and food stuffs on which four-fifths of the population were dependent fell by more than half, and this sharply curtailed the country's purchasing power. As a result of this impoverishment of the domestic market for manufactured goods, coupled with the lack of adequate tariff protection and the failure of the Government to assist in the expansion of industry, the rate of industrial growth between 1922 and 1939 was extremely slow. The number of workers in organized industry increased by only 390,000 during this entire period, and, though there was some expansion in light industries, India's steel production on the eve of the Second World War was less than one sixth that of Japan and she remained wholly dependent on foreign sources for most steel manufactures and all types of machinery.

British spokesmen are inclined to minimize Britain's economic stake in India on the grounds that British capital investments have declined sharply since 1922 and that Indians have acquired an increasing share in British companies operating in India. No exact figures are available as to the amount of private British capital invested in Indian industries and plantations; estimates range from £200,000,000 to £1,000,000,000. The actual investment of capital, however, does not tell the whole story of British influence over Indian industry. There is, for example, the fact that most of the large banks in India either are Government-controlled or are branches of British and other foreign banks, with the result that Indian industrialists find it difficult to finance any industrial undertakings of which the British do not approve. Then, too, the Government is by far the largest single purchaser of heavy industrial products in India, and its refusal to agree to buy from an Indian-owned concern has often acted as an indirect but effective veto on Indian plans for production expansion.

Another mechanism whereby the British exercise a profitable control over Indian industry is the Managing Agency system, under which a relatively small number of managing agencies promote, control, and to some extent finance a wide variety of industrial and commercial enterprises. These agencies dominate the coal, jute, and tea industries, cement, engineering, insurance, paper, and sugar, as well as the shipping industry. No matter how many shares Indians may hold in these enterprises, the managing agents run the business and receive the greater part of the profits. Though there are some Indian managing agencies, the majority and the most powerful firms are naturally British since they have the best connections with the Government and the banks.

Other sources of hidden profits that must be taken into account in estimating the real British economic stake in India include the control of the exchange value of the rupee by the London financial market, the excessively high salaries and pensions paid to British officials in India, administration of the Indian tariff system, a practical monopoly by British interests of all shipping and transhipping involving the Indian market, and various other British controls over transport and communications, insurance, industry, and trade. Despite the contention of British spokesmen that India pays no direct "tribute" to Britain, it is estimated that nearly one-twelfth of India's pitifully small national yearly income of some seven billion dollars goes into British pockets in the form of profits, commissions, interest, salaries, pensions, allowances, etc. One of the major objections of Indian industrialists to the provisions of the Indian Constitution of 1935 was that it strengthened British financial control in India and specifically prohibited the Central Indian Legislature from passing any measure which "discriminated against" British trade, industry, banking, and shipping interests operating in India.

WARTIME INDUSTRIAL "EXPANSION" — THE REAL PICTURE

THE LITERALLY global character of the Second World War placed far greater demands on India's limited production facilities than had the war of 1914–18. The threat of a joint German-Japanese drive against India and the Middle East — a threat that was not removed until the Nazi armies were defeated at Stalingrad and in Africa — made it imperative that India should be transformed as rapidly as possible into an arsenal and supply base for Allied forces operating in the Middle and Far East. The collapse of France, the destruction of British factories and shipping, the spread of the war to the Mediterranean, Africa, and Southeast Asia, all served to demonstrate the vulnerability of Britain's industrial empire — an empire highly centralized and dependent on long and perilous lines of oversea communications. If the burden on British factories and shipping was to be eased, it was clear that the industrial output of the British Empire east of Suez must be expanded. This fact was somewhat belatedly recognized by the British Government in the autumn of 1940, when the Eastern Group Conference convened at New Delhi with the announced purpose of establishing an economic base for the defense of the Eastern Empire. India and Australia were selected as most suitable for conversion into wartime industrial bases — India's geographic position and large material resources making her an ideal supply center for all areas of military operations from Egypt to Malaya.

India's industrial expansion during the Second World War has been the subject of much glowing praise, particularly in officially inspired publications and statements. Great stress has been laid on the increase in steel production to about 1,250,000 tons annually and on the wide variety of military supplies produced in India for the first time. Small beginnings were made in the manufacture of the simpler kinds of machine tools and of industrial chemicals. India supplied huge quantities of blankets, tents, uniforms, and boots to the Allied forces, and a wide variety of manufactured articles previously imported were produced in

India for the first time — e.g., various types of optical goods, cutlery, rubber goods, lubricating oils, leather goods, oxygen, apparatus, and many other items needed by the military forces.

This increase in production for military needs has been hailed as indicating a substantial expansion in Indian industrial capacity, and the protests of Indian manufacturers that the British authorities were still deliberately impeding Indian industrialization have been largely ignored or dismissed as being designed for purposes of political propaganda. But available facts do not bear out the contention that Indian industrial capacity expanded substantially during the war. Indian mills and factories derive their power from coal and electricity. The output of coal fell sharply during the past few years, and though the output of electricity increased slightly, this increase was not sufficient to offset the loss in coal production. The total supply of industrial power was therefore less than it was in 1937–38, and it is difficult to see how, under these circumstances, Indian mills and factories could have been producing more.

Many jute mills, in fact, shut down because of the coal shortage and the loss of export markets. Production of sugar, cement, and tea declined. The only major industries that showed any real increases in output were cotton textiles and steel. The overall picture, however, is that industrial activity in India at the peak of the war was less than it had been in the years 1937–38. This fact is borne out by the monthly index of industrial activity in India, compiled and published by *Capital*, the leading British-owned financial and industrial journal of Calcutta.

India's much-publicized industrial war effort, therefore, actually amounted to this: the sum-total of industrial activity did not increase, but a very large proportion of existing production — in some cases amounting to nearly 90% of the total output — was diverted from civilian consumption to military supply. The chief causes behind this singular failure to expand production were the lack of industries capable of manufacturing the necessary plant and machinery, the shortage of skilled labor, and (above all) the desire of British vested interests to make certain that not even the stress of wartime necessity could enable Indian industrialists to achieve any permanent progress that might jeopardize British control over the Indian economy.

The real economic picture in India during the war period was one of acute shortages of food grains and consumption goods brought about by the curtailment of imports and the purchase of all available commodities for war purposes. The price level skyrocketed and the general inflationary tendency was aggravated by the methods used to finance British war expenditures in India, resulting in an increase of over 500% in the volume of Indian currency. Maldistribution of available commodities, inadequate transport facilities, lack of effective price controls and rationing measures, government and private hoarding, lack of popular support for the Administration — all these contributed to a further worsening of the situation. Prices of many items increased 1,000% over prewar levels, and the general cost of living rose by 250% to 300%. While some Indians reaped enormous profits from war orders as well as from speculation and black-market operations, the vast majority of the population was reduced to a state of utter destitution. Famine and disease ravaged many parts of the country and, according to estimates based on sample surveys conducted by the University of Calcutta, killed approximately five million people and seriously affected 50 million more during 1943 and the first half of 1944. And at the end of 1944 a new famine broke out, though not of such proportions as the earlier one.

INDIA'S STERLING "ASSETS" — REALITY OR ILLUSION?

ONE OF the most publicized effects of the war on India was the shift in her financial position vis-a-vis Great Britain. As of the end of June 1945, the total value of war supplies and other goods, services, and credits obtained from India by the British Government since the outbreak of the war amounted to over $6,000,-000,000. The major portion of these supplies and services were used in the North African, Middle Eastern, and other overseas theaters of war. They were "paid for" by means of sterling credits placed to India's account in London. Of the total sterling credits thus accumulated, about $1,150,000,000 was utilized for the liquidation of India's sterling debt, and the rest "frozen" for the duration of the war. These frozen assets amounted by June 1945 to over £1,000,000,000 or more than $4 billion.

One reason for this remarkable shift in India's financial position was her large favorable balance of merchandise trade. India supplied Britain and other Allied nations with large quantities of goods through normal commercial channels, whereas Indian imports were sharply curtailed because of the shortage of shipping space, Britain's inability to supply goods, and an exchange-control policy designed to conserve the foreign exchange resources of the Empire. By this policy, Indian exporters were required to turn over their receipts of dollars and other foreign exchange to the Bank of England in return for sterling.

A second reason for the accumulation of sterling assets by India was that, in accordance with a financial agreement between the British Government and the authorities in India, the Government of India paid for all war expenditures connected with the defense of India, while the British Government paid the cost of expenditures not directly concerned with Indian defense. For example, India paid for the maintenance and equipping of all land forces stationed in India, while Britain paid and equipped Indian troops when they were serving overseas. In practice, however, the Government of India provided the rupee exchange needed for both British and Indian government expenditure, and was then reimbursed by the British Government for its share in sterling credits. It was this policy of "paying" in sterling *credits* rather than *cash* that was chiefly responsible for the enormous increase in India's sterling assets — an increase that British spokesmen constantly refer to as being the result of "the magnanimous character of British financial arrangements with India."

But, as we shall see, India's financial position is by no means so glowing and satisfactory as the British contend. To get the true picture, it is necessary to take into account the effects of the methods used to finance British war expenditures in India — methods that were possible only because of India's status as a British colony. In the first place, the Indian rupee is linked to sterling, and rupee currency may be issued by the Reserve Bank of India against its sterling reserves. Secondly, as noted above, the Government of India was required to supply the rupee funds for both its share and the British Government's share of war expenditures in India. The authorities in India raised the funds for India's share of war expenditures by the normal methods of taxation and loans; but they supplied most of the funds needed by the British Government by simply adding Britain's sterling credits to the assets of the Reserve Bank of India, which then issued a corresponding amount of new rupee currency.

This process, which the London *Economist* termed "inflationary finance of the crudest character," caused an enormous increase in the volume of Indian currency which, coupled with the sharply diminished supply of goods available for civilian consumption, resulted in a rapid and continuing rise in the Indian price level. This in turn encouraged speculation and hoarding of foodstuffs and other commodities, and greatly increased war costs, forcing the Government to print more and more currency to meet military needs, with the result that the inflationary process was accelerated. Had the British been compelled to raise the rupees needed for their own expenditures in India by the normal process of floating rupee loans, India's sterling balances in London would not be so large, but on the other hand she would not have been subjected to the disastrous inflation of her currency.

Indian economists feel that the heavy financial burden involved in this inflation, in addition to the large sums contributed by the Indian people through taxation, loans, and the diversion of the greater part of their limited production to supply the needs of Britain and the Allied Powers, should be taken into account by those who stress the "generosity" of Britain's financial arrangements with India. They contend that the accumulation of sterling assets in London, over which they have no control, does not compensate for this serious demoralization of India's internal economy. In their view, the redemption of India's sterling debt and the freezing of the sterling assets represent a forced loan wrung out of India at the cost of the welfare of the Indian people, for which they have received no adequate return.

There is no question that the entire emphasis of British wartime economic policy in India was placed on diverting Indian resources from civilian to military use rather than on measures to expand the total volume of production. This neglect of civilian needs was particularly disastrous in a country like India, where the normal level of production is barely sufficient to meet civilian requirements even in peacetime and where, as a consequence, the effects of the currency inflation were far more severe than they would have been if the inflation had been accompanied by increased production. In particular, Indians resent the fact that India was not permitted to use her large favorable trade balances in the early years of the war to finance the import of machinery and other equipment needed to expand her limited industrial capacity.

Aside from the inflationary effects of British war finance in India, there remains the question of what use India will be allowed to make of the large sterling assets she possessed at the end of the war. Because these assets have been on blocked account, the decision rests with the British Treasury, and the proposals that have emanated thus far from official and semiofficial British sources do not suggest that these sterling credits will be available to finance any extensive program of Indian industrialization. In the first place, it has been proposed that a substantial amount be deducted from the reserves to set up a capital fund that would enable the British Treasury to pay out sterling pensions, annuities, etc., to British officials retired from service in India — expenditures that now form part of the "Home Charges" of the Government of India and amount to an annual transfer of between $20 and $24 million. The remaining credits would be established as a fund — or, in other words, would be considered as a long-term loan to Britain. Repayments would be made only to the amount of the interest on this loan and would take the form of British exports to India. As the London *Economist* wrote on March 6, 1943: "The sterling resources in question must be regarded as blocked until such a time as they can be freed for financing British exports to India." It may be assumed that the character of these exports would be determined in London rather than in India, and that it would not be designed to facilitate an Indian-controlled program of industrialization.

Another fact to be noted in connection with India's sterling balances is the possibility that a large portion of these funds may be used in the postwar period to maintain the statutory exchange rate between the rupee and the pound sterling. The Reserve Bank of India is at present bound by law to maintain the exchange rate of the rupee at 1s. 6d. But once wartime controls are removed, the highly inflated rupee will fall sharply in both internal and external value because of the substantial gap between the price levels in India and in England. The only way to restore the value of the rupee to the statutory rate is to withdraw excess rupee currency from circulation. This can be accomplished by having the Reserve Bank sell sterling for rupees at the statutory rate and thereby reduce the quantity of outstanding rupees. This operation would, of course, involve a big loss because the statutory rate for rupees would be much higher than the current market rate. Thus the sterling assets which had

formed the basis for more rupee currency during the war would be sold at a loss to bring about a contraction in the volume of Indian currency — a "legal" manipulation that would successfully dispose of or reduce the Indian sterling assets. Furthermore, such a deflationary act would result in low prices, depression, and unemployment in India, would benefit British exporters who naturally prefer a high value for the rupee in terms of sterling, and would artificially drain off a large part of what India has earned during the war years.

A policy of Indian currency deflation is not the only means by which India might be prevented from utilizing the sterling credits she has amassed during the war. For example, suggestions have emanated from British financial circles that in the final apportionment of war expenditures as between Britain and India, a higher burden may be placed on India than that envisaged in the tentative financial settlement adopted in 1939, and also that a part of the British debt to India may be wiped out by the manipulation of the exchange rate between the rupee and the pound sterling. An article published in the *Manchester Guardian Weekly* of May 26, 1944, entitled "Piling Up Debt to India" is of particular significance in this connection.

The article refers to Lord Keynes's statement in the House of Lords that "in waging war without counting the cost we have burdened ourselves with an indebtedness to other countries beneath which we shall stagger." The article then goes on to declare that "we have not only thrown into the pool the bulk of the foreign assets that were built up by the savings of several generations, but have purchased abroad anything we needed for the fight and signed bits of paper absent-mindedly for anybody who sent in a bill. As a result, we have incurred a short-term overseas debt much greater than the whole of the war debt owed to the United States after the last war. A large part of it, at least £750,000,000, we owe to India as a result of *the most fantastic contract made in British history.* So long as that agreement is not revised our debt will go on rising rapidly. . . . The monetary plan assumes that three years will see us through the bottleneck. It is a bold assumption but it might prove right if there is no claim for lease-lend repayment, and if *the dishonest Indian arrangement* is stopped now. In any case, the opening left for the sterling areas needs further improvement, and *we must reserve*, in the final scheme, *the right to make any revision of our exchange rate with other* sterling countries." (Author's italics.)

It is not surprising that such comments in a paper with a long-standing reputation for liberalism struck horror to Indian ears. Not only did the *Guardian* article refer to the sterling credits amassed by India and other countries as "bits of paper" signed "absent-mindedly," but it singled out the Indian debt for specific comment. Furthermore, as we have seen, Indians did not regard the financial arrangements with Britain as either "fantastic" or "dishonest," with the ravages of inflation and famine staring them in the face. But it was the reference to a "revision of exchange" rates that caused the greatest alarm in India. India has had her exchange rate "revised" before, after the First World War. Indians are fully aware that by a manipulation of the official rate of exchange between the pound and the rupee, at least half of Britain's debt to India could be "revised" out of existence, and that much of the remainder could be eliminated by a revision of the wartime financial arrangement which would debit India for a higher share of the war costs. What was left would be repaid in the form of British exports on terms fixed in London.

It is obvious that America as well as India would be a loser if some such policy were adopted with regard to India's sterling credits. For if India were allowed to use those credits freely, she would unquestionably wish to purchase millions of dollars' worth of industrial goods and equipment in the United States. As matters stand today, however, and as they seem likely to stand tomorrow if the views expressed by the *Manchester Guardian* provide a clue to future British policy, India will be incapable of buying anything from any country except Great Britain, and then only what Britain chooses to sell.

It is significant that one of the principal demands voiced by Indian business circles is that a substantial portion of India's sterling assets be transferred to the United States and converted into dollar credits in order that India may purchase American goods after the war. Even the hand-picked Indian delegation to the Bretton Woods Monetary Conference urged that since the primary objective of the proposed International Monetary Fund was to facilitate and expand international trade, and since the United Kingdom owing to her own reconstruction needs would not be in a position to supply all of India's postwar requirements for capital goods, some means should be found to give multilateral convertibility to at least a portion of India's sterling balances in London. This suggestion was met with a prompt rebuke from the British delegation on the grounds that the question of wartime indebtedness was outside the scope of the proposed monetary fund and that the problem of India's sterling balances must be settled between India and England.

It is true that the British agreed in the summer of 1944 that in future India's dollar receipts from merchandise trade with the United States will be retained as dollar balances by the Bank of England and earmarked for India's account for postwar use. This minor concession, designed primarily to conciliate American exporters, does not affect the convertibility of the sterling assets already accumulated by India and will be of small consequence as long as Britain retains an indirect but effective control over Indian foreign trade and industrial development.

WHAT BRITAIN PLANS FOR INDIA

BRITISH STATEMENTS concerning the use of India's sterling balances are not the only indication that India's postwar industrialization will encounter serious obstacles. The reception accorded the Bombay Plan in British official and semiofficial circles, for example, gives an inkling of what may be going on behind the scenes in Whitehall and New Delhi. The first official reaction to the plan, as evidenced by the inspired comments of the London *Economist* and other journals, was one of unalloyed criticism and open hostility. This was followed by a soft-pedaling of the critical note and a somewhat labored attempt to find some good points in the plan. In February 1944, the Viceroy gave the plan the "death kiss" of official patronage accompanied by an invitation to its sponsors to a round of wining and dining. Declaring that the Government was examining the Bombay Plan with interest, Lord Wavell stated that "the views of the authors of this plan on the objects to be achieved are in principle the same as those of my Government. . . . We differ on the methods to be employed, their relative importance in the plan as a whole, the part to be played by the State and by private enterprise and the financial practicability of development on the scale contemplated within the time suggested by the authors; but our aim is similar and we welcome any sincere contribution to the problem that sets people thinking and makes them realize both the possibilities and pitfalls ahead of us."

Finally, the British authorities in India attempted to neutralize the Bombay Plan entirely by taking the whole question of postwar industrial planning under their own wing and putting forward a program of their own. On July 6, 1944, the Government of India announced the formation of a new Government Department of Planning and Development and the appointment of Sir Ardeshir Dalal as Member-in-Charge. Sir Ardeshir is a leading Indian industrialist, a member of the Government's Postwar Reconstruction Committee (since superseded by the new Department) and also one of the signatories of the Bombay Plan. According to the statement, the Government had already assembled "far-reaching plans for India's social, industrial, and economic development," through the work of various committees of experts, and the task of the new Department will be "to integrate these findings into a comprehensive national plan." This plan, however, was concerned primarily with an extensive road-building program, the extension of irrigation and hydroelectric power projects, etc., and did not contemplate either a basic change in India's agricultural structure or the establishment of Indian-owned heavy industry.

From articles in the London *Times,* the *Economist,* and other influential British journals, it would appear that two schools of thought developed in England after the publication of the Bombay Plan. One considered that industrial planning and development for India was necessary and desirable but that it should serve as a substitute for political freedom. The other held that Indian industrialization was a threat to British economy, and that some degree of political freedom might be the lesser of two evils, if thereby a program of rapid industrialization could be blocked. The *Economist* appeared to support the second school of thought, whereas both the British Government and the Government of India seemed to favor the first in the belief that proposals for postwar economic development could divert attention from the basic issue of political freedom. This was indicated, for example, in Mr. Amery's speech during the House of Commons debate on India at the end of July 1944, in which he devoted considerable time to the promise of economic planning for India. The *New Statesman and Nation* had the follow-

ing pertinent and pithy comment to make on this portion of Mr. Amery's remarks: "This new attitude, after the neglect of the past and the long adherence of Delhi to laissez faire, is certainly to be commended. But the white strangers cannot do the planning for India. Any plan that begins to cope with Indian poverty will have to shake Indians out of old habits and customs; it will have to enlist their patriotism in a mighty national effort; it will have to overcome some anti-social forces entrenched in their own society. These things a foreign bureaucracy cannot do. Only a popular national government rooted in the pride and affection of the masses could do all this. Mr. Amery, in words, disclaimed the intention of offering his economic plans, which are to run for fifteen years, as a substitute for political freedom. The suspicion haunts us, none the less, that this is precisely what he is doing, perhaps unconsciously."

In the following months, British authorities both in England and in India laid increasing stress and even enlarged on their plans for Indian economic development. By outlining ambitious programs for industrial expansion, agricultural reform, etc., to be carried out by the "Government of India," without reference to the question of who was to control that Government, the British succeeded to a certain extent in obscuring the fundamental issue of British control over the Indian economy and the fact that this control had been and inevitably would be exercised in favor of British rather than Indian interests. On April 22, 1945, the Government of India even announced a policy of "taking over" the development of major industries, such as automobiles and steel production, if private capital was not available for that purpose. This statement followed shortly after the announcement that certain large American automobile concerns were planning to establish plants in India. The Government's statement pointed out that ordnance factories, public utilities, and railways were already largely state-owned, and added that "apart from these, basic industries of national importance, such as aircraft, automobiles and tractors, chemicals, iron and steel, prime movers, machine tools, and electrical machinery, may be nationalized." This proposal sounded very modern and progressive, and in line with similar tendencies throughout Europe. But it is obviously one thing for basic industries to be nationalized by a popularly-elected and controlled government, and quite another for it to be done by a "foreign bureaucracy."

There was, moreover, some danger that the Indian industrialists would prove susceptible to this British strategy and lose sight of the fundamental question of the control of India's future development. As noted above, the Bombay Plan, when it was first issued in January 1944, was severely criticized on a number of grounds, including the fact that it dismissed far too casually the question of India's future political status. In the second part of the Plan, published in January 1945, the authors took account of some of these criticisms by calling for measures to ensure a more equitable distribution of wealth, including a graduated income tax, the establishment of a minimum wage level wherever possible, and the fixing of minimum prices for agricultural products. They also advocated certain reforms in the system of land tenure and taxation. But they still appeared to believe that industrial development would in itself provide a solution for India's agrarian problem by reducing the pressure of population on the land and furnishing a market for agricultural raw materials. There was no specific recognition of the fact that a prosperous domestic market is essential for the success of any industrialization program, and that in India such a market can be developed only by a thorough modernization of the medieval system of landownership and taxation.

Most serious of all, however, is the Bombay Plan's avoidance of the issue of political control. When the first part of the Plan was published, the introduction contained the single statement that "underlying our whole scheme is the assumption that on the termination of the war or shortly thereafter, a national government will come into existence which will be vested with full freedom in economic matters." But this optimistic assumption was hardly warranted by the political situation in India, or by the statements of British officials concerning India's future economic development. This became so clear that three leading Indian industrialists, J. R. D. Tata, B. M. Birla, and Sir Homi Mody, all signers of the Bombay Plan, subsequently made significant statements concerning the relationship of economic planning to national independence. Mr. Tata said: "Despite my enthusiasm for economic planning, I regard the issue of Indian independence as primary and, as pointed out in the Plan for Economic Development [Bombay Plan] which some of us prepared, only a National Government can put through any large scheme of economic development." In a speech before the

Calcutta Chamber of Commerce on September 22, 1944, Mr. Birla said that economic progress cannot be achieved by a politically subjugated nation and that successful industrial advancement in India depends on the early establishment of a national government. The following sharp warning was part of a long speech made by Sir Homi Mody: "If the British really think that India will accept economic development as a substitute for self-government, they are making another of those profound mistakes which proved disastrous in the past." Yet despite such statements, the second part of the Bombay Plan makes no reference whatsoever to the need for political freedom.

This failure suggests that the Indian industrialists had not yet abandoned the wavering and hesitant attitude toward the nationalist struggle that in the past had provided the British with one of their most useful instruments for maintaining control over the Indian economy. Though there is no question of the desire of the industrialists for freedom from British rule, they have on numerous occasions opposed the nationalist movement for fear that it might develop into a "social revolution" in the course of which their own power would be weakened if not destroyed. Their opposition to the demands of the Indian workers for higher wages and better working conditions has blinded them to the larger issue of political freedom for the entire nation; and to the extent that they have capital invested in land, they have also been opposed to the demands of the peasants for sharp reductions in rent and interest rates. The Indian industrialists — the very men who are most eager to develop extensive and unrestricted trade relations with the United States — are apparently unable to accept with any degree of consistency the fact that only a united nationalist movement can win freedom for India and that their position in a free Indian society must by the very fact of India's economic backwardness remain a dominant one in the foreseeable future. It is this attitude on the part of the industrialists that gives the British reason to hope that, by offering them a few minor concessions, they can win them over to the support of a "Government-sponsored" economic development program and thereby retard India's advance to independence in the economic as well as in the political sphere.

As these industrialization schemes were put forward, it became clearer than ever that if India did not emerge from her status as a political and economic colony of Great Britain, the vision of an Indian industrialization program involving the creation of a large and expanding market for all types of industrial goods would remain a vision as far as the United States was concerned. There was no question of the ability and the desire on the part of Indian leaders to undertake the economic modernization of their country. But any such program inevitably hinged on whether the future Government of India was to be British- or Indian-controlled. We must now turn, therefore, to a consideration of the political obstacles that block the way to Indian economic freedom and industrial development.

THE TECHNIQUES OF BRITISH RULE

THE FOREGOING analysis has shown that British economic policy toward India was designed to develop that country primarily as an adjunct to the industrial economy of Great Britain. Industrialization was officially discouraged, mineral and power resources remained largely undeveloped, and control of finance, trade, and transport was retained in British hands. India did indeed receive some important benefits, notably internal law and order, security from external aggression, an efficient though very costly civil service, the mechanisms of a modern economy such as railroads and communications, and (for a relatively small educated group) knowledge of Western science, industrial methods, and political thought. The vast majority of the Indian people, however, remained illiterate, disease-ridden, and impoverished. No attention was paid by the British administration to the basic problems of modernizing India's primitive, oppressive, and inadequate agrarian system, and of raising the living standards of her people.

The question that remains to be considered is the political means by which the British have been able to accomplish their economic aims in India, for it is obvious that only the retention of political and administrative power has enabled them to keep a potentially rich and powerful country in the backward economic status of a colony. According to the 1931 census, there were only 168,000 British in India, of whom 60,000 were in the army, 21,000 in business or professional occupations, and 12,000 in the various branches of the civil service. Even though the Indian people were totally disarmed, it is clear that such a small number could not rule a nation of 390 million by power alone.

India is, indeed, an outstanding example of British skill in devising administrative techniques for maintaining political control over a large, alien, and increasingly hostile population.

One such technique has been to create and protect a vested interest in the British administration among certain sections of the Indian people. These include the Indian members of the civil service, police, and army, who enjoy secure careers and relatively high pay as well as other privileges; the large landowners who were given their estates by the British and who rely on the administration to protect them from the demands of their oppressed and often rebellious tenantry; and, most useful of all, the 562 Indian Princes whose powers are guaranteed protection by the British Crown and whose territories, scattered over the length and breadth of India, have been aptly described by one of their British champions as "a vast network of friendly fortresses in debatable territory." The continued existence of these medieval autocrats, ruling two-fifths of India's territory and one quarter of her population, is unquestionably the biggest single obstacle to the development of a unified democratically governed Indian nation, and it is strictly a British-made and British-sustained obstacle.

Another technique, employed with good effect against the rising Indian nationalist movement, was the formula of repression, followed by constitutional concessions designed to win over the more moderate sections of Indian opinion. These concessions, as exemplified in the Reforms of 1909, the Constitution of 1919, and the 1935 Constitution, granted to Indians an increasing representation in the provincial and central legislative assemblies and, in the case of the 1935 Constitution, conceded a certain amount of provincial self-government. But at no point were these Indian assemblies accorded any real power to interfere in matters affecting British economic interests or the basic organization of the British regime — e.g., finance, military expenditures, foreign affairs, police, and tariff policies.

It is sometimes forgotten that the Indian National Congress was formed under official auspices in 1885 as a sop to the growing aspirations of the Indian intellectuals for a greater voice in the government of their country. But it was inaugurated only after the threat of widespread popular rebellion had been effectively quelled by the Vernacular Press Act of 1878, which abolished the freedom of the Indian press, and the Arms Act of 1879 which made it a severe penal offense for any Indian civilian to possess a weapon of any kind.

The rise of a more militant nationalist sentiment within the National Congress in the early years of the present century was first countered by the imprisonment or deportation of the more extremist leaders, the passage of a Seditious Meetings Act, and a more drastic press-control law. This was followed by the political reforms embodied in the India Councils Act of 1909, better known as the Morley-Minto Reforms. It is interesting to note that these reforms were not intended as an advance toward Indian self-government. Lord Morley, Secretary of State for India at that time, reassured the House of Lords on this point by stating that "if it could be said that this chapter of reforms led directly or indirectly to the establishment of a parliamentary system in India, I, for one, would have nothing at all to do with it." The Reforms provided for an elected majority in the Provincial Legislative Councils and an elected minority in the Viceroy's Legislative Council, but these bodies had no control over administration or finance, and their legislation could be vetoed by the Provincial Governors or the Viceroy.

The purpose of these early constitutional reforms was to enlist Indian support for British rule by gradually extending Indian participation in the British administrative machinery. There was no thought of preparing India for ultimate self-government. Lord Morley, for example, told the House of Lords on February 23, 1909: "There are three classes of people whom we have to consider in dealing with a scheme of this kind. There are the Extremists who nurse fantastic dreams that some day they will drive us out of India. . . . The second group nourish no hope of this sort, but hope for autonomy or self-government of the colonial species or pattern. And then the third section who ask for no more than to be admitted to coöperation in our administration. I believe that the effect of the Reforms has been, is being, and will be to draw the second class, who hope for colonial autonomy, into the third class, who will be content with being admitted to a fair and full coöperation."

Confronted with the resurgence of Indian nationalist sentiment during the First World War, coupled with the necessity of retaining Indian support, the British Government issued the Declaration of August 20, 1917, in which for the first time the goal of British policy in India was defined as "the gradual development of self-governing institutions with a view to the progressive realization of responsible government in India as an integral part of the British Empire." This Declaration is usually described as marking a definite shift from the previous British attitude toward self-government for India. But it must be noted that the pledge was carefully hedged by the further statement that "the British Government and the Government of India . . . must be the judges of the time and measure of each advance, and they must be guided by the coöperation received from those upon whom new opportunities for service will thus be conferred and by the extent to which it is found that confidence can be reposed in their sense of responsibility." Thus the British Government continued to adhere to the policy of enlisting the coöperation of Indians in the British-controlled administration, and made such coöperation the test of India's right to further political progress.

During the twenty-year period between the First and the Second World Wars, two legislative measures were taken to implement this declaration: the Government of India Act of 1919 and the Act of 1935 which is the basis of the present Indian constitution. The latter act has been described by British spokesmen as bringing India to the very threshold of self-government. Yet a study of its federal provisions reveals that it confirmed and enlarged the powers of a central executive responsible solely to the British Government; prohibited the proposed federal legislature from passing any measures that "discriminated against" British trade, industry, banking, and shipping interests operating in India; gave the Viceroy an unrestricted veto power and reserved in his hands complete control of foreign affairs, defense, the civil service, and police; and gave the appointed representatives of the Indian Princes such a strong representation in the federal legislature that they, plus the official, European, and conservative landlord groups, would hold an unshakable preponderance of power.

It is true that the Provincial sections of the Act granted a considerable measure of self-government. The provincial legislatures were entirely elected, with Indian Ministries responsible to them. About 11% of the population was enfranchised as compared with 2.8% under the Act of 1919. An important limitation on the activities of the Provincial Ministries, however, apart from the veto powers of the Provincial Governors and the statutory prohibition against any interference in matters affecting British interests, was the lack of funds. The Provincial Governments were made responsible for the "nation-building" services of health, education, and agricultural development; but the expanding sources of revenue such as the customs and income tax were allocated to the Central Government, while the Provinces were given as their main source of income the burdensome and inelastic land revenue. Moreover, the Provincial Ministries had no control over that portion of the budget, a large one, that covered the debt services, the salaries of the Governor and other officials, and the "defense" charges.

Anyone desirous of learning how the British Government concedes the semblance of responsible government while withholding the actuality, would do well to study the 235 pages that make up the Government of India Act of 1935, particularly the 94 sections that confer special discretionary powers on the Viceroy. Here it is sufficient to quote the verdict of a leading constitutional authority in Britain, Professor A. B. Keith: "It is difficult to resist the impression that either responsible government should have been frankly declared impossible or the reality conceded. . . . It is too obvious that on the British side the [federal] scheme is favoured in order to combat any dangerous elements of democracy contributed by British India. . . . Moreover, the withholding of defense and external affairs from federal control . . . renders the alleged concession of responsibility all but meaningless."

Another highly effective technique by which the British have countered the pressure of Indian nationalist demands has been the "scrupulous concern for minorities" that has characterized British policy ever since Indian nationalism began to assume "dangerous" proportions. The British authorities were quick to realize that India's religious divisions were a useful obstacle to the growth of a united nationalist movement and that they could also serve as an excellent justification for the continuance of British rule in order to ensure the "protection" of the minorities from the "oppression" of majority rule. Thus, in the reforms of 1909, the Moslem community was granted a separate electorate and heavily weighted representation in the new legislative councils to counterbalance the then predominantly Hindu nationalist movement. This system of "communal electorates" was extended and elaborated in each successive constitutional reform measure and reached its high point in the Constitution of 1935. Under this act the Indian electorate was divided into 19 religious and social categories, each of which was given separate representation in the Provincial Legislative Assemblies. In the proposed federal legislative assembly, this "protection of minorities" was carried to such an extreme that, even if the Hindus had won every seat that they were entitled to contest, they would still have had only 48% of the representation of British India although they constitute two-thirds of the population.

The British insist that this system of communal electorates is necessary to protect the interests of minority groups and is not intended as a "divide and rule" policy. But an examination of the allotment of seats among the various minority groups reveals that some minorities were considered to require far more protection than others, and that specially weighted representation was granted to those groups that were least closely identified with the nationalist movement. Furthermore, it is obvious that this system, whatever its intentions, serves to promote political organization along religious lines and thus fosters religious antagonism and minimizes the political and economic problems that all Indian religious communities have in common.

Another manifestation of this policy of using the minorities question to obstruct Indian progress toward national unity and self-government was the treatment accorded to the Moslem League by the British Government during the early years of the war. Despite the fact that in the elections of 1937 the League had polled only 5% of the total Moslem vote, the Viceroy and other British officials constantly referred to it as the political equal of the Congress Party and implicitly accepted both the League's claim to speak for India's 90 million Moslems and its contention that the Congress Party was seeking to establish a "Hindu Raj" that would mean political and cultural extermination for Indian Moslems. By playing up the importance of the League and accepting the extravagant and unfounded assertions of its leaders, the British authorities were able to cite the League's opposition to Congress as just cause for refusing any immediate political concessions to India. Similar use was also made of other minority groups — notably the Indian Princes — to prove that a system of democratic government based on majority rule was impossible in India, and that until these various groups could agree among themselves, it was impossible for the

British Government to consider transferring real power to Indian hands.

On the eve of the Second World War, however, the political situation in India was very different from that prevailing in 1914. The Indian nationalist movement had developed a strong mass organization, the National Congress Party, which was pledged to work for complete independence and a democratic united India including the people of the Indian States. Congress Ministries were in office in seven of the eleven provinces of British India. The experience of the two civil-disobedience campaigns of 1919–21 and 1930–34, coupled with the growth of trade union and peasant organizations, had brought about the political awakening of millions of Indian peasants and workers who, though disenfranchised, were actively supporting the Congress Party's demands for political and economic reforms. The Congress was adamantly opposed to British constitutional policy as expressed in the 1935 constitution, which it regarded as a poorly concealed effort on the part of the British to utilize communal divisions and the Indian Princes to frustrate Indian nationalist aims. The heterogeneous character of the Congress membership, embracing as it did both militant trade unionists and peasant leaders as well as conservative industrialists and bankers, had caused a certain amount of internal dissension on questions of social and economic policy and political tactics. But in the provincial elections of 1937 Congress had proved itself overwhelmingly the most powerful, most representative, and best-organized political party in India.

CHAPTER III

INDIA'S STRUGGLE FOR FREEDOM

❊

T HE CONFLICTING aims of Indian nationalism and British rule had already reached a deadlock when the outbreak of the Second World War led to an immediate heightening of political tension in India. Indian nationalists promptly demanded that Britain declare her war aims regarding India, on the ground that the Indian people should not be asked to fight in a war for freedom and democracy if they were not to share in its benefits. They further contended that the Indian people could be mobilized for the defense of their country only by a genuinely Indian government in which they had confidence. When the British authorities declined to answer the request for a statement of British aims regarding India, the Congress Ministries in the Provinces resigned in protest.

The Moslem League, on the other hand, saw an opportunity to enhance its political power and offered coöperation in the war provided it was guaranteed protection against the "Hindu majority." Encouraged by the favorable reception its claims received in official circles, the League then increased its demands and in March 1940 raised the issue of "Pakistan" — a separate Moslem state — for the first time. In the meantime, the Congress Party had made clear its sympathy with the anti-fascist cause and its intention to do nothing to embarrass the British Government. In July 1940 it went further and, abandoning Gandhi's non-violence policy, offered to coöperate actively in India's defense provided a definite date for India's independence was set and a provisional national government formed that would have the confidence of the elected members of the Central Legislative Assembly. Only such a government, Congress leaders insisted, could convince the Indian people that they had a genuine stake in the war and were not being asked to fight merely to preserve British rule.

The British Government replied, on August 8, 1940, with a

lengthy statement in which it reiterated that its ultimate goal was "free and equal partnership" for India in the British Commonwealth, under a constitution framed by Indians, "subject to the fulfillment of our obligations for the protection of minorities . . . and of our treaty obligations to the Indian States. . . ." For the time being, the Government proposed an enlargement of the Viceroy's Executive Council to include representative Indians. Since this offer in no way met the demands of the Indian nationalists and merely confirmed their suspicions that Britain intended to use the "minorities issue" to veto any political concessions, Congress withdrew its offer of coöperation. An incipient civil-disobedience campaign was crushed by the arrest of some 37,000 Congress leaders, and for more than a year the deadlock continued while the British position in Europe, the Near East, and Asia grew more and more precarious.

Japan's entry into the war and the rapid Japanese victories in Hong Kong, Malaya, Netherlands India, and Burma brought the conflict to the very gates of India and enormously increased the importance of India to the United Nations war effort. Something had to be done at once to improve the Indian situation and enlist Indian coöperation in the war. On February 15, 1942, the disastrous Malayan campaign ended with the fall of Singapore, and Japan began her advance into Burma. The British War Cabinet undertook to formulate a new offer to India, and on March 11 Sir Stafford Cripps was despatched to India to ascertain whether this new offer would secure, as Mr. Churchill put it, a "reasonable and practical" measure of acceptance and thus "promote the concentration of all Indian thought and energies" on the defense against Japan.

WHY THE CRIPPS MISSION FAILED

THIS, THEN, was the background of the Cripps offer. The question of whether the postwar provisions of the Cripps plan do in fact constitute an unrestricted offer of independence to India, as the British claim, will be discussed in a subsequent chapter. Here we are concerned with the proposals so far as they dealt with the immediate problem of mobilizing the Indian people and Indian resources against the imminent threat of a Japanese invasion. On this point the plan stated that for the duration of the war the British Government must retain control and direction of

Indian defense, but that it desired and invited "the immediate and effective participation of leaders of the principal sections of the Indian people in the counsels of their country, of the Commonwealth, and of the United Nations." The plan, however, made no definite proposals for responsible Indian participation in the defense effort, or for organizing and arming the people, or for a rapid expansion of key Indian defense industries. And it wholly ignored the basic Indian contention that only a genuinely responsible and representative government could arouse the Indian people to fight; that they would fight in defense of their own freedom but not to preserve foreign rule. The Cripps proposals represented in fact no real change in British policy as compared with the declaration of August 1940, since they offered India only a consultative relationship to the war effort and placed the customary emphasis on Britain's determination to protect "minority groups" and particularly the rights of the Indian Princes.

The Cripps proposals were rejected by every political party and group in India. During the two and a half years following the failure of the Cripps Mission, the political situation in India grew steadily worse. In August 1942 the Congress Party made a last appeal for the formation of a national government capable of mobilizing the Indian people for full support of the war, and on August 8, in understandable desperation, authorized Gandhi to invoke nonviolent civil disobedience if this demand were not granted. The Government, falsely calling the Congress resolution a plan of capitulation to Japan and choosing to define the term "nonviolent" as violence, promptly countered by arresting Gandhi, Nehru, and thousands of other Congress leaders on August 9. These arrests provoked sporadic protest demonstrations that were ruthlessly suppressed. It is true that these demonstrations were followed by acts of sabotage, but these acts were instigated and encouraged by the traitorous Forward Blocist followers of the Japanese quisling, Subhas Chandra Bose, and by Congress Socialists under the leadership of Jai Prakash Narain. The acts of these Socialists were officially repudiated by Gandhi, and Narain and his followers were disowned by the Congress Party.

These Congress Socialists of India ran a close second to the Forward Blocists in meriting the label of "pro-Japanese" and "pro-fascist." They preached indiscriminate rebellion against the British and encouraged fifth-column activities. They also carry on anti-Soviet and anti-Chinese propaganda, and have done everything possible to obstruct the trend toward Congress-League unity. Their whole policy has been aimed at maintaining the political deadlock, sabotaging national defense, and intensifying economic demoralization, in the hope that the crisis would facilitate their rise to power. In August 1944, Mr. Minoo Masani, leader of the Congress Socialists in Bombay, expressed himself as being very much displeased with Gandhi's proposals for a settlement with the Government of India and the Moslem League, on the ground that Gandhi was seeking to establish a coalition government which "would shoot Japanese, against whom Indians as such had no particular quarrel."

With all responsible Congress leaders held incommunicado in jail, it was easy for the authorities to place the blame for the violence upon Congress, declare its organization illegal, and seize its funds and headquarters. It was inevitable that the Congress Party should be seriously weakened and disorganized. The Moslem League, however, was able to capitalize on this demoralization and greatly extend its political power and influence over the rank and file of the Moslem community.

Resentment against the British increased, but the various Indian political parties, especially Congress and the Moslem League, instead of uniting to carry on the struggle, drew even farther apart and the League grew more aggressive in its demands for a separate Moslem state and in its refusal to accept a government for India in which Hindus would of necessity form a permanent majority. At that time many Congress members were convinced that the League was seeking British support to further its own ambitions at the expense of Indian freedom. On the other hand, Mr. Jinnah and other League leaders accused Congress of working for a unilateral settlement with the British that would give Congress power to ignore the League and the demands of the Moslem community for self-determination.

Political discontent and frustration in India were accompanied by an increasingly serious economic crisis that affected the welfare of millions of Indians who had remained relatively untouched by the political struggle. Acute shortages of foodstuffs in many parts of the country coupled with a sharp rise in food prices culminated in the disastrous famine that ravaged Bengal and other areas in the autumn of 1943 and again in 1944. The Government proved itself unable to take adequate measures to control food prices, check hoarding, increase food production, and improve distribution methods. In fact, many Indians contended that what they termed the Government's deliberate inflationary policy actually served to encourage hoarding and speculation because it was aimed at discouraging consumption through high prices and thereby reducing the demand to correspond with the reduction in food supplies available for civilian use. The Government was also sharply criticized for failing to take effective measures to aid the debt-ridden peasantry to expand production or open up new land.

The failure of the British authorities in India to deal effectively with the problems of food supply, transport, hoarding, inflation, and other matters directly affecting the welfare of the civilian population was the outstanding feature of the Indian economic situation in 1943 and 1944. People's Food Committees, organized by the Indian Communist Party and the trade and peasant unions, were formed in many parts of the country to urge the peasants to grow more food and to expose hoarders, but these Committees received little support from government officials and were powerless in themselves to combat the destructive activities of the big grain merchants and landlords.

On the political front, the situation remained deadlocked, with the British Government continuing to insist that it was Indian disunity alone that was preventing further progress and that Congress leaders must be kept in prison until they disavowed their resolution of August 1942. All attempts on the part of Indian leaders to arrange a meeting between Gandhi and Jinnah were thwarted by the Government. Gandhi was also refused permission to interview the members of the Congress Working Committee, despite the fact that no official shift in Congress policy could be made without such a meeting. Even President Roosevelt's personal representative, William Phillips, was refused permission to visit Gandhi and deliver a message from the President.

In February 1943 the British authorities issued a lengthy statement, known as the Tottenham Report, which was designed to prove Congress responsibility for the acts of sabotage and other disorders that followed the arrest of the Congress leaders in 1942 and which branded the Congress as defeatist and even pro-Axis. Gandhi wrote an 82-page reply refuting these charges, which he despatched to the Government in July 1943 with the request that it be published. In October the Government informed Gandhi that its statement "was published for the information of the public" and not for the purpose of "eliciting your defense," and that the Government "neither invited nor desired your comments upon it." As for publishing Gandhi's reply, the Government stated that it was not prepared to afford "any facilities for communication with the general public" or to act as "agents for your propaganda. . . . The Government does not propose to publish your letter unless and until they think fit." This time did not come until some eleven months later.

THE QUESTION OF INDIAN UNITY

DURING THIS period of political frustration and economic crisis, with the Congress Party weakened and demoralized, the activities of three political and economic groups, many of whose members also belong to Congress, were largely responsible for preventing a complete collapse of the Indian home front. These three were the All-India Trade Union Congress, the All-India Kisan Sabha or Peasant Union, and the Indian Communist Party.

The Trade Union Congress is the outstanding trade-union organization in India today. At the beginning of 1945 it comprised 416 affiliated unions with a membership of approximately 500,000. It stood for full Indian participation in the war against the Axis, for the release of all political prisoners, and for the formation of a representative national government. It urged all political parties, particularly Congress and the Moslem League, to accept the principle of self-determination of nationalities as a means to national unity. It opposed strikes and sabotage as playing into the hands of the Axis, and appealed to all workers to maintain uninterrupted production of vital war materials despite the fact that their working and living conditions steadily deteriorated. It was active in the fight for adequate price control and rationing measures to meet the food crisis, and played an important part in the establishment of People's Food Committees.

The Trade Union Congress has continued to grow in size and influence despite the official favor bestowed on its rival, the Indian Federation of Labor, which was formed with official encouragement in November 1941 under the leadership of M. N.

Roy, who also heads the Radical Democratic Party.[1] Both these organizations have consistently denounced the Trade Union Congress and the Congress Party, and the Indian Federation was rewarded for its loyal support of the Government not only with a monthly grant of 13,000 rupees for "doing propaganda to keep up industrial morale," but also by being chosen to represent Indian labor at the Philadelphia meeting of the International Labor Office in April 1944. This choice was particularly revealing inasmuch as the Trade Union Congress had represented Indian labor at all I.L.O. conferences since its foundation in 1920, and its general secretary, N. M. Joshi, was a member of the I.L.O.'s governing body.[2]

The All-India Kisan Sabha represents some fourteen provincial and local peasant unions, and its membership increased from 280,000 in 1943 to more than 550,000 in 1944, and to 825,000 in 1945. The Kisan Sabha also urged full support of the war, the release of political prisoners, and the formation of a national government. The peasant unions took an active part in organiz-

---

[1] Mr. Roy, a well-known political opportunist, was at one time a member of the Communist International, from which he was expelled. He subsequently carried on political intrigue in Europe, China, and Mexico. In 1934, on his return to India, he was arrested and sentenced to six years' imprisonment, but was released in 1936. Mr. Roy has long since lost the respect of the Indian people.

[2] December 1944 witnessed the virtual collapse of the Indian Federation of Labor as a result of the resignation of its president and vice-president, Jamnadas Mehta and Aftab Ali, who had served as the Indian labor delegates to the I.L.O. Conference in Philadelphia. Their resignations followed a further discussion of the Government's subsidy to the Federation during the meeting of the Central Legislative Assembly. Mr. Mehta had denied that the 13,000 rupees were given to the Federation, claiming that they had been paid to Mr. Roy personally. In response to questions in the Assembly, however, Dr. B. R. Ambedkar, Labor Member of the Viceroy's Council, stated specifically that the grant was made to the Federation for "the publication of printed literature, oral propaganda, visual propaganda, and the dissemination of reassuring news." He added that "I am satisfied that the expenditure achieved the result for which it was sanctioned." In addition, a member of the Information Ministry, when questioned, admitted that the Government had been subsidizing Roy's newspaper, the *Vanguard*, by purchasing 1,500 copies daily. As a result of this public exposure of the Federation's role as a mouthpiece of the Government, even the right-wing labor leaders repudiated the organization, leaving it with only Mr. Roy and his personal supporters and depriving it of whatever small claim it had had to speak for any section of Indian labor. The Calcutta Seamen's Union, headed by Aftab Ali, subsequently applied for admission to the All-India Trade Union Congress at its Madras session in February 1945 and was accepted.

ing and educating the peasants and in the formation of Food Committees to check hoarding and encourage increased food production. The Kisan Sabha insisted that to combat the food crisis it must be made "profitable and feasible for the peasantry to grow more food crops." To this end it proposed in 1942 that cultivable land then lying fallow be given for cultivation rent-free to poor peasants and landless agricultural laborers; that excessive rents be scaled down; and that peasants be provided with cheap credit facilities. The only apparent result of these constructive suggestions was that early in 1944 the Kisan Sabha was declared illegal in many parts of the country — notably in certain areas in the United Provinces and the Punjab — presumably because its demands for agrarian reforms and government aid to the peasants were distasteful to the large Indian landowners, whose interests have always received protection from the Government.

At the outbreak of the war, the Indian Communist Party was a small organization of about 4,000 members which had long been illegal in India, though many individual Communists were members of the Congress Party. In the months following the failure of the Cripps Mission, however, the increasing demoralization of the Indian people threatened to leave India defenseless in the face of Japan's continuing advance. The Communists, though fully supporting the Indian nationalist demands, recognized that India's hopes for freedom would prove futile unless Japan were defeated and therefore urged full Indian participation in the war. And the British, because they were ready to grasp at any straw that might strengthen India's defenses, legalized the Indian Communist Party in July 1942.

During the next two years, the Indian Communist Party's influence spread rapidly. Though by the end of 1944 its members still numbered only about 25,000, its influence was important in holding together an internal situation that on many occasions threatened to disintegrate into complete chaos as a result of popular bitterness and the absence of the constructive guidance of the imprisoned Indian leaders. In particular, the Indian Communists carried on a strong campaign for unity between Hindus and Moslems and for a united effort on the part of all parties and groups in India for the defeat of the Axis and the attainment of Indian freedom.

Perhaps the chief contribution of the Communist Party of

India was its exploration of the possibility of a "multinational" solution of India's intensive political problems. It recognized that the Moslem demand for Pakistan represented something more than Mr. Jinnah's personal ambitions; and that Pakistan had acquired popular support among the Moslems because it represented their genuine desire for national self-determination. The belief that a free India should consist of a voluntary federation of autonomous national states, and that only on the basis of full self-determination for all national minorities could the Indian people unite to win and maintain their freedom, gradually came to be accepted not only by many members both of the Congress Party and of the Moslem League, but also by leading foreign students of Indian affairs.

As a consequence, the years 1943 and 1944 were marked by an appreciable and growing trend toward political unity in India. By 1944 virtually all articulate sections of the Indian people had come out in support of the demand for the release of all political prisoners and the formation of a national government representing all responsible parties in order to mobilize India for full participation in the war and pave the way for her advance to full self-government in the postwar period. There was equal unanimity in opposition to the autocratic Government of India as unrepresentative, irresponsible, and unresponsive to the needs and desires of the great majority of the Indian people. This attitude was shared by the Congress Party, the Moslem League, the Liberals, the Industrialists, the Communists, the Peasant Unions, and the Trade Union Congress. Even the Hindu Mahasabha, the ultra reactionary Hindu organization, though it continued to oppose a compromise agreement with the Moslem League, had joined in the demand for the release of political prisoners and the formation of a government representing all parties.

Most important of all, there were signs of a growing recognition in both Congress and League circles that only an agreement between the two parties would enable the Indian people to put forward a united and effective demand for a solution of the present deadlock and disprove the British contention that no political progress was possible because of Indian disunity. Though the leaders of the two parties were denied an opportunity of meeting to discuss the problem, rank-and-file members on both sides were beginning to urge an agreement on the basis of full self-determination for all nationalities in India. The newly acquired mass following of the Moslem League did not share with the wealthy Moslem landlords the fear of the agrarian program sponsored by the Congress Party, and urged coöperation with their fellow peasants and workers in Congress. It may be assumed that it was pressure from this source that was responsible for Mr. Jinnah's statement on March 22, 1944, that "we Hindus and Moslems are brothers and inhabitants of one country. Our enemies think that we can never unite. But we will unite much sooner than they expect and together we shall free our country."

As far as the Congress Party was concerned, many of its leaders still clung to the belief that a strong central government was essential for India and were therefore inclined to oppose the idea of a loose federation of autonomous states. On the other hand, at the time of the Cripps Mission, the Congress Working Committee had declared that "it could not think in terms of compelling the people of any territorial unit to remain in an Indian Union against their declared and established will," and this pledge was repeated at a meeting of certain Congress leaders who were still at liberty in March 1944. Furthermore, during the sessions of the Central Legislative Assembly in the spring of 1944, representatives of Congress and the League consistently joined forces in votes of no-confidence in the existing government and in demands for the formation of a government representative of all sections of the people. Then too, many rank-and-file members of Congress were coming to believe that the granting of self-determination to the Moslems with the right of secession would strengthen rather than disrupt Indian unity and would make possible a far stronger and more effective demand for a National Government.

This change in the Indian political situation was totally ignored by the British authorities, who continued to stand on their contentions that no progress was possible because of the inability of Indian parties to reach agreement and that the Congress prisoners could not be released until they disowned their resolution of August 1942. Thus Lord Wavell, in his speech before the Central Legislative Assembly on February 17, 1944, declared that "until the two main Indian parties at least can come to terms, I do not see any immediate hope of progress." He stated further that "the demand for the release of those leaders who are in detention is an utterly barren one until there is some sign on their part of a willingness to coöperate. . . . I see no reason to release those responsible for the Declaration of August 8, 1942 until I am convinced that the policy of noncoöperation and even obstruction has been withdrawn."

This charge had become such a constant feature of British official statements on the Indian question that it is necessary to emphasize once more that the August 1942 resolution — though admittedly open to criticism in certain respects — was not the antiwar pro-Japanese document that the British authorities subsequently made it out to be, and that the outbursts of violence and sabotage that followed the arrests of the Congress leaders were neither authorized nor organized by the Congress leadership and were repeatedly denounced by Gandhi and the Working Committee. As Gandhi himself pointed out in his letters to the Viceroy, the chief demand embodied in the August resolution was for the formation of a provisional government consisting of members representing all the principal parties, and "as there is no party in the country which is not wholly anti-fascist, anti-Nazi, and anti-Japan, it follows that a Government formed by these parties is bound to become an enthusiastic champion of the Allied cause, which by the recognition of India as a free state will truly become the cause of democracy." On January 25, 1944 Mrs. Sarojini Naidu, the only member of the Congress Working Committee then still at liberty, held a press conference at which she went into great detail regarding Congress policy and the instructions that Gandhi had drawn up for offering resistance to the Japanese. Like Gandhi's communications to the Government, however, Mrs. Naidu's statement encountered the barriers of British censorship and was not allowed to be cabled abroad — an action vigorously denounced in the Moslem press as well as in papers supporting the Congress Party.

By refusing to recognize that the conditions of 1942 no longer existed, and by refusing to permit India's leaders both in and out of prison to get together and discuss the possibilities of a political agreement, the British Government laid itself open to the charge of deliberately seeking to prevent a political settlement between Congress and the League, and of attempting to accomplish the complete destruction of the Congress Party as an effective political organization. But to every criticism of its refusal to release the political prisoners or allow the Congress Working Committee to confer together and with other political leaders; of the methods employed to suppress nationalist demonstrations, including the whipping post and the machine-gunning of un-armed crowds; and of its insistence that the Indian problem was no concern of the other United Nations despite the fact that it was seriously weakening the Allied war effort in Asia, the British Government adhered to one standard reply. Repeatedly, they maintained that the plan presented to India by Sir Stafford Cripps constituted an unrestricted offer of postwar independence to India, provided that the various Indian political groups could agree upon a constitution. As a corollary to this, the British contended that Britain could not possibly transfer political power to Indian hands until this constitutional problem was solved because she was in honor bound, in the words of Lord Wavell, "to see that in the solution of the constitutional problem, full account is taken of the interests of those who have loyally supported us in this war and at all other times — the soldiers who have served the common cause, the people who have worked with us, the rulers and populations of the Native States to whom we are pledged, the minorities who have trusted us to see that they get a fair deal. We are bound in justice, in honor, and in the interests of progress to hand over India to an Indian rule which can maintain the peace and order and the progress which we have endeavored to establish."

BRITISH SINCERITY PUT TO THE TEST

THE SPECIFIC arguments used by the British to justify their refusal of Indian nationalist demands were put to the test following Gandhi's release from prison "solely on medical grounds" in May 1944. On June 12 Gandhi issued a series of proposals for reaching an agreement with the British Government and increasing India's contribution to the Allied war effort. His plan called for the establishment of a provisional Indian national government, with the Viceroy retaining complete control over military affairs, and included a pledge not to invoke civil disobedience for the duration of the war. The aim of his proposals was to ensure three things: the unhindered functioning of the Allied military command; the complete support of the Indian provisional government for the Allied war effort; and a speedy solution of the problems of production and the food crisis. Gandhi also requested permission to interview the members of the Congress Working Committee still in prison, on the ground that he could make no further move without knowing their views.

Simultaneously, Gandhi made a series of proposals to Jinnah, as the basis for an agreement between Congress and the Moslem League. These included the following major points: (1) in those areas of India where the Moslems form a majority of the population — mainly in the Northwest and Northeast — plebiscites should be held after the war to determine whether those areas should remain a part of India or form independent states; (2) in return for this, the Moslem League would coöperate with the Congress in forming a provisional national government.

Gandhi's proposals to the British Government were enthusiastically welcomed by all sections of the Indian people as giving the lie to those who had contended that Congress would not support the war. The Indian press was virtually unanimous in expressing the hope that, in response, the people of England would urge their Government to instruct the Viceroy to release the political prisoners and to open negotiations with Indian leaders for the formation of a representative Indian government. Such a move, they insisted, would not only pave the way for friendly coöperation between Britain and India in the prosecution of the war but also lay the basis for a smooth transition to complete self-government for India in the postwar period.

The response of the British Government to these proposals, however, was a prompt and decided rejection. Mr. Amery, Secretary of State for India, informed the House of Commons that Gandhi's proposals did not constitute a starting point for a profitable discussion and were "in no sense a response to Field Marshal Viscount Wavell's recent invitation to Gandhi to produce constructive proposals." Lord Wavell rejected Gandhi's request for an interview, stating that, while preliminary work might be begun on the framing of a new constitution, Indians must first reach a "gentlemen's agreement" among themselves for "a transitional government established and working within the present constitution." The Viceroy added that he would be glad to consider any "definite and constructive policy." No official notice was taken by the British Government of Gandhi's proposals for a settlement with the Moslem League. That this obstructionist attitude was not shared by all sections of British opinion is indicated by the following editorial in the *New Statesman and Nation* of August 5, 1944, commenting on "The Indian Outlook":

On reading over Friday's debate in the Commons on India, we tried for half an hour a difficult but stimulating experiment. We imagined that nature had sent us into this world with brown skins as involuntary subjects of the King-Emperor. Read from this angle, there were speeches from both sides of the House that compelled our sympathy and even our gratitude. The best of them came from the Tory benches: it was the ghastly account which Professor A. V. Hill, as a physiologist fresh from his stay in India, gave of its bill of health, its mortality from preventable diseases, its semi-starvation, its barely imaginable poverty. Seldom if ever, since the early days of the John Company [East India Company], has any Member of his eminence said so much to shatter Imperial complacency. Several of the other speeches were kindly and in their way helpful, notably that of Mr. Pethick-Lawrence,[1] who with many apologies for mentioning the subject at all, suggested, without demanding, the release of the Congress prisoners. But it was in reading not the hostile but the friendly speeches that our patience, as temporary Indians, all but gave way. No voice spoke in a tone of urgency. No Member, not even the honester of them, seemed to realize that over the greater part of India, British rule is naked autocracy. Six provinces, including some of the most populous and the most advanced, are without a vestige of self-government. And still the leaders of the party which had an electoral majority in these provinces languish in our jails untried. The Empire which dares in this way to rule its hundreds of millions without their consent has as its long range record of achievement the permanent physical misery which Professor Hill described: chalked up upon its recent score is the death of 800,000 victims of a needless, man-made famine in Bengal. Against this foreground and background Mr. Amery's lavish promises of freedom, but only after the war, moved us as temporary Indians to anger and even to nausea.

The net effect of Mr. Amery's speech was to shatter any hope that Mr. Churchill's Government will adopt a policy of conciliation. He ignored altogether the gentle, muted suggestion of an amnesty that came from the Labor Front Bench. He dismissed Mr. Gandhi's surprising and hopeful change of front on the ground that he has made no "constructive" offer. And yet he has offered peace to the Muslim League by conceding its central demand, and ended his rebellion against the British Raj by offering to serve under the Viceroy as a "constitutional monarch." What is it, then, that Mr. Amery demands? Does he expect Indians who respect themselves to serve under Lord Wavell as an autocrat? Or is he waiting for some precise lawyer's out-

---

[1] On August 3, 1945, Mr. Frederick William Pethick-Lawrence became Secretary of State for India and for Burma in the Attlee cabinet, replacing Col. Leopold S. Amery, who had held that office in the Churchill government since 1940.

line of the new relationship? If that is what he wants, it is unreasonable to demand it until the Mahatma can consult the imprisoned
Working Committee of Congress. Lord Linlithgow's refusal to meet
Mr. Nehru and Dr. Azad during the Cripps negotiations contributed
largely to their failure. Lord Wavell seems also to stand aloof at a
critical moment.

Certainly it would seem that, if the British Government had
sincerely desired to facilitate India's peaceful and rapid progress
to the status of a self-governing nation, it would have welcomed
Gandhi's proposals as a hopeful first step in overcoming the obstacles to that development, and at least gone so far as to release
the members of the Congress Working Committee and thereby
given Indian leaders the opportunity to reach that "gentlemen's
agreement" to which the Viceroy referred. It was one thing, justifiable or not, to oppose the transfer of civil administrative
power to a representative Indian government in the spring of
1942 when the war situation was extremely critical and India
was threatened with an imminent Japanese invasion. It was
quite another to refuse to consider such a move two and a half
years later when the threat to India had been removed and it
was an obvious certainty that Japan would be defeated. The argument that it would be impossible in wartime to make the constitutional change necessary for setting up a provisional national
government responsible to the Central Legislative Assembly no
longer carried the same weight. There was nothing to prevent
the British Government — as Sir Stafford Cripps himself had
pointed out as early as October 1939 — from allowing the election of a new central legislative assembly, permitting the majority parties in that assembly to form a government, and agreeing
to treat that government as though it were a cabinet in all major
matters having to do with the civilian administration. Certainly
such a government would have been more representative of and
responsive to the desires of the Indian people than the existing
autocratic bureaucracy that was responsible only to the British
Government. The only conclusion that can be drawn from the
blunt rejection of Gandhi's proposals is that the British Government was not eager to facilitate Indian progress toward self-
government and that Churchill's "we mean to hold our own"
speech was a better guide to British intentions in India than the
ambiguous and carefully guarded clauses of the Cripps offer.

THE GANDHI-JINNAH MEETING

THOUGH THE British authorities paid no attention to Gandhi's proposals for a settlement with the Moslem League, the prospect of a meeting between Gandhi and Jinnah to discuss the possibilities of a Congress-League agreement aroused the Indian people to a fever of excitement and anticipation. To appreciate the significance of this meeting, it must be realized that the British Government had successfully maneuvered these two great parties into a defensive position by insisting that a hard and fast agreement between Congress and the League was an essential prerequisite to the attainment of Indian freedom. In the daily lives of the Indian people, both on the social and economic levels and in the legislative assemblies, there was as much unity as exists in most countries; and most foreign observers were agreed that, if India were a free nation, the various economic, social, and religious problems would be handled by the normal processes of democratic procedure. In India's case, however, her people had been required to present a finished formula for future Hindu-Moslem unity, despite the fact that their efforts to attain that unity had been making what would normally be considered remarkably rapid progress. It was natural, therefore, that the Indian people attached tremendous importance to Gandhi's proposal for a meeting between the two leaders.

The proposals which Gandhi had submitted as a basis of discussion were originally drafted by C. R. Rajagopalachari, ex-premier of Madras and former member of the Congress Working Committee, who had given the question of national minorities and self-determination a great deal of study. In an article in the *Karachi Daily Gazette* on August 27, 1944, he discussed at some length the Russian handling of the national minorities problem as an example for India, because it proved that, in a country composed of many nationalities, a strong union or federation could be formed only on the basis of independence and self-determination for the federating units. He called attention particularly to the fact that in the Soviet Union each Union Republic is granted the right to secede and that, even when remaining in the Union, it is entitled to exercise functions usually associated with independent authority and that as a result "the solidarity of the U.S.S.R. has not been damaged but greatly strengthened." In conclusion, he stated that "the free people of India cannot unite in a treaty of union except on a voluntary basis, and my formula is an honest attempt to put this in tangible form."

Mr. Rajagopalachari's formula for an agreement between Congress and the Moslem League, which was accepted intact by Gandhi, contained the following points:

1. Subject to the terms set out below as regards a constitution for a free India, the Muslim League endorses the Indian demand for independence and will coöperate with the Congress Party in the formation of a provisional interim government for a transitional period.

2. After the termination of the war, a Commission shall be appointed for demarcating contiguous districts in Northwest and East India wherein the Muslim population is in absolute majority. In areas thus demarcated, a plebiscite of all inhabitants, held on a basis of adult suffrage or other practicable franchise, shall ultimately decide the issue of separation from Hindustan. If a majority decide in favor of forming a sovereign state separate from Hindustan, such a decision shall be given effect without prejudice to the right of districts on the border to choose to join either State.

3. It will be open to all parties to advocate their points of view before plebiscites are held.

4. In the event of separation, mutual agreements shall be entered into for safeguarding defense and commerce and communications and for other essential purposes.

5. Any transfer of population shall only be on an absolutely voluntary basis.

6. These terms shall be binding only in case of transfer by Britain of full power and responsibility for the government of India.

In commenting on these proposals, Mr. Jinnah denied that they met the Moslem League's demands, since they did not concede Pakistan as a right, but merely offered the opportunity to vote for it. He also criticized the failure to specify the personnel, power, etc. of the "Commission" that was to demarcate the Moslem areas, and the lack of any precise indication as to the nature of the provisional interim government in which the League was asked to coöperate. But he welcomed the fact that Gandhi had accepted "the principle of the partition of India" and agreed to meet with Gandhi to explore the possibilities of an agreement.

The tone of Jinnah's comments, as well as the text of the Rajagopalachari formula itself, was indicative of the obstacles that had still to be overcome before the two leaders could be expected to reach an agreement. They also revealed the difficulty of the task imposed by Great Britain — namely, to find an immediate and concrete formula for the solution of a problem that could best be dealt with by a process of evolution, possible only in a free India. An illuminating analysis of this problem was published on August 20, 1944 in the *People's War*, official weekly paper of the Indian Communist Party.[1] This article, written by P. C. Joshi, general secretary of the Communist Party, hailed the Gandhi-Jinnah meeting as a great event in India's national history, but warned that the final step to agreement would be a very difficult one "because it involves a complete break with their traditional mode of thought." Mr. Joshi pointed out that the Congress and the League share the common objectives of ending the political deadlock and achieving Indian freedom, but that "to the Leaguer a free India means the right to separate, to the Congressman a free India means a great and united India." And he raised the question: "Can Jinnah make Gandhi realize that there is no freedom possible except through Congress-League unity based on the acceptance of the Muslim right of Pakistan? . . . Can Gandhi make Jinnah realize that the fulfillment of the just demand of the Muslims is not possible except through Congress-League unity to fight for the freedom of all?" Unfortunately for the people of India, the answer to these questions proved to be "no."

Jinnah and Gandhi met for the first time on September 9, 1944. On September 27, after almost three weeks of conversations, the talks were abandoned without an agreement having been reached. The reasons for this failure, which came as a great shock to the people of India and their friends abroad, were clearly revealed in the correspondence between the two men during the period of their negotiations.[2] As far as Jinnah's part in the negotiations is concerned, it was evident that, when he was compelled to define what he meant by Pakistan, he spoke for the leaders of the Moslem League and not for its popular following. To this Moslem mass following, Pakistan meant self-determination for the Moslems in their homelands within the framework of a free Indian federation, and they had demanded that the League seek agreement with the Congress on this basis

---

[1] A slightly abridged text of this article was published in *Amerasia*, Oct. 6, 1944, pp. 277–285.

[2] A somewhat condensed text of this correspondence was published in *Amerasia*, November 3, 1944, pp. 307–319.

in order that the two parties might coöperate effectively in the common struggle for national freedom. The leadership of the League, however, remained in the hands of wealthy Moslem landlords who had never wanted to coöperate with the Congress and its program of agrarian reform, and were chiefly concerned with preventing the possibility of coöperation between Hindu and Moslem peasants in support of that program. In the opinion of this group, the best method to achieve this aim was to demand a completely separate state for Indian Moslems. Jinnah's correspondence with Gandhi showed that he adopted this same attitude: that he definitely opposed the idea of a federated India composed of autonomous units and insisted that India must be divided into two completely sovereign states — Pakistan and Hindustan — which could then come to agreement on matters of common concern.

As for Gandhi's part in the negotiations, he too had been subject to pressure from two sides: on the one hand, from those who adhered to the traditional Congress position that to grant the Moslem demand for autonomy would weaken the struggle for freedom from British rule; on the other, from those who argued that an agreement with the Moslems on the basis of full self-determination for predominantly Moslem areas would make possible a far more united and effective demand for Indian freedom. Gandhi's letters to Jinnah make clear that, though he had been persuaded of the necessity for a settlement with the Moslem League, he still regarded the idea of Moslem self-determination as a concession rather than a right. In other words, he was primarily concerned with winning Moslem agreement to participate in a provisional government in order to strengthen his case against the British, and only when this main goal — freedom from Britain — should be achieved would he be willing to consider a plebiscite in the Moslem areas.

Thus it may be said that both leaders undertook their conversations as a result of strong popular pressure for an agreement based on the principle of self-determination for all nationalities in India, but that neither had in reality accepted that principle. Each hoped merely to convert the other to his point of view. Gandhi thought in terms of granting just enough concessions to the Moslems to win their support in the political battle with Britain. Jinnah, on the other hand, was far more concerned with the possible future "threat" of Congress domination than with the present actuality of British rule. He therefore insisted on an unconditional and artificial partition of India, regardless of the fact that, because of the multinational character of some of the areas involved, such an arbitrary division would inevitably lead to civil strife. Furthermore, he apparently ignored the all-important fact that Indian Moslems can never hope to achieve a free Pakistan unless they coöperate with the Hindus in winning freedom from British rule.

Gandhi's inability to recognize that Hindu-Moslem unity can be attained only by an unqualified recognition of the Moslem right to self-determination and not by "concessions" granted to the Moslems, unfortunately enabled Jinnah to concentrate almost exclusively on this one issue, and to ignore or side-step other important questions, such as the character of the government he proposed for Pakistan, or how he proposed to deal with such an area as Bengal. Though in Bengal, as a whole, the Moslems are in a slight majority, Western Bengal is predominantly Hindu and it is also one of the richest and most industrialized areas in India. It is true that without the iron, coal, and jute of Western Bengal, as well as the port of Calcutta, Pakistan would be greatly weakened, but the arbitrary inclusion of these Hindu areas in Pakistan would inevitably arouse intense friction and conflict.[1]

Both Gandhi and Jinnah chose to ignore the important fact that, from the standpoint of the distribution of natural resources, India is a natural economic unit and that any program of industrialization to raise the living standards of the Indian people would require that it be developed as such. If, for example, Pakistan were to be composed solely of the areas in which the Moslems are in a majority, it would inevitably remain a predominantly agricultural state, since it would possess few industrial raw materials with the exception of oil, whereas Hindustan would possess the bulk of India's industrial wealth — approximately 90% of her coal and iron, the greater part of her manganese, copper, bauxite, etc. This would mean that Pakistan, even in the questionable event that it could free itself from British rule, would be economically dependent upon Hindustan.

But, regardless of the failure of the two leaders to rise to the

---

[1] Those favoring the "multinational" solution for India suggest that a United Bengal should constitute one autonomous unit in a free Indian federation.

level of statesmanship that had been hoped for, their meeting at least cleared the air and crystallized the issues before the Indian people. Furthermore, it is clear that the attitude of Gandhi and Jinnah did not reflect the enormously powerful demand on the part of the majority of Hindus and Moslems for a solution. Throughout their meetings, both leaders received a flood of letters from members of Congress and the League begging them to reach an agreement, and there was every reason to believe that this pressure would continue and grow in strength. Many observers in India were hopeful that, if Gandhi and Jinnah could not bring themselves to accept a solution based on full self-determination for all nationalities within the framework of a free India, other leaders with the courage to discard outmoded policies and attitudes would come to the fore.

As was to be expected, the failure of the Gandhi-Jinnah conversations to achieve some basis for agreement between the Congress Party and the Moslem League led to a further deterioration of the Indian political situation. This situation was further complicated by the well-meaning efforts of the Non-Party Leaders' Conference, a group of Indian liberals without Congress or League affiliations, to aid in the solution of the crisis. Meeting in Delhi in November 1944, the Non-Party Conference set up a "Conciliation Committee," headed by Sir Tej Bahadur Sapru, and including many prominent Indians, to "establish contact with the leaders of all parties" and then make recommendations for a workable settlement. Unfortunately, the fact that Gandhi pledged his full support to the work of this committee, coupled with the fact that the great majority of its members were Hindus, produced extremely hostile reactions in the Moslem League press, which attacked the Sapru committee as an agent of the Congress.

Faced with the obvious fact that the situation was being aggravated by extremists on both sides, the British authorities did nothing to facilitate a compromise. Members of the Congress Working Committee remained in prison where they could take no official action, and even the very moderate proposal of the Non-Party Conference that nonofficial Indians be appointed to act as advisers to the British Governors in provinces that had previously had Congress Ministries was rejected by the Viceroy. Of even greater significance was the fact that the British Government came out definitely in support of the extreme Hindu position in rejecting the Moslem demand for Pakistan. During the autumn of 1944, the Viceroy held a series of interviews: one with Jinnah; one with Bhulabhai Desai, leader of the Congress Party in the Central Legislative Assembly; and one with Vinayak D. Savarkar, leader of the Hindu Mahasabha, whose aim is known to be to strengthen Hinduism, and who had been largely responsible for the violently anti-Congress position taken by the Mahasabha in opposing all proposals for a Hindu-Moslem settlement.

What happened at these interviews was not made public, but on December 14, 1944, Lord Wavell made his annual speech to the European Associated Chamber of Commerce in Calcutta, in which he dismissed the Moslem League demand for Pakistan in the following words: "If India is still tossing with the fever of political factions, or if her political doctors decide she must undergo a major surgical operation such as Pakistan, she may miss the opportunity that is hers. I do not believe that India's condition calls for a serious operation. I should certainly try all other possible remedies first."

This statement of the Viceroy constituted further evidence of the shift in the British stand on the question of Indian unity that had been noticeable ever since the demand for Congress-League unity on the basis of self-determination for the Moslems had begun to make itself felt in 1943. Formerly, when the Congress was fighting for a United India, the main stress was placed on India's divisions, the Moslem demands for separation were encouraged, and the Cripps proposals even opened the way for the secession not only of Moslem territories but also of the Native States from the proposed Indian Union. Beginning in 1943, however, the emphasis in British official utterances shifted to a recognition of the "natural" unity of India. Thus Lord Wavell, in his speech before the Central Legislative Assembly in February 1944, stressed that "from the standpoint of defense, relations with the outside world, and the many internal and external problems, India is a natural unit."

At that time, this new line was generally regarded as marking a withdrawal of British support from the Moslem League and a bid to the ultraconservative Hindu Mahasabha, whose leaders had opposed all compromise with the Moslems and were fighting fanatically for a united India under Hindu rule. Under the leadership of Mr. Savarkar, the Mahasabha campaigned vigor-

ously against Congress-League unity and called for a united
Hindu front against the League. At its Amritsar session early in
1944, for example, the Mahasabha passed a resolution demanding that no province or community be allowed to secede from the
future Indian federation, and another resolution promising "the
Hindu ruling chiefs fullest support against any agitation against
them by non-Hindus." These activities naturally served to aggravate distrust between the Hindu and the Moslem communities,
although the Mahasabha was numerically insignificant as compared with either Congress or the League. Lord Wavell's statement of December 1944, coming so soon after his interview with
Savarkar, merely provided additional confirmation for the view
that, faced with the possibility that Congress and the League
would reach an agreement based on the recognition of the Moslem right to self-determination, the British authorities had
shifted their support to the ideas of the Hindu extremists, who
could be counted on to fight against such a Congress-League
agreement.

Another revealing clue to the official British attitude toward
the Gandhi-Jinnah meeting was provided by an editorial in the
London *Times,* following the breakdown of the conversations.
This indicated that, even if an agreement had been reached,
there was no chance that India would have won her demand for
a national government because, declared the *Times*: "There
would still have remained the problem of other minorities — the
Indian States, Sikhs, Depressed Classes, as well as those interests
still unorganized but present in varying degrees in all those
groupings connected with rural and urban labor, of which the
Radical Democratic Party is the champion." The Radical Democratic Party, as noted previously, is led by M. N. Roy, who also
heads the government-sponsored Indian Federation of Labor.
Both these organizations had served the Government of India
well as propaganda instruments, but the *Times* must have been
very confident of the ignorance of its readers if it expected them
to accept the picture of Mr. Roy as the champion of rural and
urban labor.

It is not difficult to see why the British formula that all Indian
parties and groups must be in complete agreement before India
can be given freedom should be extended to include "unorganized rural and urban labor," since this will obviously enable the
British authorities in India to offset any future agreement that

may be reached between the major parties by claiming to
"speak" on behalf of these "unorganized" millions. As the *Times*
itself frankly put it, the present Government is "a Paramount
Power in a position to assess the competing claims and correlate
them not only with one another but with the general good of
India." But the fact remains that statements such as that in the
Times, coupled with the British Government's refusal even to
consider Gandhi's proposals for a reopening of negotiations, suggest that, despite the repeated claim that Britain stands by the
Cripps offer to India, the British Government did not in fact
intend to encourage Indian progress toward self-government.
They also suggest that the Cripps plan itself is not the unrestricted offer of Indian freedom that it is so often alleged to be.

THE "JOKER" IN THE CRIPPS OFFER

THE IMPORTANT fact about the Cripps proposals is that they
make the transfer of political power to an Indian Government
conditional on a prior agreement among the Indian National
Congress, the Moslem League, the Indian Princes, and other minority groups with regard to a constitutional form of government. Failing such an agreement, any province of British India
may decide to remain outside the proposed Indian Union and
form a separate Dominion or Dominions. Furthermore, any of
the Indian States may choose to remain outside the Union and
retain their present treaty relationships with the British Crown.
These provisions are justified on the grounds that they leave the
Indian people entirely free to settle their communal differences
in any way they choose and that no large minority group will be
compelled to accept a constitution of which it does not approve.

This thesis sounds admirably democratic, but when it is applied to the Indian situation the result is to make it extremely
difficult — if not impossible — for India to attain unity and democracy, or real independence. Its major "joker" lies in its treatment of the problem of the Indian States. The States are not only
granted the right to refuse accession to the proposed Indian
Union and retain their present relations with the British Crown
but their participation in the proposed constitution-making body
is to be through representatives appointed by the Princes —
which means that the 93 million people of the States will have
no voice either in framing the constitution or in deciding whether
or not the States should join the new Union. Inasmuch as the

States stretch the length and breadth of India and in many cases consist of scattered pieces of territory within British Indian Provinces, it is obvious that, if many of them refused to adhere to the new Union, it would create an impossible administrative problem for the new Indian Government, to say nothing of their possible use as instruments for maintaining indirect British control over large parts of the country. On the other hand, it is clearly a political impossibility that there could be a workable federation between democratically governed areas of British India and the unmitigated autocracies of the States. Yet, should the people of the States rise in rebellion against their rulers and demand civil liberties at least approximating those prevailing in British India, the Princes can, by virtue of their treaties with the British Crown, demand British protection of their powers and privileges. Gandhi put his finger on this all-important aspect of the Cripps plan when he described that plan as contemplating the perpetual vivisection of India. Asked to explain his meaning, he replied: "Surely it can mean only one thing: the Cripps offer divided India into a Princely India and a democratic India. Is that not vivisection?"

In general it may be said that the Cripps proposals, as well as all the other official British statements regarding India that have filled countless books, articles, and speeches during the past three years, take the constitutional approach to the Indian problem. This approach is based on the premise that the central issue in India is to devise a constitution acceptable to all parties and groups, and it thus places the main emphasis on India's internal divisions. It is an eminently useful approach for the British because it removes from the field of discussion the basic problems of India's economic and social backwardness, the poverty of her people, and other fundamental issues that can be dealt with only by a government in which the people have confidence and which is interested in developing India for the benefit of Indians. In other words, it stresses the barriers to, rather than the urgent reasons for, Indian political freedom, and it makes possible a "plausible" argument in favor of the continuance of British rule.

Even this argument, however, rests on two main assumptions: one, that Hindu-Moslem conflict is a permanent and inevitable factor in Indian political life; and the other, that Britain is in honor bound to protect the rights of the Indian Princes against any attempt on the part of their own subjects or of the people of

British India to bring the States into the orbit of democratic government. Neither of these assumptions is tenable. The first merely serves to obscure the many basic economic and social problems common to both Hindu and Moslem peasants and workers who are seeking in increasingly large numbers to solve these problems through coöperative action. It is being refuted by the growing demand on the part of members both of Congress and of the League for an agreement on the basis of full self-determination for all minorities within the framework of a free India. And finally, it ignores the fact that in many instances so-called communal antagonism is in reality a political or economic conflict arising primarily from the poverty and the industrial backwardness that promote a fierce struggle for a share in the limited opportunities open to the Indian people. Great Britain must stand guilty of the charge of falsifying the issue of Hindu-Moslem differences and of using the issue of minorities as a means of obstructing the political progress not only of the majority but of the whole nation.

It is becoming ever clearer that British policy in the post-Cripps era was carefully calculated to weaken, and if possible destroy, the nationalist movement in India. Thousands of Congress Party leaders were kept in jail, while such elements as the traitorous Forward Blocists and Congress Socialists were left largely unmolested. It was therefore natural that, as the Congress Party disintegrated both in membership and influence, these divisive forces began to enjoy an increasing influence on the Indian political scene. By the spring of 1945 there were signs of a growing conflict within Indian nationalist ranks. The spearhead of this disruptionist movement were the Forward Bloc followers of the Japanese quisling, Subhas Chandra Bose, and the Congress Socialists, who had consistently preached sabotage against the war effort and opposed all moves toward unity between the Congress Party and the Moslem League.

It was not surprising that these groups should have been opposed to the program of the Indian Trade Union Congress, the All-India Kisan Sabha, and the Indian Communist Party — all of which constantly urged full Indian support of the war effort and unity between Congress and the League in support of the demand for a representative peoples' National Government. What was alarming was the evidence that these disruptive forces, taking advantage of the fact that all the Congress Working Committee members were still in jail (except Mrs. Sarojini Naidu), appeared to be increasing their influence within the Congress Party. At a Punjab Provincial Workers Conference at Ludhiana in February 1945, for example, the Communists were excluded while members of the Congress Socialist Party were permitted to attend. In reply to a Communist objection, it was stated that the Socialists were nearer to Congress and Gandhi than the Communists. The meeting passed resolutions expressing faith in the Congress High Command and Gandhi, and also decided to set up a Provincial Council, District Councils, and Village Centers. It was agreed that Kisan Sabhas, Trade Unions, and Student Unions should be permitted to affiliate with these Councils, but that if they declined, new parallel organizations would be set up by the Congress Party. The Communists, who had been excluded from the conference, held a separate meeting at which they expressed regret at the attitude of the main conference, denied the allegations against them, and pledged themselves to work under the Provincial Council established at the conference.

Similarly, at a meeting of the Bihar "Constructive Workers Conference," a resolution was adopted stating that the war was an imperialist struggle, and expressing faith in Gandhi's "constructive program" as the only way to achieve freedom. Following this, it was resolved that members of the Communist Party, the Kisan Sabha, and even M. N. Roy's Radical Democratic Party, should not be associated with this "constructive program" because these groups had "retarded the progress of Congress struggles for the attainment of Indian independence." According to the Indian press report, the official Congress representatives at the Bihar meeting opposed this exclusion move, but their views were apparently overridden.

This was discouraging evidence of the lengths to which the Congress Socialists, Forward Blocists, and others were ready to go in their efforts to sabotage the war and to oppose constructive proposals for the establishment of unity among the Indian people. The attitude of these groups, of course, did not represent the official policy of the Congress Party, but with the majority of responsible Congress leaders in prison and normal Congress machinery unable to function, they were making headway with their disruptive tactics which could only prove disastrous for the cause of Indian unity and freedom.

Not even Mrs. Naidu's speeches, in which she opposed the

exclusion tactics employed at these Congress meetings, succeeded in putting a brake on the disruptive movement. At the
time it was difficult to estimate how far the tentacles of this
disruptive movement would reach. The popular forces in opposition to it were strong. But it was impossible to avoid the conclusion that the British authorities were not only pleased with the
state of affairs in the spring of 1945, but that they had skilfully
maneuvered the political groups in India toward the very disunity that they so self-righteously described as an obstacle to
Indian freedom.

But the British position with regard to maintaining the autocratic powers of the Indian Princes is even more indefensible
in the modern world, where absolutism and feudal serfdom are
intolerable anachronisms. To insist that the Princes must not be
compelled to accept an Indian system of government framed
without their consent is to accept the thesis that Indian progress
toward unity and democratic government ought to be arrested
if it does not meet with the approval of a handful of feudal
potentates. Such an attitude suggests that the British Government is searching desperately for some excuse to oppose India's
advance to full self-government. On no other grounds is it possible to explain, much less justify, the repeated references to the
sanctity of the treaties with the Princes, the fulsome praise bestowed on the Princes as among "the most loyal of His Majesty's
subjects," and the denunciation of the Congress Party for its
efforts to organize the people of the Indian States and to support
their demands for civil liberties and the right to a voice in determining their future. It is not particularly to Great Britain's
credit that the Princes rank highest among the supporters of
British rule in India.

A further discouraging aspect of the Indian situation in the
spring and summer of 1945 was the existence of a news blackout
that could be fairly described as the most complete ever imposed.
The always strict press censorship was tightenend so that even
the Library of Congress was not permitted to receive Indian nationalist papers to keep up its files. No reports of the sessions of
the Indian Legislative Assembly reached the American press,
with the result that the American people as a whole were completely unaware of the fact that the representatives of the Congress Party and the Moslem League coöperated closely against
the Government, which suffered defeat after defeat on major

issues. This, of course, merely resulted in the bills being passed by Viceregal decree. This studied attempt to encourage American ignorance of and apathy toward the Indian situation was also reflected in the personnel of the Indian delegation at the San Francisco Conference, which was composed of two members of the Viceroy's Executive Council and the retired prime minister of an Indian State. While this delegation was certainly able to represent the *real* government of India — i.e., the Viceroy and the India Office — it contained no spokesmen for any section of India's 400,000,000 people whose future was certainly one of the major problems of the peace in Asia.

Behind the screen of this news blackout, new tactics for breaking the Indian political deadlock were being worked out by the British Government on the occasion of Lord Wavell's visit to London in the spring of 1945. In response to the growing criticism of Britain's unyielding and uncompromising policy toward India, and in anticipation of a general election in England, a modified version of the Cripps Plan was being considered, including a provision to make the Viceroy's Council more representative by including representatives of the Congress Party and the Moslem League.

On June 14, 1945, the British Government, headed by Prime Minister Churchill, put into official form the "Wavell Plan" for India by issuing a White Paper with new proposals for breaking the political deadlock and securing the coöperation of the principal Indian parties and groups in the administration of the country. As officially formulated, the British proposal was that pending the time when the Indian people should agree on their future form of government under the terms of the Cripps offer, the Viceroy's Executive Council should be reconstituted in such a way as to make it representative of the principal political groups. To this end, the British proposed that a conference of Indian leaders should meet and recommend to the Viceroy a list of names from which it was hoped that he would be able to choose his Council, although it was specified that the Viceroy would retain complete freedom of selection and would not be bound by the recommendations of the conference. The White Paper further proposed that all positions in the Council except that of the Viceroy and the Commander-in-Chief (who holds the post of War Minister) should be filled by Indians, and that the Viceroy should make his selections in such a way as to give "a balanced representation of the main communities, including equal proportions of Moslems and caste Hindus."

Simultaneously with this announcement, the British authorities ordered the release of the eight members of the Congress Working Committee from jail in order that they might participate in the conference of Indian leaders which was scheduled to meet at Simla on June 25. This conference opened in an atmosphere of hope, since all parties were reported to have willingly accepted the new proposals as a basis for discussion. A deadlock soon developed, however, when Mohammed Ali Jinnah, head of the Moslem League, insisted that the League alone had the right to nominate the Moslem members of the Executive Council. Congress Party leaders, on the other hand, contended that the League could not rightly claim to speak for all the Moslems of India, and this contention was supported by other Moslem leaders who were not members of either Congress or the League. The Viceroy also refused to accede to Mr. Jinnah's demand, since this would have involved the surrender of an important British prerogative, namely the Viceroy's right to choose the members of his Executive Council as he saw fit.

In an effort to prevent a breakdown of the conference, the Viceroy himself drew up a tentative list of members based on names submitted by all parties except the Moslem League. This list, though it was not made public, was reported to have included members of the Moslem League and also one non-League Moslem who was not a member of the Congress Party. The omission of a Congress Moslem from the list was said to have been intended as a concession to Mr. Jinnah, but the latter stated flatly that the League could not participate in the government except on its own terms, and the conference therefore ended in failure on July 14.

Regarded in the most favorable possible light, the White Paper can be said to constitute an attempt to give India a more representative government but not a more responsible one, inasmuch as the Viceroy's right of veto remained unrestricted and the members of the proposed new Council would be responsible to the British Government and not to any Indian legislature. The offer to transfer the departments of Finance and External Affairs to Indian Ministers constituted an advance over previous British proposals, and the release of the Congress Working Committee was at least an initial move toward making possible an agreement

among the various Indian parties. There were at least three points
about the White Paper, however, that made it difficult to accept
it as a constructive effort to facilitate India's progress toward
unity and self-government.

The first point was the carefully worded sentence excluding
the people of the Indian States from any participation in the benefits that would allegedly accrue from Indian acceptance of the
British proposals. It is, of course, true that the Viceroy's Executive Council has nothing to do with the administration of the
States. But it is also true that the future of the States is inextricably linked with that of British India, and that the British attitude toward the States constitutes one of the chief obstacles to
the attainment of a free, united, and democratic India. One of
the most pertinent criticisms of the Cripps offer is that it denied
to the people of the Indian States any voice in determining
the future constitution of India, and permitted the Indian
Princes, if they so desired, to retain their present relations with
the British Crown. The fact that the British Government felt it
necessary to include in the White Paper the statement that "nothing contained in any of these proposals will affect the relations
of the Crown with Indian states" suggested that there had been
no modification of British policy on this highly important issue,
and that the British wished to reassure the Indian Princes on
this point.

The second point was the proposal that in selecting the members of his Executive Council, the Viceroy should endeaver to
give equal representation, not to the Congress Party and the
Moslem League, but to Moslems and caste Hindus. The significance of this proposal was far-reaching. It automatically placed
primary emphasis on the communal issue and suggested that religious conflict between the Hindu and Moslem communities was
the central fact in Indian political life — a contention that was not
supported by the concurrent political developments in India.
This insistence on the necessity of *religious* rather than *political*
parity was all the more unexpected because it had been generally
believed that the new British proposals were intended to take
advantage of an agreement reached between Bhulabhai Desai
and Liaquat Ali Khan — the leaders of the Congress Party and the
Moslem League in the Central Legislative Assembly. That agreement provided for the formation of a new central government in
which Congress and the League would each have 40% of the

ministerial positions, with 20% being reserved for the smaller minority groups.

The British Government, however, chose to ignore this proposal, which would have enabled the Congress to nominate any candidates it liked, regardless of their religious affiliation, and instead insisted on religious equality. Under these circumstances, it was inevitable that Mr. Jinnah would oppose giving one of the Moslem seats to a Congress Moslem. It was equally inevitable that Congress would refuse to be represented solely by caste Hindus.

Lord Wavell could hardly have been unaware that this deadlock would arise. To any close student of recent Indian political developments in India, it was a foregone conclusion that Jinnah would insist on parity with the Congress Party, and that under the conditions of the British offer he could secure this parity only by controlling all the Moslem seats in the new government. And it was also clear that the Congress Party would maintain its traditional opposition to any division on purely religious lines, in view of its status as a nationalist political organization representing members of all religious communities.

If the British Government had really wished to make it difficult for Mr. Jinnah to successfully resist both the Congress Party and the Viceroy, the least it could have done was to propose that the Viceroy select his Council in such a way as to give equal representation to Congress and the League. In that event, Congress would have undoubtedly nominated both Hindus and Moslems for its share of the ministerial posts, while the League would naturally have nominated all Moslems. Since Congress is a nationalist and not a Hindu organization, there could have been no objection among Congress leaders if Moslems had outnumbered caste Hindus on the Council. It is true that even then Mr. Jinnah might have found other objections if he was determined to block a settlement, but he would have been deprived of his strongest argument with his Moslem followers, namely the necessity of controlling all Moslem seats in order to obtain equality with Congress.

It might also have contributed to a more successful outcome of the Simla Conference if Lord Wavell had invited a real cross-section of Indian opinion to be represented, including leaders of the Kisan Sabha and the All-India Trade Union Congress. Although it is true that these peasant and trade union organizations are not political parties in the strict sense of the term, they wield as much political influence as many formal political groups, and their combined membership is nearly one million and a half. Furthermore, many members of the Kisan Sabha and Trade Union Congress are also rank-and-file members of Congress and the Moslem League, and it is they who had been working most actively and effectively to achieve Hindu-Moslem unity on the basis of a joint approach to common economic and social problems. Their representation at Simla might well have made it difficult for either Congress or League leaders to defeat the purpose of the conference.

Perhaps the most important of the three points in the British White Paper is to be found in its early paragraphs, in which once again the British Government placed the full burden of responsibility for working out a basis for freedom upon the Indian people. As in the Cripps offer and in every subsequent British statement, the British authorities repeated that they were fully prepared to grant self-government to India if only the Indian people could agree among themselves as to the form of government they wanted and how they wished to attain it.

The fallacy of this argument has already been analyzed, but it may be emphasized once more that India has been a colonial country under the complete control of Great Britain for the past 150 years, and that under these circumstances the British Government cannot absolve itself of all responsibility for the political and economic demoralization that characterizes the current situation in India. It is also obvious that if Britain intends to defer granting freedom to India until every internal political issue is solved to Britain's satisfaction, India will never be free, for no country has ever emerged from a struggle for national freedom into a state of perfect unity and perfect political democracy.

Not that the Simla Conference could not have been a hopeful first step. The fact that the Congress Party leaders were eager to participate in a central government constituted according to the terms of the Wavell Plan, represented an important advance in their thinking since the days of the Cripps Mission. But what Nehru and other Congress leaders apparently failed to appreciate was that the British insistence on religious parity almost certainly doomed the conference to failure, and that this failure would be unjustly turned against the Indian people as a whole. It is true that when the terms of the White Paper were first published,

Congress leaders expressed strong dissatisfaction with the religious parity proposal. But they did not carry their opposition through to the logical point of insisting that the Wavell Plan be revised to conform with the prior agreement reached between Bhulabhai Desai and Liaquat Ali Khan, providing for political parity between the Congress Party and the Moslem League.

It must also be noted that the British procedure in staging the conference was open to criticism on two counts. In the first place, they released only the members of the Congress Working Committee and left thousands of other Congress leaders to languish in jail, thus making impossible a meeting of the All-India Congress Committee — the only body with power to determine Congress Party policy.

Secondly, they called the Simla Conference only a few days after the release of the Working Committee, with the result that none of its members had time to acquaint himself with the sentiment of the Party as a whole, or with political developments throughout the country. Had the British released all the Congress prisoners and given them time to meet and discuss thoroughly the problems facing the country, they might well have come to Simla better prepared to speak for their constituents, and better able to judge the strength of popular sentiment in favor of a Congress-League agreement.

The failure of the Simla Conference to pave the way for a reorganization of the Government of India on a popular and representative basis was a cause for deep regret on the part of all those who had hoped that the atmosphere of bitterness and frustration prevailing in India since 1942 might be dispelled and a way found to enable Indian leaders to begin to tackle the serious economic and social problems with which the existing Government had notably failed to deal. It was clear that those problems could be dealt with only by a government that enjoyed the confidence of the people. It was also clear that one of the major obstacles to the attainment of such a government was the failure of the leaders of the Congress Party and the Moslem League to heed the demands of their followers for a Congress-League agreement on the basis of self-determination for all minorities within the framework of a free Indian federation.

In view of this basic fact, one of the most important developments at the Simla Conference was Mr. Jinnah's open invitation to Mr. Gandhi to hold another meeting on the question of "Pakistan" for the Moslems of India. Regardless of what one might think of Jinnah's political integrity or of Gandhi's social and political theories, the fact remained that the most important problem facing the Indian people was to achieve an agreement between the Congress Party and the Moslem League that would enable them to present a united front to the British Government. Over and over again it had been proved that when Indian leaders met in conference with British authorities, they always came out on the losing end because they themselves were disunited.

There was every evidence, moreover, that among millions of Hindu and Moslem peasants and workers, there was a genuine desire to coöperate in winning political freedom and in the solution of economic and social problems that affected both communities alike. And there was good reason to hope that if Gandhi and Jinnah failed once more to lay the basis for such coöperation, the task would be taken up by younger leaders who were less burdened with the heritage of the past, and who were willing to recognize that, as Nehru stated in an interview following his release from jail, "politics in terms of religious communities are inconsistent with either democracy or any modern conception of politics or economics." In another interview Nehru declared that new and younger groups were arising in India whose influence would be felt, and included Gandhi, Jinnah, and himself in the generation "that is going out." It remained to be seen whether this "older generation" could rise to the heights of statesmanship demanded by the situation in India, or whether India's political progress would have to await the emergence of a "new generation" of leaders better equipped to meet the high standards set by Britain as the price for India's freedom.

The failure of the Simla Conference was at the time overshadowed by the sweeping victory of the Labor Party in the British elections. At this writing (late August 1945), it is impossible to predict accurately what effect that victory will have on the Indian situation. However, the King's speech to Parliament on August 15, written by Prime Minister Attlee, contained the general pledge that "in accordance with the promises already made to my Indian peoples, my Government will do their utmost to promote, in conjunction with the leaders of Indian opinion, the early realization of full self-government in India." The words "in accordance with the promises already made" can refer only to the terms contained in the 1942 Cripps proposals. That the

new Labor Government in its early days did not take a very advanced approach to the Indian problem is further indicated by
the fact that both Prime Minister Attlee and Sir Stafford Cripps
wholeheartedly supported the terms set forth in the White Paper
of June 14. It is also well known that both Attlee and Cripps are
staunch advocates of dominion status rather than full independence for India, even though they must be aware that under dominion status the Indian people would probably fare more like
the Africans in the Union of South Africa than like the Canadians
in the Dominion of Canada.

But though there was no indication of a radical change in British policy toward India, there were signs that the new Government might adopt a different approach from that of its predecessor. Reports from London suggested that elections would be held
in India to re-establish representative government in the provinces, that all political prisoners would be released, that the electorate would be broadened, and that no one political party would
be permitted to obstruct the course of the elections. It was even
reported that the elections would be held for the added purpose
of convening a constituent assembly as recommended in the
Cripps proposals. As a beginning, this program had within it the
possibility of at least some change in the British approach to the
Indian problem. But the fact remained that this problem could
not be dealt with in a vacuum, without regard to Britain's world
position and particularly her relations with the United States. No
British Government can single-handedly undertake to aid in the
development of a free and expanding Indian economy without
the assurance of American coöperation. Its most sincere efforts
can be rendered futile if Britain is compelled to shape her policies
in terms of economic and financial rivalry with the United States.
Thus, the prospect of a new and more constructive British effort to solve the Indian problem merely served to underline the
urgent necessity of Anglo-Indian coöperation in the freeing of
India and other colonial areas from economic and political
bondage.

BRITAIN WITHOUT A COLONIAL INDIA

THE INESCAPABLE conclusion of any thorough study of the Indian
problem is that there is no immediate likelihood of India's being
freed from colonial bondage. Mr. Churchill's pronouncement
that he "did not become the King's First Minister to preside over

the liquidation of the British Empire" was far from being an expression of the moment. All the evidence points to the fact that throughout the war the British Government used every available technique for ensuring that India will remain a subject nation: physical suppression, imprisonment, economic pressure, financial maneuvering, a "divide and rule" policy, censorship, and intensive domestic and foreign propaganda. Chief among the activities of the British propaganda machine in the United States was the fostering of the absolutely erroneous belief that the Indian National Congress Party was pro-Japanese and pro-Axis. The effectiveness of this propaganda, coupled with the great need for Allied unity in the war against fascism, made it easy for the Indian problem to be pushed into the background as far as American public opinion was concerned.

But as we cross the threshold into the momentous postwar years, India looms ever larger as a problem demanding solution. So long as India remains a British colony, the seeds of future economic and military conflict will be present. A colonial India, moreover, cannot be anything but an obstacle to the expansion of world trade. Unable to develop her agricultural and industrial resources or to raise the standards of living of her people, India cannot provide a prosperous market for the products of her own and foreign industries. She cannot constitute either a new economic frontier for America or an expanding market for British industry.

Britain's reluctance to relinquish her political and economic stranglehold on India strikes many observers as short-sighted as well as stubborn. Even some British industrialists, realizing that India is drying up as a source of British revenue, are seeking to find an alternative to the theory of Empire self-sufficiency. Herbert Morrison, Britain's Home Secretary in the Churchill cabinet and Lord President of the Council in the Attlee cabinet, declared some months ago that "the myth of a self-sufficient empire has gone the way of other historical illusions, and I hope and believe that British common sense has said goodbye to it forever." On another occasion Mr. Morrison denounced the idea of imperial preference as "based on the utterly false assumption that there is a fixed amount of trade to be done and that if somebody else does it, we won't. The truth is that there lies before all nations the possibility of a tremendous expansion in world trade, as in industry at home."

Unfortunately, Mr. Morrison's constructive views on this issue are supported only by that section of British manufacturers who are especially interested in expanding their export trade. He does not represent the views of the dominant monopolistic section of British vested interests. And yet even these interests must realize that, despite Britain's privileged position in the Indian market, British revenue from India has been steadily decreasing.

As a source of raw materials, India has continued to supply about 5% of Britain's total imports, but as a market for British manufactures she has declined sharply in importance. Britain exported to India 15% of her total exports in 1913, 10.7% in 1929, 7.2% in 1938, and 6.9% in the first half of 1939. India's dependence on British sources of supply also diminished markedly, not only as a result of the increase in Indian production of cotton textiles and other commodities, but also because of increasingly severe competition from other countries, notably Japan, in the India market. In 1913–14, India obtained 64% of her imports from Britain; in 1928–29, 45%; in 1937–38, 30%, and in 1940–41, only 21%.

Though Britain retained the power to regulate the exchange rate between the rupee and the pound in such a way as to favor British exports to India, India maintained a favorable trade balance vis-à-vis Great Britain amounting to roughly $44 million annually during the period 1936–39. This is the typical result of a colonial economy in which the market is gradually saturated because the colony is maintained as a raw-material source and there is no development of productive facilities designed to raise the people's purchasing power. Indian poverty and industrial backwardness have meant steadily diminishing returns for British industry. As we have seen, the major emphasis has been placed on increasing Indian production of a few money crops for export, with little or no attention being given to the requirements of the domestic market. India's major commercial and industrial centers are located at or near seaports, and all railways and roads are designed for the transport of goods between the interior and the coastal centers. There is no adequate trade and transport system for distributing domestic production in the home market. Most of India's 730,000 villages have not been reached by metaled roads or railways, and internal trade is still further hampered by the customs barriers erected by the Indian States. Freight rates are so high that peasants are discouraged from growing a surplus for shipment to other Indian centers. Furthermore, the production of money crops for export has largely by-passed India's villages, and the vast majority of her agricultural population have no share in Indian wealth and are not consumers of modern industrial products.

The economy imposed on India by British rule has in fact failed to develop the consuming power of 70% to 80% of the Indian people. England, which is more than twice as densely populated as India, has succeeded in developing an annual purchasing power of £97 per capita, while that of India (even including the foreign population) is less than £6. Indian prewar imports amounted to only $1.55 per capita annually and her exports to only $1.65 (1938), while Britain's amounted to $83.05 and $41.30 respectively (1939). Britain will be vitally dependent on an expanding export trade in the postwar period to make up for the loss of income from overseas investments and from financial and shipping services, and her only hope of finding these new export outlets lies in the development of an expanding world economy and increased purchasing power in the hitherto backward areas of the world. Throughout the nineteenth century, British prosperity was due in large measure to the fact that British capital was invested in the development of other countries, including the United States, and the fact that the resulting increase in those countries' wealth created a corresponding increase in Britain's foreign trade. It is a well-known economic axiom that trade between industrialized nations is more extensive and profitable than trade between industrialized and backward nations. As early as 1812, Lord Castlereagh acknowledged that "Great Britain has derived more real commercial advantage from North America since the separation than she did when that country was . . . part of her colonial system." Britain's new balance-of-trade position arising out of the financial and other losses incurred during the war merely emphasizes her need for aiding in the development of India as an expanding market for all types of industrial products. Why then should Britain not welcome a large-scale development program for the expansion of India's agricultural and industrial production?

The answer to this question may seem self-evident, but it is far from being that. Britain is certain to emerge from this war with her prewar economic structure seriously undermined. As a manufacturing nation dependent on imports for the bulk of

her raw materials and food supplies, Britain relied for her prewar prosperity on her export trade, her income from overseas
investments, and her shipping, financial, and commercial services. It is a foregone conclusion that she will emerge from this
war in a much weakened financial position vis-à-vis the United
States. It is estimated that as a result of the war Britain will have
lost roughly half her normal prewar income. Certainly one of
the consequences of Britain's weakened position will be to put
her at a disadvantage in meeting American competition in world
markets.

. In an effort to overcome the expected loss in Britain's traditional form of income, some adjustments to this changed external
position are already being made internally through the expansion of the domestic market for industry, increased food production to lessen dependence on imports, and the diversification
of export products. But the fact remains that Britain will not
willingly relinquish any part of her empire or sacrifice the immediate though ever decreasing benefits of imperial control, for
the sake of a future problematical return, unless she is assured
that the other major powers will coöperate in creating an expanding world economy. The question of India's economic future in particular will be considered in the light of the economic
policies adopted by other major powers, especially the United
States.

Britain faces two alternatives in her future economic policy
with regard to India. She can either decide to return to a preferential bilateral system of interempire agreements, or she can
choose to coöperate in the development of an expanding world
economy that would involve not only technical and financial aid
to backward areas but also free access to raw materials, markets,
and investment opportunities. During the war Britain made
preparations for a revival of a restricted, bilateral trading system
with many countries both within and outside the British Empire.
India was by no means the only country to have amassed a
substantial blocked sterling account in London. Large contracts
were concluded with a number of colonies, Dominions, and
other countries in the sterling area by which Britain agreed to
purchase their entire output of cotton, wool, butter, tea, etc.,
irrespective of whether these commodities could be shipped to
England before the end of the war. All these purchases were
credited to the blocked sterling account of the country con-

cerned, which means that in the postwar period these British creditors may be forced to buy from their debtor and thus restrict their trade relations with other countries.

A system of imperial preference unquestionably holds out definite attractions for Great Britain. Under the Ottawa Agreements it secured for Great Britain a "safe" or privileged market for about 50% of her total exports and gave Empire countries a guaranteed outlet for more than 40% of their exports. Britain has not the huge internal market of the United States to furnish an outlet for the greater part of her industrial products, nor has she anything comparable to American domestic sources of raw materials and food. Furthermore, Britain does not any longer possess the captial resources to undertake the economic development of India single-handed, nor can she afford to invest large sums in development projects that may not yield an immediate return. It is therefore unrealistic for Americans to expect that Britain will give up India and the system of colonial exploitation unless we do our part in creating an alternative system of world economic relations.

Suggestions have emanated from official British circles to the effect that Britain intends to maintain the system of imperial preference in the postwar period. These hints, coupled with frequent references to the strengthening of imperial ties, the continued restriction of Indian industrial expansion, and the rigid limitations placed upon Indian imports of capital goods, have disturbed many Americans. They see in them evidence that Britain intends to approach the problem of the postwar world from the standpoint of the rival strength and resources of other nations rather than from the standpoint of international collaboration. But it must be emphasized that one of the chief reasons why many British statesmen feel the need for creating a stronger imperial bloc and, in particular, for retaining a privileged position in the Indian market, is their fear of an American reversion to economic isolationism or an American drive to replace Britain in world markets.

Even the attitude of the British working class towards freedom for India is closely related to the problem of Anglo-American relations. Throughout the years of British rule over the greatest empire in the world, the upper section of the British working class supported colonial exploitation and willingly accepted some of its spoils. This compromise with imperialism on the part of labor reached its greatest heights during the years of bloody suppression of India's struggle for freedom by the two earlier Labor Governments under Ramsay MacDonald. Even today the British Labor Party maintains a relatively conservative outlook toward India. Although many individual or independent British unions have passed resolutions supporting Indian independence, the British working class as a whole has been influenced by certain of the tory arguments. They have been told that, if Britain were to relinquish control of India and her other colonies, the United States would certainly grab them for exclusive American exploitation. In such an event, the argument continues, England — which is so poor in natural resources and depends so much on foreign trade and investment — would become a tenth-rate, isolated little country in which everyone including the workers would suffer a sharp reduction in living standards.

If we accept the probability that capitalism will remain for some time the dominant form of economy in most of the world, and if there is merit in the contention that a liberated but weak colonial nation would become a temptation to a trade-hungry and all-powerful America, then even the conservatism of the British Labor Party can be understood only in the light of complex world relations. It becomes ever clearer that the solution of the Indian problem involves not only Britain and India but the United States as well. If the American people wish to live in a world free from bitter commercial conflicts and colonial exploitation, and if American industrialists want India free to develop an expanding industrialized economy that can furnish a profitable outlet for the products and capital of the industrialized nations, we shall have to prove by specific agreements on questions of trade, currency, transport, etc., that we are ready to coöperate in creating a world economic system in which the English people can enjoy a high standard of living and Britain can maintain her position as a great industrial and trading nation without having to depend upon a closed imperial bloc and upon the exploitation of a subject India.

Thus America has definite responsibilities with regard to India's future, just as it is Britain's responsibility to renounce the nineteenth-century mentality still prevalent in upper circles in England, to cease maintaining that the Cripps offer as it now stands is a genuine offer of freedom to India, to refrain from withholding the fruits of Allied victory from any nation simply because it has been rendered defenseless by decades of colonial subjection, and to express openly to the world and particularly to the United States a willingness to coöperate in the creation of that new system of economic relations which is so essential to world security and prosperity. Only then can we hope for the kind of international coöperation that will lead to the development of India as a new economic frontier not only for ourselves but also for the peoples of India, Britain, and the world.

The urgent need for some step to break the Indian deadlock was recognized by William Phillips, President Roosevelt's personal representative in India, one of whose letters to the President was quoted in Chapter I. While Mr. Phillips was still in India he wrote the President setting forth his proposals as to what that step might be. The full text of this letter was eventually published by Drew Pearson in his column of November 9, 1944, and is of such importance that it seems desirable to quote it in full:

March 3, 1943

Dear Mr. President:

Gandhi has successfully completed his fast, and the only result of it has been increasing bitterness against the British from large sections of the people. The Government has handled the case from the legalist point of view. Gandhi is the "enemy" and must not be allowed to escape from his just punishment, and at all cost British prestige must be maintained. Indians look at it from a different angle. Gandhi's followers regard him as semidivine and worship him. Millions who are not his followers look upon him as the foremost Indian of the day and feel that, since he has never had an opportunity to defend himself, it is a case of persecution of an old man who has suffered much for the cause which every Indian has at heart — freedom for India. And so presumably Gandhi comes out of the struggle with an enhanced reputation as a moral force.

The general situation as I see it today is as follows: From the British viewpoint their position is not unreasonable. They have been in India for 150 years and, except for the mutiny of 1857, generally speaking, internal peace has been maintained. They have acquired vast vested interests in the country and fear that their withdrawal from India would jeopardize those interests. The great cities of Bombay, Calcutta and Madras have been built up largely through their initiative. They have guaranteed the regime of the Princes, who control territorially about one-third of the country and one-fourth of the population. They realize that new forces are gathering throughout the world which affect their hold over India, and they have therefore gone out of their way, so they believe, to offer freedom to India as soon as there are signs that the Indians themselves can form a secure government. This the Indian leaders have been unable to do and the British feel that they have done all that they can in the circumstances. Behind the door is Mr. Churchill, who gives the impression that personally he would prefer not to transfer any power to an Indian government before or after the war and that the status quo should be maintained.

The Indians, on the other hand, are caught in the new idea which is sweeping over the world, of freedom for oppressed peoples. The Atlantic Charter has given the movement great impetus. Your speeches have given encouragement. There is thus a complete deadlock, and I should imagine that the Viceroy and Churchill are well satisfied to let the deadlock remain as long as possible. That is, at least, the general impression in most Indian circles. The problem, therefore, is: can anything be done to break this deadlock through our help? It seems to me that all we can do is to try and induce the Indian political leaders to meet together and discuss the form of government which they regard as applicable to India, and thus to show that they have sufficient intelligence to tackle the problem.

We cannot suppose that the British Government can or will transfer power to India by the scratch of a pen at the conclusion of the peace conference unless there is an Indian Government fit to receive it. The question remains, therefore, how to induce the leaders to begin now to prepare for their future responsibilities. There is, perhaps, a way out of the deadlock which I suggest to you, not because I am sure of its success, but because I think it is worthy of your consideration.

With the approval and blessing of the British Government, an invitation could be addressed to the leaders of all Indian political groups, on behalf of the President of the United States, to meet together to discuss plans for the future. The assembly could be presided over by an American who could exercise influence in harmonizing the endless divisions of caste, religion, race, and political views. The conference might well be under the patronage of the King Emperor, the President of the United States, the President of the Soviet Union, and Chiang Kai-shek, in order to bring pressure to bear on Indian politicians. Upon the issuance of the invitations, the King Emperor could give a fresh assurance of the intention of the British Government to transfer power to India upon a certain date as well as his desire to grant a provisional set-up for the duration. The conference could be held in any city in India except Delhi.

American chairmanship would have the advantage, not only of expressing the interest of America in the future independence of India, but would also be a guarantee to the Indians of the British offer of independence. This is an important point because, as I have already said in previous letters, British promises in this regard are no longer believed. If either of the principal parties refused to attend the conference, it would be notice to all the world that India was not ready for self-government, and I doubt whether a political leader would put himself in such a position. Mr. Churchill and Mr. Amery may be obstacles, for, notwithstanding statements to the contrary, India is governed from London, down to the smallest details.

Should you approve the general idea and care to consult Churchill, he might reply that, since the Congress leaders are in jail, a meeting such as is contemplated is impossible. The answer could be that certain of the leaders, notably Gandhi, might be freed unconditionally in order to attend the conference. The British may even be searching for a good excuse to release Gandhi, for the struggle between him and the Viceroy is over, with honors for both—the Viceroy has maintained his prestige; Gandhi has carried out his protest against the Government by his successful fast, and has come back into the limelight.

There is nothing new in my suggestion except the method of approach to the problem. The British have already announced their willingness to grant freedom to India after the war, if the Indians have agreed among themselves as to its form. The Indians say they cannot agree because they have no confidence in the British promises. The proposed plan perhaps provides the guarantee required by the Indians, and is in line with British declared intentions. Possibly this is a way out of the impasse which, if allowed to continue, may affect our conduct of the war in this part of the world and our future relations with colored races. It may not be successful, but, at least, America will have taken a step in furthering the ideals of the Atlantic Charter.

Sincerely yours,
(*signed*) WILLIAM PHILLIPS

Although it apparently was not practicable to broach this proposal to the British Government at the time Mr. Phillips made his report, his suggestion may yet prove to be an effective method of dealing with the Indian impasse, provided that it is expanded to include a general economic agreement between

England and America that will make possible effective Anglo-American coöperation not only in India's economic development but also in all other dependent and semidependent areas of the world.

But though it may be that, in the not too distant future, a way will be found by which India can attain both political and economic freedom, the United States faces a problem the solution of which cannot be indefinitely postponed. The next few years of probable prosperity must be used to lay the basis for that constructive coöperation with the unindustrialized areas of the world which will enable our economy to function without a disastrous recession. Fortunately for the American people, India is not the only country capable of becoming an important new economic frontier for the American economy. China, the most populous country in the world, has finally freed herself from foreign control and is therefore in a position to undertake an extensive program of economic development in the postwar period. The next section of this book is therefore devoted to an examination of China's potentialities as a market for American goods and capital, and of the factors, both favorable and adverse, that will influence the future course of Chinese economic development.

PART TWO

CHINA'S ASSETS AND LIABILITIES

❀

CHAPTER IV

CHINA AS A NEW ECONOMIC FRONTIER

❁

A S A NEW economic frontier for the United States in the postwar period, China's assets are first and foremost her political independence and her consequent ability to undertake a program of economic development and to offer equal opportunities to the goods and capital of other nations without having to accord special rights and privileges to any one of them. In addition, China has a vast population, extensive natural resources, and an urgent need for all forms of capital and consumer goods. It may be argued that China like India is in the midst of a serious political crisis that threatens her internal unity and stability. But, as we shall see, there are powerful forces working for a successful solution of this crisis, and the United States is in an excellent position to give these forces encouragement and support.

The following appraisal of China's industrial potential is based on the assumption that the pledges of the Cairo Conference will be carried out — that "all the territories Japan has stolen from the Chinese, such as Manchuria, Formosa, and the Pescadores shall be restored to the Republic of China." This means that in terms of territorial possessions and natural resources, China will emerge from the war more powerful than she has ever been in modern history. And it is obvious that in a country of China's vast size and huge population, a nation-wide program of industrial development together with the construction of thousands of miles of railways and roads, the building of power plants and other public utilities, the construction of an adequate communications system, and the modernization of agricultural methods would require the import of enormous quantities of capital goods and raw materials. It is also clear that, as increased agricultural production, industrial progress, and the development of mineral and power resources served to raise the living standards of the Chinese people, the expansion of the consumer market through a steadily increasing demand for all types of goods and services would guarantee the fiscal solvency of such a program.

China's industrial resources may not be so varied and extensive as India's, but they are sufficient to ensure a far higher level of economic prosperity than any but a handful of the Chinese people has ever experienced. Although China's mineral resources have been only partly surveyed [1] and present estimates will undoubtedly be revised upwards in the light of new discoveries, China's known coal reserves are conservatively estimated at more than 260 billion tons,[2] of which 127 billion are located in Shansi, 72 billion in Shensi, 20 billion in Manchuria, and the remainder scattered throughout the rest of China. Iron-ore reserves total nearly 2 billion tons with an iron content estimated at between 600 and 700 million tons. Of these reserves approximately 1,500 million tons are located in Manchuria, underlining the importance of that area in China's future industrial plans. China is the world's leading producer of tungsten and antimony and possesses lesser though substantial amounts of tin, copper, gold, magnesite, molybdenum, and mercury. China is also the leading producer of high-grade talc, valuable industrially as a lubricant and filler; and the possessor of large amounts of exceptionally pure clay and such nonmetallic minerals as salt, limestone, sulphur, and gypsum, as well as building stone and cement materials. Her known oil reserves are negligible, being estimated at less than 1% of those of the United States, but this deficiency could be at least partly offset by the development of a synthetic-fuel industry based on her abundant coal supplies. The extensive oil-shale deposits of Manchuria, which have been of such great service to Japan's war machine and are estimated to total 7,628 million tons, also constitute an important addition to China's potential fuel supply. Like India, China possesses immense potential hydroelectric power resources, estimated at 22 million horsepower. It has been estimated that the Yangtze River alone could be harnessed to make the world's largest power plant, producing five times as much power as our own Grand Coulee dam. Furthermore, in the near future it will be possible to learn to what extent the Japanese had succeeded in developing China's mineral and other resources in

[1] Judged by American and European standards, not more than one-third of China has been explored geologically.

[2] Some estimates are four times this figure.

occupied areas. It is known, for example, that Japan had developed still further the extensive magnesite deposits in southern Manchuria and had produced fluorspar from mines in Chekiang and possibly also in Shantung. Aluminum plants were reported to be operating in Manchuria, using local bauxite ore. Formosa, too, had been developed into a large center of chemical industries producing fertilizers, alcohol, vegetable oils, paper, charcoal, mineral oil, and refined camphor.

China is also capable of creating a strong agricultural base for her prospective industrial structure. Despite the severe handicap of primitive methods of production, an ancient and oppressive system of landlord-tenant relations, and the lack of adequate transport and credit facilities for the marketing of agricultural products, China already produces a wide variety of food grains and substantial quantities of agricultural products that could serve as the basis for light industries and for export — e.g., cotton, wool, silk, tea, wood oils, vegetable oils, bristles, hides and skins, egg products, and soy beans. Moreover, China's position in this respect will be strengthened in the postwar period by the addition of the agricultural resources of Manchuria and Formosa, which will substantially increase her output of wheat, rice, soy beans, sugar, and tea.

China thus possesses the natural resources to support a very considerable degree of industrial expansion. As in the case of India, the outstanding characteristic of the Chinese economy has been the wide gap between potential resources and the actual level of economic development. In the prewar period, China exclusive of Manchuria had only about two million industrial workers. Her annual coal production did not exceed 20 million tons, her pig-iron production averaged about 148,000 tons, and her steel production about 50,000 tons. Less than 1% of her potential hydroelectric power resources was developed, and she possessed virtually no heavy industries of any kind. In addition to cotton, silk, and woolen textiles, the only Chinese-owned modern industries that had made any progress were flour milling, sugar refining, oil pressing, and the manufacture of cement, glass, paper, matches, and cigarettes. And even in these light industries, China was dependent upon imports for from 50% to 70% of her needs. Furthermore, many of China's modern industries were engaged only in the preliminary processing of raw materials, while the final manufacture of consumers' goods was still carried on largely in small-scale industries and household workshops operating without benefit of modern machinery.

Then, too, China's industrial development was confined almost exclusively to the coastal areas and treaty ports while the resources of the vast interior remained inaccessible and undeveloped. The absence of a modern system of transport was in fact one of the major obstacles to China's transition from a local to a national economy. China had only 12,000 miles of railway (including the Manchurian lines), or 1 mile for every 753 square miles of territory, whereas even India had 1 mile for every 28 square miles.

As a result of this industrial backwardness and the lack of transport facilities to make possible the development of mineral and other resources in the interior provinces, China remained an overwhelmingly agricultural nation with four-fifths of her population dependent on the land for a livelihood. Moreover, China's agrarian structure, like India's, was ill fitted to sustain this burden. China's rural economy before the war was characterized by an oppressive system of landlord-tenant relations under which the peasant was forced to surrender from 40% to 70% of his crop to the landlord; by heavy taxation; by usurious interest rates ranging from 30% to 80%; by primitive methods of cultivation and low yields per acre; by excessive parcellization of the land, which prevented the employment of modern production methods; by the increasingly swift concentration of land ownership in the hands of a constantly narrowing section of the population; and by a rapid increase in the number of totally landless peasants. Surveys of agricultural conditions in various parts of China showed that no less than 65% of the peasant population either were landless or possessed such small holdings that they could not make a living. It was estimated that, for the country as a whole, 81% of the cultivable land was owned by 13% of the rural population, while in some areas the concentration of ownership was much higher. Famines, floods, and droughts also added to the peasant's burden. Even in the best of years, he was unable to progress much beyond the bare level of subsistence because of the crushing burdens imposed by the landlord, tax-collector, money-lender, and merchant.

These conditions condemned the vast majority of China's peasants to chronic and abject poverty. Millions sought relief by emigration; other millions swarmed to the coastal cities to provide an inexhaustible supply of appallingly cheap labor for Chinese and foreign industrial enterprises. Large sections of arable land were left uncultivated and China was compelled to begin importing food in substantial quantities. These conditions naturally meant that China's internal market became increasingly impoverished. Even the most optimistic estimates put China's national income at $25 billion, while more realistic observers placed it at between $10 and $12 billion or about $25 per capita, with the vast majority of the population possessing little or no money income of any kind. In contrast, the United States enjoyed in 1944 a per capita income approximately 50 times as high. Until this basic agrarian problem is solved and China's farmers are freed from the crushing burden of an outmoded and backward economy, China cannot hope to produce adequate supplies of food for her people and sufficient quantities of raw materials for industry and export, nor can she create an expanding domestic market with which to support her proposed industrial development program.

PAST OBSTACLES TO CHINESE INDUSTRIALIZATION

THE CONTINUED industrial backwardness of prewar China was due primarily to foreign domination of her industry, finance, and trade, through the system of treaty ports, extraterritoriality, foreign concessions, and the control of the chief sources of Chinese government revenue as security for foreign loans. It is true that the establishment of modern industrial and commercial enterprises in the treaty ports had led to the emergence of a Chinese industrial and banking class, but this group was too weak financially and too inexperienced to compete successfully with the strongly organized and better financed foreign enterprises, and its members were for the most part compelled to accept the role of compradors (agents or brokers for foreign capital).

The extent of foreign control over China's economy prior to 1937 is sometimes forgotten. China's cotton industry was more than half controlled by British and Japanese capital. Her banking system was dominated by British, American, and Japanese interests, and her railways by British, European, and Japanese capital. Foreign-owned coal mines produced almost half of China's total annual output, and most of the iron mining in China Proper was controlled by Japanese capital with the entire output earmarked for export to Japan. More than two-thirds of all the steam tonnage engaged in Chinese shipping was owned by foreign interests, and a large share of China's foreign trade was handled by foreign import and export firms and financed by foreign banks. And, finally, the Chinese Government's financial and industrial policies were subject to constant foreign pressure exerted through supervision of revenues, control of the foreign-exchange market by foreign banks, and the political and economic strings attached to the financial credits extended by foreign countries. The dominant role played by foreign capital in China's prewar industrial structure was in turn responsible for its other main features. These included the artificial concentration of modern industrial enterprises in the coastal centers, while the interior remained backward and undeveloped; the limiting of Chinese industry almost entirely to small and undercapitalized light industries; and the inability of the Chinese Government to offer protection to domestic industry.

In the years immediately preceding the outbreak of the war in 1937, the Chinese Government had begun to lay plans for the establishment of basic industries outside the treaty port areas, but unfortunately it chose to concentrate these enterprises too close to the coming battle areas — in the provinces of Hunan, Hupeh, and Kiangsi. With the spread of the war to the Yangtze Valley, China was forced to abandon these embryonic industrial bases and remove to the interior such equipment as could be salvaged. In fact, the Japanese advance to the line of the Pei-ping-Hankow-Canton railway resulted in the loss of virtually all of China's industrial plant, forcing the Chinese Government to fall back on the undeveloped and backward areas of the interior. In addition to the huge material devastation resulting from military operations, this loss of the coastal areas, together with China's isolation from outside sources of material aid, caused a sharp decline in the political influence of the Chinese industrial and banking class, which had absorbed Western ideas of industrial progress. The economic basis of the Chinese Government was thus shifted to the feudal-minded landed gentry of the interior, whose economic and political power depended on maintaining China's oppressive agrarian system, and who were therefore opposed to industrial progress and agricultural reforms.

On the other hand, China's forced retreat to the interior was

in certain ways beneficial, in that it drew attention to the hitherto ignored resources of that area and stimulated the idea of a
genuinely nation-wide program of economic development. The
migration of millions of Chinese from the coastal centers to the
interior served also as a great leavening force in bringing to
formerly isolated areas knowledge of conditions in more advanced centers and in creating a far stronger sense of national
consciousness. The Chinese people were awakened by the war
to a new appreciation of their country — its potential resources
and the need for developing these. They were inspired with the
idea that they were fighting a war of resistance *and* reconstruction, and both goals took on a definite and concrete meaning in
the minds of many who had never before concerned themselves
with conditions outside their own village.

Furthermore, to offset the liabilities of wartime material destruction, the ravages of inflation, and the impoverishment of
the people, China in the postwar period will possess certain
assets that she could not count on before the war. For one thing,
the system of extraterritoriality and foreign control over Chinese
economic life is a thing of the past, and China will therefore be
able to establish industrial enterprises without facing the competition of specially privileged foreign firms. Then, too, the restoration of Chinese control over the industrial centers along the
coast will mean a revival of the power and influence of the more
forward-looking bankers and industrialists. In addition, China
will be in control of Manchuria — one of the most highly industrialized areas of the world.

Thus, though China has emerged from the war confronted with
an enormously difficult task of economic reconstruction, she will
face this task with greater political freedom and more extensive
economic resources than she has ever before possessed in her
modern history. Her needs for all forms of capital and consumer
goods as well as for such construction materials as steel, iron,
and copper will be virtually limitless, and she will undoubtedly
hope to obtain the greater part of such imports from the United
States. Already many American business firms are looking to
China to afford an important outlet for American heavy industry
in the form of machinery and machine tools, railway equipment,
steel mills, power plants, and many other forms of industrial
goods.

There is, of course, the question of how such extensive imports could be financed. It is clear from the previous listing of China's resources that, unlike India, she does not possess exportable commodities of sufficient value or in sufficient quantities to pay for the imports of industrial equipment that she will require. Possible financial reparations from Japan and remittances from overseas Chinese would help in part to meet her balance of payments. But reparations are by their very nature temporary, and as China becomes more and more prosperous there will inevitably be a tendency for overseas Chinese to return to their homeland and for large-scale emigration to cease.

In time, therefore, other methods will have to be found to enable China to pay for essential imports. One such method would be a steady flow of American and other capital investment to China in sufficient amounts to balance the difference between exports and imports. The importance of converting an excess of American exports into long-term capital investment cannot be overemphasized; this has already become recognized as sound practice. In a report issued on November 28, 1944, for example, the Committee on International Policy of the National Planning Association stated that "failure of this country to export capital at a rate substantially greater than one billion dollars a year would be little short of disastrous." It then recommended a budget for 1950 in which American exports would total $10 billion and imports $6 billion, with the difference covered by $300 million in service items and the balance of $3,700,000,000 by net capital outflow of which $3 billion would be represented by long-term capital investments abroad. Regardless of whether $3 billion is an adequate sum to achieve the desired results, the proposed technique may be the only means available, at least for the time being, to expand trade with such impoverished and backward countries as China.

Provided that China coupled her industrial development program with measures designed to raise the living standards of her agricultural population, foreign capital investments would be protected by the existence of a continuously expanding internal market as new resources were opened up and both industrial and agricultural production increased. In time, moreover, as other backward areas are developed, China herself could become an exporter of raw materials and consumer goods to these new markets and thus build up credit balances with which to pay for her imports from the United States and other industrial nations. This process of evolution from a backward agricultural economy to that of a modern one, from a poor country to a rich one, is far from being novel. In fact it is the very process by which all great industrial nations have reached their goals. The outstanding example is the United States, which grew from a tiny agricultural nation in 1800 to the giant industrial and financial power of today in large measure as a result of capital supplied by foreign investors.

There will unquestionably be economists and businessmen who will be disturbed by this or that detail regarding American participation in China's economic development. And there will be many who will be put off by the seeming complexity and risk of the undertaking, even though they are in agreement regarding its fundamental importance. But the alternative to making a sincere effort to solve this problem is economic chaos for China, for America, and for the world. American ingenuity has solved big problems before and can do so again. We must not be dismayed or discouraged by China's poverty, backwardness, and disorganization, especially since it is this very backwardness that gives America her great opportunity to solve a problem that has vexed the American economy for the past three decades.

It may truly be said that realistic coöperation between America and China could provide the solution for many of the world's economic ills and enable the postwar world to remain stable and at peace. The liberation of China from her economic and political stagnation and paralysis will make it easier for other backward nations to follow suit. An economically strong and politically independent China could act as a powerful incentive for the freeing and rehabilitation of other countries. A strong and progressive China could serve as model, champion, and inspiration to other countries struggling to raise themselves from the mire of poverty and exploitation to a level on which they too can make an important contribution to world prosperity and peace. The industrialization and modernization of China would be only the first step in a mathematical if not a geometric progression. It would give the initial momentum to a process that could be continued and accelerated by the freeing of India, of the countries of Africa and Southeast Asia, and of other subject nations.

CHINA'S POSTWAR PLANS

CHINA'S LEADERS are already busily engaged in formulating ambitious plans for their country's postwar economic development, all of which allegedly derive their inspiration from the program laid down over twenty years ago by Dr. Sun Yat-sen as the goal of the Chinese nation. In his book, *Three Principles of the People,* Dr. Sun emphasized that the goals for China were nationalism, or political independence; democracy, or government by and for the people; and the people's livelihood, or economic welfare. In his *International Development of China,* he elaborated a vast blueprint for the economic development of China involving extensive financial and technical participation by foreign powers.

One of the most important recent statements of China's postwar economic aims is that contained in Chiang Kai-shek's book, *China's Destiny,* first published in March 1943. Here the Generalissimo, while recognizing that the complete fulfillment of the nation's "Industrial Plan" may require 30 to 50 years or even longer, outlines the goals to be achieved in the initial ten-year period of reconstruction. Among other things, the goals set for this ten-year period include the building of 12,500 miles of railway and 16,875 miles of highway, 225,000 miles of telegraph lines, 3,000 locomotives, 44,000 railway cars and 450,000 automobiles and trucks, more than 3 million tons of merchant shipping, power plants with a capacity of nearly 11 million horsepower, and an increase in mineral production aimed at an annual output in ten years' time of 150 million tons of coal, over five and a half million tons of iron and steel, one and three quarter million tons of mineral oils, and so on. In addition, Chiang's program calls for the establishment of a machinery and machine-tool industry and a large expansion of the Chinese textile industry. Vast quantities of raw-material imports are also contemplated, judging by Chiang's estimates of the amounts required for the ten-year program: e.g., 8 million tons of iron, 26 million tons of steel, more than 500 million tons of coal, 13 million tons of gasoline, and 25 million tons of fuel oil — amounts far beyond China's capacity to supply. These figures may be unrealistically large, but they give some indication of the potential vastness of the China market.

There is, however, one serious flaw in the ambitious blueprints emanating from Chungking. They appear designed to superimpose an elaborate and costly industrial structure and transport system upon an unstable and impoverished economic base. There is no doubt that China needs railways, factories, power plants, a merchant marine, and heavy industries. But unless the Chinese people are sufficiently prosperous to use the new transport facilities and to purchase the products of the new industries, China cannot hope to establish a sound and enduring economic structure. It may in fact be said that while the Chinese Government's postwar plans adhere faithfully to Sun Yat-sen's dicta regarding large-scale development projects financed by foreign capital, they ignore his equally important contention that the aim of Chinese policy should be to raise the living standards of the people. One can search through every official plan and proposal without finding a mention of the most basic problem of postwar reconstruction — namely, the radical reconstruction of China's semifeudal agrarian economy, without which a prosperous internal market cannot be created. This glaring omission leads us to a consideration of the economic and social aims of the men who control the present Chinese Government and also of those whose aims and plans are more in accordance with American needs and principles.

CHAPTER V

THE RULERS OF KUOMINTANG CHINA [1]

❀

THE YEARS 1939 to 1945 witnessed a disturbing transformation in the political situation in China, as compared with the early days of the war with Japan. After ten years of bitter civil war, the months preceding the outbreak of hostilities in July 1937 had been notable for a rapprochement between the Kuomintang and the Chinese Communists, culminating in an entente or "united front" which was officially established in September 1937. The urgent need for a program of united national resistance to the invader was recognized by all parties and groups in China, and during the first year of the war the Kuomintang modified its repressive policies in a number of respects. Civil liberties were largely restored. Freedom of the press, speech, and assembly was granted to all parties including the Communists, and many political prisoners of the civil war era were released. The high point of political unity was reached at the Emergency Session of the Kuomintang Party Congress, held at Hankow in March 1938.

This session adopted a "Program of National Resistance and Reconstruction," which was accepted by all non-Kuomintang parties as forming the basis for a genuine united front and as holding out the promise of an immediate extension of political and economic democracy. As a temporary measure, pending the convening of a Constitutional Assembly, one of the articles in

---

[1] The term Kuomintang China is commonly used to denote all of China except the Border Regions and guerrilla areas. It is the area in which the Kuomintang — the only legal political party in China — is able to maintain exclusive political power. Before Japan's defeat, the Border Regions, as their name implies, were located on the borders between Free and Occupied China. The guerrilla areas were scattered throughout Occupied China behind the Japanese lines. In the Border Regions and guerrilla areas, coalition governments existed in which all parties participated.

this Program provided for the formation of a People's Politica'
Council, and this Council met for the first time in July 1938.
Though purely advisory in character, with its members appointed by the Kuomintang, the Council included representatives of all important minority parties including the Communists
as well as important leaders with no party affiliation. Its formation was therefore hailed as marking a definite if limited advance
toward a more democratic process of government.

With the fall of Hankow and Canton at the end of 1938, however, the Chinese Government was compelled to retreat into the
backward and undeveloped provinces of the interior. An important result of this retreat, as we noted previously, was that it
destroyed the economic power and political influence of the
industrialists, traders, and bankers who had been engaged in
modern enterprises in the coastal areas and were in many respects relatively progressive in outlook. It is true that China's
predominantly agricultural and therefore highly decentralized
economy enabled her to resist successfully a powerful enemy
and remain a national entity despite the occupation of her richest
and most developed areas. So long as Chinese armies could retreat into relatively self-sufficient areas, they could not be permanently defeated. Had China possessed an industrialized and
interdependent national economy, it is questionable whether she
could have suffered the serious amputation she did and still
avoided complete conquest. But this same nonmechanized,
agricultural, and decentralized economy of the interior also gave
the reactionary landlord-usurer-merchant class an opportunity
to gain a monopoly of power. This group became the economic
mainstay of the Kuomintang regime, and its influence on the
Government's policy was soon evidenced in a sharp reaction
from the progressive tendencies that had characterized the Hankow period, resulting in a tightening of the party dictatorship,
the suppression of civil liberties, open hostility toward all non-
Kuomintang parties and groups, and the adoption of anti-Communism as a shield behind which to institute a period of repression unmatched in Chinese history.

From 1939 onwards, control of the Kuomintang and of the
Chungking Government (which is appointed by the Party) was
concentrated increasingly in the hands of the extreme right wing,
headed by the two Chen brothers, Chen Li-fu and Chen Kuo-fu,

and commonly known as the "CC" clique.[1] Chen Kuo-fu occupied the influential post of head of the Board of Organization of the Kuomintang and was also chief of the personnel section of the Kuomintang's Central Political Institute, while Chen Li-fu, as Minister of Education, was responsible for the system of "thought control" and surveillance by the Party's secret police that inaugurated a reign of intellectual terrorism throughout Kuomintang China. The "CC" clique was able to maintain its control over the Party and the Government because it controlled the Party police and also dominated the Central Executive Committee of the Kuomintang — the real policy-making body of China. This Committee is chosen from delegates elected by the Kuomintang membership to the Party Congress. But there has been no election to a Party Congress since 1935, so that for the past ten years the Central Executive Committee has been chosen by a group of men elected during one of the most reactionary periods of modern Chinese history when civil war and political repression were at their height. It is significant that some of the delegates elected to the 1935 Party Congress subsequently went

---

[1] The two Chen brothers are nephews of the late Chekiang war lord, Chen Chi-mei, who helped Sun Yat-sen against the Manchus and was a patron of Chiang Kai-shek. The principal rival of the "CC" clique in the struggle for power within the Kuomintang is the "Political Science Group" (Cheng Hsueh Hsi). Though no longer a formal organization as it had been in the early days of the Chinese Republic, this latter group is composed of well-trained intellectuals who aspire to a role similar to that of the old scholar-mandarin class. They share the view that China will never become a democracy but must fall back on the old system of rule by an intellectual élite. They have been described as a kind of "professional free-lance bureaucracy" clustering around one dominant individual in whose service they hope to shape Chinese policy. In 1940, there were more than fifty "Political Scientists" in high positions in the bureaucracy; several were in the Cabinet and others occupied posts as provincial governors. Though extremely conservative in outlook, this group is not so reactionary as the "CC" clique. They do not oppose western ideas or techniques, provided that these can be adapted to Chinese customs and institutions. They have no organization or machine comparable to that of the "CC" clique, nor do they enjoy the support of any popular groups, their influence being largely personal. Prominent members of the Political Science Group include General Chang Chun, Governor of Szechwan; Dr. Weng Wen-hao, Minister of Economics; Wang Chung-hui, elder statesman and important adviser to the Generalissimo; Chang Kia-ngau, High Adviser of the Executive Yuan; Wu Ting-chang, ex-governor of Kweichow and owner of a controlling interest in China's leading paper, *Ta Kung Pao*; and O. K. Yui, Finance Minister.

over to the Japanese to join the leading Chinese quisling, Wang Ching-wei.[1]

The Kuomintang membership in 1945 was approximately four times that of 1935. Many of the ablest and most forward-looking men in China had joined the Party after the outbreak of the war either for political protection or from patriotic motives. But none of these new members could vote or take any part in formulating the Party's policies. Many of them were strongly opposed to the reactionary policies of the ruling clique. They believed that Chinese unity could be maintained and strengthened only by an extension of political democracy in both the Party and the Government and by economic reforms to win the support of the people. But they were powerless to break the stranglehold of the ruling clique, whose policies were designed with one aim and one aim only — to maintain their monopoly of political and economic power and to suppress, by force if necessary, all demand for a modification of their dictatorship. From 1939 onward, the disastrous results of this policy, both for China and for her Allies, became clearly apparent not only in the military but also in the political and economic spheres.

From the military point of view, perhaps the greatest disservice done to China's cause was the continued military blockade of the Border Regions and guerrilla areas in North and Central China by approximately half a million well-trained Central Government troops that might otherwise have been employed against the Japanese.[2] The reasons for maintaining this blockade were simple. The right-wing elements in the Kuomintang were alarmed by the growing popular support for the agrarian reforms, democratic electoral procedures, and political education programs introduced in these areas. They therefore determined to prevent the spread of this program to Kuomintang China and, if possible, to bring about the destruction of the guerrilla forces by denying them all access to outside sources of food, munitions, and medical supplies.

---

[1] Wang Ching-wei died in a Japanese hospital on November 10, 1944, and was replaced as puppet head of the Nanking Government by Chen Kung-po.

[2] For a long time the Kuomintang authorities denied the existence of such a blockade. When they eventually admitted it, they claimed that the number of blockading troops was much less than half a million. But even General Ho Ying-chin admitted in an interview in 1943 that the figure was 250,000. On May 1, 1945, Mao Tse-tung stated that "at one time these troops numbered 797,000."

This blockade failed in its major purpose. The guerrilla troops under the leadership of the Eighth Route and New Fourth Armies grew in strength, expanded their operations against the Japanese, and increased their popular following in the "occupied areas," despite frequent attacks against them by Kuomintang troops as well as innumerable "mopping-up" campaigns by the Japanese. The blockade and the political aims and outlook that it represented did, however, accomplish other results that seriously weakened the Allied cause in Asia. In the first place, it denied to China's American allies the use of the strategic areas captured and controlled by the guerrillas in North China. Lacking bases in North China, the 14th Air Force was unable to touch even the periphery of Japan's "Inner Defense Zone" in Manchuria, Korea, and Japan Proper, and it was not until the giant B-29's were put into service that raids upon Japan's main industrial centers became possible.

Another result of the policy pursued toward the guerrilla forces was to bring China to the verge of civil war on numerous occasions and to facilitate Japan's military advance in North China. In fact, there was considerable evidence to support the charge that the Kuomintang regime feared the economic and political program of the guerrilla areas more than it did the Japanese. What disturbed the landed bureaucracy of Chungking above all else was the fact that the extraordinary economic, political, and military progress made in the Border Regions and guerrilla areas was accomplished under the leadership of the Chinese Communist Party. A fact known to few foreigners is that as early as 1940 a lengthy document setting forth "Measures to Solve the Communist Problem" was prepared for the guidance of high-ranking political and military leaders of the Kuomintang and circulated secretly.

This document laid great stress on the necessity of restricting the military and political activities of the Communists and of bringing the Border Regions and guerrilla bases under the direct control of the Kuomintang. It declared, for example: "The so-called 'Shensi-Kansu-Ninghsia Border Area Government' of the Communist Party is to be absolutely denounced. The Central Government decidedly takes this to be a local issue and gives instructions to the provincial governments of the respective provinces to freely take all measures necessary to restore their sovereign rights and interests. . . . The local governments in the

North China guerrilla areas should be immediately transferred to the Branch Office of the Party [Kuomintang] and the Political Council of the Hopei and Chahar War Areas."

Particularly revealing, however, were the methods suggested in the document for accomplishing the desired purpose of eliminating the Communists as a political and military force. One of the main points stressed was that the Central Government should not appear to be involved in the conflict; that the work should be entrusted to local party officials and military leaders. Thus the document, after recommending the despatch of "loyal and efficient troops" to North China "to strengthen the military force of our party in this area and to restrict the expansion of the communists," stated: "Concerning the attitude of the various party, civil, and military organizations, the Central Government must appear to be generous, the local authorities must be cautious and strict, and the lower officers and members must engage in vigorous struggle. Concerning the distribution of work, the party headquarters and members must do the fighting work, the government taking the position of mediator, while the troops are the driving force. . . . In disposing of Communist cases, the various party, civil, and military organizations must assign the work to loyal members of our party so that absolute secrecy may be kept." Other suggested methods included the strict enforcement of "measures promulgated by the Central Government to prevent the activities of non-Kuomintang parties"; the organization of "special societies to be merged into communist organizations"; and the use of "all effective methods to demolish as much as possible the organizational, communication, and publications distribution network of the communists."

When this remarkable document came to the attention of the British Embassy, then headed by Ambassador Sir Archibald Clark-Kerr, one of its leading members took it directly to Chiang Kai-shek for an explanation. The Generalissimo informed him that it had been prepared by a clique in the Kuomintang and submitted to the Central Executive Committee but that the Committee had, of course, rejected it and that it did not in any sense constitute the official policy of the Chinese Government. The fact remains, however, that the document itself specifically stated that the Government was not to appear involved in the work of crushing the Communists, and that the actual policies pursued by local Kuomintang civil and military officials during the past five years bear a remarkable resemblance to the policies and methods suggested in the document.

Numerous cases have been reported, for example, where Kuomintang troops have been ordered to follow a policy of "anti-Communism first and resistance second." Many Americans find such reports hard to credit, as indeed they are. Not long ago I attended a private dinner at which a well-known Chinese general was also present. During a discussion of Far Eastern events, he was asked the following questions: "General, leaving aside the ultimate justification of your Government's military blockade against the Eighth Route and New Fourth Armies, it is certainly true that Chinese men and women among the guerrilla and partisan troops are fighting the Japanese and are being wounded in the process. Ordinary humanitarianism would seem to require that these wounded and helpless Chinese should be given medical supplies, and thousands of Americans have contributed money for the purchase of such supplies. On what grounds, then, does your Government refuse to permit such medical aid to go through the blockade?"

His unhesitating reply was simple and explicit: "Would you send medical aid to your enemy? We consider the Communists to be the enemies of the State, therefore greater enemies than the Japanese." The General's reply left those present so shocked that no one thought it worth while to ask him the obvious question: "And do you think that if the Japanese defeated China there would remain such an entity as a Chinese State? Wouldn't it be the better part of wisdom first to ensure the existence of a State before you fight for control of it?"

In view of this attitude on the part of Kuomintang leaders, it is not surprising that preparations continued to be made for the destruction of the two famous guerrilla armies as a political and military force as soon as China's allies should have attended to Japan's defeat, if not before. Toward that end, available military supplies were diverted from the sagging fighting front to the blockading forces or hoarded for future use.[1] The Chinese Gov-

---

[1] A large part of these supplies went to arm the forces of General Tai Li, head of Chungking's secret military police. Tai Li is estimated to have a total of 180,000 plain-clothes agents, of whom probably 40,000 are full-time operatives and the remainder special contact men. The addition of uniformed agents would bring the total of Tai Li's operatives to approximately 300,000. He is the real head of Chinese military intelligence, and controls the use of all communication facilities in China — e.g., railroads, trucking companies,

ernment continued to maintain an army of millions of troops that it could not adequately feed, train, or equip — presumably with an eye to the future struggle for power — and ignored suggestions from American military leaders that this army be reduced to manageable size. Finally, close and friendly relations were maintained by the Central Government with various Chinese puppet leaders, both civilian and military, pending the time when these traitors could join the campaign against the popular forces that sought to establish a new and democratic regime.

There is, in fact, a large accumulation of evidence that certain picked Central Army troops and commanders were encouraged to go over to the Japanese. Ostensibly the mission of these troops was to enter occupied areas for the purpose of maintaining as much control as possible and preventing the Japanese from gaining complete dominance. In reality, however, there were two reasons for this maneuver. First, these troops joined with the Japanese in fighting the Chinese Communist forces. The second and more long-term objective was to ensure that there would be Kuomintang military control over these areas following Japan's defeat. The Eighth Route Army's records are replete with evidence obtained from captured Kuomintang puppet troops indicating that their coöperation with the Japanese was part of a deliberate plan on the part of the Kuomintang authorities. Of an estimated 800,000 puppet troops, over 500,000 are said to be "Chungking-planted" puppets — the rest being those recruited by the Japanese themselves.

The Chungking authorities, of course, were not unaware that these troops would be a more effective controlling force within China after Japan's defeat if they had actually fought the Japanese. But they preferred to make certain that these troops would not be decimated in the war, and would therefore be available later for use in the expected civil conflict. This charge may sound fantastic, but the fact remains that on at least two occasions

---

airlines, and radio. His agents operated in all parts of Free and Occupied China, and on occasion did useful work in checking on Japanese activities, but their main job has been to discover and wipe out all forms of opposition to the Chungking regime. A certain proportion of American supplies to China was given to Tai Li in return for information regarding the Japanese, but it is reported that most of this information proved valueless, and that the greater part of the supplies was stored away in Tai Li's warehouses, presumably for ultimate use in regaining control of liberated areas from guerrilla troops. Tai Li's men were also heavily involved in the smuggling trade between Free and Occupied China.

early in 1944 the then Chinese Minister of Information, H. C. Liang, broadcast to the Chinese people urging them not to be too disturbed by the fact that substantial numbers of Chinese troops were going over to join the puppet forces of Japan, because, when the time came for Japan's final defeat, these puppet forces would certainly desert their Japanese masters and prove true patriots. By taking for granted the ultimate patriotism of the Chinese puppet troops, his statements constituted an inducement to other Chinese troops to desert for economic or political reasons with the assurance that their actions would be excused and their patriotism remain unquestioned.

Of even greater significance in this connection was the statement by Dr. Wang Chung-hui, one of the most influential men in the Chungking Government and a trusted adviser of the Generalissimo. Dr. Wang is reported to have declared in October 1943 that he hoped and expected that after the war the Chinese Government would issue a general amnesty for Chinese puppet officials in the occupied areas. He admitted that some of the leaders, such as Wang Ching-wei, would have to be punished, but said that Chen Kung-po would be a "doubtful case." (Subsequently, following the death of Wang Ching-wei in November 1944, Chen Kung-po became head of the Nanking puppet regime.) Wang Chung-hui is at present chairman of the "Far Eastern and Pacific Sub-commission" of the United Nations War Crimes Commission, and is also said to be the real foreign minister of China, so his views in this connection are of special importance. The whole strategy of the "Chungking-planted" puppets was clearly demonstrated following Japan's surrender, when Chiang Kai-shek called upon the puppets to "maintain order" in the "occupied areas" pending the arrival of Central Government troops, and when the puppets suddenly became known in official statements from Chungking as the "underground," although for years there had been nothing underground about their activities as instruments of Japanese rule. A. T. Steele, in a despatch from Chungking published in the *New York Herald Tribune* of August 14, 1945, made no bones about stating that in recovering control of Japanese-occupied areas, "the Chungking government is counting on assistance from Chinese puppet troops. . . . It is no secret that many puppet officials and army officers are in league with Chungking, and plan to declare allegiance to the central government when the opportunity is ripe. These will be expected to hold their garrison areas against Communist pressure until central government troops arrive."

It must be emphasized that there was not the slightest indication that the Chungking Government, despite its tolerant attitude toward the Chinese puppets, was contemplating any form of compromise peace with Japan. Whatever else might be said of Chiang Kai-shek's aims for China, no one could question his determination to free his country from all forms of foreign domination. But Chiang's record as a political leader during the previous eighteen years had been notable for his skill in playing off one opposing force against another. And there was every indication that he favored a policy of allowing America to defeat Japan, while he preserved the greater part of his military power to suppress any opposition to his regime that might arise after the Japanese had been driven out of China. To this end it was "logical" that he should maintain close relations with Chinese puppet officials and with the Kuomintang troops "planted" in occupied China, with a view to the quick restoration of Kuomintang power in those areas, after Japan's defeat. It was also "logical" that these "planted" puppets should be ordered to coöperate actively in "anti-Communist" campaigns.

Sensational evidence that Chungking was negotiating with Chinese puppets along these lines was provided in September 1944, when Governor Lung Yun of Yunnan intercepted a letter to the Generalissimo from General Tang Sheng-ming, puppet governor of Hunan, with a copy addressed to General Tai Li. This letter indicated that General Tang had assumed the post of governor with the approval of Chungking, and it offered Chiang the following alternatives: either he could become an American "puppet" or he could withhold his forces and allow the Americans to fight the Japanese single-handed. In the latter event, Japan would refrain from attacking Chungking and allow Chiang to concentrate his armed strength for use in maintaining his power in the postwar period. In addition to this concrete example of negotiations, there were persistent rumors throughout the spring of 1945 that three important representatives of the Nanking puppet regime were actually in Chungking, putting forward peace proposals on behalf of the Japanese. One of these three was reported to be Yuan Tso, chief of the Kiangsu Education Department and a protégé of the Japanese Navy.

The fact that the enemy's puppets could visit China's capital with impunity, and that the Chungking Government regarded Chinese puppet troops more as potential weapons against Chinese opposition forces than as instruments of the Japanese, did not, of course, indicate direct collaboration with Japan. But American observers in China considered that Chungking's maneuvers amounted to playing Japan off against the United States for the sake of Chungking's future power, and they also believed that the policy of "planting" puppet troops to combat partisan forces in the liberated areas not only weakened China's war effort, but would seriously complicate possible American military operations against Japan on the Chinese mainland. In a famous despatch to the *New York Times* dated October 31, 1944, Brooks Atkinson put the case succinctly when he wrote in part: "No diplomatic genius could have overcome the Generalissimo's basic unwillingness to risk his armies in battles with the Japanese. . . . The Chinese Government hedges and hesitates over anything involving the use of its armies. Foreigners can only conclude that the Chinese Government wants to save its armies to secure its political power after the war."

Moreover, there were also many evidences of serious military demoralization in Kuomintang China that could be attributed directly to the Chungking Government's failure to mobilize the country's resources, its refusal to train and organize the people for guerrilla warfare, its pernicious and corrupt system of conscription, and its inability to control many of its frontline commanders who had reverted to the status of local war lords more interested in exploiting the areas under their control than in fighting the Japanese. China's armies were poorly equipped, miserably fed, and in many cases badly led. The extent to which the Chungking regime had allowed its armies to deteriorate was strikingly manifested in the disastrous Honan campaign of May 1944, and in the subsequent Japanese drive southward into Hunan, Kwangsi, and Kiangsi.

In the Honan campaign, a Japanese force not exceeding 100,-000 troops utterly destroyed 600,000 Chinese troops under the command of General Tang En-po, but it was not the military disaster that made this campaign such a disgraceful episode in China's history. The outstanding feature of the Honan campaign was its political implications, notably the fact that the Chinese peasants turned on their own army and fought against it. These peasants had suffered for more than two years from the oppressive treatment of the troops quartered in that area, who had ruthlessly extorted grain from the people during the serious famine period. As a result of these extortionate demands, together with the cruelty with which the peasants were impressed into the army's services, the people of Honan had only the utmost contempt and hatred for the Chinese troops. The final blow came when, at the outset of the campaign, most of the trucks available to the 1st War Zone Command (Honan) were used by army officers and civilian officials to evacuate their families and personal belongings to Sian, while the local government seized the peasants' oxen and ox-carts for army transport purposes. This infuriated the peasants to the point where they began to disarm first individual soldiers, and then whole units of troops. It is reported that at least 50,000 rifles were seized by the peasantry under the slogan "Better the soldiers of Japan than the soldiers of Tang En-po," and that many of these peasants subsequently formed guerrilla bands.

Chinese officials, however, blamed the series of Chinese defeats in the summer and autumn of 1944 entirely on the failure of China's allies to supply her with sufficient material aid. The implication of some of their statements seemed to be that China had fought enough — that it was now up to her allies to bring the war to a successful conclusion. This sentiment might have been excusable if the Chinese Government had done everything possible to strengthen China's powers of resistance and if it had not continued to put obstacles in the way of its allies. The Government, however, had not only failed to win the support of its own people, but had also failed to make effective use of the American equipment it received, and had obstructed American efforts to gain military intelligence about the Japanese by refusing to allow observers to visit the fighting fronts in both Kuomintang and guerrilla areas. Not until late in the summer of 1944 was an American military mission permitted to visit the guerrilla areas in North China, and even then the mission was restricted to the gathering of information under the guidance of official "interpreters." In view of these facts, attested to by numerous observers in China, it was impossible to accept the Chinese contention that China's military demoralization from 1941 onward was due chiefly to her failure to receive outside aid, and that it was now up to her allies to pull her through. Instead, Americans were reluctantly forced to the conclusion that the Chungking regime was, in the words of Brooks Atkinson of the *New York Times,* "a moribund anti-democratic regime that is more concerned with maintaining its political supremacy than in driving the Japanese out of China."

The policies pursued by the Kuomintang on the economic and political fronts also served to support this conclusion. Economically, by the middle of 1945, China faced collapse not only because of the hardships wrought by eight years of war, but also because of the Government's inability or unwillingness to take effective steps to check the disastrous currency inflation, and the hoarding, speculation, and profiteering indulged in by landlords, merchants, and others who either were powerful in the Kuomintang or had close connections with leading Party members. The centralization of all economic power in the hands of the ruling bureaucracy had discouraged private enterprise and stifled the development of much-needed productive forces — a notable instance being the increasing restriction of the activities of the Chinese Industrial Coöperatives. Industrial and handicraft production had declined sharply because it was more profitable to speculate in raw materials than to invest in industrial enterprises. The Government had failed to make any effective effort to tax adequately the incomes and profits of the landlords and merchants, and its tax-collection machinery was reported to be so corrupt and inefficient that not more than half the revenues collected actually reached the Government. Though Government officials occasionally denounced hoarding and profiteering, no real attempt was made to crack down on those who engaged most freely in these activities. Nor did the controlling bureaucracy make any effort to deal with the fundamental economic problems of Kuomintang China, notably the rapid concentration of land holdings, the extortionate rents and interest rates exacted from the peasants, and the impact of inflation, particularly on the professional and salaried classes.

Another evidence of demoralization and corruption in high circles was the continued trade with Japanese-occupied areas. This trade involved the import of semiluxury items and the export of food and raw materials that were of great value to the Japanese, such as rice, wool, tungsten, tung oil, and other commodities. It was even reported that, in certain areas, local commanders had allowed military equipment to be sold to the Japanese. This illicit traffic, at first carried on surreptitiously, grew to such profitable proportions that in January 1944 the Chungking Government decided to control it openly. At least, this would seem to be the only logical explanation of the report that four government banks were organizing a CN$150,000,000 company with an original capital of some CN$20,000,000 to conduct trade with the occupied areas in order "to combat commodity shortages in Free China." This company was organized in June 1944, under the name of the International Hsing Yeh Co., and was headed by Tu Yueh-sheng, famous before the war as the Opium Czar, banker, and leader of the Shanghai underworld. Particularly active in this trade were the Central Trust of H. H. Kung's Central Bank and the Central Relief Administration dominated by Tu Yueh-sheng and Wang Hsiao-lai.

According to reliable reports, wolfram, tin, and quicksilver were being exported to Hong Kong during 1944 in as large quantities as transport facilities would permit. Copper was being sold to Indo-China, and raw cotton was exported to Japanese-occupied areas in China where it was spun into thread or cloth and resold to Free China, with the Japanese making a profit on both transactions. In a number of areas, tobacco and opium were being grown specially for export to Japanese-held areas. Most shocking of all was the trade in rice, which was being exported in substantial quantities to Canton, Kwangchouwan, Hankow, Shanghai, and elsewhere despite acute shortages in Free China, because the Japanese paid higher prices for it. Chinese farmers were starving in many parts of China, and even their seed rice had been confiscated by the army, yet a few wealthy landlords who controlled large stocks of rice continued to make high profits by selling it to the Japanese. The Japanese, on the other hand, were selling only two items to the Chinese that could be called essential — cloth and thread; other items being such luxuries as toiletries, cigarettes, silk, clocks, and lipsticks.

This development of profitable commercial relations with the enemy was, of course, an important contributory factor to the decline in military morale, the growing distrust and hatred with which the people regarded their own military leaders, and the increasing ease with which the Japanese advanced. All American observers in China during 1944 and 1945 were agreed that the Japanese were making effective use of the military and political disunity in China to disrupt Chinese resistance by political and economic means. As early as May 1941, the Chinese had lost

the battle of Chungtiao Shan in South Shansi and Northern
Honan mainly because Japanese armies had already learned to
utilize Chinese political friction and economic disorganization.
The people in this area had been overtaxed and their grain
seized by the army. Surreptitious trade had flourished with
Japan, with the result that the Japanese were able to send many
agents into the area in the guise of Chinese merchants, and thus
obtain information that was invaluable to them when they finally attacked. Furthermore, the people of the area gave no support to their own troops, with the result that the battle was won
by the Japanese with very little loss to their fighting forces.

In every subsequent campaign, the Japanese showed the same
ability to make use of Chinese disunity, and in each case the
Chinese defense plans were handicapped or rendered useless
by the fact that the armies and the people were hostile to each
other, and that the front lines had been infiltrated and corrupted
by trade with the occupied areas. In most cases, the Japanese
accomplished their objectives without the use of heavy weapons,
except to reduce isolated strong points, and relied on guerrilla
tactics of infiltration and progaganda. There was even a report
that, in the Hunan battle late in 1944, the Japanese advanced by
buying territory from the Chinese commander for so much rice
for each square mile. Thus one can justly conclude that in the
campaigns of 1941–45, it was the enemy who developed the
tactics and strategy that should have been developed by the
defenders. The Japanese, who had the military equipment with
which to carry on mechanized warfare, found it more advan-
tageous to use the simpler type of guerrilla offense, while the
Chinese troops for whom mechanized war was impossible because of lack of equipment, but for whom guerrilla warfare
should have been a natural weapon, were unable to mobilize
even a guerrilla defense, much less an offense. Such was the
penalty that Chungking had to pay for its failure to mobilize
and arm its own people — a failure that reaped its bitterest dividends in the disastrous campaigns of 1944, which resulted in the
loss of all American air bases in Southeast China.

As a result of this increasing military and economic demoralization, stimulated by open corruption and blatant inefficiency
on the part of the bureaucracy, resentment against the existing
regime spread rapidly during 1944, accompanied by an increasingly strong and openly voiced demand for democratic reforms

that would give the people a voice in the government. These opposition forces included many different groups representing all
shades of political opinion, but they were united in the belief
that only a genuinely representative government supported by
the people could deal effectively with the urgent political, economic, and military problems confronting China; that only such
a government could establish internal unity, restore national
morale, and carry out effective measures against the economic
abuses that were being tolerated and even openly encouraged
by the reactionary clique in power.

The ruling clique, however, refused to heed this demand for
political reform and continued to use repressive measures to
prevent the growth of any effective opposition movement. All
minority parties and groups were suppressed and denied legal
status. The People's Political Council remained completely im-
potent, its membership hand-picked by the Government and its
recommendations ignored. The various secret-police organizations were steadily strengthened and carried on constant espionage against all those suspected of "dangerous thoughts." Oc-
cupants of government posts and students going abroad were
required to undergo preliminary training at the Kuomintang's
Central Political Institute in order that they might be certain
to conform to the "orthodox" interpretation of Kuomintang
"doctrine."

Efforts were also intensified to prevent the spread of "radical"
ideas among Chinese university students and to ensure unquestioning acceptance of Kuomintang party doctrines as enunciated
by the "CC" clique. Teachers were in no position to oppose this
trend because the inflation had made their fixed salaries wholly
inadequate and they were dependent for their very existence
on the rice rations granted them by the Government. Those who
dared to make a stand on behalf of freedom of speech lost their
jobs and many were imprisoned. It is an open secret that the
four American professors who went to Chungking in the autumn
of 1943 to teach at the Postgraduate School of Journalism sponsored by Columbia University were surprised and shocked at
what they had to face in their efforts to teach the evolution and
meaning of the principles of freedom of speech and of the press.
Having gone to China under the impression that they were to
work for the Chinese Government to aid in preparing Chinese
journalism students for further study abroad, they found that

the School was affiliated with the Kuomintang's Political Training Institute and was intended primarily to provide the Party with more efficient press agents and propagandists. Furthermore, the students themselves were carefully chosen for soundness on Party lines and were paid by the Party, while the selection of those who were to receive further training abroad was to be made by Party officials. No news of the School's progress has been made public since it opened in October 1943, except that Professor Harold L. Cross, dean of the School, did not continue in that position after the first term. Later, Rodney Gilbert of the *New York Herald Tribune* undertook the task of being dean of the school, which finally closed its doors in the fall of 1945. Another evidence of the lengths to which the Kuomintang rulers endeavored to carry their policy of "thought control" was the plan for "supervising" the thoughts and actions of Chinese students studying abroad, which aroused so much criticism in American academic circles that it was abandoned for the duration of the war.

The policies pursued by the Kuomintang in suppressing minority political parties will be discussed later. But to complete the picture of political regimentation it is necessary to add a few facts about the position of organized labor in Kuomintang China. During the early years of the Chinese revolution there was a rapid growth in trade union organization, and labor unions took an active part in the revolutionary movement of 1925–27, the high point of their activity being the famous sixteen months' general strike in the Hong Kong-Canton area involving 250,000 workers. In 1927, the All-China Trade Union Federation claimed a membership of nearly three million workers, but the split in the Kuomintang marked the beginning of a ten-year period of civil war and of ruthless repression in which many thousands of trade union leaders lost their lives. All unions were crushed, although spontaneous strikes, frequently of a political character, occasionally occurred in various parts of the country, notably the one-day general strike of Shanghai workers in 1936 in protest against Japanese aggression as well as the Government's continued refusal to offer united resistance to Japan.

Following the outbreak of war, the Government modified its repressive attitude toward labor unions to some extent, but it still maintained the policy of keeping union activities under its own control. Thus, even in 1938 when the Chinese Association of

Labor was organized, it was formed under government auspices. In 1940, control of labor affairs was transferred to the Ministry of Social Affairs headed by Ku Cheng-kang, a leading member of the "CC" clique. On May 5, 1942, the Government adopted the National Mobilization Act, which was almost identical in its provisions with Japan's General Mobilization Act and which gave the Government power to outlaw strikes and conscript labor. Subsequently, a special series of regulations governing labor policy "in time of emergency" were enacted and later embodied in a new National Labor Union Code promulgated on November 20, 1943. The most important feature of this new code was that it made membership in Government-controlled unions compulsory for all workers. "Supervision and control" of all unions were vested in national and local organs of the Ministry of Social Affairs, which was empowered to dissolve any union for "serious violations." Workers in government and defense enterprises might belong only to special unions, with no right to strike and only limited powers of collective bargaining. Ordinary unions were technically permitted to strike under some circumstances, but they were held responsible for "refraining from actions disturbing to social tranquility," and strikes were not allowed in "periods of emergency" as determined by the Government.

Although the Chinese Association of Labor is officially declared to have a membership of over 500,000, chiefly composed of postal employees, this membership is largely on paper and the Association performs no function in China. Its president, Chu Hsueh-fan, is a former protégé of Tu Yueh-sheng, ex-head of the Shanghai gangs that carried out the work of destroying the Shanghai unions in 1927. Chu Hsueh-fan's only role is to serve as a spokesman for China at international labor conferences and to raise funds for his union from overseas. It is well known that he exercises no power whatsoever in China and that the Chinese Association of Labor performs none of the functions of a trade union federation since all power to determine labor conditions, wages, working hours, etc., rests with the Ministry of Social Affairs.

Some of the most disturbing features of Chinese Government policy in the period from 1939 through 1945 could, of course, be attributed to temporary wartime conditions. But there were also certain aspects of Kuomintang policy that threatened to have a very direct and adverse bearing on China's postwar development. This was not only true in the realm of political democracy, but applied also to official Chinese pronouncements concerning China's postwar economic aims.

Both official and semiofficial spokesmen constantly stressed the thesis that China is a predominantly agricultural country with special historical characteristics that are so deeply ingrained in Chinese society that they must inevitably determine the character of China's future development. From this premise they reasoned that, since these characteristics are a product of China's particular type of agrarian economy, that economy must remain the basis of any future economic structure. Their views concerning China's future development may be summarized as follows: First, China will remain a predominantly agricultural country. Second, light industry for the production of consumer goods will be widely decentralized, with thousands of small producing units scattered throughout the country and financed either by private capital or by individuals acting in coöperation with the Government. Finally, there will be a few large centers of heavy industry under centralized bureaucratic control.

The economic philosophy underlying these theories was perhaps most clearly demonstrated in Chiang Kai-shek's book *Chinese Economic Theory*, published early in 1943 and used as a text-book in the Kuomintang's Central Training Institute. Like *China's Destiny*, this book emphasizes the great superiority of ancient Chinese civilization over Western culture, and strongly deplores the fact that certain Chinese scholars have accepted Western economic theories. "Most so-called scientific thinkers tend to treat lightly the things of their own country and to esteem highly all which is foreign. . . . They have forgotten the fact that China has herself had a long historical development, her own special geographical environment, and her own economic laws and principles on which the country developed. This tendency is very much to be regretted." Much space is devoted in the book to praising the economic theories of the ancient Chinese sages, and glorifying the economic and social structure of ancient China, in which the village was both the economic and the military unit. Though admitting the necessity for modern industrial development, the book emphasizes the necessity of subordinating private enterprise to control by a bureaucratic government, condemns the principles of free enterprise and individual initiative, and insists that "a government which manages people's affairs

. . . is the foundation of the philosophy of national economics." The whole tone of the book is strongly paternalistic and feudal in outlook, and the social and economic ideology that it outlines in exceedingly vague and rhetorical terms can perhaps best be described as fascism adapted to a semi-feudal agrarian economy.

These views were not shared by the more progressive Chinese industrialists and bankers, who believed that if China was to take her place as an equal among the great powers, she could do so only on the basis of an expanding economy that would give full scope to private ownership and initiative and provide for a prosperous internal market. They also recognized that China could not hope to develop such an economy until her agrarian system had undergone some very radical changes. During the war, however, this group had no strong base or support in China, whereas the political power of the semifeudal landlord class greatly increased.

This landed bureaucracy, as we have seen, was bent on maintaining its enhanced power. The landed gentry are well aware that the existence of large-scale industrial plants throughout the length and breadth of China, able to attract millions of workers away from the land, would constitute a most serious blow to their economic power. Obviously, a system of decentralized small-scale or cottage industry would be the best safeguard against any disturbance of China's present agrarian system. Moreover, the development of a few large industrial centers under the control of a government in the hands of a reactionary oligarchy not subject to democratic control could further prevent the growth of an independent class of industrialists as well as an independent industrial working class, both of which would constitute a threat to the dominant position of the feudal-minded landlord class.[1] The more one studies the official pronouncements regarding China's postwar economy, the more one is struck by their similarity to the economic structure of modern Japan in which a bureaucratic-government-controlled heavy industry was artificially grafted on a semifeudal agrarian base. As E. H. Norman points out in his study of *Japan's Emergence as a*

---

[1] Even the billion-dollar postwar industrialization plan for China, drawn up by officials of the U.S. Foreign Economic Administration at the request of the Chinese Government and completed in March 1945, does not take cognizance of this basic aspect of China's economy.

Modern State, Japan's economic development following the Restoration of 1868 was characterized by two phenomena: "First, the stunting of the growth of a capitalist class and its consequent dependence on a section of the feudal ruling class, and second, the social transformation from a feudal to a capitalist economy carried out with the minimum of social change in agrarian relations."[1]

The interlocking of landlordism, banking, and government has long been recognized as an outstanding feature of Japan's political and economic structure, resulting in a highly centralized control by a small ruling oligarchy. Japan's industrial achievements have been notable, but they have been accomplished at the cost of an impoverished peasantry, a large surplus agricultural population, a severely limited internal market, and excessively low living standards for the majority of the Japanese people. Admittedly, conditions in China are very different from those in which Japan undertook to modernize her economic structure at the end of the last century. But if the present ruling clique in China is able to preserve the present system of landlord-peasant relations, while superimposing a few large, bureaucratically controlled modern industries on this backward agrarian base, China will develop an economy as unbalanced and unhealthy as that of prewar Japan. It is characteristic of official China's economic perspective that her spokesmen have repeatedly mentioned with envy Japan's prewar position as the leading exporter of low-priced cotton textiles. They maintain that, as part of her share of reparations, China should be given these erstwhile Japanese export markets. Obviously, China can support such an export trade only on the basis of a very cheap labor supply stemming from the existence of an impoverished and landless peasantry. If China's economic future is to be based on a foundation of coolie labor and prewar living standards, she cannot possibly develop the type of expanding internal market that is so vital to a healthy and effective coöperation between her and the United States as well as other industrial countries. No basic postwar issues will be solved by the mere act of transferring American prewar export totals from Japan to China.

---

[1] E. H. Norman: *Japan's Emergence as a Modern State* (New York, 1940).

CHIANG KAI-SHEK AND "CHINA'S DESTINY"

THE FOREGOING description of the aims and practices of the Kuomintang's ruling clique during the six-year period from 1939 through 1945 may be of only historic interest before this book appears in print. Certainly, it is the author's sincere hope that it will be. It is clear, however, that the cleavages between the right-wing elements in the Kuomintang and the democratic forces in all China are too deep to be healed by superficial compromises. But whether or not any basic political changes take place in China in the near future, it is nevertheless essential that the American people should be fully aware of the serious nature of the political and economic crisis from which China is suffering, and of the long and difficult road that the Chinese people have still to travel before China can be expected to become a strong, prosperous, and democratic nation.

What the situation boiled down to by the middle of 1945 was that there was already an undeclared civil war in China. That war was not, as many people believed, a conflict between the Kuomintang and the Chinese Communists for control of the Chinese State. Rather, it was a conflict between a small but powerful element in the Kuomintang that opposed any extension of political democracy and favored an authoritarian, one-party dictatorship, and those groups both within and outside the Kuomintang that wanted a genuinely democratic form of government in which all minority parties would be permitted to function. The political and economic program that had been introduced in the guerrilla regions was one of democratic government and moderate land reforms, designed to enlist the support of all sections of the population. This program, as all foreign visitors to those areas have attested, was in no sense Communist, but it did represent a definite challenge to the political and economic philosophy of the ruling clique within the Kuomintang, who wished to preserve the old land system intact and had no desire to relinquish their monopoly of political power by democratizing the Chinese Government.

Nor did there seem to be much hope for a change in the philosophy of this ruling clique, judging from the opinions expressed in *China's Destiny*, the book in which Chiang Kai-shek himself discusses China's internal problems and her future development. When this book was first published in March 1943, it shocked many Westerners by its strong antiforeign tone, its bitter and provocative denunciation of all opposition groups, its insistence that the Kuomintang alone must lead China, and its generally hostile attitude toward the tenets of Western democracy and individual liberty. At that time, however, it was recognized that Chinese leaders had some reason to feel that they had not been treated as equal partners in the Allied war effort, and that some of the extreme views expressed in the book might be due to this sense of isolation and to a resultant bitterness against any and all groups that appeared to challenge the Government's authority. After the Cairo Conference, however, it was hoped that the Generalissimo might modify his position, and this hope was strengthened by the news that the book had been withdrawn from circulation.

China's Destiny was not only subjected to severe attacks from foreign critics but was also criticized widely though guardedly in Kuomintang China. When he became aware of the rising tide of criticism among Chinese intellectuals, students, and even among his loyal followers in the Government, Chiang Kai-shek decided to take the bull by the horns. He ordered all important government officials to send him written and signed appraisals of *China's Destiny*. After studying all of these official "criticisms," he was surprised and delighted to find that, except for minor points, the contentions of the book received complete support from his critics. Thus reinforced and armed with unanimous official backing, a revised edition of *China's Destiny* was published in January 1944 with only minor alterations to distinguish it from the first edition. In the new version North Burma, including the Hukawng Valley, as well as the Liuchiu Islands, was added to the map of China that in the earlier version had included Hong Kong, Outer Mongolia, Tannu Tuva, and Tibet. A few of the stronger passages attacking the Western Powers were toned down somewhat, and a few other passages slightly altered. Otherwise *China's Destiny* remained the same as the earlier edition — a narrow and short-sighted special interpretation of history, patterned to suit the needs of an autarchic bureaucracy fighting bitterly to maintain power. It is significant that Chungking has refused permission for the publication of an English-language version of either the first or the revised edition. But regardless of the devious ways of a power-obsessed ruling clique, *China's Destiny* can no longer be regarded as the product of a momentary irritation but must be recognized as a deliberate and carefully drawn-up set of principles by which the aims of China's present rulers must be judged.

China's Destiny maintains that foreign aggression was responsible for all China's troubles during the past hundred years. Everything is blamed on the "unequal treaties" and on China's military, political, and economic domination by the Western Powers and Japan. In making this point, Chiang Kai-shek pictures the "old China" before the coming of the foreigners as a "golden world" in which the economic and political system and the political and social concepts embodied in Confucian philosophy were virtually ideal. He is particularly lavish in his praise of the achievements and policies of such Confucianist statesmen as Tseng Kuo-fan — who is regarded by liberal Chinese as a traitor for having helped the Manchu dynasty to suppress the Tai-ping Rebellion.[1] There is absolutely no recognition of the fact that it was the despotic system of government and the feudal agricultural economy of this "old China" that oppressed the Chinese people and rendered them incapable of resisting foreign aggression. It is significant that the Japanese selected the *Analects* of Confucius as their principal weapon of psychological warfare in China, and made every effort to revive the Confucian system of social ethics in the areas under their control. They were well aware that for more than two thousand years the Emperors and Mandarins of China had used the moral precepts of Confucius to enforce unquestioning obedience by the people, and they chose "classical Confucianism" as the ideal method of combating nationalism and democracy in China.

Dr. Sun Yat-sen himself pointed out that "the former weakness and decline of China was due to the harsh oppressions of absolutism," and that "it is impossible to make China strong and

---

[1] The Tai-ping Rebellion was a great peasant uprising in the middle of the nineteenth century that was precipitated by the early years of foreign penetration but that had its roots chiefly in the intolerable economic conditions prevailing within China. By 1850 this uprising reached the proportions of a mighty antidynastic peasant rebellion that swept northward from Kwangsi Province and established its power in the Yangtze Valley for a period of eleven years. The final defeat of the Tai-pings occurred in 1865, with Tseng Kuo-fan and Li Hung-chang being remembered as the arch betrayers of the Chinese people. Tseng Kuo-fan, representative of the landed interests, and Li Hung-chang, leader of the new comprador class, succeeded in preserving the Manchu dynasty only with foreign military and naval aid.

prosperous save by promoting the principle of democracy." But the author of *China's Destiny* glorifies the virtues of ancient China and makes no secret of his hostility to the modern political and economic thought of the West. In his view, China has suffered greatly because of the obsessions of many of her scholars with the "libertarian theories" of the West that are wholly "unsuited" to Chinese society. What China needs, according to Chiang Kai-shek, is not more individual liberty but to be bound together rigidly so that individuals may not enjoy the "liberty" of "grains of sand." "The fact should be appreciated that the democratic system we speak of for China is not on the pattern of the nineteenth-century individualistic and class democracy of Europe and America." Moreover, Chiang makes it clear that the Kuomintang alone is to supply this "binding force." "To the Kuomintang is entrusted the destiny of China." It is the duty of all sincere patriots to join the Kuomintang, and any opposition to the Kuomintang during the period of "political tutelage" is branded as "traitorous feudalism."

As for China's future economic development, *China's Destiny* makes no mention of the need for a reform in China's agrarian system, but concentrates on the ambitious program of industrial development described in the preceding chapter. There is no recognition of the fact that an expanding internal market is essential for sound industrial development and that such a market can be achieved only if the peasants are freed from the crushing burdens and restrictions of a feudal economy.

It is not surprising that the publication of *China's Destiny* was greeted with dismay in those American circles that had access to its contents. For months previous to its publication, American students of Chinese affairs had expressed concern over the suppression of liberal forces in China and the growing influence of the more reactionary elements within the Kuomintang. Among those who took this stand were many who had staunchly supported the Chinese Government in the past and could in no sense be regarded as Communist sympathizers. Their view was and is that the preservation of Chinese unity and the strengthening of democratic forces in China were essential not only for the success of the war effort in Asia but also for the emergence of a strong and stable China as a bulwark of Far Eastern security in the postwar world.

In *China's Destiny*, however, they found no support for the trend toward greater political unity and democracy that had appeared so promising in the early months of the Sino-Japanese war, but rather an outspoken demand for the strengthening of the Kuomintang dictatorship and the suppression of all groups seeking political and economic reform. This fact, combined with the strongly antiforeign tone of the book, disturbed many foreign observers who had counted upon Chiang Kai-shek to combat the forces of reaction and emerge as the true leader of a united democratic China. Raymond Gram Swing, for example, in an important analysis of the Chinese situation, pointed out that it used to be thought that Chiang looked forward to the introduction of true democracy after the war, but that doubts have been raised by the publication of *China's Destiny*, which now becomes "the official guide and text-book for the Kuomintang. . . . In spirit it is an antiforeign book. It is also anti-imperialist . . . but it does not much differentiate between American policy and imperialism and it is not friendly to the tenets of Western liberalism. On the subject of democracy, Chiang writes that there can be other types of it than the Western kind, and states that the destiny of China rests with the Kuomintang. In other words, while there can be other factions in theory, China will keep the one-party system, continuing its youth movement and presumably its rigid controls. There is no mention in the book of land reforms. So there is no basis in this doctrine on which to build hopes for what we should consider a democratic movement in which the agrarian radicals would have some political weight."[1]

The sections of *China's Destiny* that most clearly reveal the political and economic aims of the ruling section of the Kuomintang, however, are not those dealing with the iniquities of foreign imperialism, or even those glorifying the virtues of "ancient China." Such misinterpretations of history, if left to the mercy of time, would like so many other false historical theses prove harmless through neglect. But *China's Destiny* also contains a call to action in that section of the book devoted to a history of Kuomintang-Communist relations. Here, with discouraging clarity, is painted the picture of future civil strife in China if this bitter, distorted, and irreconcilable approach continues to dominate Kuomintang policy toward the so-called "Communist problem."

---

[1] Broadcast of August 11, 1943, published in full in the September 1943 issue of *Amerasia*, pp. 281–84.

Among other things, Chiang Kai-shek charges the Chinese Communists with responsibility for the split in the Kuomintang in 1927, for fomenting civil war and obstructing China's economic development in the 1927–1937 period, and for precipitating the Japanese invasion of China. As to the current status of Kuomintang-Communist relations, Chiang provides the following justification for the forcible liquidation of the Communists and their supporters: "During this period of military rule and political tutelage the gathering together of military force under any name whatsoever or in support of any policy to divide our territory may be described, if not as the militarism of the warlords, at the very least as feudalism. . . . If this partition of the territory by force and this militarist anti-revolutionary condition continues, then the politics of the nation cannot follow a straight course and the period of military rule cannot be brought to its conclusion. . . . Why are our internal parties not willing to abandon their armed division of territory and give up their attitude of feudalistic militarism? Can they be reckoned as Chinese? Can they be reckoned as a political party? In what country of the world is there a political party which follows a policy of armed force and division of territory, impedes the national unification of its country and prevents the governmental system from entering its proper course? . . . I have always advocated that the National Government should adopt a lenient attitude toward all shades and divergencies of opinion in the country and seek to bring about an understanding by fair means. But if there is no willingness thoroughly to alter the feudalistic militarism and no determination radically to abandon division by armed force, then no leniency can have any effect and no *reasonable solution* can be found." (Author's italics.)

THE CHINESE REVOLUTION, 1925–1945

CHIANG KAI-SHEK's accusations against the Chinese Communists constitute only one of many attempts on the part of leading Chinese officials to use the so-called "Communist problem" in China to obscure and distract attention from the basic issue of political democracy and to disparage all popular demands for democratic reform. In addition, however, they present a highly distorted and misleading interpretation of Chinese political history during the past two decades.

Kuomintang-Communist history covers a period of more than

twenty years. Twice during this period the two parties coöperated, and in coöperation achieved some of the greatest triumphs
in China's modern history — namely, in the Nationalist Revolution of 1925–27 and in the first year of resistance to the Japanese
in 1937–38. Between these two periods of coöperation, however,
stretched a decade of bloody civil strife during which the Kuomintang's obsession with anti-Communist campaigns greatly facilitated Japan's encroachments in Manchuria and North China
and blocked the widespread popular demand for united national
resistance against foreign aggression.

In 1924, the Kuomintang was reorganized and the first period
of coöperation between the Kuomintang and the Chinese Communists was initiated under the leadership of Dr. Sun Yat-sen.
This reorganization was accompanied by the formulation of a
new revolutionary program against both foreign imperialism and
the old feudal system in China, a reorganization in which Chinese Communist leaders took an active part. Together the two
parties formed a revolutionary army and under the military leadership of Chiang Kai-shek carried through the famous Northern
Expedition that overthrew the warlords and freed China from
some of the shackles of foreign imperialist control. Throughout
this period, the Chinese Communist Party played an active part
not only on the fighting fronts but also in organizing the peasants
and workers to support the nationalist forces.

Up to 1927, the Chinese revolutionary movement embraced all
nationalist groups in China — industrialists, bankers, landlords,
workers, and peasants. With the success of the Northern Expedition and the capture of Shanghai, however, the right-wing
groups under the leadership of Chiang Kai-shek turned against
the peasants and workers and their Communist and trade union
leaders in a ruthless blood purge. This purge, which began on
April 12, 1927, in Shanghai,[1] cost the lives of tens of thousands of

---

[1] Even in 1926, when Chiang Kai-shek was leading the nationalist armies
in the Northern Expedition, he had already made an agreement with the
Ching Pang secret society in Shanghai, headed by Tu Yueh-sheng. In the
spring of 1927, when Chiang's forces occupied Shanghai, the Ching Pang
gangs rose according to plan and, acting in coöperation with Tai Li's
Blueshirts, served as a fifth column which enabled Chiang to seize the
Chinese city, destroy the Chinese Communists, and break up their mass
labor organizations. Tu Yueh-sheng took the lead in organizing these activities, having borrowed the necessary weapons from the Chief of Police
of the French Concession, and thus became firmly established as a personal

Communists, revolutionary workers and peasants, as well as many members of the Kuomintang who wished to carry through the revolution to its logical conclusion not only against foreign imperialism but also against the feudal elements in the Chinese economic and social structure.

In *China's Destiny*, Chiang Kai-shek explains this disastrous split in the Chinese nationalist movement by claiming that "the Communists broke faith with the Kuomintang and fomented class war." It is not surprising that this accusation has provoked bitter indignation among the Communists and others who clearly remember the unprovoked slaughter of unarmed workers and peasants in the streets of Shanghai and elsewhere at the hands of gunmen. Actually, the split occurred because the reactionary elements in the Kuomintang — supported financially by the Shanghai bankers, many of whom had comprador relations with foreign interests — did not want the revolution carried to a point that would undermine their own political and economic power. In addition, the conservatives in the Kuomintang overestimated their own strength vis-à-vis foreign imperialist interests and believed that they no longer needed the support of the workers and peasants. The Chinese Communists and the left-wing sections of the Kuomintang, on the other hand, had trusted too blindly in the pledges of unity made by the right-wing leaders and had thus failed to realize the importance of preparing the workers and peasants for the subsequent betrayal. As a consequence, the attack from the right wing caught them unprepared and disorganized. There is no question in the minds of disinterested students of the period, however, that the action of the right-wing groups constituted *the* betrayal of the Chinese Revolution, and that, by alienating the support of the workers and peasants and precipitating civil conflict, it weakened China and made her an easy prey to the machinations of the foreign powers. It was not an accident that Japanese aggression took on its most militaristic aspects soon after the break in the Chinese united front.

For ten years after the break in 1927, the Kuomintang suppressed all demands for an extension of political democracy and for united national resistance to Japan, and instead concentrated on a series of military campaigns against the Communists and

---

and political supporter of Chiang Kai-shek. Tu and other prominent Shanghai bankers subsequently helped to finance Chiang's efforts to establish a right-wing nationalist government.

their supporters, first in Central and South China and then in the Northwest where the Communist forces were driven in 1934–36. It is true that during this period the Kuomintang also contributed to the political progress of China through the centralization of government, the elimination of provincial war-lordism, the formation of a national army, currency reforms, and the extension of the transportation system. But the work of the Kuomintang was only one of many factors responsible for the awakening of China, and in many respects its policies weakened rather than strengthened China for the inevitable struggle with Japan.

Though one would never learn it from the pages of *China's Destiny*, the Chinese Communist Party also made important contributions to China's political progress by acting as a leavening force on the people as a whole and particularly on the Chinese peasantry. Having established a Chinese Soviet Republic with headquarters in Kiangsi, the Communists introduced a democratic election system based on extensive adult suffrage and the secret ballot, and carried out a land policy that equalized possession of land among the peasants.[1] Every effort was made to secure intelligent participation by the people in the processes of government. Public meetings were held before each election at which government and party representatives made reports, followed by criticism and general discussion. The people were also given the right to recall their representatives. In addition, the Chinese Soviet regime instituted many other economic and social reforms of a constructive character. Most important of all, it created a strong democratic citizens' army trained to enlist the coöperation of the people by educating them in the meaning of China's struggle for freedom. The Chinese Soviets thus established the pattern for guerrilla warfare based on the organized support and coöperation of the civilian population that was later to prove so successful in the operations of the Chinese guerrillas against the Japanese.

Following the Chinese Soviet Government's retreat to the Northwest in 1934–36 and the entry of Kuomintang troops into the erstwhile Communist areas, the *New York Times* correspondents, Hallet Abend and Anthony Billingham, made the following comments on its policy: "The Communist regime pro-

---

[1] The land policy of these earlier days has since been radically modified. The new land policy of the present Border Regions will be described in a later section.

vided more in the way of social services than does the present provincial government. Taxation was less under the Reds than it is now, and was levied more equitably. . . . Present officials ruefully admit that a considerable part of the people are more friendly to the Reds than to the Government, that the farmers regularly supply information to the Communists and give them food and shelter, but refuse coöperation with the government forces. . . . The Communists not only established schools in every town and village in Fukien but made education compulsory for adults as well as children. In regions recovered from the Reds it was found that almost the entire population had been made literate."[1]

This period of civil war in China also witnessed the Japanese conquest of Manchuria and steady Japanese inroads into North China, while the Chinese Government continued to play for time and appeased the Japanese in a series of agreements, notably the Shanghai Truce, the Tangku Truce, and the Ho-Umezu Agreement. The Government justified its policy on the grounds that national unification must come first before resistance to Japan could be undertaken. Many different groups in China, however, opposed this view and insisted that unification by coercion would never succeed and that the only possible way to unify the country was by resisting Japan and thus welding the Chinese people together in a common struggle for national liberation. These groups also argued that by continuing internal warfare the Government was wasting manpower and resources and bankrupting the country, thereby failing to create a strong economic base for resistance against Japan. The great nation-wide student movement of 1935 was one of the chief manifestations of this increasingly powerful demand for a program of united national resistance to Japan.

In August 1935 the Chinese Communists proposed to the Central Government that a united front be formed of all anti-Japanese elements to resist further Japanese penetration. This proposal went unheeded for more than a year. But important sections of the Kuomintang became so convinced that continued appeasement of Japan would be disastrous and that no ordinary appeals would be heeded by Chiang Kai-shek that they engineered his kidnaping in Sian in the fateful month of December

---

[1] H. Abend and A. Billingham: *Can China Survive?* (New York, 1936), pp. 239–40.

1936. The Chinese Communists, believing that Chiang was *the* man to lead a united China against Japan, buried their bitter memories of ten years of bloody suppression, and quickly came to his aid. They were the chief factor in securing Chiang's release from his captors.

During the early months of 1937, negotiations were carried on between the Kuomintang and the Communist Party that culminated in the manifesto issued by the Communists on September 22, 1937, and acknowledged by Chiang Kai-shek in a formal statement on September 23. The Chinese Communist Manifesto embodied the following seven points:

1. In order to safeguard the independence and freedom of the Chinese nation, a national war of liberation shall be proclaimed.

2. A democratic form of government shall be set up; a National Convention shall be convoked to draft and promulgate a constitution and to formulate fundamental policies for the salvation of the nation.

3. In order to promote general welfare and to make possible a life of happiness for the people, relief shall be afforded to those suffering from famine or flood, social life shall be stabilized, industries connected with national defense shall be expanded, and grievances of the people shall be redressed.

4. The Communist Party is prepared to fight for the realization of Dr. Sun Yat-sen's revolutionary principles because they answer the present-day needs of China.

5. The policy of insurrection which aims at the overthrow of the Kuomintang political power, the policy of land confiscation, and the policy of Communist propaganda shall all be disowned and discontinued.

6. With the disappearance of the Chinese Soviet Government, a system of political democracy shall be put into practice, so that the country may be politically united.

7. The former Red Army which has been reorganized into the Eighth Route Army shall be under the control of the National Military Council, and ever ready to be sent to the front.[1]

In his statement acknowledging this declaration, Chiang Kai-shek declared that "the points contained in it such as the discontinuance of the policies of insurrection and Communist propaganda, the disappearance of the Soviet Government, and the reorganization of the former Red Army, all tend to strengthen the National Government in its resistance to foreign invasion. . . . The reference made by the Communist Party to its readiness to

---

[1] See *The Chinese Year Book 1938–39*, pp. 339–40.

fight for the realization of Dr. Sun Yat-sen's revolutionary principles shows further that the efforts of the entire nation are directed to one single aim." Chiang concluded by expressing the
hope that the Communists "will sincerely carry out what is contained in the declaration and . . . work in unison with the rest
of the nation to accomplish the task of national salvation." Since
these two statements formed the basis of the so-called United
Front agreement, it is important to note that Chiang Kai-shek's
statement made no reference whatsoever to the first three points
in the Communist manifesto calling for the immediate establishment of democratic government and economic reforms.

Because the Kuomintang-Communist agreement of September
1937 was never embodied in a single document officially accepted by both sides, interpretations of the rights and obligations of both parties to the agreement inevitably differed and a
wide area of controversy developed. The Communists claimed
that, in return for their willingness to give up their soviet government and become a special administrative district under central
government authority, to incorporate their troops in the National
Army, to abandon the policy of land-confiscation, propaganda
against the Kuomintang, and so on, the Central Government had
agreed to the introduction of the democratic political system in
China. The Kuomintang leaders, on the other hand, refused to
admit that the "united front" agreement involved anything more
than a recognition by the Communists of the Central Government's authority. Furthermore, the Kuomintang claimed that the
Chinese Communists had not lived up to their part of the agreement. Thus in September 1943, in his statement on the Communist issue before the Kuomintang Central Executive Committee,
Chiang Kai-shek accused the Communists of "failing to live up
to the pledges made in their declaration of September 1937 supporting a National United Front," and stated that "if the Chinese
Communist Party can prove its good faith by making good its
promises, the Central Government will once more treat it with
sympathy and consideration."

The Chinese Communists, on the other hand, pointed out that
even before the September declaration, the Chinese Soviet Republic had been reorganized as the government of the Border
Region of Shensi-Kansu-Ninghsia and the National Government's authority in that area had been formally recognized; that
the Red Army had been reorganized as a unit of the national

army acknowledging the supreme authority of the Military Affairs Commission; and that Chiang Kai-shek had appointed Generals Chu Teh and Peng Teh-huai as commander and vice-commander respectively. Furthermore, they contended that the "united front" agreement specified that the new Border Region Government should have full legal status as a special administrative district — a contention supported by the fact that the Executive Yuan of the Central Government in 1938 approved a measure establishing the legal status of the Border Region, although this measure was never officially promulgated.

The failure to reach a specific agreement as to the terms of united front coöperation also gave rise to continued disputes over the operations of the Communist-led armies and guerrilla troops. The military task assigned these units in 1937 was that of reoccupying and organizing territories behind and between the Japanese lines. But the successes achieved by the Eighth Route Army in the North and by the New Fourth Army in the Yangtze Valley in regaining territory from the Japanese, together with the rapid increase in the number of guerrilla and partisan fighters who flocked to their support, alarmed the leaders of the Kuomintang. They regarded these successes not as victories over the Japanese, but as the entrenchment of a rival political power over an increasingly large area, and they were particularly disturbed by the political and economic reforms introduced in these guerrilla areas.

As a result, the united front had become a dead letter by the end of 1939. A strict military blockade was imposed against the guerrilla areas and Border Regions in the North, and in the winter of 1940–41 the New Fourth Army suffered an attack by Central Government troops in which most of its leaders were either killed or captured. Following this "incident" the Government ordered the complete dissolution of the New Fourth Army; but the Communists refused, and the New Fourth continued to operate as an effective fighting force against the Japanese in the coastal regions north of the Yangtze River. During 1942 and 1943 further clashes took place along the borders of the Communist-controlled areas, and in the summer of 1943 the Kuomintang forces manning the blockade were strengthened and the forcible dissolution of the Border Region governments and the liquidation of the Communist-led armies was openly advocated in Chungking.

Actual civil war was averted partly because of fear of American public opinion and official American disapproval, but chiefly because of the strength of the Communist-led forces and the reluctance of some of the blockading officers and troops to attack. In July 1943, the order for an attack was actually issued to Hu Tsung-nan, the general in command of the blockading troops. General Fu Tso-yi, next in command, hurried to Chungking to warn against the wisdom of such a move, arguing that his troops were not sufficiently strong militarily to make the attack successful, and also that he was not certain of the loyalty of his troops in such a campaign. He was supported in this stand by two other generals, whereupon the Generalissimo called for Hu Tsung-nan to report for a consultation. Asked whether the Communist forces could be defeated in one month, General Hu replied with a categoric "no." When the one month was raised to two, the reply was "perhaps." The order to attack was thereupon rescinded. Obviously, two months is not a long time, but in those critical days it was long enough for world public opinion to become aroused. Victory had to be attained quickly if the plan was to be successful. Some Chinese, accustomed to the language of their militarists, offer another interpretation. They believe that when General Hu Tsung-nan replied "perhaps" to the "two month" question, he really meant that success could not be achieved at all.

This situation, which was obviously detrimental to the Allied war effort, was justified by the Chungking Government on the ground that the retention of special local authority and armed forces by the Chinese Communists was incompatible with national unity and could not be tolerated. The Kuomintang leaders also accused the Communists of having "recruited new forces and occupied new territories without the approval of the supreme command." They charged that the Communists had made the war an excuse to expand their party's power, and that they were aiming at the overthrow of the Kuomintang and the establishment of a Communist state in China.

To these charges, the Communists replied that they had agreed to the dissolution of their independent forces and administrative areas in 1937 only in return for the Kuomintang's promise to put into effect political democracy throughout the nation — granting free speech, free press, free assembly, and legal status to all minority parties. They announced that they were perfectly willing to give up their armed forces and special districts to government control, provided that the government was one representing all sections of the people and all parties. In the absence of any such guarantee, however, they were inclined to believe that the real aim of the Kuomintang was to eliminate them entirely as a political force, and they were confirmed in this view not only by the continued military blockade and attacks on Communist forces by Government troops, but also by the treatment meted out to the minority parties in Kuomintang China.

As to the Kuomintang charge that the Communist armies had been enlarged and new territories conquered without the Government's approval, it may be noted that, though this had unquestionably occurred, the expansion of the Communist area of operations had never taken place in Free China. It had been achieved entirely in the Japanese-occupied areas; and the guerrilla forces, together with partisan troops and militia recruited from the people of those areas, had succeeded in immobilizing some 300,000 Japanese troops. It is obvious that if the Eighth Route and New Fourth Armies had abided by their original allotment of 45,000 and 13,000 troops respectively, they could never have accomplished this task. Had these armies refrained from expanding their forces and areas of operation in "occupied" China, some 300,000 Japanese troops would have been freed for an attack on the Central Government forces. In that event, a Chungking or even a National Government in China might not have survived for long.

Furthermore, there was overwhelming evidence to indicate that the Communists had gone a long way toward fulfilling their pledge with regard to the realization of Sun Yat-sen's three principles of nationalism, democracy, and the people's livelihood, while the Kuomintang had not made a single step in that direction. In the guerrilla areas, democratic methods of government had been introduced, the system of land ownership and taxation revised for the benefit of the people, and private industry and trade encouraged; whereas in Kuomintang China civil liberties had been increasingly curtailed, one-party government was still the rule, the power of the landlords to exploit the peasantry had increased rather than diminished, and control of industrial resources and production was monopolized by the ruling bureaucracy.

This sharp contrast between the actual political and economic conditions prevailing in the two areas had led many American students of Chinese affairs to feel that instead of the terms "Kuomintang" and "Communist" China, the basic distinction between the two regions would be more accurately described by the phrases "autocratic or feudal China" on the one hand and "democratic or progressive China" on the other. This contention raises two important questions that will be discussed in the following chapter: What are the political and economic aims of the Chinese Communists? Is Communism really the central political issue in China, as leading Kuomintang spokesmen would have us believe?

CHAPTER VI

IS COMMUNISM THE ISSUE IN CHINA?

❇

As KNOWLEDGE of the political and economic program instituted in the guerrilla areas gradually filtered through to the United States, many Americans came to the conclusion that the Chinese Communists were really not Communists at all, but rather agrarian revolutionists whose aim was merely to achieve a radical change in the feudal structure of Chinese agriculture. Raymond Gram Swing, for example, in the broadcast quoted in Chapter V, stated that "these are not Marxian Proletarians, these so-called Communists, they are agrarian radicals, trying to establish democratic practices and particularly to break up the great estates, so that the farm worker can have individual status and own property. . . . They should not be called Communists, whatever their origin may be. . . . At the same time that the Kuomintang has gone to the right, the Communists have become versed in the democratic art of compromise."

Mr. Swing went on to say that the Communists had rejected the Kuomintang demand that they disband their administration and their army because "if they lose their identity they lose their cause, and abandon hope of introducing their social and economic reforms in all China. And they do not believe that as a minority party they would be allowed to exist. . . . If the Communists were to come into Central China and serve as a minority and opposition party they would have to have a guarantee that they were to be allowed to function. But the only convincing guarantee that Chiang could give them would be to show an interest in their reforms. . . . But that is out of the question, because Chiang Kai-shek derives most of his power from the very landlord class which the Communists are seeking to dethrone." Spokesmen for the Kuomintang however, have insisted that the democratic policies introduced by the Communists are simply a blind to attract a popular following and that their real aims are to overthrow the Kuomintang and establish Communism throughout China. It is therefore important that the American people should be able to judge the validity of both the above contentions regarding the nature of the Chinese Communist program.

Perhaps the best way to explain the position of the Chinese Communists is to say that they accept the Marxist interpretation of a country's political and economic development. According to this interpretation, a semicolonial and industrially backward country cannot possibly achieve communism or socialism without an intervening stage of development, and furthermore, it is not in the power of any group of people to disregard this historical truth. In China's case this means that the Chinese people must strive first to win freedom from foreign domination and establish their national independence, and second, that they must lay the foundations for modern economic development by an agrarian revolution that will free the peasants from their present semi-feudal relations to the landed gentry class. Chinese Communist leaders contend that the attainment of these two objectives requires a democratic political system that will allow all sections of the people a voice in the government and will also grant full opportunity to private initiative and free enterprise in the development of China's economic resources. They believe, however, that there should be more government supervision and control than there was in early capitalist development in the West in order to avoid the worst abuses of industrialization and the unrestricted exploitation of natural resources.

In his "New Democracy," [1] for example, Mao Tse-tung, leader of the Chinese Communist Party, states that the economic policy of a democratic China should be based on the principle enunciated in the declaration of the First Kuomintang Congress, in 1924 which states: "enterprises, foreign and Chinese, that possess a monopoly character or that due to their large scale are beyond the individual's power to establish, such as banks, railways, aviation companies, etc., shall be run and managed by the state, so that private capital cannot manipulate the life of the people." Mao elaborates this by stating that a democratic Chi-

---

[1] Appeared originally as an article under the title "The Politics and Culture of New Democracy" in the January 15, 1941 issue of the magazine *Chinese Culture* published in Yenan. Subsequently reprinted as a pamphlet entitled *New Democracy*. Published in the United States under the title *China's New Democracy* (New York, 1944).

nese Government "will not confiscate other capitalist private property, nor will it restrict the development of that capitalist production that does not control the life of the people. . . . It will adopt certain measures to confiscate the land of big landlords and distribute it to the peasants that are without land or have too little of it, to realize Dr. Sun's slogan 'land to those who till it.' . . . This is different from establishing a socialist agricultural system for it only turns the land into the private property of the peasants. . . . The economy of China should never be monopolized by a 'minority of the people.' We can never let the few capitalists and landlords control the life of the people."

When China attains the status of a modern industrial nation with a genuinely democratic form of government, the Communists believe that there will naturally exist all types of political parties from conservative to radical. During this stage of China's development, the Chinese Communist Party will play the same role that Communist parties have played in Western countries such as England, France, and the United States. In the meanwhile, however, and for a long time to come, they contend that Communism or Socialism is not the issue for China. One prominent Chinese Communist has said that he does not foresee Communism in China for at least a century. The major problem is to attain national unity and national freedom, and to establish a progressive democratic government that will enable all sections of the Chinese people to participate freely in the construction of a strong and prosperous society. In an interview with an American correspondent in July 1944, for example, Mao Tse-tung declared that China needs three things: (1) to drive out the Japanese; (2) to realize democracy on a national scale by giving the people fundamental liberties and a government elected by the people; and (3) to solve the agrarian problem so that capitalism of a progressive character can develop in China. It is on the basis of this analysis of China's needs that the Communists challenge the Kuomintang's theory of one-party rule.

In this connection, it may be noted that the Chinese Communists have encouraged private enterprise in the areas under their control, and have urged that Chinese industrialists be allowed greater freedom in Kuomintang China in order to stimulate production. In the Border Regions, rent reduction has been substituted for the former policy of confiscation of land, not only to retain the support of the landlords in the war but also to make investment in industry more attractive than in land. In the Communists' view, the "restriction of private capital" as advocated and practiced by the Kuomintang bureaucracy has stifled industrial development at a time when it is most urgently needed. Furthermore, they believe that the restrictions imposed on the industrialists have weakened their ability to challenge the power of the landlord-bureaucrat regime, and have thus served to strengthen the most backward and oppressive elements in the Chinese economy. That this encouragement of private industry is not merely a wartime measure was emphasized by Mao Tse-tung in the interview quoted above, during which he declared that "it is a matter of mutual benefit to adopt proper treatment of capital after the war. This applies not only to Chinese capital but also to foreign capital. Private capital must have opportunity for broad, liberal development."

On the political front as well, the Chinese Communists contend that bureaucratic centralization tends to retard China's development into a modern democratic nation because it obstructs rather than encourages the participation of the Chinese people in their government. They maintain that all sections of the people, with the exception of the feudal elements, have a stake in achieving national independence and a more progressive social system. Industrialists, bankers, workers, peasants, and professionals alike suffer in varying degrees from the existence of a feudal agrarian system that prevents the use of modern methods of production and the expansion of the internal market, and therefore they should coöperate in changing that system. The defeat of Japan will result in China's winning independence from foreign control, but it will not automatically enable China to build up a prosperous and expanding economy. This task can be accomplished only if China is united under a genuinely democratic political and economic structure.

Official spokesmen for the Kuomintang have sought to obscure and discredit all demands for at least the beginnings of democratic government by branding them as "Communist-inspired," but this charge can hardly be leveled against the statements of Dr. Sun Fo, son of Dr. Sun Yat-sen and president of the Legislative Yuan. In the spring of 1944, Sun Fo made a speech before the Central Training Institute of the Kuomintang in which he made it clear that the extension of democracy and not "the Communist problem" constitutes the central issue in Chinese domestic politics. Declaring that if Sun Yat-sen's principle of democracy is ever to be realized in China "there must be a fundamental readjustment of methods within the Kuomintang itself," Sun Fo pointed out: "We must recognize that in the past we ourselves unwittingly assumed the attitude and habits of a ruling caste. . . . The number of our party members is less than one per cent of the total population of the country. The Kuomintang is an infinitesimal portion of the population. But we have come to regard ourselves as if we were the sovereign power in the state, entitled to the enjoyment of a special position and to suppress all criticism against us. The whole civilized world is fighting dictatorship and tyranny which breed fascism and aggression. . . . For these reasons we should revise our own psychological approach to internal problems and correct our own attitude of intolerance. To build a genuinely democratic state, policies must be freely discussed in our debates, and all views, ideas, and criticisms must be allowed to be expressed as fully as possible." Summing up his criticism of the Kuomintang for failing in its appointed task of preparing the people for democratic government, Sun Fo declared that "we have already spent sixteen years in political tutelage, yet there is not one member of a *hsien* [county] council nor one *hsien* administrator who has been elected to his office by the people of the *hsien.*"

Several months later, Sun Fo made an even more critical attack on Kuomintang policy. Declaring that "Chinese politics cannot be divorced from the main current of international thinking, which is toward democracy and liberalism," he added that China's friends abroad generally are not conservatives, and that "it may be said that the leftists, not the rightists, have given us sympathy from the beginning." In the early years of the Kuomintang, its activities and followers were "naturally of the Left," but after the Northern Expedition of 1926, "there was internal dissension in the party, culminating in the movement to expel the Communists. . . . To oppose the Communists we opposed the Left and identified ourselves with the Right. This has been the great error committed by our party. From our initial mistake we have developed reactionary tendencies for the last decade. . . . The most important task for the party is to bring about real democracy within China. We must get off the wrong track and turn back to the left. The party's ideal has always been to achieve true democracy and to oppose militarism, autocracy, and despotism. We must return to our original way and proclaim ourselves with pride as true revolutionaries."

Discussing the relation of postwar industrialization in China to political democracy, Dr. Sun Fo declared: "Without political democracy in our country, it will be difficult to bring about an ideal industrial economy. To obtain foreign funds we must first win the confidence of foreign countries . . . we should clearly show our democratic ways so that we shall enjoy the confidence and support of our friends and dispel their doubts and suspicions. . . . If China does not hasten to complete her democratization, her industrialization will not be achieved. Without industrialization there will be no national reconstruction. Without national reconstruction the revolution will have failed. Failure of the revolution will mean that the party has not fulfilled its mission in history."

The fact that Sun Fo could be so outspokenly critical of Kuomintang policy, and that foreign correspondents were permitted to cable extensive excerpts from his speeches, might seem to indicate that the suppression of free speech and the rigidity of Chinese censorship were not so severe as its critics had maintained. There were, however, a number of reasons to account for the exceptional treatment accorded the statements of Sun Fo. First, the publicity given them may well have been designed to allay foreign criticism and convince foreign observers that freedom of speech still flourished in China. This conclusion is supported by the fact that the scripts of his speeches released to the foreign correspondents differed considerably from the original Chinese texts; in one case there was absolutely no similarity between the two. Second, Sun Fo may have been used as a "safety valve" by the ruling clique, to enable the liberal elements in the Kuomintang to give expression to their pent-up discontent with the policies of the regime. Three, Sun Fo, though he commands widespread popular respect, has never had a personal clique or following among the government bureaucracy and was presumably in no position to make an effective bid for control of the party machinery. Four, as the son of Sun Yat-sen, he occupies a unique position of prestige which would make it extremely difficult for even the highest authorities to muzzle him.

Thus the fact that Sun Fo's statements were allowed circulation abroad could not be taken as definite evidence of a change of heart on the part of the ruling clique. But the statements themselves were of great importance nevertheless. They showed that Sun Fo and other liberal leaders in the Kuomintang were keenly aware of the reactionary trend in Kuomintang policy, and also that they were increasingly sensitive to criticism of the Kuomintang, both within China and abroad. Furthermore, Sun Fo's statements emphasized the fact that this criticism was not pro-Communist, but that it arose from a desire to see China maintain and strengthen her national unity, as well as from the knowledge that the suppression of political and civil liberties by the Kuomintang was not directed only against the Communists but against all non-Kuomintang parties and groups. An outstanding example of this fact is provided by the history of the Federation of Chinese Democratic Parties.

THE "LITTLE PARTIES" CHALLENGE
ONE PARTY RULE

IN THE SPRING of 1941 a number of the "little parties" in Kuomintang China united to form the Federation of Chinese Democratic Parties with a program calling for the immediate extension of political democracy as essential to China's continued unity and resistance. Included in this Federation were the National Socialist Party, the Young China Party, the Third Party, the Rural Reconstructionists, and the Vocational Education Group. Though small in numbers, these parties had considerable prestige and numbered some prominent Chinese leaders among their members. The following brief description of the history and program of these various parties shows the broadly inclusive character of the Federation and indicates that extremely conservative as well as liberal groups in China had been antagonized by the dictatorial and reactionary character of the Kuomintang regime.[1]

The National Socialists are a party of intellectuals, consisting mainly of university professors of conservative outlook. Their program is grouped under the headings of Nationalism, Reformed Democracy, and Socialism, but its content is conservative. Its concept of government contains much less of popular

---

[1] A detailed account of the history, composition, and aims of the Federation and its constituent groups was published in *Amerasia*, April 25, 1943, pp. 97–117, based on information taken from *Parties and Groups in the War of Resistance* by Chang Che-i, Hankow, 1939 (in Chinese), with additional information supplied by individual members of these parties.

democracy than is contained in the basic principles of the Kuomintang, though it is well in advance of actual practices in the Kuomintang China of today. The "socialism" in its program is most nearly comparable to that of the conservative Radical Socialists of prewar France, which it resembles in its assurances regarding the retention of private property, especially small-scale private property. The war brought the Party out of its academic isolation and forced it to take a stand on the key issues of national unity and resistance. And, although some of its most reactionary members went over to the Japanese, the remainder have grown steadily stronger in their demand for united resistance and political democracy. The principal leaders of the party are Chang Chun-mai (Carson Chang) and the noted Catholic publicist Lo Lung-chi, who was active in the anti-Japanese student movement of 1935.

The Young China Party grew out of the "Young China Study Association," a group of Chinese students formed after the First World War as part of the widespread movement to study Western thought and science for application to China's problems. Among them were Tseng Chi, Li Huang, and Tso Shung-cheng, present leaders of the Young China Party. From the outset the Young China Party strongly opposed the Communists, and even considered the contemporary Kuomintang a far too radical group. It made no effort to mobilize a mass following, but concentrated on recruiting support from intellectuals, officials, and military officers. After the success of the Northern Expedition, the Young China Party went partly underground, but retained some influence in Szechwan, particularly in the provincial army. In 1938 the Young China Party, like the National Socialists, pledged its support to the anti-Japanese war and the Three People's Principles, and in return was recognized by the Kuomintang as a group whose assistance in the war would be welcomed. The Party is still a right-wing group, but the circumstances of the war, the need for national unity, and its recognition that this requires the democratization of China's wartime government have made it an active member of the Federation.

The "Third Party" was the only organized section of the Kuomintang which, even after the 1927 split, continued to uphold the "Three Great Policies" which, together with the Three People's Principles, were willed to the Kuomintang by Dr. Sun Yat-sen: alliance with the U.S.S.R. in foreign policy, a united front with the Communist Party in internal politics, and assistance to the workers and peasants. This group never regarded itself as having seceded from the Kuomintang, but the exigencies of underground work caused it to change its name frequently and it was known at various times as the Chinese Revolutionary Party, the New Party, the Workers and Peasants Party, etc. The name "Third Party" was given it by the right-wing Kuomintang veteran, Wu Chih-hui. The Party fought for united anti-Japanese resistance long before the outbreak of the war, and has consistently urged the formation of a united front of all parties and the immediate convocation of a National Assembly "to lay down the political basis for the anti-Japanese war." Its economic program advocates fundamental agrarian reforms to promote the mobilization of the peasantry. During the first two years of the war, members of the Third Party were given considerable opportunity for political activity. One of its leaders, Huang Chi-hsiang, became Vice-Director of the Political Department of the National Military Council, and two others were members of the first People's Political Council. But, as a result of the Party's protest against the attack on the New Fourth Army in January 1941 — which was stronger than the protest of any other of the constituent parties of the Federation — it was deprived of its seats in the People's Political Council.

The Rural Reconstructionists represent that group in China which takes the educational, administrative, and productive reconstruction of the village as the starting point for national reform. Of the two main schools of thought in the Chinese rural reconstruction movement, one emphasizes education and the other is concerned with promoting the political activity of the people. The best-known exponent of the first group is Dr. James Yen, while the second group is headed by Liang Shu-ming, promoter of experiments in village self-government in Honan and Shantung. Liang is the principal representative of the Rural Reconstructionists in the Federation. They are not strictly speaking a political party but they have been a progressive force in China for many years and their pupils have been taught to recognize both the possibility of and the need for democratic unity in China. Moreover, their experience with village self-government had given them confidence in the ability of the people and a knowledge of the procedures by which local anti-Japanese mobilization was achieved during the war.

The Vocational Education Group consists of the personnel of a large network of vocational schools established during the past twenty years in the province of Kiangsu under the leadership of Huang Yen-pei. The schools were originally financed by Kiangsu bankers and industrialists, and as a result this group adopted a reactionary position during the 1923–1927 revolution, backing the war lord Sun Chuan-fang against the nationalist armies. The victorious Kuomintang, however, did not suppress their activities and the number of schools went on increasing. Most of them were captured by the Japanese, but work has continued in new units established in Free China. Huang Yen-pei himself is said to be held in high esteem by the Generalissimo and other Government officials, and perhaps because of the dependence of his schools on official support he has been the most cautious of the leaders of the Federation.

Thus the Federation of Democratic Parties included one radical, two liberal, and two definitely conservative groups. The significance of its formation lay in the fact that it represented the first organized protest within Kuomintang China against the complete monopoly of political power by the Kuomintang, and also demonstrated that the Chinese Communists were not alone in their criticism of repressive Kuomintang policies. The leaders of these various "little parties" were disturbed by the progressive curtailment of civil liberties in Kuomintang China, the rapid widening of the rift between the Kuomintang and the Chinese Communist Party, the obvious determination of the Kuomintang to weaken or eliminate the influence of all other parties, and the trend in Chinese politics toward civil war.

The leaders of the small parties were keenly aware that the preservation of national unity was essential for continued resistance; that civil war must inevitably mean surrender to the Japanese. And they were also convinced that political unity could not be achieved by force, but required that all parties and groups be given a responsible share in the conduct of the Government. Since these small parties were individually too weak to exert any influence, they determined to unite in support of a joint program and plan of action that would give them greater weight in the fight for political unity and democratic government.

The Federation of Chinese Democratic Parties was formally established on March 25, 1941. In view of the oppressive political atmosphere prevailing in Chungking at that time, it was decided that the Federation's propaganda center should be located outside Kuomintang China in Hong Kong, and that it should begin its work secretly. A ten-point program was adopted, calling for the immediate extension of political democracy and an end to one-party control over the State. This program denounced the lack of democracy as the chief menace to Chinese unity, and attacked the Kuomintang's use of the national army, civil administration, and exchequer for purely party purposes. It condemned the activities of the secret police as being directed not against spies and traitors but against non-Kuomintang patriots, criticized the bureaucratic corruption and profiteering that stifled China's war economy, and called for immediate improvement in the food, living conditions, and pay of soldiers at the front.

With regard to the abolition of one-party rule, the program advocated that the Government's influence should not be used to promote the power of any one party in schools and cultural organizations; that official personnel should be selected on the basis of the "best and ablest," and that the use of national political power for the purposes of party recruiting should be prohibited; that the practice of paying party expenses out of National and Local Government revenues should be abolished; and that the "New District System" of local government, by which members of district advisory councils and the headmen of villages are selected by Kuomintang-controlled examinations instead of by popular election, should be altered.

This ten-point program was published in the Federation's daily paper *Kwang Ming Pao* in Hong Kong on October 10, 1941, together with a lengthy preamble. This preamble explained that the Ten Points were published as an initial step towards the coalition of all democratically minded groups and people in an effort to solve the crucial problem of national unity. If China was to be powerful, said the declaration, she must first have unity. Looking back over the history of the Republic, the preamble continued, it became evident that China had been truly unified only at moments of maximum effort for internal progress, such as the anti-Manchu revolution of 1911 and the great national revolution of 1925–27. On each of these occasions, the victorious national armies had been the instrument not of one party but of the true national interest. China's past history proved that when national policy served the interests of the people, no internal force was needed to unite the nation. Coöperation among parties became automatic. But, unfortunately, this unity was gradually lost. The Government put less and less faith in the people and more and more in military power alone. It was not the purpose of the Federation to fix the blame for this situation. But it was their conviction that everyone must work to rectify it, and it was their hope that the Kuomintang would take the lead. Two concepts were basic to the reform of national policy: political power must be made truly democratic, and the army must be made truly national.

The publication of this program elicited a widespread favorable response from overseas Chinese, non-Kuomintang leaders, and also from the more liberal elements within the Kuomintang itself. The policy adopted by the ruling element in the Kuomintang, however, was to avoid calling the people's attention to the Federation and its program. Within China, all news of its proposals was strictly censored, and the Chinese Government made every effort to get a number of leaders of the Federation ejected from Hong Kong. Having ascertained that the Federation's activities originated in Chungking and that its executive committee included two of the five members of the Presidium of the People's Political Council, the Hong Kong Government replied that no basis could be found for the suppression of its activities in Hong Kong or for the deportation of its leaders.

At the November 1941 session of the People's Political Council, Federation members planned to advance a new proposal for internal political reforms in accordance with the Ten-Point program, but were informed that the Generalissimo did not wish the proposal to come up for discussion. Thus by the outbreak of the Pacific war and the fall of Hong Kong, the Federation had not achieved any of the internal political reforms it advocated nor had it attained any sort of legal status. Yet its program continued to gain new adherents because of the basic interest of the Chinese people in the growth of unity and democracy. From this point of view, the Federation could be said to speak for the vast majority of the citizens of China who are not organized into any party.

In May 1944, the Federation again issued an urgent appeal for the immediate introduction of a democratic form of government, stating that "the need for China to become a democracy has passed beyond the stage of theory: it is a fact. . . . The formation of a democratic system must not be postponed until after the war. . . . If democracy is not realized during the war, then what we shall obtain after the war will not be democracy but the division and ruin of our country and suffering ten or a hundred times that of today." Declaring that all the recent discussions on the subject of democracy have remained limited to "empty words" while "regulations against the people's freedom remain numerous," the Federation urged that what the Kuomintang must consider is how to yield its prerogatives and special position and return them to the ranks of the people. "A truly patriotic revolutionary party cannot remain opposed to its own people."[1]

As a first step, the Federation suggested that the number of non-Kuomintang members of the People's Political Council be increased in accordance with the proportions fixed when the Council was first established in 1938, and that these members be chosen by their respective parties and groups instead of being appointed by the Kuomintang. Further, it proposed that the powers of the People's Political Council be increased and particularly that it have a voice in the drafting of the budget. "If even this cannot be done, the whole idea of the so-called carrying out of democracy by the Government must be distrusted and the likelihood of the so-called enforcement of constitutional government within one year after the war will be even more distrusted."

After dealing at some length with the urgent need for internal unity not only to strengthen China's powers of resistance but to win the confidence of China's allies, the Federation's statement urged that "Kuomintang-Communist relations must be improved under the principle of democracy," pointing out that "the views repeatedly expressed by the Chinese Communist Party have never gone beyond democracy," and that "various preparations now being made by the Kuomintang are also presumably aimed at the realization of democracy." In addition to this major need, the Federation demanded that prompt measures be taken to deal with the economic crisis, including the dismissal of corrupt and inefficient officials, the mobilization of popular organizations to participate in the prevention of hoarding and the control of commodities, and aid to private factories in securing materials and fuel so as to stimulate production instead of the "present

---

[1] This statement, entitled "Views and Policies of the Federation of Democratic Parties Regarding the Present Situation," issued in Chungking in May 1944, was printed in *Pacific Affairs*, September 1944, pp. 330–336.

attitude of indifference to the existence or extinction of factories."

The publication of this statement by the Federation reflected the growing dissatisfaction and unrest in Kuomintang China over the Government's refusal to grant legal status to non-Kuomintang parties, despite the widespread conviction among all sections of the people that the democratization of the government was essential for the solution of the grave internal problems with which China was faced. Before considering the strength of this opposition movement, it may be helpful to examine the reasons why so many Chinese distrusted the Government's promise that constitutional government would be introduced within one year after the war, and why that distrust was not entirely removed by Chiang Kai-shek's New Year's message of January 1, 1945, in which he declared that "we must prepare for the convening of a People's Congress within this year [1945] to adopt and promulgate a constitution," or by his subsequent announcement, on March 1, 1945, that the constitutional assembly would be convened on November 12, 1945.

"CONSTITUTIONAL" GOVERNMENT — KUOMINTANG-STYLE

THE CONSTITUTIONAL issue has long been a subject of controversy and debate in China. Those who opposed any immediate extension of political democracy contended that the great majority of the Chinese people were incapable of dealing intelligently with complex problems of administration and that the period of "political tutelage" under the Kuomintang must be continued until China should be thoroughly unified and the people better educated. Those who urged the immediate introduction of representative government, on the other hand, argued that the extension of political democracy was essential to cement national unity and to deal with China's urgent social and economic problems. They contended further that the very fact that the Kuomintang regime had been compelled to resort to repressive measures to preserve its power and stifle public criticism was part of the evidence that the Chinese people were ready and eager to practice democracy.

The history of China's progress toward constitutional government can be summarized briefly. In his *Fundamentals of National Reconstruction,* Dr. Sun Yat-sen outlined three stages for China's political development: military rule, political tutelage, and constitutional government. During the period of political tutelage, the people were to be prepared for self-government under the leadership of a broadly representative, nationalist party embracing all sections of the population — the kind of party that the Kuomintang was in his lifetime. When more than half the provinces had become fully self-governing, a Constitutional Assembly or "People's Congress" was to be held in order to adopt a constitution, and this was to be followed by the election of a new Central Government responsible to a National People's Congress.

This theory of three stages in China's political development has been the official policy of the National Government of China since 1927. In 1928, the period of military rule theoretically came to an end with the establishment of the National Government at Nanking. The stage of political tutelage was then officially inaugurated with the announced aim of preparing the Chinese people for local self-government by 1935. In May 1931, the Kuomintang called together a People's Convention in Nanking at which a provisional constitution was adopted, and it was agreed that the Kuomintang should continue to exercise the governing power on behalf of the Chinese people until political education had become sufficiently widespread to permit the calling of a Constitutional Assembly. At the meeting of the Kuomintang Central Executive Committee in 1932, it was decided to summon such a Constitutional Assembly in March 1935. Subsequently this was postponed to November 1936, and then to November 1937. In the meantime, Kuomintang legal experts had drawn up a draft constitution to submit to the Constitutional Assembly. This Draft Constitution was published by the National Government on May 5, 1936. Following this, two statutes governing the organization of the Constitutional Assembly and the election of delegates were promulgated by the Government on May 14, 1936, and were subsequently issued in revised form on April 30, 1937.

More than two-thirds of the delegates had already been selected when the outbreak of the war with Japan resulted in the indefinite postponement of the Constitutional Assembly. As a temporary measure, the People's Political Council was organized in the spring of 1938. As noted above, this was a purely advisory body, with its members appointed by the Kuomintang. But it did include representatives of minority parties and non-party leaders. At the fourth session of the People's Political Council in September 1939, the question of introducing constitutional government was again raised. Many members of the Council were disturbed by the reversal of the trend toward political democracy that had appeared so hopeful only the year before. Civil liberties were being increasingly curtailed by the Government, the political concentration camps were filling up, and tension between the Kuomintang and the Chinese Communist Party was increasing. Members of the minority parties represented in the Council, as well as many non-party leaders, were convinced that the only way to preserve national unity in the face of Japanese aggression was to give all parties and groups a responsible share in the conduct of the Government. The Council therefore petitioned the Government to fix a date for the convening of a Constitutional Assembly in order that a representative form of government might be established. As an interim measure, the Council urged that the political status of all citizens (with the exception of traitors) be declared equal in the eyes of the law.

The Government made no response to this latter request, but at the meeting of the Kuomintang Executive Committee in November 1939 it was agreed that the Constitutional Assembly should be convened in November 1940. On September 25, 1940, however, the Government announced that because of wartime difficulties the meeting of the Assembly would once again be postponed. During the next three years, the political and economic crisis in China steadily deepened, power was concentrated increasingly in the hands of the right-wing bureaucrats and the landlord-merchant class, all popular movements were suppressed, and on several occasions the danger of open civil strife between the Kuomintang and the Chinese Communists appeared imminent.

Against this dark background of political and economic crisis, the Kuomintang Central Executive Committee held its 11th Plenary Session in Chungking in September 1943 and passed a resolution stating that within a year after the war, a "People's Congress" would be convened to adopt a constitution and set a date for its enforcement. In announcing this decision, Chiang Kai-shek expressly stated that when constitutional government was established, all political parties would enjoy equal rights and freedoms before the law, with the Kuomintang retaining no special privileges.

This public declaration that the Kuomintang would not attempt to maintain its monopoly of political power after the war was hailed in some quarters as an important advance toward political democracy in China. It has also been repeatedly cited by official Kuomintang spokesmen as proof that the ultimate aim of the Kuomintang is to establish a genuinely democratic government. Why, then, did this pledge fail to satisfy those parties and groups in China who were eager to achieve a democratic solution of China's political crisis?

In the first place, the Kuomintang resolution postponed the convening of a Constitutional Assembly until after the war on the ground that it was impossible to consider the introduction of a democratic system of government as long as such a large part of China remained in enemy hands. But, even granting the plausibility of this excuse at the time, many Chinese questioned whether such policies as the restriction of freedom of speech and assembly, the "thought control" imposed on Chinese students and teachers, and the suppression of all opposition parties and groups were intended as preparation for ultimate democratic practices and the extension of equal rights to all. Just as disturbing was the fact that the Kuomintang's resolution did not propose the election of a new Constitutional Assembly with full power to draft a constitution for China. Instead, the Kuomintang leaders proposed to convene an Assembly, most of whose members were chosen by the Kuomintang before the war, and one that was expected to adopt a constitution drawn up by Kuomintang legal experts and published by the Government in 1936. In other words, both the proposed Assembly and the constitution that it was expected to ratify were purely Kuomintang creations of a prewar vintage and did not take into account any of the far-reaching wartime political changes in China.

Furthermore, the provisions governing the membership of the Constitutional Assembly were such as to give the Kuomintang a decisive preponderance of power and to deny adequate representation to other political forces. According to these provisions, the Constitutional Assembly is to have some 1,681 delegates. Of these, 665 are to be selected on a regional basis under the supervision of the local officials of the Kuomintang. Of the others, 330 are to be chosen by professional and trade organizations, but only by those organizations that were recognized as legal by the Kuomintang in 1937. This excludes many organizations formed during the war both in Kuomintang China and in the guerrilla areas. And finally, 240 delegates are to be chosen directly by the National Government — i.e., the Kuomintang — and 155 by special methods. This last group is to comprise 45 delegates from Manchuria and Jehol, 24 from Mongolia, 16 from Tibet, 40 from overseas Chinese, and 30 from the army, navy, air force, and institutes of military education. In addition, all members and reserve members of the Kuomintang Central Executive Committee and the Central Supervisory Committee are to be ex-officio delegates, whose numbers would complete the grand total.

In the view of non-Kuomintang leaders, these provisions, particularly those providing for appointed and ex-officio delegates, were contrary to democratic principles and would enable the Kuomintang to dominate the Assembly's actions. They maintained that a wholly new Constitutional Assembly should be elected on a nation-wide basis with no one party having the right to appoint delegates or to supervise their election. They supported this contention by pointing out that many of the delegates chosen in the prewar period had since died, disappeared, withdrawn from public life, or gone over to the Japanese.

The minority parties and non-party leaders found further cause for dissatisfaction in the provisions of the Draft Constitution which is to form the basis of discussion at the Constitutional Assembly. The chief criticism against this Draft Constitution is that it does not provide for sufficient popular control over the Central Government. The President of the Chinese Republic is given very extensive regular and emergency powers. Superior to the executive, legislative, judicial, examination, and control branches of the Central Government, he is responsible only to a Triennial National Congress. He appoints the President and Vice-President of the Executive Yuan as well as its various Ministers and Commissioners — e.g., of Finance, Foreign Affairs, Economic Affairs, etc. — who are responsible only to him. Holding office for six years and eligible for reëlection, he is commander-in-chief of the armed forces, can declare war, make peace, negotiate treaties, appoint and remove civil and military officials, declare a state of emergency, and do "whatever is necessary to cope with the situation, provided that he shall submit his action to the ratification of the Legislative Yuan within three months after the issuance of the orders." These powers are qualified in each case by the phrase "in accordance with law."

Chapter II of the Draft Constitution specifically guarantees a long list of civil liberties and rights, but, unlike the American Bill of Rights, each clause is qualified by the phrase, "which shall not be restricted except in accordance with law." Since "law" is defined as "that which has been passed by the Legislative Yuan and promulgated by the President," this qualification leaves the way open for a serious curtailment of civil liberties at the discretion of the President and the Legislative Yuan. Even the further broad provision that "only laws imperative for safeguarding national security, averting national crisis, maintaining public peace and order or promoting public interest may restrict the citizens' liberties and rights" does not modify the qualifying clause "in accordance with law," since almost any action could be justified under these definitions.

It is when we come to the powers of the National Congress, however, that we find the chief cause for the contention that the Draft Constitution would not establish a genuinely democratic government. Delegates to this Congress are to be elected by universal, equal, and direct suffrage and by secret ballot for a term of six years. The Congress is given the power to initiate laws, hold referenda on laws, to amend the constitution and to elect the President and Vice-President of the Republic, as well as the Presidents and members of the Legislative Yuan. However, the Congress is to be convened by the President only once in every three years for a period of one month, although extraordinary sessions may be convened at the instance of two-fifths of the members or by the President. Barring such special sessions, members of the Congress would have only two opportunities to exercise their political powers during their six-year term of office, with only very limited control over the Government in the interim years. This feature of the Draft Constitution has been sharply criticized by many Chinese leaders as undemocratic and as paving the way for a virtual dictatorship by the President. In their view, the National Congress should have more powers over the legislative and executive branches of the Central Government and should certainly meet oftener than every three years if it is to exercise any real control.

The system of local government proposed in the Draft Constitution has also been a target of criticism, particularly the sections providing that the only duties of Provincial Governors will be to execute the laws and orders of the Central Government and supervise local self-government, whereas Chinese Provincial

Governments have hitherto always enjoyed a large measure of autonomy in local affairs. Furthermore, Provincial Governors are not to be elected by the people of their provinces but appointed and removed by the Central Government. These provisions are in line with the prevailing trend toward the centralization of all political power in the hands of the Central Government, and many Chinese believe that, in view of the widely differing conditions in various parts of China, such centralization will tend to hamper rather than to encourage the fullest development of the country.

A detailed study of the provisions of the Draft Constitution reveals that its effect would be the establishment of a strong bureaucratic Central Government responsible in a general way to the people as a whole, but removed as far as possible from direct popular control over its legislative and executive actions. This is not surprising in view of the fact that the Draft Constitution is the work of the leading legal experts of the Kuomintang rather than the product of any widespread popular discussion, and that it was drawn up in 1934–35 when the Kuomintang was still striving to establish full control over the country and was far more interested in setting up a strong central administration than in paving the way for greater popular participation in the government. Furthermore, the Draft Constitution clearly reflects the views of those Kuomintang leaders who believe that the Chinese people are not ready for genuine democratic government, and that the actual administration of government must be kept in the hands of a "competent" bureaucracy.

In view of the above facts, it becomes easier to understand why Chiang Kai-shek's pledge of March 1, 1945 did not wholly satisfy those who were urging the need for greater political democracy as an immediate necessity. For there was nothing in the Generalissimo's statement to indicate that he envisaged the election of a new and genuinely representative Constitutional Assembly, or that the Draft Constitution of 1936 would be discarded in order to allow that Assembly to have a free voice in determining a constitution that would more effectively guarantee popular control over the Government.

In the absence of any such commitments, Chiang Kai-shek's March 1 speech did little to alleviate the immediate political crisis or to convince the people of China that they were going to be given a really responsible share in the government of their country. Democratic government can never become a reality unless the people of a country are permitted to participate in the process of establishing it. And there was no question that in Kuomintang China the people's participation in the conduct of their government was diminishing rather than increasing. Until that trend should be reversed, there was little reason to hope for the early establishment of genuinely representative government in China.

To Americans who were vitally interested in seeing the emergence of a democratic, economically strong, and politically united China as the surest guarantee of a stable and prosperous postwar order in Eastern Asia, the continued failure on the part of the Chinese Government to reverse the trend toward reaction and dictatorship was discouraging. But the situation in China was by no means so dark as it might seem to one who concentrated solely on developments in Chungking and on the policies and aims of the ruling clique. That clique stood for the "old China" that opposed modern progress, scorned the people, and clung to the privileges and powers of a feudal autocracy based on an impoverished and oppressed peasantry. There was, however, a "new China" that was growing in power and determination, and demanding democratic progress and reform in both the political and the economic spheres. The aims, accomplishments, and prospects of that "new China," discussed in the following chapter, are matters of great concern to the American people, for America cannot have a fruitful friendship with the "old China."

CHAPTER VII

A NEW CHINA CHALLENGES THE OLD

❈

THUS FAR this survey has dealt primarily with the darker and more discouraging aspects of the situation in China — the obstacles that must be overcome before China can emerge as a strong and democratic nation, capable of providing a new economic frontier for the industrial nations of the world. The appraisal of Chinese Government policies may seem excessively pessimistic and critical, but it must be emphasized once again that China can never create an expanding market for the products of her own as well as foreign industries without a thoroughgoing program of agrarian reform. As Henry Wallace told a gathering of Chinese agricultural experts during his visit to Chungking in June 1944: "No large country with a wide range of climate, making possible diversified agricultural production, can be industrially strong or sound unless both its agricultural technique and the agricultural part of its society are progressive and prosperous." And it is certain that no such program of agrarian reform will be undertaken by a bureaucratic government in which the landed gentry hold a monopoly of political and economic power. China can become a new economic frontier only if she establishes a genuinely democratic system of government so that the Government's participation in and regulation of economic development is in the interests of the people as a whole and not those of a small feudal-minded section of the population.

The development of a democratic and forward-looking China will obviously require the concerted effort of all liberal and progressive elements in Chinese society. And by the autumn of 1944, the prospects for such a concerted effort appeared brighter than at any time since 1938, despite or perhaps because of China's desperate military plight. Large and potentially powerful groups were becoming increasingly resentful of the continued dictatorship of a regime that had notably failed to deal effectively with China's basic economic and political problems.

These opposition forces included many of the younger army officers, small merchants and businessmen, professors, students, and professional workers, members of the "small parties," the Chinese Communists and their co-workers and supporters in the guerrilla areas, and last, but not least, the generally liberal elements in the Kuomintang itself represented by such men as Sun Fo. In a class by herself, feared and ostracized by the Kuomintang bureaucracy, but with immense personal prestige, was Madame Sun Yat-sen, who continued to fight courageously for the realization of the democratic principles and policies of her husband, and did not hesitate to criticize the repressive policies of the existing regime. Madame Sun is justly called the greatest and bravest individual in China. At times when affairs in Kuomintang China were at their darkest, she alone kept the flames of freedom and liberty from being entirely extinguished. Her voice of protest has never wavered for one moment since the fateful days of April 1927 when the national revolution was betrayed by some of her husband's most trusted associates.

In addition to this mounting political opposition, there was increasing discontent among the peasants in Kuomintang China, manifested most dramatically in the peasant rebellion that broke out in Kansu Province in February 1943. The chief causes of this rebellion against the Central Government were the excessive taxation in kind, the forcible and undemocratic methods of conscription into the army, and the onerous system of labor conscription by which every four families were required to provide the Government with the work of one man each day, together with implements, mules, etc. The peasants' resentment was directed primarily against officials appointed from outside the province, especially Governor Ku Cheng-lun, whom they accused of trying to impoverish and enslave the people of Kansu. It was estimated that nearly one million took some part in the rebellion, and the situation in Kansu is still far from tranquil. Some of General Hu Tsung-nan's troops were moved into Kansu to quell the rebels, but the peasants took to the hills and carried on guerrilla warfare. These rebels were in no way led or assisted by the Chinese Communists; in fact, the Communists offered to assist the Government in solving the Kansu problem, but this offer was refused.

Thus by the autumn of 1944 the Chungking Government had lost virtually all the popular support that it had enjoyed during the early part of the war. The only groups on which it could still rely were the rural gentry, those military officers who remained personally loyal to Chiang Kai-shek, the higher ranks of the bureaucracy, and the merchant-bankers who had close connections with the government bureaucrats. Foreign observers estimated that if free elections were held in China, a minimum of 75% to 80% of the vote would be cast against the existing regime. Furthermore, though the opposition groups in Kuomintang China were not unified and represented widely differing political views and economic interests, they were tending to draw together on the basis of their common demand for a modification of the system of political dictatorship that denied them any voice in the government of the country.

OPPOSITION FORCES IN KUOMINTANG CHINA

THIS UNIFICATION process was, of course, opposed by the Government with every means at its disposal, but the strength of the opposition movement was growing. The Federation of Chinese Democratic Parties, which had changed its name to the Chinese Democratic League, was functioning with relative freedom in Kunming because it had enlisted the support of General Lung Yun, chairman of the Yunnan Provincial Government. Furthermore, the Federation for the first time was seeking a concrete agreement with the Chinese Communists for concerted action in support of its program, which was described as the achievement of internal unity through the establishment of a "democratic form of government in which there will be decentralization and recognition of local interests somewhat along federal lines, with the Federation of Democratic Parties forming a middle party between the Kuomintang and the Communists." Other points in this political program, on which it was hoped that all dissident political groups in China could unite, were the release of political prisoners, abolition of political police, and continued close coöperation with the United States.

In addition to General Lung Yun, the League had gained the support of a number of provincial military leaders who were critical of the Chungking Government's policies and disagreed with its attitude toward the Chinese Communists. These included Marshal Li Chi-shen, chairman of the Military Advisory Council in Chungking; General Huang Hsu-chu, chairman of the Kwangsi Provincial Government; General Liu Wen-hui, chairman of the Sikang Provincial Government; and General Teng Hsi-hou, Pacification Commissioner for Sikang and Szechwan. The Federation had also gained the sympathy, though not the active coöperation, of the important Kwangsi leaders, Generals Li Tsung-jen and Pai Chung-hsi. Even in Szechwan — the province in which one would expect the Central Government's influence to be strongest — the most powerful militarists, such as Generals Pan Wen-hua and Yang Sen, had become actively critical of the Government by the end of 1944 and the great majority of Szechwan newspaper editorials either criticized the Government or demanded the institution of democracy.

This inclusion of the provincial militarists in the opposition forces disturbed some foreign observers who did not regard them as hopeful champions of democratic progress. But though one reason for their support of the demand for democratic government may have been their desire to escape from Central Government control, there was also evidence that they were sincerely concerned over the weakness of Chungking's military leadership. Furthermore, whatever their reasons, the fact remained that the support of these generals gave strength and a more inclusive character to the demand for a coalition government, and that, if this demand should prove effective, these provincial militarists themselves would of necessity be subjected to the influence of a new national unity and forced to modify whatever personal ambitions they might harbor.

A second important development in Kuomintang China during 1944 was the reported move on the part of military leaders in Southeastern China to set up a "Southeastern Government of Joint Defense," embracing the provinces of Kwangsi, Kwangtung, Fukien, Chekiang, and Hunan. The stated aims of this proposed regime were: to establish democratic government in place of the existing dictatorship; to coöperate more fully with China's allies; and to carry out general popular mobilization. This embryonic movement reflected the growing dissatisfaction on the part of the commanders in Southeastern China with the ineffectiveness of Chungking's military administration in the face of the Japanese drive into Kwangsi, and a belief that drastic reforms were needed if China was to take an active part in the forthcoming allied offensive against Japan.

The rapidity of the Japanese advance into Southeastern China prevented this separatist tendency from crystallizing into a definite political movement in 1944.[1] But there were strong indications that it might in time become the spearhead of a radical reorganization of China's political structure. For twenty years, Chiang Kai-shek's chief source of power had been his ability to force recalcitrant war lords to relinquish their semiautonomous power over the provinces of China and submit to the authority of a Central Government. But the kind of Central Government that the Generalissimo had been instrumental in developing was one that excluded these provincial leaders from all participation except on the Generalissimo's terms. Twenty years ago the existence of a number of semiautonomous provinces was unquestionably a serious handicap in the development of a strong China. But, as of 1945, a movement toward greater decentralization may have within it the roots of a democratic federal system in which local interests would be better represented. Such a development could, for example, pave the way for bringing the Border Regions — which are already semiautonomous in character — into the central Chinese political structure, and their participation would do much to safeguard its democratic character.

Among the generals sponsoring this plan for a "Southeastern Government of Joint Defense" were Marshal Li Chi-shen; General Hsueh Yueh, Governor of Hunan and commander of the 9th War Zone (East Hunan and Kiangsi); General Yu Han-mou, commander of the 7th War Zone (Eastern Kwangtung and Southern Fukien); and General Chang Fa-kuei, commander of the 4th War Zone (Western Kwangtung and Kwangsi). As Li Chi-shen was also an active supporter of the Chinese Democratic League, there was the possibility that he would seek to coördinate the programs of the two groups. Since most of the above names are presumably unfamiliar to Americans, a brief who's who of some of these generals and of the leaders of the Federation of Democratic Parties may be useful to indicate the broad political scope of the opposition movement gathering weight in Kuomintang China.

Marshal Li Chi-shen is an important Kwangsi general who achieved early fame as commander of the famous Fourth Army

---

[1] A military consequence of this movement was the organization, along the Kwangsi-Kwangtung border, of a guerrilla army estimated by some to total 50,000 rifles under the over-all command of Marshal Li Chi-shen and under the active command of Generals Tsai Ting-kai and Liang Hsu-min.

immediately preceding the Northern Expedition of 1926. In the 1927 split he joined the right-wing faction, took the lead in suppressing the Canton uprising in December 1927, and ultimately served as Director of Military Training in the Nanking Government in 1932–33. In November 1933, he rebelled against Chiang Kai-shek and became chairman of the abortive "People's Government" at Foochow. Li was expelled from the Kuomintang in February 1934. With the outbreak of war with Japan in 1937, he hurried to Nanking and offered his services to Chiang. He became successively a member of the National Military Council and, in 1942, a member of the Supreme National Defense Council. In September 1943, his failure to attend the meeting of the Central Executive Committee of the Kuomintang in Chungking was attributed to his fear of leaving Kwangsi because the conservative elements in the Kuomintang were after his scalp. Li's appointment as Chairman of the Military Advisory Council in Chungking in December 1943 was believed to be a further attempt to lessen his influence in Kwangsi. At the beginning of 1944, it was reported that the conservative Kuomintang leaders in Chungking were seeking to liquidate the power and influence of the three Kwangsi leaders — Li Chi-shen, Li Tsung-jen, and Pai Chung-hsi — or at least to "quarantine" Kwangsi militarily as had been done with the Communist areas.

General Hsueh Yueh, the "little tiger," is a native of Kwangtung Province and served as a divisional commander under Pai Chung-hsi during the revolutionary campaigns of 1925–27. In January 1939 he was made commander of the 9th War Zone with headquarters at Nanchang, and in March he became governor of Hunan Province. Hsueh Yueh was the commander of the Chinese forces that defeated the Japanese at Changsha in October 1939 and again in October 1941 and in January 1942. In February 1944, he was promoted to the rank of full general in recognition of his meritorious service. During the Japanese drive in the Hunan-Kwangsi area in September 1944, the performance of Hsueh Yueh's troops was reported to be "the shining exception" to the general military ineptitude that characterized the Chinese command. Hsueh Yueh had never been identified with the Kwangsi-Kwangtung faction in previous disputes with the Central Government, but is reported to have become increasingly critical of Chungking's policies, particularly with regard to the Kuomintang-Communist dispute. Early in 1944 he was quoted as saying: "Many prominent Chinese military leaders are critical of the Chungking Government's policies, and Americans who are interested in Chinese political affairs should devote some attention to the activities of the 'so-called Communist forces,' who are perhaps not so dangerous to the future of China as they are said to be by the Kuomintang."

General Lung Yun is a typical old-style reactionary Chinese war lord who for years fought to keep the influence of the Central Government out of his province of Yunnan. He steadfastly refused to come to Chiang's assistance during the early years of the war, but in 1941 two of his subordinate generals, Sun Tu and Lu Tao-yuan, finally switched their allegiance to Chiang Kai-shek, and, aided by the ill-fated Burma campaign of 1942, the power of the Central Government was gradually extended over Yunnan. With the arrival of General Chen Cheng in Yunnan in March 1943 with over 50,000 Chungking troops, the "nationalization" of Yunnan was completed, although Lung Yun remained as governor.

General Yu Han-mou, commander of the 4th War Zone, has been the military boss of Kwangtung Province since 1936 when its erstwhile semi-independent militarist ruler, Chen Chi-tang, was forced to flee. In March and April 1942, General Yu directed an extensive punitive campaign against the Kwangtung guerrilla forces operating in the area between Canton and Hong Kong, shortly after they were instrumental in aiding the escape from captured Hong Kong of many important foreign and Chinese citizens, including Madame Yu Han-mou.

General Chang Fa-kuei, a native of Kwangtung and commander of the 4th War Zone, achieved his greatest fame as commander of the Nationalist 12th Division and then of the Fourth Army. It was under his leadership that the Fourth Army became popularly known as the "Ironsides," for its heroic exploits in the Northern Expedition in 1926–27. Subsequently, General Chang was one of the leading officers responsible for the unusually brutal suppression of the Canton Commune. At present he is said to be in complete accord with the view of Marshal Li Chi-shen. He has a reputation for being very generous to his troops and very popular with them.

Among the leaders of the Federation of Democratic Parties, the most influential is said to be Dr. Lo Lung-chi, former editor of the *I Shih Pao*, a Catholic daily paper in Tientsin that was famous for its liberal views. Dr. Lo was at one time professor of political science at the National Peking University and a member of the People's Political Council, but was ousted from both positions by Chiang Kai-shek in 1941 because of his criticism of the Kuomintang. Perhaps its most popular leader is the Federation's present chairman, Chang Lan (also known as Chang Piao-fang). During most of his lifetime Chang has been a fearless liberal of the old school, one-time Governor of Szechwan, and since 1938 a member of the People's Political Council. Other prominent leaders of the Federation are Chang Chun-mai (Carson Chang) of the National Socialist Party, Tso Shun-sheng of the Young China Party, Liang Shu-ming of the Rural Reconstructionists, Huang Yen-pei of the Vocational Education Group.

THE ACHIEVEMENTS OF GUERRILLA CHINA

THUS THE pressure for a change in the existing regime in favor of a more representative form of government was growing in Kuomintang China. During 1944, however, the program of these opposition forces was confined to paper plans and occasional statements. In Guerrilla China, on the other hand, the leaders who advocated a more democratic system of government for China had actually put into practice a political and economic program governing the lives of some ninety million Chinese. The policies and achievements of these guerrilla governments cannot, of course, be taken as a precise indication of what might be expected from a liberal and broadly based government in postwar China, because conditions at that time will have changed greatly and many new problems will have arisen as a result of the restoration of the coastal areas and Manchuria to Chinese control. But there is no doubt that the policies adopted in the guerrilla areas will exercise a lasting influence on millions of Chinese, and that the people of those areas that have taken an active part in defeating Japan will insist on having a strong voice in determining the future development of their country. It is therefore important that the American people should have some idea of what has actually been accomplished in the guerrilla areas, not only in terms of military resistance against Japan, but also with regard to the political and economic measures instituted under the leadership of the Chinese Communist Party.

As noted previously, the Chinese Communist position is that China's immediate needs are first, freedom from foreign domination, and second, a democratic political and economic structure. The question that naturally arises is whether they have actually carried out these theories in practice in the areas under their control. In March 1945 there were nineteen of these areas, including six Border Regions and thirteen less highly organized "liberated areas," stretching all the way from the borders of Manchuria and Mongolia in the north to Kwangtung Province and Hainan Island in the south.

In addition to the regular troops of the Eighth Route and New Fourth Armies, numbering about 910,000, the guerrilla forces included more than two million armed militia and partisan troops, and as of the spring of 1945, these forces claimed to have liberated a total of more than half a million square miles and 95 million people from Japanese control. Millions of Chinese in the guerrilla areas were also organized into various civilian defense bodies that coöperated in various ways with the guerrilla armies. It is estimated that from twelve to fifteen million Chinese participated actively in guerrilla warfare in either a military or a civilian capacity, whereas the membership of the Chinese Communist Party was only about 1,200,000.

The most important Communist-led area is the Shensi-Ninghsia-Kansu Border Region with its capital at Yenan, the headquarters of the Communist Party and the Eighth Route Army. This area, lying west of the Yellow River, had been heavily bombed but never invaded by the Japanese, and it is here that the Communist program has been most fully carried out. Next in importance is the adjacent Shansi-Chahar-Hopei Border Region, with its capital at Fuping in Western Hopei. This region had been the scene of some of the bitterest fighting between the guerrilla forces and the Japanese, and constitutes the largest single area controlled by the guerrillas.

In the guerrilla areas deepest within the Japanese lines and most subject to constant attack, the political and economic program is naturally less fully developed, but in each of these areas the principles of administration and popular mobilization introduced in the main Border Regions have been followed as closely as possible. A summary of the achievements of these Border Regions will therefore suffice to indicate the general character of the political and economic program developed under the leadership of the Chinese Communists. The following account is based on the reports of foreign observers who have had the opportunity to study conditions in these areas at first hand.[1]

All foreign observers who have visited the guerrilla forces are agreed that the main secret of their military success has been the wholehearted support that they have received from the civilian population. That support and coöperation constitute the best possible proof that the program instituted under the leadership of the Chinese Communists effectively meets the needs and desires of the Chinese people, and that the Communist theory as to China's more long-term needs — namely, national unity and a democratic form of government — was perfectly suited to the immediate military need of mobilizing all sections of the people for united resistance.

Politically, the guerrilla program emphasized universal education and genuinely representative government. Village councils were elected on the basis of universal adult suffrage, and these councils elected representatives to the district and regional governments. Members of the Communist Party were pledged not to accept more than one-third of the elected positions in any local or regional government. Of the remaining two-thirds, an effort was made to have one-half Kuomintang and the rest non-party representation, although in many areas there were not sufficient Kuomintang members to make this possible. Also in a few places there were not enough Communists for them to attain a representation of one-third. As a result of this policy, the administration of the various guerrilla areas and border regions were carried out by coalition governments in which all parties and classes were represented. In the Shensi-Kansu-Ninghsia Border Region, for example, the *New York Times* correspondent

---

[1] Among these foreign observers are: Col. Evans Carlson, U.S.M.C.; Stanton Lautenschlager, for many years a Presbyterian missionary and teacher in China; Professor William Band, head of the Physics Department at Yenching University; Lieutenant George Uhlmann of the Fighting French Navy and one-time French vice-consul at Mukden; Guy Martel Hall, manager of the Peiping Branch of the National City Bank of New York; Mr. C. Brondgeest, a Dutch engineer; Michael Lindsay, a tutor in the Department of Economics at Yenching University; Edgar Snow, Ralf Sues, Agnes Smedley, and the half-dozen foreign correspondents who visited the guerrilla areas in the summer of 1944. Although the author's own visit to Yenan and surrounding territory took place in the summer of 1937, he had the opportunity of witnessing the formative period of the united front and of studying the character of the leaders as well as the rapid economic and political changes that even then were taking place.

in a despatch from Yenan dated July 12, 1944 reports that "the network of People's Councils, which elect local officials, is a great pyramid going right down to the villages. Of 9,967 village councillors in fourteen districts 5,549 are poor peasants, 2,435 are middle peasants, 690 are rich peasants, 502 are hired laborers, 394 are industrial workers, and the rest are laborers, gentry, and merchants. Of these the Communists number 2,477 or 24 per cent." In the Shansi-Chahar-Hopei Border Region, the influence of the Communists was reported to be less than in the area governed from Yenan because of the presence of a large number of intellectuals from Peiping and Shanghai who were not members of the Communist Party. The chairman, vice-chairman, and chief of the education department of the Shansi-Chahar-Hopei Border Government, for example, were members of the Kuomintang, and a large proportion of other civil officials were non-party men.

The economic program in the guerrilla areas also reflected the Communist theory that what China needs is to lay the foundation for modern economic development and individual free enterprise in which all sections of the population can coöperate. Moderate agrarian reforms were introduced to relieve the peasants of excessive rent and interest charges, and to ensure that every family possessed land of its own to till. But the rights of landlords who chose to remain in the guerrilla areas were recognized and protected; the payment of equitable rents was made obligatory; and though some large estates were broken up, landlords were permitted to retain enough land to rent some of it out to other farmers. Only the estates of absentee landlords and those who had gone over to the Japanese were confiscated and redistributed to the peasants. Private industry and trade were given every encouragement, although it was necessary to initiate various state-controlled industrial projects to meet the basic economic needs of the area.

Mao Tse-tung, leader of the Chinese Communist Party, in an address to the People's Political Council of the Shensi-Kansu-Ninghsia Border Region on November 21, 1941, summed up this economic program as follows: "Regarding agrarian problems, on the one hand we advocate a policy of reducing rents and interest so that the peasants can have clothing and food; on the other hand, we are also carrying out a policy of recognizing the payment of rents and interest as obligatory so that the landlords can also have clothing and food. Regarding the relation between labor and capital, on the one hand we are realizing the policy of helping the workers so that they may have food and clothing, while on the other hand we are also carrying out a policy of industrial development, which will provide the capitalists with profits." On another occasion, Mao Tse-tung emphasized that "State economic enterprises and coöperatives ought to be developed, but the main thing for the present is not State enterprises but private enterprises. It is to afford the opportunity for the development of an economy based on liberalism."

An interesting example of how this program worked in practice was given by Harrison Forman in a despatch to the *New York Herald Tribune*, dated Mitze, August 24, 1944. "Mitze," declares Mr. Forman, "is one of the most prosperous little towns I have ever seen in my travels throughout the length and breadth of China. Mitze, with a population of about 10,000, is about 200 miles northeast of Yenan. . . . It was market day as I entered the south gate in the late afternoon. The city's long single street was thronged. In contrast to the monotonous blue of other places in China, here all wore white homespun, since dyes are unobtainable. . . . I saw no patched garments, no underfed bodies, and no beggars. Even the children wore shoes, almost without exception, which is a sure sign of prosperity anywhere in China.

"Mitze, which next to Yenan is the largest town in the Border Region, is a comparatively new city. The shops are well stocked, the shop fronts freshly painted, and the flagstoned street cleanly swept. After being quartered in the primary school — a substantial building much better than the average elsewhere in China — I walked down the street and talked to the shopkeepers and merchants. All spoke enthusiastically and sincerely of the new democracy the Communists have brought here. Mitze is well known for its rich landlords with their privately owned enterprises, who, undisturbed, have actually been encouraged by the Communists. The Rugmakers House of Chow — Six Brothers — is typical. They started business last year with a capital of only 60,000 yuan, local currency (about 300 American dollars). Today they are incorporated with a capital of 30,000,-000 yuan ($150,000), and the Border Region Government is a substantial stockholder, having purchased one-third of the shares, though it exercises no control over the business and has no members on the corporation's board of directors. All the workers also are shareholders and receive bonuses and divide extra yearly dividends among themselves. This surely is not communism in Soviet Russia's definition of the term, for any man can start his own business, a business which is permitted to develop into a profitable venture, as in any other capitalist state."

Another interesting example is provided by conditions in the town of Suiteh, as reported by the *New York Times* correspondent in a despatch dated August 22, 1944: "In Suiteh the new regime was established after the war began and land ownership remained unchanged. The landlords, retired military and civil officials, scholars and gentry, who gave luster to the city's reputation as the greatest cultural center of North Shensi, are still here and still in power, though reduced, in the administration. An Wen-hsiang, president of the Suiteh People's Political Council, is a typical country gentleman of the old school. His 400 acres of land have been in his family's possession for 1,000 years. . . . He had fought all his life against corruption, gambling, and opium and was impressed with the fact that Communist administrators were free of all these vices. When the Eighth Route Army beat back Japanese attempts to cross the Yellow River toward Suiteh he decided to support the new regime. Lowered farm rents and increased production followed and banditry ceased, he said. When asked what he thought of communism he replied: 'Once I went to Shanghai where the rich live in great houses in luxury that leads to degeneration while ricksha coolies run their hearts out for a few coppers. I was shocked by such inequality between rich and poor. If the Communists can remedy such conditions I am for them.'"

A new taxation system was introduced in the Border Regions in 1941 consisting of a progressive income and property tax with rates varying from 7% to 65%. In 1942, the exemption limit was lowered and the rate on high incomes reduced somewhat. The only other taxes are local levies for education and relief purposes, and those levied on imports and exports which are designed more for trade control purposes than for revenue. Unlike the armies in Kuomintang China, the guerrilla forces are not permitted to confiscate grain or other supplies from the people. All taxes, paid chiefly in grain, are collected by the various local governments, stored locally, and issued to the army supply department or government organizations against grain tickets given out by a special government department. As these local governments are popularly elected, the people have a voice in determining the amount of taxes levied and the amount of grain given to the troops. A further advantage of this system is that the army's grain reserves are widely scattered among the villages. Michael Lindsay reports, for example, that "under normal conditions in the base areas the army gets its grain from the local supply department, but in the guerrilla areas or during a Japanese offensive each unit carries its own grain tickets and can get supplies from almost any village. In the guerrilla areas the general policy is to keep the amount of Chinese taxes at about one-eighteenth of the Japanese taxation. . . . The occupied areas also make quite large voluntary contributions." [1]

In addition to these political and eocnomic reforms, the Border Region Governments and the more highly organized guerrilla base areas established a number of "mass movement" organizations through which they carried out the work of popular organization and political education. There are five civilian organizations — farmers, workers, youth, women, and children — and two military: the self-defense corps and the militia. Membership in these organizations is very large, and in addition to their work in support of the armed forces, the members carry on extensive educational activities. Local leaders give political instruction and encourage educational and cultural activities as well as the use of improved methods in agriculture and so on. They also endeavor to secure popular coöperation in applying new reforms. To quote Mr. Lindsay again: "By providing this local leadership, which educates the people and maintains close contact with the government, the associations have been largely responsible for the excellent popular morale and the rapid social progress which has been made." Foreign observers reported that in the program of political education carried out among the people, the entire emphasis was on the need for a national united front against Japan, and that no attempt was made to teach Communist doc-

---

[1] Mr. Lindsay, a former teacher at Yenching University, lived in the Shansi-Hopei-Chahar Border Region for more than a year following Pearl Harbor and is now in Yenan serving as a radio technician. His report on the military, political, and economic conditions in the Chinese guerrilla areas, entitled "The North China Front," was published in two issues of *Amerasia,* March 21 and April 14, 1944, with the permission of Mr. Lindsay's father, Professor A. D. Lindsay, Master of Balliol College, Oxford, and of the London *Times,* which published extracts from the report.

trines or encourage anti-Kuomintang sentiment. These foreign observers also agreed that as a result of this political education program and their experience in the actual work of government, the people of the Border Regions are far more aware of both national and international problems than is the case with the average Chinese in other parts of China.

The position of labor unions in the guerrilla areas is simply one phase of this general policy of popular participation in all phases of the administration and development of these areas. Union membership is voluntary and officers of the unions are elected by the membership. The principal unions are the General Labor Union in the Shensi-Kansu-Ninghsia Border Region and four other federations operating mainly in "occupied" territory — i.e., the Shansi-Chahar-Hopei Labor Federation, the Southeastern Shansi Federation of Unions, the Federation of the Taihang Range Unions, and the Labor Federation of the Chengting-Taiyuan and Tatung-Pukow railways. Estimates of the total union membership range from 600,000 to 1,000,000, although these figures include many agricultural laborers and handicraft workers.

All factories in the Border Regions are unionized, the unions' chief function being to ensure the enforcement of the labor contract with the management and to represent the workers in collective bargaining. The unions also carry on educational work in an effort to eliminate illiteracy and educated the workers in the political phases of their struggle against the Japanese. They also coöperate with the government and factory owners in operating technical training classes and conducting research in order to develop improved methods of production with the primitive equipment that is available. Wages are fixed by special wage-fixing committees composed of representatives of the management and the union. Workers are penalized for tardiness and absenteeism but enjoy many benefits under the Labor Protection Law, such as vacations with pay, dismissal allowances, medical treatment, and hospital fees, all of which are borne by the management.

Industrial development is naturally very limited and manufacturing facilities are extremely crude, since there was virtually no industry whatsoever in these areas before the war and since during the war it was impossible to import industrial equipment. Recent reports, however, indicate a steady growth in the num-

ber of small-scale industries and coöperatives manufacturing
such essentials as woolen and cotton cloth, soap, paper, glass,
and agricultural implements. Other essential commodities that
could not be produced in the guerrilla areas were obtained by
trade with the occupied territories, but this trade was strictly
controlled. Imports of luxuries and exports which could be of
military value to the Japanese were forbidden, while imports of
"semiluxuries" — i.e., goods not absolutely essential — and exports
of goods that might be of some indirect value to the Japanese
were heavily taxed.

One of the most important achievements of the Border Regions has been the increase of argicultural production through
the reclamation of waste land, improved production methods,
and the policy of requiring agricultural labor from every able-
bodied person, including soldiers and officials. Among the things
that most impressed all the foreign correspondents who arrived
in the Shensi-Kansu-Ninghsia Border Region in the summer of
1944 was the fact that agricultural production was plentiful and
the people appeared healthy and well fed. Brooks Atkinson of
the *New York Times,* for example, writing from Yenan on September 23, 1944 declared that: "To an American, many aspects
of Yenan are pleasantly familiar. Just now the air is buoyant
with autumn elixir. . . . Many crops are being harvested, like
corn, buckwheat, pumpkins, tomatoes, onions, beans, cotton,
tobacco, millet and hemp. Everywhere there is good fruit in
abundance, grapes of good size and color, pears that are somewhat less juicy than Americans like, and small red apples with
a fine astringent flavor. With so much provender available in
a sparsely populated area the people look better fed, huskier,
and more energetic than in other parts of China. They also carry
fewer burdens on shoulders and backs."

The correspondents reported that an intensive campaign was
being waged against "loafers," while honors and rewards were
showered on "production heroes" — farmers and workers who
had made outstanding records in production or devised more
efficient methods. Everywhere on the walls of Yenan was carved
the slogan, "Move Your Own Hands!" and the epithet *ehr liu tze*
or "loafer" was applied with derision and scorn to those few who
refused to join in the effort to make the area self-sufficient. As
one correspondent put it: "We have come to the mountains of
North Shensi to find the most modern place in China," while

another who was brought up in China said: "I find myself continually trying to find out just how Chinese these people are."

Harrison Forman reported in July 1944 that "primary consideration has been placed upon food production. A vast acreage of waste lands has been reclaimed. (The cultivator is given title to lands he opens up.) Last year alone, a million *mow* (six *mow* equals one acre) were reclaimed, while this year it is expected that another million *mow* will be reclaimed. . . . Preferential treatment is given to immigrants and refugees, who are helped through three years of tax exemption. The provision of agricultural loans is intended for the purchase of more plowing oxen and farm implements. . . . All garrison army units have gone into production and already have become self-supporting for the greater part of their necessary expenditures, some units entirely so. . . . Members in institutions and schools also devote a certain number of hours a day to production. . . . With everyone, including the soldiers, in production to one degree or another, the burden on the people has been lightened. Last year the grain tax collection amounted to only 10 per cent of the total production. Including taxes for local education and relief levies, total taxation amounted to 14 per cent of the farmers' income. Commercial taxes are fixed at 13 per cent of the net profits."

Similarly, the *New York Times* correspondent reported that the barren country of northern Shensi has been transformed into "an area of intensive cultivation, stock breeding, and handicraft industry. . . . The reclamation of great expanses of waste land was accomplished not only by the local residents but also by garrison troops who work on the land throughout the summer and train in military units throughout the winter. The soldiers are able to feed themselves without imposing any burden on the peasantry."

The visiting correspondents were also impressed by the freedom of discussion and lively debate that characterized a meeting of the Border Region Government together with the Standing Committee of the Regional People's Council. Both these bodies were elected by the People's Council, the region's highest authority. The Chairman of the Government, Lin Tsu-han, is a Communist, but the Vice-Chairman is a non-Communist. Members of the Council included a peasant, a merchant, a landlord, an intellectual, a tenant farmer, a doctor, an army officer, a cultural worker, a shop clerk, and a Moslem mullah. Of the 24 members attending the meeting, eight were Communists and the rest non-party men.

These political and economic policies, coupled with the broad program of popular education, enabled the guerrilla forces to achieve remarkable military successes despite the difficult material conditions under which they were compelled to operate. Blockaded both by the Japanese and by Central Government troops, they were forced to depend almost entirely on munitions and equipment captured from the Japanese. Yet their excellent intelligence service, based on the loyal coöperation of the civilian population, enabled them to withstand innumerable "mopping-up" campaigns by vastly better armed Japanese troops. During the period 1939–45, they occupied the full attention of more than 300,000 Japanese troops and some 800,000 puppet troops, and accounted for nearly half the total casualties inflicted on the Japanese by all Chinese armed forces. Unable to equip their troops for large-scale offensive operations, they fought thousands of small battles and skirmishes, disrupted Japanese communication lines, and recaptured large areas behind and between Japanese garrison points and railway zones.

According to the latest available reports issued by Yenan, the record of the Eighth Route, New Fourth, and other anti-Japanese guerrilla forces during the past eight years (up to March 1945) is indicated by the following figures:

Enemy Losses	Eighth Route (North China)	New Fourth (Central China)	Kwangtung (South China)	Total
Japanese casualties	384,960	124,345	2,129	511,434
Puppet casualties	296,966	158,405	2,854	458,225
Japanese captured	2,886	942	52	3,880
Puppets captured	235,754	44,978	1,764	282,496
Japanese deserters	166	38	18	222
Puppet deserters	69,602	34,300	718	104,620
Total Enemy Losses				1,360,877
Eighth Route, New Fourth, and Kwangtung Army Losses				
Wounded	211,381	73,886	402	285,669
Killed	112,245	47,993	829	161,067
Total				446,736

The guerrilla forces were, of course, severely restricted in their tactics by the shortage of ammunition and lack of offensive weapons. This point was emphasized by General Chu Teh, commander of the Eighth Route Army, in an interview with Brooks Atkinson of the *New York Times* in September 1944, during which he pointed out that "if we could get guerrilla arms, like rifles with telescope sights, and sufficient small-arms ammunition, we could develop guerrilla warfare on a much larger scale. Since we have had long experience in the use of captured Japanese equipment, we could make effective use of the Japanese equipment that Americans have already captured in other areas. If we were sufficiently armed with some light artillery and anti-tank guns, we could destroy the whole Japanese communications system." The Chungking Government, however, refused to allow Japanese equipment captured by American forces to be shipped to the Communist areas.

The effectiveness of Chinese Communist control over the areas which they had recaptured from the Japanese was vouched for by many foreign observers, particularly American airmen who had been forced down in "occupied China" and rescued by the Communist-led guerrilla forces. The reports of these men fully substantiated the Communist claim to the control of virtually the entire countryside in those parts of North and Central China that were under nominal Japanese occupation. Some of the air crews traveled as far as 1,000 miles by daylight in Communist-held territory from points as far distant as the seacoast just south of the Manchurian border. Others were rescued from points close to Shanghai, Hankow, Canton, Nanking, and Taiyuan — all important Japanese bases. These men reported that in traveling through "occupied" China under the escort of the guerrillas, no attempt was made to conceal them except when crossing railways or in the immediate vicinity of Japanese garrison points, and that everywhere the people turned out to welcome them. They also testified to the extent of Communist control by stating that in some cases it took more than a week of steady travel to cross areas completely controlled by the partisans in which there were no Japanese forces whatsoever.

All reports by both civilian and military observers that visited the Communist-led Border Regions and guerrilla areas during 1944 supported the conclusion that the Chinese Communists were sincere in their professed desire to see the establishment of a genuinely democratic form of government, and the carrying through of a thorough program of agrarian reform, and that they were working hard to put this program into practice. These observers were also agreed that the condition of the people in the guerrilla areas, whether judged from the standpoint of economic welfare or democratic rights, was far ahead of that of the average Chinese in those parts of China controlled by the Kuomintang, whose leaders continued to oppose agrarian reforms and ruthlessly suppressed civil liberties.[1]

The final question to be considered is the relations between these Communist-led areas and the Chungking Government. Before reviewing the course of Kuomintang-Communist negotiations from May 1944 to their breakdown in February 1945, however, it may be well to conclude this appraisal of the guerrilla areas with Michael Lindsay's estimate of the future relations between the guerrilla areas and Kuomintang China, since he has been in an excellent position to evaluate the real nature of the Communist program. He wrote:

There is nothing in the present developments in North China which would not fit into a democratic China after the war. The elaborate political organization which has aroused a great deal of suspicion is really a necessary condition for carrying on guerrilla warfare against a superior enemy. A policy of introducing communism in North China would be unworkable and would alienate popular support while a separatist movement would demand a complete reversal in political education and would almost certainly split the existing organization. . . . The risk of future civil strife depends very largely on the form of postwar Chinese Government. . . . A Central Government, which tried to abolish democratic institutions and restore the former exploitation of the peasants by powerful landlords and moneylenders working with corrupt officials, would certainly meet with the universal opposition of the North China population and might well cause a civil war. On the other hand, a democratic government which confirmed and extended the present reforms would find no reason for conflict. It would find, in fact, that North China had changed from one of the most backward to one of the most progressive areas in China.

---

[1] The American correspondents that visited Yenan in the summer of 1944 obtained many long interviews with Chinese Communist leaders concerning the political and economic problems confronting China. Unfortunately, however, a great deal of this material was suppressed by Chinese Government censorship and never reached the American press. When the correspondents returned to Chungking, they complained that more than half their reports had been suppressed. Chiang Kai-shek's response to this protest was to issue an order, on October 15, 1944, prohibiting all foreign correspondents from visiting the Communist areas in the future.

KUOMINTANG-COMMUNIST NEGOTIATIONS

THE KEY political issue in China during 1944 was the question of Kuomintang-Communist relations and the possibility of an agreement between the two parties that would enable China to mobilize her full resources for the war against Japan. Negotiations were begun in May 1944, with the Communists urging immediate democratic reforms, the release of political prisoners, funds and equipment for the Communist-led armies, and recognition of the legal status of the Border Region Governments and guerrilla base areas. The Kuomintang representatives countered by agreeing to arm and equip ten divisions of the Communist forces, provided that these were concentrated in a specified area and made subject to direct orders from Chungking. They also demanded that the Shensi-Ninghsia-Kansu Border Region be placed under the direct administration of the Executive Yuan, and that all other guerrilla base areas behind the Japanese lines be dissolved. Finally, they insisted that the Kuomintang must remain in sole control of the government for the duration of the war, and that the immediate convening of a constitutional assembly and the establishment of democratic government was impossible so long as a large part of China remained in Japanese hands.

Thus, the negotiations remained deadlocked, but by September 1944, when the People's Political Council met in Chungking, the many-sided pressure for some relaxation of the stringent party dictatorship of the Kuomintang had apparently begun to have some effect. Brooks Atkinson, *New York Times* correspondent in Chungking, reported that "never before have delegates to the People's Political Council spoken so sharply to Government Ministers about corruption, inefficiency, repression, the shocking treatment of Chinese soldiers and other evils of the moribund regime, and never before have Chinese newspapers reported speeches and criticisms so fully." On September 15th, the problem of Kuomintang-Communist relations was openly discussed under Government auspices for the first time when Lin Tsu-han, Communist representative, gave the People's Political Council an account of his negotiations with the Government representatives, and General Chang Chih-chung followed with an account of the negotiations from the Government's point of view. Mr. Lin stated that the fundamental points at issue between the Communists and the Central Government were (1) the immediate establishment of democracy, and (2) the size and disposition of the Communist armed forces. He contended that to fight a total war the people must be mobilized and that this could not be done until the Central Government took the first steps toward democracy by granting freedom of speech, legalizing other political parties, and establishing local self-government. With regard to the second point, Mr. Lin pointed out that the Government was willing to authorize and equip only ten divisions, or about 150,000 troops, whereas the Communist-led forces then numbered some 570,000 plus more than two million guerrilla fighters. The Communists believed that any such drastic reduction in numbers would open up large areas to the Japanese. A similar objection applied to the Government's demand that all guerrilla governments behind the Japanese lines be dissolved, since this would obviously play into the hands of the Japanese and eliminate an extremely important source of support for any future Allied offensive against Japan. In concluding his address, Mr. Lin appealed for the immediate formation of a coalition government in order that China's total resources might be concentrated against Japan. Since this demand was one that had been consistently voiced by the Chinese Democratic League and other liberal leaders, Mr. Lin's appeal evoked a widespread favorable response, indicated by the fact that on the day after this session of the People's Political Council, China's leading independent newspaper, *Ta Kung Pao,* stated: "The Chinese people want to be the inhabitants of a democratic country with a constitutional government. As such we demand national unity, political freedom, and economic equality."

In a highly illuminating despatch commenting on this statement and on the Chinese political situation in general, Brooks Atkinson reported on September 16, 1944 that "six weeks ago this crisp statement on China's sorest needs could not have been published. . . . The causes of the recent change in the tone of political life are matters of speculation . . . but it is obvious that China's military situation is increasingly dangerous. Whatever the rights and wrongs of the Central Government-Communist feud may be, the resulting fact is that China is unable to bring her full military strength against Japan. The Communist armies have neither the equipment nor freedom to fight the Japanese efficiently. Between 200,000 and 300,000 Central Govern-

ment troops who might conceivably have prevented or mini-
mized the Honan disaster have wasted many manpower years
in blockading the Communists." Atkinson also noted that "many
political and intellectual groups are clamoring for recognition
or for a chance to participate in the Government. . . . Other
things that vex China are an alarming decrease in industrial
production and motor transport, inefficiency in the military organization, continuing inflation, the widespread corruption in
taxation, the manner of conscription of army recruits, and the
too-large number of public servants."

Pointing out that China's one-party government is in the final
analysis a "one-man government," Atkinson concluded that "no
radical improvement can be expected in China until the Generalissimo changes the government and eliminates musty ideas
that have stagnated the regime. . . . It is a serious reflection on
the Kuomintang that China has not developed new public servants for many years; the Old Guards are not only older but also
more guarded as time goes on." He acknowledged that quite
apart from the Government's willingness or unwillingness to
establish a constitutional, democratic regime, there were many
practical reasons why so radical a change would be difficult
during wartime when two-thirds of China was occupied by the
Japanese, but "the Generalissimo could form a coalition government now without altering organic law. He has authority enough
and personal prestige enough to take into the government representatives of the unrecognized parties, popular cultural societies,
and independent liberals. . . . Excepting the current change
in the tone of the censorship there is no concrete evidence that
any decisive change is going to be made in the administration
of this tired, impoverished, loosely knit, sprawling State. But it is
exciting to speculate on things that might reasonably happen."

Other expert foreign observers of conditions in China shared
Mr. Atkinson's opinion that the situation in China was bad but
not hopeless, and that the one man with the power to make possible a definite change for the better was Generalissimo Chiang
Kai-shek. There was also an increasing feeling among correspondents and other American observers in China that American
influence could and should play an important role in influencing
the policy of the Chinese Government, and that liberal Chinese
were looking increasingly to the United States for encouragement and support. A. T. Steele, veteran Far Eastern correspond-

ent of the *Chicago Daily News,* reported after a six weeks' visit
to China in the summer of 1944 that "thousands of Chinese hope
and believe that American influence will have a profound effect
in persuading China's rulers to follow the paths of democracy
instead of fascism, to avert civil war and to modernize China's
army. Some suggestions by Chinese are: reorganize the government to eliminate unessential services; take drastic measures
to improve Sino-Soviet relations and solve the Communist-Kuo-
mintang issue; remove inefficient and corrupt officials; hasten
preparations for the democratization of China; and intensify
efforts to enlist the people as a whole in the war. . . . The one
man with sufficient power to make any or all of these possibilities
come true is Chiang Kai-shek."

An incident illustrating the hope and faith of certain sections
of Chinese in American support was the fact that during the
visit of Henry Wallace to Chungking in June 1944, a group of
Chinese university students risked the severe penalties of open
criticism of the regime and sent Mr. Wallace a personal letter as
well as an open letter addressed to the American people. In this
second letter, the students sharply condemned the "fascist" and
distatorial policy of the Government, the persecution of all liberal and left-wing elements, and the system of repression and
espionage directed against the students and faculties of China's
universities. They affirmed their belief that the responsibility
for combating these trends and building a democratic state in
China rested primarily with the Chinese people themselves; but
they contended that other countries, and particularly the United
States, also had a duty to fulfill in this connection, and they appealed to the American people and their Government to take a
strong stand in support of a democratic government for China,
and to give all possible aid to those groups that were wholeheartedly fighting the Japanese.

The Communist position during these negotiations was best
summed up in a speech by Chou En-lai in Yenan on October 10,
1944.[1] Chou emphasized that the policies pursued by the Kuomintang — the failure to mobilize popular participation in the
war, the refusal to institute democratic government, the repression of civil liberties, the policy of passive and partial resistance
and of depending solely on foreign aid — had resulted in an

---

[1] The full text of this speech was published in *Amerasia,* March 23, 1945.

unprecedented military, political, and economic crisis in Kuomintang China. He then stated that, to meet this crisis, the Chinese Communists proposed "the immediate convocation of an Emergency Conference on National Affairs by the National Government, to be attended by the representatives of all groups for the abolition of one-party dictatorship, the establishment of a coalition government, and the reversal of past erroneous policies." According to the Communist plan outlined by Chou, the representatives to this Emergency Conference should be elected by all anti-Japanese parties (Kuomintang, Communist, and others); all anti-Japanese armies; all local governments, including those in the liberated areas behind the Japanese lines; and all people's organizations of a nation-wide character. This Conference should adopt an administrative program on the basis of Dr. Sun Yat-sen's Three People's Principles, and on the basis of this program a coalition government of all parties and groups should be established to take the place of the present one-party dictatorship. This Coalition Government should have the power to reorganize the Supreme Command, and to invite representatives from the main sections of the armed forces to form a United Supreme Command. Furthermore, "the Coalition Government shall, after its formation, immediately proceed to prepare for the convocation of a People's Congress based on genuine universal franchise within the shortest possible time, thereby guaranteeing the realization of constitutional government."

After describing in detail the military achievements of the Communist-led guerrilla forces, Chou En-lai concluded: "We believe that the only correct program to overcome the present crisis and to answer China's immediate needs consists of a reorganization of the Government and the High Command, the establishment of a Coalition Government of all parties and a United High Command, and the abolition of all defeatist military commands and fascist political decrees. We insist upon the National Government's recognition of all the anti-Japanese troops and all democratically elected governments behind the enemy lines. We oppose unconditionally the elimination of hundreds of thousands of these forces and of the popular governments."

GENERAL STILWELL'S RECALL

AMERICAN ATTENTION was focussed on the increasingly serious political impasse in China, and its relation to the Allied war ef-

fort, by the recall of General Joseph W. Stilwell from the China-
India-Burma theater and the resignation of the American Ambassador to Chungking, Clarence E. Gauss, at the end of October 1944. In the flood of newspaper and radio comments evoked
by Stilwell's recall, the American public in general were for the
first time made aware of the darker side of the picture so far as
China's political and military situation was concerned. Unfortunately, much of the publicity accorded to this event made it
appear as if some sudden and disastrous crisis had arisen in
China, or as if the crisis had been provoked by tactless and un-
skillful diplomacy on the part of the American Government
which was accused by some of having attempted to dictate to
the Chungking Government.

Actually, the situation that led up to General Stilwell's recall
was no new development, but was the result of the steady process of military and political deterioration already described.
When General Stilwell arrived in China in the spring of 1942
to take up his duties as chief of staff to Chiang Kai-shek and
commander of American forces in the China-India-Burma theater, he had previously spent more than ten years in China and
had taken the trouble to learn no fewer than eleven Chinese dia-
lects. He knew and admired the Chinese people, and was convinced that the Chinese armies could and should play a major
role in the defeat of Japan on the Asiatic continent. In his view,
this strategy would not only be the quickest and most effective
method of achieving Allied victory against Japan, but would
also serve to unite and strengthen China.

Starting from the initial premise that the Chinese armies must
be aided to play a more active part in the campaign against
Japan, Stilwell's main objectives were (1) to see that the best
possible use was made of the limited resources that China possessed, and (2) to get more supplies to China by reopening a
land route through Burma. From the outset, however, he encountered serious obstacles — the principal one being the fact
that the Chungking Government was not eager to risk its armies
in battle against Japan because it wished to save them to ensure
its political power after the war. For this reason, Chinese officials were far more inclined to favor the strategy advocated by
General Chennault, commander of the United States 14th Air
Force, who believed that the main effort against Japan in China
should be made by air power, and therefore that the greater

part of the limited supplies reaching China should be used to strengthen his air force. All he asked of the Chinese was food for his men and airfields, and he did not concern himself specifically with what use the Chinese made of their land forces. This strategy of relying chiefly on American air power to do the job of defeating Japan in China was entirely agreeable to the Chinese Government. Better to retain control of a devitalized and weak China, protected by a ring of American bombers, than to risk losing control of a strong and united nation exerting all its energy to mobilize the people for victory in the war. Such were the mental processes of a landed bureaucracy fearful of losing power and distrustful of its own people.

General Stilwell, on the other hand, believed that it was of primary importance to improve China's combat efficiency, reopen a supply road through Burma, and get China back into the war as an effective fighting force. He viewed this as a purely military problem, but it immediately compelled him to cope with delicate and complicated political issues. In his effort to develop the Chinese armies into an efficient and unified fighting force, for example, he was confronted with the fact that supplies intended for the fighting fronts were being diverted to the troops blockading the guerrilla areas or were being hoarded for future use. The blockade itself not only prevented American forces from making use of the strategic areas controlled by the guerrillas, but also served to immobilize large numbers of Chinese troops that might otherwise have been fighting Japan.

Stilwell was also seriously handicapped in his efforts to reopen a supply route through Burma by the failure of the British to undertake a large-scale amphibious campaign or to give full support to his proposed land offensive. The British failure to undertake amphibious operations against Burma in 1944 was generally attributed to the lack of adequate shipping and naval strength, but it was known that the British authorities were not overenthusiastic about Stilwell's idea for a land offensive using Chinese troops. The reason for this was suggested in a report by John Davies, Jr., State Department representative on Stilwell's staff, who made a detailed investigation of the situation for his chief and whose report was commented on in Drew Pearson's column of September 9, 1944. According to Pearson: "Davies hinted that the British did not want to go back to Burma until they could take it back by themselves. To have Burma retaken through the initiative of the United States and China, he indicated, would not help British politics and prestige." British strategy was reported to call for the defeat of Japan by naval and air power first, and then the recovery of Japanese-occupied territory without disturbing the political situation in those areas more than was absolutely necessary. There was also evidence that some British official circles believed that Chinese participation in the reconquest of Burma would lead to Chinese demands for territorial compensation in Northern Burma — an area that for many years was a matter of dispute between Britain and China. One report states that at the second Quebec Conference, Prime Minister Churchill requested Stilwell's removal, but that General Marshall flatly refused. According to this same report, the British desire for Stilwell's recall was a strong contributory factor in his ultimate removal, although the main cause was unquestionably the situation in China.

The Burma campaign was also the occasion for serious differences between General Stilwell and Chiang Kai-shek. The two Chinese divisions in Burma were nominally under Stilwell's command but, according to one observer, their operations were frequently slowed down because "they were waiting for orders from Chiang." The most serious crisis arose, however, when Stilwell began his twin offensives against Myitkyina and Mogaung and requested support from Chiang's divisions on the Chinese side of the Salween River. Chiang was reluctant to allow these divisions to cross into Burma and delayed sending these reinforcements for more than two months despite urgent and heated pleas from Stilwell. The ostensible reason for Chiang's reluctance was that he did not wish to weaken the Central China front, but it was also reported that he did not want Chinese troops to fight for Burma unless he was given some assurance of a *quid pro quo* from the British.

It was with regard to the internal situation in China, however, that both General Stilwell and Ambassador Gauss encountered the most serious difficulties in their efforts to encourage effective Chinese participation in the war. Stilwell recognized that, unless the internal disunity that was hamstringing China's war effort could be replaced by a genuinely united effort on the part of all Chinese armed forces, the war against Japan might be greatly prolonged. He therefore urged on Chiang Kai-shek the importance of uniting the regular Government troops and the Chinese guerrillas into a single striking force against Japan. To this end, he wanted the blockade against the guerrilla areas lifted and American military supplies and liaison officers despatched to the guerrilla areas. In the diplomatic field, Ambassador Gauss supported Stilwell in urging the need for political unity and for measures to counteract the growing opposition to the Chungking regime that was developing throughout Free China as a result of the Government's dictatorial and repressive policies and the openly corrupt character of much of its administration. Mr. Gauss suggested to the Generalissimo that one means of allaying this popular discontent and providing the basis for a united war effort would be the establishment of a representative "war council" in which all important political groups would share responsibility for the conduct of the war. This proposal, which seemed like a workable compromise between the Chinese Communists' demand for a genuinely representative coalition government and the Kuomintang's insistence on the maintenance of one-party rule, was at first considered favorably by Chiang Kai-shek, but was later rejected.

These negotiations between Stilwell and Gauss on the one hand and the Generalissimo on the other continued for almost two years, and a good deal of personal bitterness was inevitably engendered in the process, as the requests of the two American officials were repeatedly refused or ignored and Chiang Kai-shek came to feel that the American Government was attempting to dictate Chinese policy. At this juncture, early in July 1944, President Roosevelt is reported to have urged the Generalissimo to permit an American general to take command of all the Chinese armies in order to avoid serious consequences from the growing Japanese offensive. General Stilwell was recommended for the post, and Stilwell was shortly thereafter made a four-star general. But apparently Chiang Kai-shek insisted that political issues must be settled first. In an effort to aid in settling these issues, Major-General Patrick Hurley was sent to China in September as the President's personal representative. It is believed that Hurley's appointment was recommended by Harry Hopkins. Although at first Hurley was friendly with Stilwell, he soon accepted the Generalissimo's point of view, and in the name of "Chinese-American unity" suggested Stilwell's recall. General Stilwell was then recalled and Ambassador Gauss's resignation was accepted. Lieut. Gen. Albert C. Wedemeyer became commander of American forces in the China theater, and General Hurley was appointed American Ambassador to Chungking.

Shortly after General Stilwell's recall, a number of changes were made in the Chungking Government, including the removal of General Ho Ying-chin, H. H. Kung, and Chen Li-fu from their positions as War Minister, Finance Minister, and Minister of Education, respectively. Since these three men ranked among the leaders of the most reactionary wing of the Kuomintang, their removal was hailed in some quarters as marking a decided change for the better in China's political situation, and as evidence that Chiang Kai-shek had determined to liberalize his regime. Actually, however, these Cabinet shifts involved no real change in the political structure of Kuomintang China. Dr. Kung retained his post as Vice-President of the Executive Yuan, and his successor as Finance Minister, O. K. Yui, is known not only as a "Chiang man" but also as a "Kung man." Chen Li-fu was transferred to the head of the organization board of the Kuomintang Party, an influential post where he could continue to exercise supervision over all Party personnel. Furthermore, the appointment of Dr. Chu Chia-hua to succeed him as Minister of Education did nothing to reassure those who had disliked Chen Li-fu's Gestapo-like methods of political surveillance and "thought control." Chu Chia-hua was educated in Germany and is an admirer of the Nazi form of government and an advocate of a strict one-party state for China. Though he is not a member of the "CC" clique, his influence is hardly less reactionary.

Furthermore, though General Ho Ying-chin was replaced as War Minister by General Chen Cheng, he retained his position as Chief of Staff, a far more influential post in China than that of War Minister. Ho Ying-chin is an arch-reactionary with whom anti-Communism is an obsession. To him as much as to any single Chinese leader may be attributed the responsibility for the "anti-Communism first and resistance second" policy pursued by many of the Central Government's armies, and the insistence on preserving Chungking's forces for a final show-down with the Chinese guerrillas. It was not surprising, therefore, that General Ho should have been decidedly unreceptive to American appeals for a unification of China's fighting forces against Japan.

General Chen Cheng, on the other hand, although he commanded many anti-Communist campaigns during the middle thirties, has a well-deserved reputation not only as one of China's ablest field commanders but as an extremely popular and, since 1937, a relatively liberal leader. Before his appointment, he was the leader of a group that demanded a thoroughgoing reorganization of the Chinese Army; the reduction of the number of divisions from almost 350 to 250, with these divisions brought to full strength; stripping all military commanders of concurrent political posts; a radical reorganization of the feeding and medical care of the troops, etc. It appeared extremely doubtful, however, whether he would be able to reorganize the army command in view of the fact that Ho Ying-chin had made a practice of appointing divisional and army commanders who were loyal to him personally. The fact that Ho was a graduate of and at one time Chief Instructor at the Whampoa Military Academy gives him great influence with the large group of army officers who were "Whampoa cadets," whereas Chen Cheng, though he was once an instructor at Whampoa, is a graduate of the Paoting Military Academy and therefore does not have the same following among the "Whampoa cadet" clique.

These Cabinet shifts were followed by the appointment of T. V. Soong as Acting President of the Executive Yuan, making him the second ranking official in the Chinese Government. This appointment was widely hailed as an encouraging move, since Soong enjoyed a reputation for liberalism and was reported to be far more "moderate" in his view regarding the possibility of a compromise with the Chinese Communists. In reality, however, there was little basis for this satisfaction. In the first place, Soong had been given no real official status; he was merely filling in for Chiang Kai-shek during the military crisis in order that the Generalissimo might give his full attention to military matters. Furthermore, Soong had no real following in China, and, though frequently giving verbal support to liberal groups, had never taken any positive action to back up his words. In fact, on numerous critical occasions in the past he had shown himself both hesitant and indecisive. His appointment, therefore, did nothing to alter the opinion of the many foreign observers who regarded the Cabinet changes as being largely a gesture made in the hope of allaying criticism both within China and abroad.

That this view was also shared by prominent Chinese liberals was demonstrated in a speech delivered on November 24, 1944, by Dr. Chang Hsi-jo, head of the Political Science Department of the Southwest Union University at Kunming, before more than a thousand students. Dr. Chang is prominent in liberal circles in Kunming, was an early follower of Dr. Sun Yat-sen, and served for a time in a high position in the Ministry of Education. He had previously attracted widespread attention by his lectures on "Modern China and Constitutionalism" in which he had made the "revolutionary" statement that a system of law without democracy is an empty shell.

Dr. Chang's November 24th speech, commenting on the recent Cabinet changes, was notable for its frank criticism of Chiang Kai-shek, its major conclusion being that the only solution for China's current crisis lay in a sharp curtailment of the Generalissimo's powers. Though admitting that the Cabinet changes showed Chiang's awareness of popular dissatisfaction with the Government, Dr. Chang maintained that the changes themselves were totally inadequate to accomplish any basic revision of policy. Furthermore, he declared that the responsibility for China's demoralization did not rest with the reactionary leaders of the Kuomintang, but with the Generalissimo himself. Giving full credit to Chiang Kai-shek for his contributions to Chinese unity, Dr. Chang accused him of subordinating China's welfare to his personal ambitions and to building up his personal political machine — the Kuomintang; of seeking to deify himself before the Chinese people; and of attempting to regiment thought and stifle criticism.

Dr. Chang pointed out that Chiang Kai-shek had taken upon himself the right to dictate every phase of Chinese life, and had surrounded himself with second-rate officials who were content to be "yes men." Some of the major abuses that have resulted from this monopoly of power were listed by Dr. Chang as follows: the failure to introduce constructive agrarian reforms; corruption and incompetence in the army; and the system of "thought control" and restrictions on freedom of speech. Asking whether the perpetrator of such policies could be rightly considered superhuman, Dr. Chang boldly advised his students to think of Chiang Kai-shek simply as a human being who should not be regarded as above criticism. He also emphasized that Chinese liberals should not look to the Kuomintang for voluntary reforms, because the party is simply Chiang Kai-shek's personal retinue and entirely subject to his commands. In Dr. Chang's view, the Government's policy during the past few years clearly indicated that Chiang Kai-shek and the Kuomintang were increasingly preoccupied with only one thing — the maintenance in power of the Generalissimo and the party.

To meet this situation, Dr. Chang proposed that the National Government should call a meeting of representatives of all political and cultural groups in China, and that this convention should elect a council to exercise executive authority in the Government and curtail the power of the Generalissimo. The convention should also set up machinery for the establishment of a representative legislative body to which both Chiang Kai-shek and the executive council would be responsible. He admitted, however, that he was not very hopeful that any such step would be taken, unless Chiang Kai-shek himself should modify his determination to remain a dictator.

The general impression that the Cabinet changes did not indicate any change in Kuomintang policy was strengthened by the continued failure to reach any basis of political settlement with the Chinese Communists, despite the increasing gravity of the military situation. On November 10, 1944, at the request of Ambassador Hurley, Chou En-lai returned from Yenan to Chungking and presented the Communist proposals for the formation of a democratic coalition government to the Generalissimo. These proposals were rejected, and the Government made a counter offer to give the Communists some representation in the Government in return for placing the Communist armies under Chungking's control. This was not satisfactory to the Communists, who did not want representation in the existing regime but a genuine change in the character of the Chinese Government that would give representatives of all parties an actual voice in determining policy.

Following Chou En-lai's return to Yenan, Mao Tse-tung made a speech before the People's Political Council at Yenan on December 15, in which he declared that the Kuomintang-Communist negotiations had not "attained the least result" and appealed to the people of China to demand a national convention of all parties in order to secure "a democratic coalition government." Stating that "our sole task is to coöperate with the Allies in overthrowing the Japanese invaders," Mao declared that the task of the Chinese people in 1945 is to "rise as one man to demand that the Kuomintang authorities change their present policy so that a democratic coalition government can be set up. . . . As soon as there emerges a Chinese central coalition government which really puts democracy into practice and can mobilize and unify all anti-Japanese forces in China, the anti-Japanese war of resistance and the liberation of the Chinese people will come very quickly." Commenting on the American landings on Leyte and other military successes, Mao warned against allowing Japan to score further gains in a divided China. "The Japanese invaders will certainly resort to stratagems to induce capitulation of the Chinese Government through China's capitulators," he declared. Claiming that the Yenan regime alone had carried out the principles advocated by Dr. Sun Yat-sen in the revolution of 1911 for the creation of a "new democracy," Mao added that the Communists had been able to unite people of all walks of life into a "heroic army which had shattered all enemy offensives," and was now about to launch a counteroffensive "to recover vast lost territory."

From the American standpoint, the continued failure of the two major parties in China to agree on some basis of united action presented a serious problem. It was the sincere hope of all American friends of China that ways and means could be found to bring the central armies of China to sufficient fighting strength to take a leading role in the land offensive that both Admiral Nimitz and General Wedemeyer had declared to be essential for Japan's defeat. The fact remained, however, that as a result of Japan's successful drive to cut China in two, the Chungking Government had lost control over the coastal areas of China. In those areas, as well as in North China, the only Chinese forces were the guerrillas and the partisan units operating under Communist leadership. Thus, from the view of immediate military needs, it was obviously in America's interests to have established close relations with the Communist-led armies — a politically difficult task so long as the rift between Chungking and the Communists continued. In addition to this immediate military need for an agreement between the Kuomintang and the Communists, there was the more long-term desire to see China become a strong and united nation in the postwar world. These two aims were, of course, closely related, since it was obvious that the effectiveness of Chinese participation in the war would have a very direct bearing on China's future unity and strength.

American observers in China — both official and unofficial — had long argued that the United States should adopt a more positive policy in support of American aims and interests with regard to China. Specifically, they urged that the United States should not only give military and technical assistance to the Chinese guerrillas, but should also make clear its intention of supporting all groups and individuals in Kuomintang China having the courage to demand a more democratic political system and a program of agrarian reform. They argued that it would certainly be possible for the American Government to indicate to Chungking that American postwar economic aid to China would not be extended to strengthen the power of the Chinese landed gentry, or to build up monopolistic state enterprises under the control of a narrow bureaucratic regime; that America is interested in the development of a free and progressive economy in China under a democratically constituted government, because only with such an economy can the United States enjoy mutually beneficial relations, and only such a government can ensure political unity and stability in China. By using its influence to encourage political and economic reforms in China, the American Government could aid China to become, in fact as well as in theory, the leading power in Eastern Asia as well as a strong and friendly ally and a new economic frontier of inestimable value to the future prosperity of the United States.

During the period when the United States was represented in China by General Stilwell and Ambassador Gauss, American policy was directed along these general lines. Both Stilwell and Gauss believed that China could and should play a major role in the final offensive against Japan, and were apparently hopeful that Chiang Kai-shek could be persuaded to relax his strict dictatorship and make at least some concessions to the growing demand for a representative coalition government. American pressure was also exerted for a relaxation of the blockade against the Communists, with the result that in the summer of 1944 an American military mission headed by Col. David D. Barrett was at last permitted to visit the guerrilla areas in North China. The missions of Henry Wallace and Donald Nelson to Chungking were also indicative of the American Government's efforts to improve the political and economic situation in China by urging much-needed reforms in the interests of the Allied war effort.

Throughout this period, there was no sign that the growing opposition to the Chungking regime was directed against Chiang Kai-shek personally. Even the Communists and others who were sharply critical of the practices of the ruling clique continued to

acknowledge him as the undisputed leader of China; their demand being that he cease to act as the dictatorial head of a single party and place himself at the head of a coalition government
representing all parties and groups. It may strike some readers
as strange that, in view of Chiang's economic and social views
and his long record as the leader of an admittedly autocratic and
repressive government, he should still have been regarded as *the*
man under whose leadership a united China could emerge. It
must be borne in mind, however, that no man can remain for
long at the head of a government unless he is by and large the
spokesman for the dominant social forces in his country. In the
case of China, these dominant forces were the landed gentry and
the bureaucracy, and Chiang was their chosen and successful
representative. But it was believed that Chiang's political agility
and his strong desire to remain the leader of China would enable
him to adapt himself to the fact that the democratic forces were
beginning to supplant the feudal-minded landlord class as the
dominant element in Chinese society.

Certainly, a recognition by Chiang Kai-shek that he could
hope to remain the head of a strong and influential nation only
by adjusting himself to the demand for an abolition of one-party
dictatorship would have gone a long way toward solving both
the political crisis in China and the problem of effective military
coöperation between American and Chinese fighting forces. Unfortunately, however, developments in China during the first
seven months of 1945 indicated not only that Chiang Kai-shek was
unwilling to modify his intransigent attitude, but that he had
been strengthened in his power to oppose the demands of the
prodemocratic forces by the new policy adopted by the representatives of the American Government — Ambassador Hurley
and General Wedemeyer. As a result, the political impasse in
China became even more serious, and the criticism of the opposition forces was directed for the first time against Chiang personally.

Before turning to an examination of these developments, however, some reference must be made to the Chungking Government's resentment at American criticism of Chinese conditions.
There is no doubt that American public opinion became increasingly critical of China during 1944. The emergence of a strong,
progressive, and prosperous China is of such vital importance to
the future peace and prosperity of Asia and the world that it was

almost inevitable that those Americans who spoke or wrote about the Far East should have expressed their alarm when they saw the trend of official Chinese policy apparently set for political repression and the retention of a backward and impoverished agrarian system.

It is also understandable that many Chinese officials should have resented such criticism as an unwarranted interference in China's affairs, in view of the fact that for one hundred years China had been exploited by the stronger industrial powers of the West. But these same officials might have recognized that the war had wrought an important change in China's international position. The Western Powers had renounced all extraterritorial rights and cancelled the unequal treaties. The Cairo Conference, as far as it could go politically, had assured China of a prominent place in the postwar world and accepted her as one of the four Great Powers. Certainly these were momentous changes and, if Chinese officials had accepted them as such, they might have realized more clearly that so long as the actions of one nation have the power to affect vitally the lives of the people of another, active interest in the internal affairs of that nation should not be construed as "unwarranted interference."

During the years prior to 1940, for example, when the American Government was pursuing an appeasement policy toward Japan, the Chinese Government through numerous officials in the United States took an active part in the attempt to influence official and public opinion in favor of a different policy. There was no resentment on the part of the American people or even in official circles at this direct "interference" in our "internal" affairs. On the contrary, millions of Americans supported these Chinese propagandists and helped them politically and financially. Subsequently, the Chinese authorities on frequent occasions took an active and direct interest in American politics, as, for example, during the visit of Madame Chiang Kai-shek to this country in 1943. Even today the Chinese Government maintains in the United States perhaps the largest (though by no means the most effective) propaganda machine of any foreign power.

IMPASSE IN CHINA

THE STORY of developments in China during the first six months of 1945 is a complicated one in which three main threads are closely interwoven: the negotiations between the Kuomintang and the Communists, which were resumed on January 25 and broke down completely on February 15; the measures taken by Chiang Kai-shek to counter the growing demand from all sides for the immediate establishment of a coalition government; and the effects of American policy and actions on the Chinese situation.

It soon became clear that the recall of General Stilwell and Ambassador Gauss marked the beginning of a new American policy in China. In the first place, General Wedemeyer, though an able military leader, lacked the intimate knowledge of Chinese conditions that his predecessor had possessed and was inclined to take an extremely conservative stand on political issues, and political conservatism when applied to China easily leads to the support of ultrareactionary elements. But it was Ambassador Hurley's complete lack of knowledge of China and her problems that upset the hopeful policy instituted by General Stilwell and Ambassador Gauss, with the result that by August 1945 the internal situation in China had reached a new low, and American policy toward China had reached an impasse filled with dangerous potentialities.

When General Hurley first arrived in China to take up his duties as Ambassador, he seems to have believed that the Chinese Communists were justified in their demands for a basic change in the character of the Chungking regime to make it more representative of all political forces in the country. Early in November 1944, for example, he flew to Yenan for a series of conferences with Chinese Communist leaders concerning the possibility of unifying China's fighting forces against Japan, and of establishing the principles upon which a permanent unified China might be built. As a result of these discussions, a draft agreement, reported to have been written by Ambassador Hurley himself, was drawn up and unanimously approved by the Central Executive Committee of the Chinese Communist Party.

The terms of this draft agreement, which was signed by Mao Tse-tung on November 10, 1944, appear to have been largely a repetition of previous demands put forward by the Chinese Communists for the formation of a genuinely representative government for China. It specified that the Kuomintang and the Chinese Communists would coöperate in unifying all the fighting forces of China, and that the present government of China would be reorganized into a coalition government in which all the anti-

Japanese parties and groups would be represented. This new government would at once initiate a democratic program involving extensive reforms in the military, political, and economic spheres. At the same time, the National Military Council — the supreme military authority in China — would be reorganized so as to include representatives of all sections of the Chinese armed forces. The new coalition government would pledge itself to support the Three People's Principles of Dr. Sun Yat-sen, and would undertake to pursue policies designed to promote political democracy and economic progress, and to guarantee civil liberties, such as freedom of speech, freedom of the press, freedom of assembly and association, and freedom of religion. It would also undertake to release political prisoners and abolish the system of secret police and political concentration camps. The draft agreement also stipulated that all Chinese armed forces would receive equal treatment from the new government, and would pledge themselves to obey the orders of the government and of the reorganized National Military Council. Furthermore, any supplies or equipment received from foreign nations would be distributed equitably among the various units of the Chinese fighting forces. Finally, under the new coalition government, all anti-Japanese parties in China would be given legal status.

At the time, Ambassador Hurley must have felt that the terms proposed in this draft agreement were reasonable and, as he himself is reported to have remarked, in accord with "good old-fashioned Jeffersonian democratic principles." But when Chiang Kai-shek flatly rejected these proposals and offered instead to give the Communists one or two positions in the Chungking Government if they would place their armies under Chungking's control, Hurley was easily won over to the Chungking position. This could only have been due to his inability to comprehend the real issues at stake in the Chinese situation. These issues were fundamental ones — the issue of democracy versus dictatorship; of feudalism versus modern economic progress — on which no compromise was possible. There can be no such thing as halfway democracy, or partial civil liberties, or a strong, modernized economy based on a feudal and oppressive land system. But Ambassador Hurley failed to recognize this basic fact. As a result, he soon came to regard the Chinese Communists as unreasonable in their refusal to modify their demands. He could not understand, for example, why the Communist leaders were unwilling to reduce the number of their troops and place them under Chungking's control, and he accepted as justifiable Chiang Kai-shek's contention that no government could tolerate the existence of an independent army.

Certainly it would be both intolerable and inconceivable in the United States that a political party should have armed forces under its command. But China is not the United States. In the first place, the "National Army" is, in reality, a Kuomintang Party Army, so that, when the Communists were ordered to incorporate their forces into this Army while the one-party dictatorship was still in force, they were actually being asked to accept disbandment as a political party. It is well known that no party or group in China ever exercised political power unless it was supported by armed force. Intellectually speaking, the "Political Science Group" is probably the most influential in Kuomintang China; yet it has no real power because it has no military backing. It was not a question of theory but of fact. And so long as the fact was that political power in China depended on the control of armed force rather than popular support, it was hardly reasonable to expect that any political party would voluntarily sign its death warrant by surrendering its forces to the command of a rival party, particularly when it was convinced that the leaders of that party were merely seeking to perpetuate their power. Ambassador Hurley is reported to have described the Chinese Communist Army to a group in Washington by saying: "They're members of a political body. Let me put it this way — it's as if all of us Republicans were armed." But he might well have considered how he would feel about the Republican Party being armed if the United States Army were under the complete and exclusive control of the Democratic Party, and the Republicans' only chance of continued existence as a political entity lay in their control of armed power.

Ambassador Hurley, however, apparently succumbed to Chiang Kai-shek's argument that the chief threat in all Asia was the "Red Menace"; that it was both useless and dangerous to make any concessions to the Chinese Communist demands, and that American military and economic aid should be confined strictly to the Chungking regime. It was obvious, for example, that American landings on the coast of China would be greatly facilitated if close working relations had previously been established with the guerrilla forces in the coastal areas, and also that the guerrillas in North China could constitute a valuable adjunct to any land offensive against Japan if they were given a minimum of equipment and technical aid. Yet in February 1945, General Wedemeyer announced that he was not empowered to give military aid to the guerrilla fighters of the Chinese Communists, and that all American officers in China were required to sign a statement that they would not give assistance to individuals or organizations other than those affiliated with the Chungking Government. This latter order, of course, applied not only to the Communists but also to those provincial military leaders who had come out in support of the demands of the Chinese Democratic League.

Just previous to this announcement, the headquarters of the Chinese Central Armies was established at Kunming, and General Ho Ying-chin — whose removal from the post of War Minister had been regarded by many as an important concession to the critics of the Chungking regime — was appointed Commander-in-Chief of all Chinese ground forces, with Governor Lung Yun of Yunnan as Deputy Commander. The explanation given for these actions was that they were intended to prepare the way for a Chinese offensive in concert with the expected American landings in China. In other words, American military policy in China at the time seemed to be aimed solely at strengthening the Central Armies in the South with such equipment as could be brought in from India, while all efforts to utilize the Chinese forces in the North had apparently been abandoned.

One of the immediate effects of this Hurley-Wedemeyer policy was to convince Chiang Kai-shek that the United States Government was definitely committed to exclusive support of the Chungking regime, and would no longer exert pressure in favor of concessions to any opposition group. As a result, his attitude toward the Communists immediately stiffened, and he became increasingly intransigent in his refusal to make any concession to the demands for the establishment of a coalition government.

Kuomintang-Communist negotiations were resumed on January 24, 1945 when, once again at Ambassador Hurley's request, Chou En-lai returned to Chungking from Yenan, announcing that the purpose of his trip was to "propose to the National Government, the Kuomintang, and the Chinese Democratic League that a conference of all parties and groups should be held," preparatory to the convening of a "National Affairs Conference, so as formally to discuss the organization and steps leading to a coalition government." The proposals which Chou was instructed to submit to the Kuomintang as a basis for an agreement were summarized by him as follows: "Immediate abolition of the one-party dictatorship, establishment of a democratic coalition government and a united high command, recognition of the legal status of all anti-Japanese parties and groups, repeal of all laws suppressing popular freedom, abolition of the secret political police, release of political prisoners, cessation of the blockade of the Border Region, and recognition of the legal status of anti-Japanese troops and popularly elected governments in the liberated areas."

Two points are worth noting about these statements. In the first place, they indicated that the Communists were adhering closely to the demands presented to the Kuomintang on many previous occasions, and had not "upped" these demands as Chiang Kai-shek subsequently accused them of having done. The second point of significance was Chou's inclusion of the Democratic League among those groups to which he intended to propose the convening of an all-parties conference. Though the League had for some time been seeking to establish a working agreement with the Communists, this was the first indication that the Communists considered the League a major political force.

During the negotiations that followed, Chiang Kai-shek flatly refused to agree to the demand for the immediate formation of a coalition government, insisting that the Kuomintang must retain complete political power until a constitutional assembly could meet and draft a constitution. As "concessions" to the Communist demand for immediate democratic reforms, the Chungking Government offered to include a Communist representative on the National Military Council, and to set up a Wartime Political Council in the Executive Yuan on which the Communists and other parties could have representation. It further proposed that a three-man commission, composed of one Government officer, one Communist, and one American officer, be established to arrange for the incorporation of the Communist forces into the National Army. The Government also suggested that "to allay the Communists' fears" an American general might be placed in command of the Communist forces under the supreme command of Chiang Kai-shek.

The Communists rejected these "concessions" as in no way meeting their demand for the end of one-party dictatorship and the establishment of a genuine coalition government and united military command. They pointed out that neither the National Military Council nor the proposed Wartime Political Council had any real power to determine policy, and they were adamantly opposed to placing their armed forces under Kuomintang control, and to sacrificing the popular governments that had been established at such cost in the liberated areas. Furthermore, the failure of the Chungking regime to institute even the beginnings of democratic reforms confirmed their belief that the promise to introduce constitutional government, contained in Chiang Kai-shek's New Year's Message of January 1, 1945, was only a maneuver to obscure the real determination of the ruling clique to preserve its monopoly of power. The negotiations therefore broke down completely in the middle of February, and Chou En-lai returned to Yenan.

During this period Chiang Kai-shek, encouraged by the assurance of American support, was also maneuvering to undermine and weaken the opposition forces in Kuomintang China, particularly the Democratic League. In his New Year's Message he had attempted to pacify them with the promise that a constitutional assembly would be convened within the year, if war conditions permitted. But on January 15, the League issued a statement which showed that its members were far from satisfied with this pledge.[1] This statement pointed out that to convene a constitutional assembly, most of whose members had been appointed by the Kuomintang before the war, was no guarantee that a constitution deserving full popular support would be drafted, or that national unity would be achieved. The statement then repeated the major points in the League's program, i.e., the immediate termination of the one-party dictatorship and the establishment of a coalition government; the calling of a conference of all political parties and groups to set up a wartime national government and prepare for the calling of a genuine people's congress and the drafting of a constitution; a guarantee of civil liberties; the granting of legal status to all political parties and the release of political prisoners; abolition of secret police and concentration

---

[1] This statement was the first League document to be signed by the National Salvation Association, the largest liberal mass organization in Kuomintang China and headed by Shen Chun-ju.

camps; equal treatment as to arms, supplies, and training for all armed forces in the country, and a unified military command; and the abolition of "thought control" and a guarantee of academic freedom.

Chiang Kai-shek next endeavored to weaken the League by giving some of its principal military supporters important positions in the Chungking bureaucracy. Governor Lung Yun of Yunnan, as noted above, was made Deputy Commander-in-Chief of all Chinese ground forces. General Pan Wen-hua, a leading Szechwan war lord, was appointed Governor of Szechwan, and General Yang Sen, another Szechwan militarist who supported the League, was made Governor of Kweichow. There was no indication, however, that these maneuvers succeeded in weakening the League's opposition to the Chungking regime. General Pan Wen-hua refused to accept the governorship of Szechwan, and editorials in the Chengtu and Kunming papers continued to be extremely critical of the Government's policies, and in January the leaders of the League were reported engaged in drawing up a final platform for a coalition government that would take over the administration of national affairs. Marshal Li Chi-shen, the most prominent military leader in the League, who was living in Chaoping in Yunnan early in 1945, was said to have received assurances of coöperation from Generals Pan Wen-hua, Hsueh Yueh, Liu Wen-hui, Yu Han-mou, Lung Yun, Teng Hsi-hou, and Feng Yu-hsiang.

This did not mean, of course, that these provincial military leaders were ready to engage in armed conflict with the Chungking forces. For the most part, they supported the League's platform because of their resentment at the Central Government's attempt to control the resources and man power of their respective provinces, and to exclude them from a voice in Government decisions. Some of them, however, were sincerely convinced that the Chungking regime was incapable of conducting the war efficiently, even going so far as to criticize Chiang Kai-shek's own ability as a military leader. And though their opposition presumably presented no real military threat to the Central Government, it could not be dismissed as totally insignificant.

For the time being, however, it was clear that the extreme right wing of the Kuomintang was firmly in control of the Chungking bureaucracy. The Cabinet changes of October 1944, which had been hailed in some quarters as an encouraging sign, had proved completely meaningless. General Chen Cheng as War Minister was entirely helpless, all effective power over army organization and administration remaining in the hands of General Ho Ying-chin. Similarly, T. V. Soong's influence was becoming increasingly negligible, it being reported that all cables and documents addressed to him as Foreign Minister were first scrutinized either by the Generalissimo or by Dr. Wang Chung-hui, who had become foreign minister in all but name.

Perhaps the most conclusive indication that Chiang Kai-shek had once more become entirely adamant in his determination to preserve the Kuomintang's monopoly of political power was provided by his speech of March 1, 1945, before the Preparatory Commission for the Inauguration of Constitutional Government, in which he announced that a constitutional assembly would be convened on November 12, 1945.[1] This speech was notable not only for its unconditional condemnation of the Chinese Communists, but also for its explicit statement that both the membership and the work of the constitutional assembly would be controlled by the Kuomintang.

With regard to the Communists, Chiang accused them of being solely responsible for China's lack of unity. "Before the Japanese invasion we were a united nation. Today, but for the Communists and their armed forces, we are a united nation. There are no independent war lords or local governments challenging the central authority." Though reiterating his earlier statement that "the solution of the Communist question must be through political means," Chiang made it clear that he regarded the Communists as traitors to their country. In stating the Government's position in the negotiations, he claimed that "no sooner is one demand met than fresh ones are raised," and that to accede to the demand for a coalition government would "not only place the Government in open contravention of the political program of Dr. Sun Yat-sen" but would lead to friction and chaos, and to the collapse of the central authorities, because "there exists in our country no responsible body representing the people for a government to appeal to."

After enumerating the concessions offered to the Communists, the Generalissimo declared that their rejection of these offers showed that they were insincere in their desire to coöperate in

---

[1] The full text of Chiang Kai-shek's March 1st speech, together with that of the Communist reply, was published in *Amerasia*, April 6, 1945.

the war. He also advanced the customary Kuomintang argument that the Government was willing to grant legal status to the Communists "as soon as the latter agree to incorporate their army and local administrations in the National Army and Government." In conclusion, he announced that, subject to the approval of the Kuomintang Party Congress scheduled to meet in May 1945, a national assembly would be convened on November 12th to inaugurate constitutional government, following which "all political parties will have legal status and enjoy equality." In the meantime, however, the Kuomintang "definitely cannot abdicate to a loose combination of parties."

Read with reference to its political background, Chiang's speech was in essence a repetition of all his previous speeches. And it was a serious blow to the many Chinese and foreigners who were agreed that the evils and abuses which were hamstringing China's war effort could be remedied only by democratic political reforms that would curb the power of the ruling clique. As far as the Communist question was concerned, it was an unconvincing attempt to discredit the Communist demands and to prove that the Communists were not deserving of support. The claim that no other forces challenged the Government's authority, which was clearly incompatible with the growing following of the Democratic League, could only be interpreted as meaning that the Communists alone possessed sufficient armed strength to constitute an effective opposition. The reasons why the Government's "concessions" were wholly inadequate to meet the critical situation have already been mentioned, but it may be noted once more than the Communists had not presented "fresh demands" and that none of their original requests had ever been met.

The most important point about Chiang's speech, however, was his flat rejection of the demand for the formation of a coalition government *before* the convening of the constitutional assembly — a demand put forward not only by the Communists but also by the Democratic League and other Liberal groups. The point at issue here was a basic one, namely whether China's political future was to be determined by a Kuomintang-nominated and Kuomintang-controlled assembly, or whether other parties and groups were to have a voice both in the election of members and in the deliberations of the constitutional convention. On this point, Chiang showed himself adamant. All power was to remain with the Kuomintang, and the other parties were not even to be given legal status until after the assembly had met and the constitution had been adopted. It was not surprising, therefore, that his speech did nothing to relieve the political crisis or to reassure those who were interested in seeing China achieve a genuinely democratic form of government.

It is interesting to note that the Japanese fully appreciated the significance of this issue, and were apparently well pleased at the prospect that Chiang's stand would result in further disunity and conflict in China. A Domei broadcast from Tokyo on March 13, 1945, for example, informed the people of Greater East Asia:

The positions taken by Chungking, which refuses to give up one-party government, and Yenan, which demands the creation of a coalition government before instituting the constitutional government, do not warrant any hope of rapprochement between the two factions. . . . On March 1, Chiang Kai-shek announced the failure of his negotiations with Yenan, and at the same time revealed that a National Congress will be held in November to decide on the question of the constitutional government. If the National Congress is to be held without the settlement of the Yenan-Chungking impasse, it is clear that the meeting will be held according to the desires of the Kuomintang Party, and, although the National Congress is supposed to realize the institution of a constitutional government, the procedure of the conference will surely be directed toward the Kuomintang's monopolization of the government. Thus, the aftermath of this National Congress will clearly see a further intensification of the struggle between Yenan and Chungking and with other parties.

The immediate aftermath of Chiang's speech demonstrated how sharply the political situation had deteriorated since the recall of General Stilwell and Ambassador Gauss in the preceding autumn. The Chinese Communist statement, issued in reply to the speech, not only attacked the reactionary elements in the Kuomintang for their "fascist and defeatist military and political policies," but singled out Chiang Kai-shek himself as the chief spokesman for this reactionary clique, characterized his accusations as "lunatic remarks" and "gangster talk," and declared that his "personal dictatorship" had led China into its present crisis and "must end immediately." As for Chiang's promise that measures with regard to the convening of the constitutional assembly would be referred to the People's Political Council for consideration, the Communists declared that "everyone knows it [the

Council] is nothing but a purely ornamental organization appointed by Dictator Chiang Kai-shek. . . . Since its foundation, the People's Political Council has never had the slightest power to decide any question. . . . The Chinese people must resolutely oppose a packed national convention and demand the immediate ending of Chiang Kai-shek's one-man dictatorship and the setting up of a democratic coalition."

THE AMERICAN DILEMMA

As FAR as American policy in China was concerned, it appeared to have reached a serious impasse. For a number of years, the basic aim of that policy had been to mobilize the combined strength of the Kuomintang and Communist fighting forces against Japan by bringing about an agreement between Chungking and Yenan. And with the prospect of American landings on the coast of China for an offensive against Japan's main industrial centers on the continent, the need for the coöperation of the Communist-led guerrilla forces in the North was obvious, since the lack of such coöperation would have meant a prolonging of the war and the unnecessary sacrifice of American lives. Yet Ambassador Hurley and General Wedemeyer had given Chiang Kai-shek reason to believe that he could rely on exclusive American support for the Chungking Government, and this had encouraged him to adopt an intransigent attitude toward the Communists and thus sharply reduced the chances for a reconciliation between the two factions. The American Government was, in fact, placed in a position where it could take steps to arm and equip the guerrillas only at the risk of an open break with Chungking.

The unfortunate results for the United States of the failure on the part of some of its leading representatives to grasp the real nature of the Chinese problem was also becoming manifest in the economic field. Great hopes had been aroused when, in the summer of 1944, the Generalissimo had invited Donald Nelson to aid in the organization of a Chinese War Production Board to stimulate and regulate Chinese industrial production. Mr. Nelson had previously inspected Chinese factories in and around Chungking, and had reported to the Generalissimo that they were operating at only from 30% to 70% of capacity because of bureaucratic corruption, factional disputes within the Kuomintang, and the fact that far higher profits could be made from speculation in raw materials. A Chinese WPB was therefore established under the direction of the Chinese Minister of Economic Affairs, Dr. Weng Wen-hao, and in November 1944 Mr. Nelson returned to China with a staff of American experts to aid in its organization.

During the first week-end after their arrival, Mr. Nelson's assistants drafted the organic law for the Chinese War Production Board, which was approved by the Generalissimo and subsequently by the Executive and Legislative Yuans. This law was the product of the American officials' experience with red tape and diffused authority in the operation of the American War Production Board. Apparently wholly unaware that one of the major criticisms of the Chinese economic set-up was its excessive degree of bureaucratic centralization, which stifled private initiative and placed all power in the hands of a few strategically placed bureaucrats, they wrote a law that put virtually unlimited economic powers in the hands of the head of the Chinese War Production Board. He was given complete control not only over the production of war and essential civilian supplies, but also over priorities, the allocation of materials and man power, the import and export of critical materials, transportation priorities, stock-piling of war materials, and the requisitioning of materials, facilities, and products for war use. The law also provided for a committee of war production finance, including cabinet ministers and representatives of Government banks, but stipulated that the final authority in this committee should rest with the chairman, and the chairman of the WPB was made ex-officio chairman of the finance committee. The WPB was also given authority to obtain from both public and private industrial and commercial concerns all data, records, and other information necessary to carry out its functions.

Here was centralization of control carried to an extreme that even the Chinese bureaucracy had not attempted to legalize. And here was concrete evidence of the danger of applying American experience to Chinese conditions. It is one thing to eliminate red tape and organizational overlapping in a democratic government like that of the United States. It is quite another to give unlimited power to a single bureaucrat in a country that had not yet secured even the beginnings of popular control over Government policies, particularly when the officials who were to exercise these sweeping powers were the very ones responsible for the conditions that the WPB was intended to rectify. The results were decidedly unfortunate. As of the spring of 1945, the Chinese WPB was reported to be almost completely ineffective. Speculation and hoarding of raw materials continued unabated, and the "galloping inflation" that had been undermining the Chinese economy had reached such alarming proportions that Leon Henderson was dispatched from Washington to advise on measures to check it.

America, then, was faced with the serious deterioration of political and economic conditions in China on the eve of the final land offensive against Japan. The extent to which American policy had contributed, directly or indirectly, to this state of affairs was a debatable one, but one thing at least seemed clear — American military leaders had apparently abandoned the idea that China's armed forces could play a major role in the final defeat of Japan. Only on this assumption was it possible to explain the decision to refrain from arming the guerrilla forces in the North, and to confine American military aid to the training and equipping of selected Chinese forces in the South.

The general line of argument in support of this new policy was as follows: the Japanese armies had to be defeated on the mainland of China, but Chinese forces could not accomplish this task without a long period of training, and the American public was in no mood to support such a prolongation of the war. Thus a large American army had to be used to do the job quickly. It was assumed that the principal battle zone would be in North China, where the Japanese were expected to make a desperate stand to defend the approaches to Manchuria and Korea — the sites of their chief industrial centers on the continent and also ideal bases for an amphibious invasion of Japan Proper.

A plausible case could, of course, have been made for counting out China's fighting forces as a major factor in the war in the interests of a quick victory over Japan. And such a policy would also have obviated the necessity of overriding Chungking's objections to military aid for the Communist-led forces. On the other hand, there were serious disadvantages both for the immediate future and for the postwar period. In the first place, it was clear that the Communist-led troops in the North could have provided valuable assistance if given a minimum of equipment. This opinion, shared by all foreign observers who had visited the guerrilla areas, was strongly reasserted by Raymond P. Ludden, a foreign service officer of the State Department, who returned to this country in March 1945 after a seven-month trip in Communist-controlled territory with a military intelligence unit of the American army which established a permanent base in this area. Mr. Ludden told a story of hundreds of thousands of well-trained Communist troops fighting incessant guerrilla warfare against the Japanese. He reported that the Communists were seriously short of supplies, but "would put to good use any material they got." He also emphasized that the Communist armies enjoyed popular support wherever they went, and that this support "was on too large a scale and too widespread to be merely window-dressing." The Eighth Route Army, according to Mr. Ludden, "is highly regarded by the people, who consider it the central force, both military and political, in this vast region."

It is not without significance that the State Department permitted Mr. Ludden to present his informal report to the press at a time when both General Wedemeyer and Ambassador Hurley were in Washington stating their views on the Chinese situation. It was perhaps an indication that the United States had been brought precipitately and unexpectedly to the impasse in its relations with China which it had tried for so long to avoid. There was every indication that the State Department was by no means in unanimous agreement with Ambassador Hurley's handling of the political situation in China. For if the United States refrained from aiding the guerrilla forces of the Eighth Route and New Fourth armies out of deference to Chungking's attitude, it would not only be depriving its own soldiers of valuable aid in the war, but might well antagonize millions of Chinese who had established genuinely democratic institutions in the guerrilla areas, and whose aims were far more in accord with American interests than were those of the reactionary bureaucracy in Chungking.

Ambassador Hurley, however, returned to Chungking in April 1945, apparently unshaken in his belief that the only way to promote unity in China was by unconditional and exclusive support for the Chungking regime. On his way back, he stopped in Moscow and was reported to have interviewed Marshal Stalin on the Chinese question, apparently in the hope that pressure could be brought to bear on Yenan in order to obtain agreement for the Hurley-Chungking policy. The very naïveté of such an approach was amazing, to say the least. And if General Hurley cherished the belief that he could obtain a pledge of Soviet support for his policy in China, he must have been disillusioned by an article published shortly after his visit in the influential Soviet journal *War and the Working Class*, which analyzed the Chinese political situation in terms that were hardly complimentary to the Chungking Government.

Though Ambassador Hurley was content to accept at its face value the Generalissimo's assertion that he was working to achieve unity and democracy in China, and though he took steps to ensure that no criticism of the Kuomintang regime should emanate from the American Embassy staff in Chungking, the military and political situation in China by August 1945 provided no grounds for his optimism, and no justification for his "personal diplomacy." On the contrary, there was abundant evidence that internal disunity in China had reached more dangerous proportions than ever before, and that by a policy of exclusive aid to a regime opposed by a majority of the Chinese people, the United States was contributing to the outbreak of large-scale civil war in China.

The best proof of this serious state of affairs was provided by two speeches delivered during the first week in May: one by Chiang Kai-shek at the opening session of the Sixth National Kuomintang Congress in Chungking, and the other by Mao Tse-tung at the closing session of the Seventh National Congress of the Chinese Communist Party at Yenan.[1] Chiang's speech was notable on three counts. In the first place, it ignored completely the problem of relations between the Kuomintang and the Chinese Communist Party and made no reference whatsoever to the demands of opposition groups in Kuomintang China for the immediate establishment of a coalition government. Secondly, it dwelt at length on the Kuomintang's plans for the inauguration of constitutional government and the "return of political power to the entire people," which would allegedly be accomplished by the Kuomintang-controlled "National Congress" scheduled to meet in November 1945. Thirdly, it emphasized the Kuomintang's intention of promoting the welfare of the people, preventing monopoly and exploitation, and "eliminating the cause of the class struggle."

On the first point, no comment seems necessary. With regard

---

[1] Summaries of both speeches were published in *Amerasia*, May 18, 1945.

to the second, it may be pointed out again that only a constitutional assembly elected by all sections of the Chinese people, and free to draft a constitution, could accomplish a "return of power to the people," and that this was not the kind of assembly that the Kuomintang proposed to convene. As for promoting the people's welfare and eliminating monopoly and exploitation, the Chungking Government's policies during the preceding eight years had tended in precisely the opposite direction, and the official pronouncements concerning China's economic future had made it abundantly clear that what the Kuomintang leaders envisaged was a bureaucratic centralization of economic power, with state-controlled modern industries superimposed on China's semifeudal agrarian structure.

In marked contrast, Mao Tse-tung put forward specific proposals for the attainment of political unity; emphasized the undemocratic character of the proposed "National Congress"; and outlined in detail the policies that should be followed by a democratic coalition government in both domestic and foreign affairs, illustrating his points with references to actual achievements in the guerrilla areas. Mao's main thesis was that China needs a democratic coalition government both during and after the war in order to mobilize and unify the forces of resistance, collaborate effectively with China's allies, and lead the Chinese people in building up a strong, unified, and prosperous country. A continuation of the dictatorship by reactionary elements within the Kuomintang, he maintained, will not only prevent democratic reforms and effective mobilization, but will also lead to civil war.

Mao described the Kuomintang's plan to convene a constitutional assembly while refusing to allow the establishment of a coalition government as a "mockery of democracy," and as designed to give the Kuomintang leaders an excuse to take punitive action against anyone who opposes the decisions of this assembly. He then proposed that in order to promote the establishment of a coalition government, "a conference of people's representatives from all parts of liberated China should be called in Yenan as soon as possible to discuss measures for unifying the activities of all liberated areas, giving leadership to the anti-Japanese democratic movement . . . and promoting the unity of the entire country." After comparing conditions in the liberated areas with those under Kuomintang rule, and calling attention to the existence of the Kuomintang-planted puppet troops, Mao emphasized that what the Chinese people want is not "absolutist unification by dictators," but "democratic unification by the people."

In outlining the domestic policies of a new, democratic China, Mao proposed a continuation of those already in practice in the liberated areas — that is, encouragement of all productive forces, reduction of rent and interest rates, protection of workers' interests coupled with guarantees of legitimate profits to employers, religious freedom, the elimination of illiteracy, and respect for the language, literature, customs, and religious beliefs of national minorities.

With regard to the "diplomatic problems" confronting China, Mao expressed full support of the principles of the Atlantic Charter and the resolutions adopted at the Moscow, Cairo, Teheran, and Crimea Conferences, and suggested the following four-point policy for a settlement of the Chinese and Far Eastern questions: "First, the Japanese aggressors must be defeated, and Japanese fascism and militarism and the causes producing them thoroughly exterminated; there must be no half-way compromise. Second, the last vestiges of fascism in China must be exterminated. Third, domestic peace must be established in China, and civil war must not be allowed to recur. Fourth, the Kuomintang dictatorship must be abolished. After its abolition it should at first be supplanted by a provisional democratic coalition government, fully supported by the entire country. Then after all lost territories have been recovered, a regular coalition government should be established through free and unrestricted elections."

Mao urged that the Chinese Government abandon its attitude of enmity toward the Soviet Union and take steps to improve Sino-Soviet relations, declaring that "we believe that without the participation of the Soviet Union it is not possible to reach a final and thorough settlement of the Pacific question." Expressing sincere thanks for the great efforts of America and Britain in the common struggle against Japan, he added: "We request the governments of the United Nations, especially the governments of America and Great Britain, to pay serious attention to the voice of the vast majority of the Chinese people, and not to let their diplomatic policy go against the will of the Chinese people and thereby lose their friendship. If any foreign government aids China's reactionary clique in opposing the democratic cause of the Chinese people, a grave mistake will have been committed."

As for the other countries of the Far East, Mao urged that after

Japan's unconditional surrender the people of Japan should be aided and encouraged to establish a democratic regime, without which the thorough extermination of Japanese fascism and militarism is impossible. . . . "The decision of the Cairo Conference to grant independence to Korea is correct and the Chinese people should aid the Korean people to attain liberation and freedom. . . . America has already granted independence to the Philippines. We hope that Great Britain will also grant independence to India because an independent, democratic· India is necessary for the maintenance of world peace." With regard to Burma, Malaya, the Dutch East Indies, and Indo-China, Mao· declared: "We hope that Great Britain, America, Holland, and France, after helping the local peoples to defeat the Japanese, will grant them the right of establishing independent democratic regimes in accordance with the policy advocated at the Crimea Conference with regard to liberated areas in Europe."

The views expressed by Mao Tse-tung take on added weight and significance in the light of the large increase in the strength of the Communist Party and the armed forces under its leadership. The membership of the Party itself had grown from 800,000 to 1,200,000 in the space of a year and a half, while during the preceding six months the regular troops of the Eighth Route and New Fourth Armies had increased from 570,000 to 910,000, despite constant casualties. This increase, moreover, had occurred during a period when the Central Chinese Armies were losing more territory to the enemy than at any time since the early days of the war. The Communist-led armies apparently enjoyed such great prestige among the Chinese people that they were able not only to expand their forces but also to move into those areas from which the Central Armies had been expelled and regain control of a large part of them for the Chinese people.

Perhaps the most noteworthy point in Mao Tse-tung's speech was his proposal that "a conference of people's representatives from all parts of liberated China" be held in Yenan. The implications of this proposal were far-reaching. According to the latest Communist figures, there were nineteen such areas, including six "Border Regions" and thirteen "liberated areas," located in North, Central, and South China, with a combined population of more than 95,000,000. Although in Mao's speech the purpose of such a conference was described as the coördination of their joint war effort and the encouragement of organized resistance in the occupied areas, a more detailed analysis of the deliberations of the Communist Party Congress suggests that the calling of such a conference would be designed as a direct political countermove to the convening of the Kuomintang-controlled "National Congress" in November 1945. Although there was apparently no plan to set up a separate government embracing all the liberated areas, there was good reason to believe that the Chinese Communist Party and their followers did not intend to accept the decisions of a constitutional assembly controlled by a party that refused to grant them legal status and was openly engaged in laying plans for their ultimate destruction. It was therefore reasonable to assume that one of the chief purposes of the conference proposed by Mao Tse-tung would be to organize popular opposition to the holding of an unrepresentative constitutional assembly and to any decisions adopted by such an assembly. It could also be assumed from Mao's remarks that the Yenan regime and its millions of supporters were preparing for the possibility that Chiang Kai-shek would use their opposition to the decisions of *his* "National Congress" as an excuse to treat them as rebels against a legally constituted regime. In that event the stage in China would be set for civil war.

There was no improvement in the Chinese political situation during the months immediately preceding Japan's surrender, and no modification of the Hurley-Wedemeyer policy of exclusive aid for the Chungking regime, even when American-armed [1] Chinese troops under General Hu Tsung-nan engaged in large-scale fighting with Communist-led forces in July in Shensi and under Yen Hsi-shan in August in Shansi. A climax was reached when, following Japan's first peace offer of August 10, General Chu Teh, commander-in-chief of the Communist armies, ordered his troops to arrange for the disarming of all Japanese and puppet troops in the Communist area of operations. This action was promptly denounced by Chiang Kai-shek, who ordered the Communist armies to "remain at their posts and wait for further instructions," and commanded Chu Teh "never again to take independent action." Simultaneously, a Chungking Ministry of Information spokesman announced that the Chinese Government would hold Japan "strictly accountable" for any arms that she or her puppets

---

[1] On August 3, General Wedemeyer admitted it was "probably true" that some Chinese government troops fighting Communist troops were using American weapons.

"might surrender to any organization or party other than officers or men duly authorized by the Chinese Government."

By this action the Chungking regime made it clear that it was more fearful of the Chinese people in the liberated areas than of the Japanese and puppet troops, and that it was determined at all costs to prevent the Communist-led armies from asserting their control in the areas they had liberated from Japan. This was borne out by the message sent by Chiang Kai-shek to General Yosuji Okamura, commander of Japanese forces in China, on August 16, stating that "upon cessation of hostilities, Japanese troops are temporarily permitted to retain their arms and equipment for the maintenance of public order and communications, and must wait for military instructions from General Ho Ying-chin, Chinese military chief of staff."

The Chinese Communists protested against the Chungking order that they "remain at their posts" as being "contrary to the national interest" and "beneficial only to the Japanese invaders and traitors who have turned against their country," and proceeded to launch a drive against Japanese positions in North China, which in many cases were manned chiefly by Chinese puppet troops.

That the United States was closely involved in the gathering internal crisis in China was indicated by the fact that American transport planes were used to fly Kuomintang troops and officials to key points in occupied China to prevent their recovery by the Communist-led forces. There was thus serious danger that the United States might find itself directly involved on one side of an internal Chinese conflict. This was, in fact, the logical fruit of a policy that had failed to promote Chinese unity, and had encouraged the Chungking Government to believe that it could rely upon American support in its efforts to crush all popular opposition to its dictatorship. Had the full weight of American influence been exerted in favor of the formation of a coalition government in China prior to the end of the war, the American Government would not have found itself in the unenviable position of having to aid a repressive Chinese regime in suppressing a large section of the Chinese people.

At this critical moment came the announcement on August 26 of the terms of the Treaty of Alliance between China and the Soviet Union, followed by Mao Tse-tung's acceptance of Chiang Kai-shek's invitation to come to Chungking for a conference.

Much of the press comment on the treaty took the line that there was now no danger of internal conflict in China because the Soviet Union had renewed its recognition of the Government of China, which at the time was still the Chungking regime, and had pledged adherence to the principle of noninterference in Chinese affairs. According to this interpretation, the treaty was "a blow at the Communists" that greatly weakened their position vis-à-vis Chungking.

This conclusion was unwarranted. In the first place, the Communists had received no material aid from the Soviet Union during the war; such strength as they possessed derived from the wide popular following they had won during the war and there was no reason to assume that this support would diminish or disappear. Secondly, there was no reason to believe that the Soviet Union had intended to give Chungking carte blanche to suppress internal opposition by any means it chose. And, finally, the sources of unrest and conflict in China remained unchanged. The small ruling clique in Chungking was still determined to crush all opposition to its dictatorship, while the forces opposed to that dictatorship, of which the Communists were only one, were equally determined that it must be replaced by a democratic government in which all parties would be represented.

The success or failure of the negotiations between the Generalissimo and Mao Tse-tung to pave the way for a permanent settlement of China's internal conflict appeared to rest primarily upon Chiang Kai-shek's willingness and ability to modify the Kuomintang's hitherto adamant insistence on remaining the sole political power in China until after the establishment of "constitutional" government under purely Kuomintang auspices. Admitting Chiang's great skill at political compromise, the question was whether he had the actual power to reach a basic agreement with the Communists and other opposition groups whose views and aims concerning China's future political and economic structure were so diametrically opposed to those of the ruling clique. It was not a question of good intentions or sincerity, but of where Chiang himself derived his poltical power, and whether those sources would permit him to carry through such promises as he might make in the interests of national unity and progress.

The real key to the situation lay in the fact that Chiang Kai-shek's power stemmed from the landlord-usurer class that was bent on preserving China's medieval, semi-feudal economy. So long as that economy remained intact, and so long as that group remained politically dominant, there was no likelihood that Chiang could reach a basic settlement with the democratic forces of China. For should he attempt to do so, he would be faced with a revolution from the right. However, the democratic forces in China had become so strong that a revolution from the right could not be permanently successful. The day was past when Chiang Kai-shek could hope to base his power exclusively on a narrow and reactionary segment of Chinese society. If he was really sincere in his utterances about democracy for China, and if his claim of vast popular support for his principles was justified, there was only one way for him to prove it, and that was to throw the country open to a free expression of opinion. If Chiang chose this method, he might still be able to emerge as the head of a new, united China with a government based upon broad popular support instead of upon armed force and the terroristic activities of the Kuomintang's secret police.

It appeared entirely possible that the negotiations between the Generalissimo and Mao Tse-tung would result in some temporary, stop-gap arrangements to tide over the immediate threat of civil war. But close students of China were convinced that so long as Chiang Kai-shek received support solely from the proponents of an economic structure that was both reactionary and oppressive, no compromise that he might reach with the advocates of a modern, democratic China would be of any lasting value. In view of the United States' vital interest in the emergence of a unified, democratic China, it was all the more unfortunate that Chiang's unwillingness to trust himself to the free expression of Chinese opinion had been strengthened in the months immediately preceding the end of the war by open and unconditional American support for this attitude.

The American people have certain definite aims in the Far East. They want stability, peace, and opportunities for profitable economic relations with the peoples of Eastern Asia, and China is obviously the key to the attainment of these goals. Only if China is strong, democratic, and prosperous can she serve both as a powerful stabilizing factor and also as a valuable ally for America in both the political and the economic spheres. The United States cannot afford to become impatient with the difficulties confronting American-Chinese relations. Nor can it afford to let the personal political ideology of any one of its representatives interfere with the constructive policy that has been slowly developing. For several years, General Stilwell and Ambassador Gauss and their respective staffs had painstakingly accumulated a vast store of honest information, on the basis of which a forward-looking policy was well in the making. Nothing has occurred since their recall to justify abandoning the effort to promote China's unity and to strengthen her economic and political structure.

A weak, divided, and economically backward China will not only be a liability in the postwar era, but might well play into the hands of those who favor a restoration of the prewar balance of power in the Far East. Such a China would be a standing invitation to political and economic rivalries among the industrialized powers, and particularly to a resurgence of Japanese expansionist ambitions. For it must be emphasized that American-Chinese relations are and will continue to be strongly influenced by the general international political situation in the Far East, and particularly by the decisions reached regarding the postwar treatment of Japan. It may be stated as an axiom that China's future development will be circumscribed to a large degree by the political and economic structure of postwar Japan. And it is far from certain that Japan's military defeat will result in the permanent elimination of those features in her society that have hitherto driven her to a war-promoting series of grandiose aggressions. Powerful forces within the Western Powers are seeking for the impossible formula of destroying Japan's military power without at the same time weakening her political "reliability" in the prewar power politics sense of the word. This problem, which will be considered in the following chapters, is perhaps the Number One problem of the postwar Far East, not only because in point of time it will be the first to present itself for solution, but also because that solution will be the test of the kind of political and economic structure the United Nations intend to establish in the Pacific.

PART THREE

CREATING A TRUSTWORTHY JAPAN

❋

CHAPTER VIII

WAR-BREEDING FORCES IN JAPAN

❁

AT THE BEGINNING OF 1945, Allied proposals concerning the treatment of a defeated Japan were still confined mainly to generalities and were concerned primarily with the destruction of the most flagrantly aggressive elements in Japanese society. The Cairo Conference had limited itself to the pledge that Japan would be stripped of all territories gained by aggression since 1895. In his Christmas Eve broadcast of 1943, President Roosevelt had reiterated that peace with Japan would involve "the restoration of stolen property to its owners," and that it must ensure "the permanent elimination of the Empire of Japan as a potential force of aggression." In October 1944, on the occasion of the landing of American troops in the Philippines, a White House statement declared that we have the will and power to teach Japan "the cost of treachery and deceit, and the cost of stealing from her neighbors. With our steadfast Allies, we shall teach this lesson so that Japan will never forget it. We shall free the enslaved peoples. We shall restore stolen lands and looted wealth to their rightful owners. We shall strangle the Black Dragon of Japanese militarism forever."

In these and many similar statements, the emphasis was solely on the elimination of Japanese military power. This was in marked contrast to the principles enunciated by President Roosevelt in his broadcast of December 1943 regarding the political approach to the question of postwar Germany. The President declared that the conferees at the Teheran meeting "were united in determination that Germany must be stripped of her military might and be given no opportunity within the foreseeable future to regain that might." But he added that "the United Nations have no intention to enslave the German people. We wish them to have a normal chance to develop in peace, as useful and respectable members of the European family. But we most certainly emphasize that word 'respectable' — for we intend to rid them once and for all of Nazism and Prussian militarism and the fantastic and dangerous notion that they constitute the 'master race.'"

Thus two additional principles were added to the basic determination to crush German military power: the old German leadership must go, and on this basis the German people will be given a normal chance for peaceful development and be accepted as useful members of the European community. In subsequent statements the President elaborated these principles by stressing the fact that Prussian militarism, Nazism, and the great cartels of modern Germany had been the driving force behind German aggression and German military power.

The failure to apply similar principles to the question of the postwar treatment of Japan reflected the fact that in both England and America there was less fundamental thinking with regard to the basic elements in the Japanese economic and social structure that had made Japan an aggressive and predatory power throughout her modern history. The main emphasis in the proposals emanating from official and semiofficial sources was on the elimination of Japanese militarism and the destruction of Japan's military power, with no apparent recognition of the fact that the military "extremists" were merely a manifestation rather than the primary cause of Japanese aggression. In other words, Allied leaders were deeply concerned with the problem of how to render Japan incapable of aggression, but paid comparatively little attention to the even more important problem of encouraging the development of a Japan that would not need nor wish to solve its problems by military force.

In England, this failure to go to the roots of the matter with regard to the establishment of a lasting peace in the Far East was reflected chiefly in the scarcity of comment on the subject of postwar Japan — official British statements being confined to reiterated pledges that Britain would do her full share in bringing about Japan's defeat. It was also reflected in the official ban placed on criticism of the Japanese Emperor and in the reported statement of a "British expert on Far Eastern affairs" to the effect that "any British Government would normally dislike so radical a disturbance of the status quo as the substitution of an unstable republic for the present throne in Japan."[1] Then, too, there was

---

[1] Quoted by Frederick Kuh in a despatch to *PM*, dated London, December 25, 1943.

the ill-judged remark in 1944 of Captain Oliver Lyttelton, British Minister of Production, that "America provoked Japan to such an extent that it was forced to attack." Although this extraordinary comment was hastily modified by the British Foreign Office, it clearly reflected a reluctance to dig deep into the basic causes of Japanese aggression.

The American approach to the problem of Japan naturally differed from the British. The United States had never had a prolonged alliance with Japan, it did not have the same kind of political and economic stake in the prewar status quo in Eastern Asia, and it did not share the instinctive British support for a monarchical system of government. Thus, though there was a similar lack of specific official comment on the basic causes of Japanese aggression, there was also a strong though still vaguely expressed feeling among the American people that there was something wrong with Japan which could not be cured simply by a military victory.

This feeling was clearly evidenced in the reaction to the early speeches of Joseph C. Grew, whose ten-year ambassadorship in Japan was abruptly ended on December 7, 1941. While stressing the power and fanaticism of the Japanese militarists, Mr. Grew also expressed in the months immediately following his return to this country the view that the Emperor and other "moderate" elements in the Japanese ruling class had opposed the policy of aggression against the United States and Britain, and that the system of emperor-worship in Japan might be an asset rather than a liability if the militarists were eliminated and power transferred to this "moderate" peace-loving group. These views aroused widespread criticism in the American press, and even the *New York Times,* customarily a staunch supporter of the State Department, took Mr. Grew severely to task for his suggestion that we "sponsor an autocratic theocracy incapable of developing a real democracy based on self-government by the people and therefore always subject to domination by cliques that control the Emperor." The *Times* added that the idea of Japanese racial supremacy based on the emperor-worship cult "confronts us with even more difficult but no less dangerous problems than nazism and fascism, which we are pledged to eradicate."

It is known that, as a result of this strongly adverse criticism, Mr. Grew was advised by the State Department to refrain from making further speeches on postwar policy toward Japan. It is also a matter of record that the Department modified its former attitude toward the Emperor so far as our political warfare against the Japanese people was concerned. Previously, American propaganda material had endeavored to convince the Japanese people that their Emperor was the victim of the unscrupulous militarists who had deceived him and thwarted his genuine desire for peace.[1] But by the middle of 1943 the new State Department policy consisted of two points. On the one hand, the Deparment was not committed to the support of the Emperor, this being a question to be decided by the Japanese people themselves after the elimination of the militarists. On the other hand, the Emperor was not to be openly attacked in American propaganda, on the ground that he might be useful in discrediting militarism by putting the blame for Japan's defeat on his military advisers, and then giving the powerful weight of his Imperial sanction to the policies of a new "moderate" Japanese Government. There was no specific indication as to what groups were expected to undertake the formation of this new "moderate" government. But in the midst of this shift in official American policy on the question of the Emperor, there occurred a highly significant change in the Far Eastern Division of the State Department.

Until May 1944, the leadership in the Far Eastern Division had been in the hands of men who knew China better than they knew Japan. As the war in the Pacific speeded up and the hour of Japan's defeat drew nearer, however, it was natural that the Government should wish to enlist the services of men who knew Japan intimately, and that therefore the men who had held important diplomatic positions in Japan before Pearl Harbor should be given important posts in the Far Eastern Division. But there was occasion for considerable comment and speculation when this group was given what seemed like the dominant power in that Division.

---

[1] For example, Senator Elbert Thomas, broadcasting in Japanese in the summer of 1942, informed the Japanese people that "you and your Emperor have been betrayed by the war lords, who have seized power from the rightful holders of it." See also *Amerasia*, January 7, 1944, pp. 6–8, for text and comment on a Japanese-language pamphlet, reported to have been dropped by American planes among Japanese soldiers, quoting two Imperial Odes to prove the Emperor's desire for peace and proclaiming that the militarists "treasonably deceived His Majesty."

Not only did former Ambassador Grew replace Dr. Stanley K. Hornbeck as Director of the newly constituted Office of Far Eastern Affairs, but in addition to Mr. Grew, Joseph W. Ballantine, a former counselor of the American Embassy in Tokyo, was appointed Deputy Director; Eugene H. Dooman, who had spent sixteen years in the diplomatic service in Japan and was counselor of the Embassy from 1938 to 1941, was made a special assistant to Mr. Grew; and Earle R. Dickover, former first secretary in Tokyo, became chief of the Japanese section. These appointments were generally taken to mean that the day-to-day direction of American Far Eastern policy had been transferred from the so-called "China crowd" headed by Dr. Hornbeck, who had been in charge of the Far Eastern Division since 1928, to men whose diplomatic experience in the Far East had been chiefly if not entirely in Japan.

The real significance of this shift in personnel, however, was not that Mr. Grew and his colleagues were pro-Japanese or anti-Chinese, but that they were known to support the view that there is a "moderate" peace-loving element in the present Japanese ruling class that can be trusted to form a "reliable" government in postwar Japan. This confidence in the existence of a "moderate" element was clearly revealed in Mr. Grew's published record of "Ten Years in Japan." [1] In his introduction to the book, for example, he states that "the present book will not have served one of its purposes if it does not bring home to my readers the fact that there are many Japanese today who did not want war, who realized the stupidity of attacking the United States, Great Britain and the other United Nations, who did everything in their power to restrain the military extremists from their headlong and suicidal aggressions." A perusal of the book reveals that the "many Japanese" to whom Mr. Grew refers were prominent members of the ruling oligarchy, including the Emperor himself, members of the Court circle, leading industrialists and financiers, and foreign-office officials, with whom he was in close contact throughout his stay in Tokyo.

It is significant that at no point in his carefully prepared record did Mr. Grew suggest that the unbalanced Japanese economic structure, with its extreme concentration of capital in the hands of a few powerful monopolies and its impoverished internal

---

[1] Joseph C. Grew: *Ten Years in Japan* (New York, 1944).

market, had anything to do with the policy of aggressive imperialism pursued by Japan throughout her modern history. He did not appear to think it worth mentioning that the civilian leaders of Japan with whom he enjoyed such friendly social relationships were also directors and stockholders in the great financial and industrial concerns that not only equipped the Japanese war machine but also reaped enormous profits from Japan's colonial conquests. Nor did he refer to the popular forces that had fought a determined though losing battle against a system of autocratic rule at home and aggression abroad. There is not a word, for example, about the strike wave in Japanese war industries in 1941, and only the briefest mention of the 1937 election results, which showed widespread popular opposition to the Government's policy of aggression.

Mr. Grew seemingly did not regard the people of Japan as an important political force. Instead, he devoted himself tirelessly to the cultivation of the civilian members of the Japanese ruling class, whom he regarded as the sole hope of curbing the militarists. Even when the Konoye Cabinet fell in October 1941 and General Tojo became Premier, Mr. Grew reported that Prince Konoye had resigned in the belief that "the conversations with the United States would make more rapid progress if our Government were dealing with a Prime Minister whose power was based on a commanding position in and on support of the Army." On October 25, 1941, Mr. Grew noted in his diary that a "reliable Japanese informant . . . who is in contact with the highest circles" had told him that just before the fall of the Konoye cabinet, the Emperor had ordered the armed forces to pursue a policy which would guarantee that there would be no war with the United States. Accepting this statement at its face value, he comments that "the Emperor's stand necessitated the selection of a Prime Minister who would be in a position effectively to control the Army, hence the appointment of General Tojo who, while remaining on the Army active list, is committed to a policy of attempting to conclude successfully the current American-Japanese conversations."

Thus, up to the very last minute before the long and carefully planned attack on Pearl Harbor, Mr. Grew clung to the hope that the "moderate" elements would prevail. But what is far more important is the fact that, though disillusioned in this hope, he and his colleagues either retained unshaken their belief that the "moderates" were sincerely opposed to the policy of aggression, or else were trying to justify their assiduous cultivation of this group. Only on one or other of these assumptions can we explain their continued insistence that, once the militarists have been eliminated, some unspecified "liberal" element will emerge and that the Emperor, freed from the control of the "extremists," will serve a useful purpose by giving his Imperial sanction to the policies of this new ruling group.

It is true that Mr. Grew in a speech delivered on October 27, 1944, warned the American people to beware of a "premature and enticing" compromise peace offer from Japan, and stated: "There are many shrewd, level-headed, coldly-calculating Japanese — including not only some of their statesmen but also men such as those who built up the great business houses and shipping companies and industrial concerns of Japan. . . . These men are almost certain to make an attempt to save something from the wreckage." Mr. Grew further predicted that as a first move toward seeking such a compromise peace, the Japanese would appoint as prime minister some former statesman who they believe is "labeled in our minds as a liberal, reinforced by an ostensibly liberal cabinet." Furthermore, in his statement before the Senate Foreign Relations Committee on December 12, 1944, following his appointment as Under Secretary of State, Mr. Grew flatly denied that he had ever advocated retaining the Japanese Emperor as the leader of a postwar government in Japan. Declared Mr. Grew: "With regard to the institution of the Emperor, I do not think that anyone is yet in a position to determine definitely whether it is going to be an asset or a liability. . . . I have never held or stated that the Japanese Emperor should be retained after the war, nor have I ever held or stated that the Japanese Emperor should be eliminated after the war. I believe this problem should be left fluid until we get to Tokyo." He added, however, that it was impossible to predict the impact of defeat on the Japanese mind, and that "the Emperor may be the only element in Japan capable of exerting a stabilizing influence."

But it is one thing to propose that the question of the Emperor should be left to the Japanese people to decide; it is quite another to suggest, as Mr. Grew did, that we should consider making use of the Emperor as a "stabilizing influence" in order to prevent any social upheaval in Japan after the war. Similarly, it is one thing to recognize that Japanese business and financial leaders may seek to escape the full effects of military defeat; it is quite another to recognize the inherently untrustworthy character of the economic system of which these men are the product. To single out men whom we should not trust is purely negative; a positive policy requires that we indicate those forces and groups in Japan that we regard as trustworthy and pledge them our support. As of the end of 1944, there was no evidence that the State Department had taken this latter step. In fact, there was good reason to believe that even Mr. Grew's suspicions with regard to Japan's great business monopolies were not shared by his colleagues in the Far Eastern Division [1] so far as their views on Japan's postwar economic structure were concerned; that they were still interested in making a "durable" peace with the Japan that they knew, rather than with a Japan in which all sections of the old leadership had been replaced.

It is, of course, impossible to state with certainty the reasons that led to the change in the Far Eastern Division's personnel, but it is known that Dr. Hornbeck favored a "tough" peace with Japan that would transform her into a purely agricultural nation incapable of waging modern war, and that his views were strongly opposed by Mr. Dooman and other members of the so-called "Japan crowd." It is also generally agreed that Dr. Hornbeck, though strongly anti-Japanese in his approach to Far Eastern problems, was also rabidly anti-Russian. He did not recognize the necessity of strengthening the democratic forces in China. In his absorption with crushing Japan's military power without at the same time changing the political character of the Far East, he failed to see that a reactionary, disunited China was not the alternative to a fascist-militarist Japan. If this was the case, it may be assumed that he was unable to put forward convincing and constructive proposals for a postwar settlement in Asia.

Another factor that almost certainly entered into the decision to alter the Far Eastern Division's personnel was the recognition that the United States would unquestionably have to take the leading part in determining future Allied policy toward Japan. It was no accident that the change came at a time when the Chungking Government's fortunes were at a low ebb, and when,

---

[1] Mr. Grew was succeeded as Director of the Far Eastern Division by Joseph W. Ballantine, with Eugene H. Dooman assuming the post of Special Assistant to Mr. Ballantine.

furthermore, very justifiable criticism was being leveled at the Chungking regime for its refusal to democratize the government, its harsh suppression of all opposition parties and groups, and its unwillingness or inability to adopt constructive measures for increasing industrial and agricultural production. With the beginning of a powerful naval and air offensive against Japan's outer rim of defenses, coupled with the launching of the final stage of the offensive against Germany, preparations for the peace settlement in Asia as well as in Europe had to be begun. Under the circumstances, China did not inspire sufficient confidence in her ability to take a strong prodemocratic stand. Despite her eight years of indomitable resistance, China was too disunited and too weak to be a powerful and constructive political factor in the peace settlement with Japan.

Thus in addition to the obvious need for men capable of dealing with Japanese problems, the temporary weakness and reactionary character of the Chinese Government made it easier for those who viewed the future of the Pacific primarily in terms of Japan to assume positions of leadership in the State Department. The fact remains, however, that those entrusted with the responsibility for laying the basis of the peace in the Far East were men whose contacts were not only almost exclusively with Japan, but were limited strictly to one narrow section of Japanese society — the small upper class — and whose experience led them naturally to think of the Japanese economic and political structure from the standpoint of that class. It was therefore highly questionable whether their service in Japan had prepared them to understand the needs and aspirations of the Japanese people, or had qualified them to evaluate correctly the forces that were basically responsible for Japanese aggression. And, by the same token, it was also questionable whether they were any better fitted than their predecessors to estimate China's potentialities as a force for peace and progress in the Far East.

As far as the postwar treatment of Japan is concerned, however, the basic question that confronts the American people is whether or not we can expect Japan to become a peaceful and prosperous member of international society by the simple procedure of defeating and discrediting her militarists and by stripping her of all territories acquired by aggression. The argument that the militarists have been solely responsible for Japanese aggression, and that it would be difficult, unnecessary, and unprofitable to alter the basic political and economic structure of Japan, finds ready acceptance, of course, in those business and financial circles that enjoyed profitable relations with the great Japanese business houses before the war, and also in those circles that regard any modification of Japan's oppressive economic system or her autocratic method of government as tantamount to unbridled revolution. An impartial study of modern Japanese history, however, reveals that the militarists have been only the most aggressive proponents of an expansionist policy that developed inevitably from the political and economic structure established at the time of Japan's transition from feudalism to a modern capitalist economy following the Meiji Restoration of 1868.

THE ROOTS OF JAPANESE AGGRESSION

THE REAL key to Japan as an aggressor nation lies in the fact that ever since the Restoration, which overthrew the feudal regime of the Tokugawa clan and nominally centralized all power in the hands of the Emperor Meiji, Japan has been ruled by a small interlocking oligarchy composed of militarists, industrialists, bankers, landlords, and bureaucrats, and that each of these groups has had a stake in preserving an autocratic political system and supporting a policy of aggressive foreign expansion. The Meiji Restoration, which set the stage for Japan's emergence as a modern industrialized state, was carried out by one section of the feudal aristocracy (headed by the Satsuma and Choshu clans) in coöperation with the wealthy merchants and money-lenders of Osaka, including the Mitsui and Sumitomo families. This coalition was faced with the enormously difficult task of rapidly transforming a weak, disunited, feudal country into a modern centralized state with sufficient industrial strength to resist foreign domination and escape the fate that had befallen China at the hands of the Western Powers. The speed and efficiency with which the Meiji leaders destroyed the power of the feudal lords, suppressed internal revolts against their regime, and established the basis of a modern industrial structure has long been hailed as one of the most remarkable achievements in world history. But the fact that the task had to be done quickly left a deep impression on the subsequent course of Japanese development. As E. Herbert Norman points out: "The fact that Japan had to create in a generation what other nations had spent centuries to accomplish meant that Japan had not the time to afford such luxuries as liberal institutions. Japan skipped from feudalism into capitalism omitting the laissez-faire stage and it political counterpart, Victorian liberalism. Thus speed was determining element in the *form* which modern Japanese govern ment and society assumed. The *speed* with which Japan had simultaneously to establish a modern state, to build an up-to date defense force in order to ward off the dangers of invasion to create an industry on which to base this armed force, to fash ion an educational system suitable to an industrial modernized nation, dictated that these important changes be accomplished by a group of autocratic bureaucrats rather than by the mass o the people working through democratic organs of representation . . . The autocratic or paternalistic way seemed to the Meij leaders the only possible method if Japan was not to sink into the ranks of a colonial country."[1]

The pattern of autocratic rule was paralleled in the economic sphere by a close interlocking of the State, the former feudal nobility, and the merchant-banking class in the industrial devel opment of modern Japan. This alliance was the culmination o the tendency in feudal Japan for the leading merchants to seek political protection from the feudal authorities in return fo: financial favors. The feudal regime of the Tokugawas, which held power in Japan from 1615 to 1868, had imposed a stric policy of "seclusion" which prohibited all intercourse with for eign nations and thus prevented the Japanese merchants from accumulating capital through foreign trade and from colonia plunder. And, because they were confined to internal trade and money-lending, their chief customers were consequently the feudal nobility. Thus the prosperity of the merchant-banker group was closely linked with that of the feudal nobles and war riors, their customers and debtors. Furthermore, many of the merchants themselves had invested their profits from trade and usury in land, and had become landlords in their own right. In addition, some of the most prosperous merchants had become members of the ruling caste through adoption into *samura* families, while many impoverished feudal warriors (*samurai*) solved their economic difficulties by entering the families of merchants. This gradual infiltration of merchants into key posi tions within the feudal hierarchy became very important toward the end of the Tokugawa regime in bringing about the coöpera-

[1] E. H. Norman: *op. cit.*, p. 47.

tion between the big merchants of Osaka and the leading anti-Tokugawa clans of Choshu and Satsuma.

Thus even before the Meiji Restoration, the economic interests of the merchant-banking class were closely allied to those of the feudal nobility, and in the agrarian settlement undertaken after the Restoration the aristocracy and the merchants united in suppressing peasant revolts that had as their chief aim the final eradication of feudal rights and privileges. Furthermore, the abolition of the feudal structure in Japan was achieved by a compromise between the new regime and the old feudal nobility whereby the feudal lords were paid off in government bonds, with the result that the most powerful lords were transformed from territorial to financial magnates. With this newly acquired capital, they invested in banks, industries, or landed estates and became members of the financial oligarchy. Their power as semi-autonomous rulers was destroyed, but at the same time they were given a vested interest in the new regime. The Government also assumed responsibility for the debts owed by the feudal lords to the merchants and money-lenders. These debts were met by the issue of government bonds, and the funds received by the bondholders enabled them to invest in new industrial projects or in land. Thus the handful of wealthy merchant-banking families and the more powerful of the former feudal lords joined forces as landlords, bankers, and industrial stockholders under the paternalistic protection of the State, while many of the poorer *samurai* found employment in the government bureaucracy or in the newly established army and navy. This was, as Mr. Norman points out, the final stage in that "union of the yen and the sword" that was already evident in the Tokugawa period and that has been an outstanding characteristic of modern Japan.

The agrarian settlement of the early Meiji period is basic to an understanding of the modern economic structure of Japan not only because of its effects in cementing a permanent alliance among the landlords, the banking groups, and the State, but also because it was responsible for the special features of modern Japanese agriculture: excessively high rents, fragmentation of holdings, primitive technique, and the existence of a large surplus agricultural population that provided an inexhaustible reservoir of cheap labor for Japanese industry. The removal of the feudal ban on the sale and division of land, though it nominally made the peasant a free landholder, actually paved the way for the dispossession of the peasantry by legalizing the processes of forced sale, mortgage, etc. Prior to the abolition of the feudal system, the Japanese peasant cultivated his land and turned over a percentage of his harvest to his feudal lord. But the Meiji Government needed a fixed source of revenue, and therefore substituted a land tax based on the assessed value of the land and payable in money by the landowner. If a bad crop, fluctuations in the price of rice, or other factors beyond his control made it impossible for the small independent producer to meet this tax payment, he was compelled either to sell his land or to turn to the village usurer for assistance, thereby plunging himself into debt and eventually losing his land by foreclosure. Tenant farmers, on the other hand, still paid a high rent in kind to the landlord who, after deducting the amount needed to meet the land tax, retained the remainder as clear profit.

The dispossession of small peasant proprietors for debt or failure to meet the land tax proceeded rapidly, and by 1892 nearly 40% of the total cultivated area in Japan was being worked by tenant farmers. A similar process of peasant expropriation had, of course, taken place in England following the industrial revolution, but there it had been followed by an increase in the scale of farming, and by a large-scale migration of the rural population to the cities to find employment in the new industries. In Japan, however, the concentration of land ownership did not result in any absolute decrease in the number of agricultural households working the land or any increase in the scale of agricultural production. There were a number of reasons for this unusual situation. For one thing, the excessively high rents extracted by Japanese landlords made them prefer to keep as many tenants as possible on their land rather than to consolidate their holdings and undertake large-scale production. For another, Japanese industry was never sufficiently developed to provide employment for the entire surplus agricultural population. This was partly the result of the special factors governing the development of modern industries in Japan, but it was also due in large part to the very existence of this large surplus agricultural population. Industrial capital was scarce and costly in Japan, and many Japanese manufacturers preferred to avoid the expense of constructing large modern factories by farming out piece-work jobs to the peasant families — a fact which explains the important share contributed by tiny factories and household workshops to Japan's total industrial production. Furthermore, it may well be that the large financial trusts, which controlled the supply of capital available for industrial development in Japan, consciously kept that development restricted to a level that would ensure the continued existence of a large reservoir of cheap labor. It must be remembered that many of Japan's financial and industrial leaders were also large landlords and thus stood to benefit doubly from this oppressive system of agrarian relations: as landlords, because the pressure of population on the land enabled them to keep rents and interest rates high, and as industrialists because this same surplus population in the countryside enabled them to keep industrial wages low. As one Japanese economist frankly expresses it: "Existence of up-to-date factories with high technical efficiency side by side with millions of small farms amply supplying these factories with skillful but low-wage manpower constitutes the backbone of the national economy of Japan."[1] It also constitutes, as we shall see, the "backbone" of Japan's aggressive foreign policy.

Thus the results of the Meiji land settlement were to preserve essentially feudal relations on the land, with a vast number of small peasant proprietors, tenants, and part owners cultivating minutely parceled plots of land, paying high rents and extortionate interest charges, and supplementing their inadequate earnings by household industry or by sending one or more members of the family to seek employment in the cities. That conditions in rural Japan have not improved since the early years of the Restoration is indicated by the figures for landholding just before the war. In 1938, for example, nearly half the best arable land in Japan was owned by some 3,500 large landlords. The Imperial family alone owned more than three and a half million acres. At the other end of the scale were some five and a half million poverty-stricken farm households. Of the owners and part owners, more than three million held less than 2.5 acres apiece, and more than two million held less than 1.25 acres, while nearly half of all land cultivated in Japan was worked by tenant farmers. Rents averaging 50% to 60% of the crop were still common, and usurious interest rates added enormously to the mounting burden of agricultural debt.

[1] Shiroshi Nasu: *Aspects of Japanese Agriculture*, Institute of Pacific Relations (New York, 1941), p. 10.

Turning now to the industrial development of modern Japan we find that its main characteristics were: extensive participation of the State in the original development of key industries, and the concentration of economic power in the hands of a small financial oligarchy working in close coöperation with the State. Since the first aim of the Meiji leaders was to strengthen Japan's defenses against foreign military and commercial domination, they were primarily concerned with the development of *strategic* industries — i.e., industries related to military and naval power and manufacturing industries designed to compete against foreign products in both the foreign and the domestic market. At the time of the Restoration, however, only a handful of merchants and bankers had accumulated sufficient capital to finance such large-scale enterprises, and these financial magnates were reluctant to risk their wealth in costly and unproven undertakings. Instead they loaned money at profitable rates to the Government, which itself employed foreign technicians and undertook the establishment of mines, arsenals, factories, shipyards, chemical plants, and other industries deemed necessary for national defense, as well as a State-controlled transportation system. When these enterprises had been developed to a high level of technical efficiency, the State turned most of them over to a few trusted banking groups at extremely low prices. The mining and silk-reeling industries, for example, were transferred to private operators before 1890. The Government, however, continued the policy of subsidizing strategic industries and also retained a large measure of control over the Japanese economy through the establishment of semiofficial companies jointly owned by State and private capital, as well as through the Government-controlled banks, railways, shipyards, arsenals, etc.

This process of State-subsidized industrial development laid the basis for the fabulous power and wealth attained by the vast, monopolistic family enterprises — the Mitsui, Mitsubishi, Sumitomo, Yasuda, and a few other great trusts, collectively known as the *Zaibatsu*, or financial oligarchy. These concerns got their start by acting as financial backers of the Meiji regime in creating an industrial base to support Japan's military power and make possible her belated entry into the world of aggressive imperialist rivalries. It was to them that the State handed over many of its industrial enterprises, and they continued to be the recipients of large subsidies and profitable government contracts.

CAN WE TRUST A ZAIBATSU JAPAN?

THE ROLE which the *Zaibatsu* have played in shaping both the foreign and the domestic policies of modern Japan — their relations with the militarists, the Emperor, the Japanese political parties, etc. — is worth careful study because it seems clear that even if the militarists are eliminated as a political force in postwar Japan, the natural result will be the emergence of a Japan dominated by these great industrial and financial combines. The *Zaibatsu* and the militarists have been the two major forces in Japanese politics throughout modern Japanese industry and, as we shall see, the control of the *Zaibatsu* over the Japanese economy has been greatly strengthened as a result of the war. Remove the militarists and it is certain that unless definite steps are taken to prevent it, the result will still be a *Zaibatsu*-controlled Japan. It is therefore important to estimate what such a Japan would be likely to mean in terms of maintaining peace and assuring economic prosperity for the peoples of Eastern Asia, including Japan.

From the outset, the *Zaibatsu* were active partners of the militarists and bureaucrats in furthering Japan's expansionist ambitions. This was not surprising in view of the fact that their industrial enterprises were founded with the sole purpose of building up Japan's military power, and that furthermore the impoverished people of Japan were incapable of providing an adequate market for the products of modern large-scale industries. The *Zaibatsu*, being closely linked with the landlords and the former feudal nobility, naturally did not attempt to expand the internal market by relieving the peasants of the burden of feudal relations, nor had they any desire to raise the living standards and purchasing power of the workers in an industrial setup so completely dependent for its profits on low wages. Thus they were entirely ready to support a campaign for the acquisition of colonies that would secure them new markets and controlled sources of industrial raw materials — a campaign that soon led Japan into the first of a continuing series of wars for the domination of the Asiatic continent.

For the *Zaibatsu*, war proved a highly profitable business. The Sino-Japanese war of 1894–95, the Russo-Japanese war of 1904–5, and the Second World War, which for Japan spanned the years 1931 to 1945, brought them fat war contracts. The large indemnities received from China and Russia also went into their pockets in the form of government contracts, and the annexation of Formosa and Korea, and the acquisition of the South Manchuria Railway Zone and the Kwantung peninsula, gave them new controlled markets and sources of raw material. These early successes convinced the industrial and financial magnates of Japan that they could solve their economic problems by a policy of foreign expansion that would have the added advantage of diverting the attention of the Japanese people from their own impoverished and oppressed state.

This conviction was strengthened by Japan's extremely profitable participation in the First World War. Though she failed to enforce the Twenty-One Demands that would have transformed China into an exclusive Japanese colony, she was second only to the United States as a supplier of the Allies and enjoyed an even greater relative increase in foreign trade. The total tonnage launched by the Japanese shipbuilding industry increased from 85,000 tons in 1914 to 646,000 tons in 1919, and earnings from Japanese shipping services rose from 27 million yen to 360 million yen in the same period. Between 1913 and 1918, the capital investment in Japan's national economy increased sevenfold and her exports of manufactures more than doubled as she acquired new markets in India, Southeast Asia, and Latin America while her rivals were occupied with the struggle in Europe. In 1913, Japan had been a net debtor on international account to the extent of 1.2 billion yen. By the end of the war, she had become a creditor to the extent of 1.4 billion yen and in addition had imported about 600 million yen of gold. Thanks to Japan's vast war profits and small war expenditures, the *Zaibatsu* were able to expand their operations in every field of industry, trade, and finance. And this extraordinary development took place during a war in which Japan had done almost no fighting, sent no troops to Europe, and sustained only 1,210 casualties (dead, wounded, and missing).

During the 1920's, the so-called "Liberal Decade" in Japan, the economic and political power of the *Zaibatsu* was strengthened, Japan enjoyed a brief period of quasi parliamentary government, and there was a conflict between the advocates of a "positive" policy of aggression on the Asiatic continent and those favoring a more "moderate" policy of economic penetration, if possible without the use of armed force. On the basis of these three facts, some Western commentators have drawn the conclusion that the *Zaibatsu* favored democratic government and peaceful economic relations with the rest of the world, in opposition to the military "extremists" who demanded a dictatorship at home and the establishment of Japanese domination in Eastern Asia by military means.

This conclusion is definitely erroneous. There is no question that the power of the *Zaibatsu* increased enormously during this period in both the economic and the political spheres. By 1930, the House of Mitsui's commercial transactions alone were greater than the total State revenue of Japan. More than 50% of the banking capital of Japan was held by the eight leading monopolies — Mitsui, Mitsubishi, Sumitomo, Yasuda, Shibusawa, Kawasaki, Yamaguchi, and Konoike — and the Big Five together held nearly 40% of the total bank deposits, nearly 30% of the total loans, and nearly 45% of the total security investments, in addition to their preëminence in heavy industry, shipping, foreign trade, and the exploitation of colonial resources. The increasing economic strength of these great combines was paralleled by a corresponding growth in their political power, as illustrated by the Kato Government of 1924–25. Both Premier Kato and Baron Shidehara, the Foreign Minister, were related by marriage with the Iwasaki family which controlled the Mitsubishi interests, and two other cabinet members were directly associated with that firm. The influence of industrial and financial interests also penetrated the ranks of the Imperial Household, hitherto the exclusive preserve of the Satsuma-Choshu military nobility, and resulted in the formation of a pro-Mitsubishi clique including Count Makino, Lord Keeper of the Imperial Seal, and Baron Ikki, Minister of the Imperial Household. Prince Saionji, last of the *Genro* (Elder Statesmen) was also sympathetic to the business interests because of his relation to the Sumitomo family.

It is also true that during the twenties, political parties achieved an unprecedented importance in Japan. The franchise was gradually extended until by 1925 all males over 25 years of age were permitted to vote, and during the period from 1925 to 1931, six consecutive governments were formed by party leaders holding majorities in the Diet's lower house. But the attitude of the *Zaibatsu* toward this development of party government was by no means one of enthusiastic support for popular government. They accepted party government as a necessary evil and used it as a weapon for improving their own position within the ruling oligarchy. In their view, it served as a useful safety valve for the intense social discontent that arose after the war. The Rice Riots of 1918 and the strike wave of 1919 had shown the depths of this discontent, and the *Zaibatsu* were glad to allow it to find a harmless outlet in a strictly regulated system of parliamentary government. There was, of course, no danger that the power of the *Zaibatsu* would be impaired, since the Japanese constitution provided ample safeguards against any real democratic control of the government. And to make doubly sure, the leading *Zaibatsu* maintained a financial stranglehold over the two major political parties through lavish contributions to their campaign funds. The Mitsui interests dominated the Seiyukai, while the Minseito was controlled by Mitsubishi.

Thus the most important fact about the growth of parliamentary government during this "liberal decade" is that control of the parties and the parliament remained in the hands of the ruling oligarchy. And that control was used to suppress any demand for changes in Japan's political structure that would give the people real power. Those daring to advocate even the most minor economic or social reforms found themselves subject to the dangers of police "surveillance" and occasional beatings by "patriotic" thugs. It is significant that when the law granting universal male suffrage was passed in 1925, the Government almost immediately passed a "Peace Preservation Act" giving the police full power to arrest anyone suspected of harboring "dangerous thoughts" concerning changes in the "national structure." In this way the authorities successfully forestalled any movement for democratic reform that might have resulted from enlarging the electorate from 2,800,000 to 13,000,000 voters.

Finally, the controversy over a "positive" policy of aggression as against a "moderate" policy of economic penetration by all means short of war was not a conflict between the army "extremists" on the one hand and the "moderate" and peace-loving business interests on the other. The *Zaibatsu* themselves were sharply divided on this issue. The Mitsui interests, who controlled the Seiyukai Party, also had close connections with the dominant clique in the Japanese Army. These groups were aligned in support of the "positive" policy of aggressive expansion on the continent at the expense of China and the Soviet Union. The leading advocate of this policy was General Baron Tanaka, head of the

Seiyukai until his death, and author of the famous Tanaka Memorial, which presented a detailed program for world conquest by Japan.

Opposed to this policy were the Mitsubishi interests, whose military connections were chiefly with the Japanese Navy — a natural result of Mitsubishi's extensive shipbuilding and merchant-marine interests. At that period Mitsubishi had extensive interests in foreign trade throughout Eastern Asia, and its directors believed that the goal of Japanese economic domination in that part of the world could be best achieved by "peaceful penetration" rather than by the program of armed aggression advocated by Baron Tanaka and his army colleagues. Mitsubishi's chief spokesman was Baron Kijuro Shidehara, who served as Japan's Foreign Minister in six out of the seven cabinets that held office between June 1924 and December 1931, and his name is frequently applied to the policy of "moderate" expansion pursued by Japan during that period. Those who maintain that there really are "moderates" and "liberals" within Japan's ruling oligarchy frequently cite Shidehara as an example. But the real truth of the matter is that Shidehara was only a tool of a certain section of the *Zaibatsu* that for a brief period favored this "moderate" policy as the best method of achieving their expansionist aims. When support for this policy weakened after 1930, Shidehara ceased to exercise any political influence.

From 1930 onward, there was no notable opposition to a policy of aggressive expansion from any section of the *Zaibatsu*. Although increasing pressure from the militarists was in part responsible for this, economic considerations were decisive in convincing Japan's financial leaders that it would be more profitable to throw in their lot wholeheartedly with the advocates of a campaign of territorial conquest. The world-wide economic depression after 1929 hit Japan hard; the value of Japanese foreign trade being reduced by nearly half between 1929 and 1931. Under these circumstances, even the most "moderate" business leaders began to look with approval on the army's plans for the seizure of new colonial markets, particularly as these plans involved the expenditure of substantial sums in the form of war contracts to industry.

The attitude of the leading *Zaibatsu* at the time when Japan undertook the first step in her campaign of conquest — the invasion of Manchuria — was summed up by Mr. Ginjiro Fujiwara, then head of the Mitsui paper monopoly, who in July 1944 became Munitions Minister in the Koiso Cabinet. Declaring that "diplomacy without force is of no value," Mr. Fujiwara advocated *Zaibatsu* support for Japan's militarists on the following grounds: "No matter how diligent the Japanese may be, no matter how superior their technical development or industrial administration may be, there will be no hope for Japan's trade expansion if there is no adequate force to back it. Now the greatest of forces is military preparedness founded on the Army and Navy. We can safely expand abroad and engage in various enterprises, if we are confident of protection. In this sense, any outlay for armament is a form of investment." [1]

The *Zaibatsu* soon found that this investment yielded very gratifying returns, as the Army and Navy authorities expended ever larger sums for the rapid expansion of Japanese heavy industries. Navy contracts alone totaled 378 million yen in 1936 and 473 million yen in 1937. The substantial share of these contracts awarded to the Mitsubishi shipyards and Mitsubishi Heavy Industries gave them a valuable stake in a "positive" policy of continental expansion. For all the *Zaibatsu*, "patriotism" became an increasingly profitable business.

This is not to say that there were no disagreements between the *Zaibatsu* and the militarists. But these disagreements did not concern the main objective to which both were committed — the domination of Eastern Asia by Japan. Such disputes as arose were confined entirely to questions of timing and method, and the control and development of the conquered territories. When Japan launched her campaign for the conquest of China in July 1937, she did so under a civilian government headed by Prince Konoye and having the full support of Japanese big business.

The role of the *Zaibatsu* as agents and beneficiaries of Japanese aggression is summed up by Professor G. C. Allen, well-known British authority on Japan, as follows: "The rise of the *Zaibatsu* has depended upon privileges extended to them by the Government and upon their ability to provide the State with financial and other resources in times of stress. They have all benefited from colonial exploitation, and in each of the great wars in which Japan has been engaged they have earned large profits, both from the provision of loans and from supplying war ma-

---

[1] *Spirit of Japanese Industry*, p. 134. Cited by William Henry Chamberlain in his *Japan Over Asia* (New York, 1936), pp. 245–6.

terials. In other words, they have been the necessary instruments of national policy and have reaped a considerable share of the rewards attending the success of that policy. . . . Whatever Government is in office must depend upon the *Zaibatsu* for the resources and expert knowledge needed to carry out its program of political and economic expansion. The Kwantung Army cannot develop Manchukuo without their help. The Admiralty and War Office can only extend armaments by utilizing the *Zaibatsu* factories, and these orders serve to increase their profits. . . ."[1]

The power of the *Zaibatsu* derived not merely from their close association with the State, but also from the fact that they operated extensively in banking, industry, trade, shipping, mining, and every other form of economic activity. Each giant trust was organized both horizontally and vertically into holding companies controlling sources of raw materials, all stages of production, transport, warehousing, and distribution, as well as the banking facilities to finance its own operations. The extent to which the *Zaibatsu* dominated the financial, industrial, and commercial life of Japan before the present war is indicated by the following facts. In 1937, the four leading *Zaibatsu* banks (Mitsui, Mitsubishi, Sumitomo, and Yasuda) possessed more than one-third of the total deposits in non-Government banks, and their trust companies held some 70% of all trust deposits. Furthermore, through investments or loans, these financial institutions controlled many smaller banks and public utilities, as well as many manufacturing enterprises and trading companies in addition to those which they operated directly. A decisive share of Japan's total foreign trade was conducted by their trading companies, and they had large amounts of capital invested in shipping, shipbuilding, colonial enterprises, engineering, mining, metal manufacture, textiles, sugar-refining, and flour-milling.

It has been estimated that the Mitsui family alone controls over 15% of Japan's industry. And if one were to include the houses of Mitsubishi, Sumitomo, and the next five smaller families, as well as the Imperial Household and the Ministry of Finance, the figure would rise to 70%. The Mitsui family, tracing its extraordinary wealth to its seventeenth century monopoly of trade between Osaka and Tokyo, was the banker for the Imperial Restoration in 1867–68. Today, Mitsui controls one of Japan's

[1] G. C. Allen: Part II of *The Industrialization of Japan and Manchukuo 1930–40*, edited by E. B. Schumpeter (New York, 1940), pp. 629–643.

strongest private banks, insurance companies, shipping lines, mines, power companies, spinning and weaving mills, and a vast commercial organization. The older family of Sumitomo got its start toward great wealth through its control of copper mines in the sixteenth and seventeenth centuries. Its interests today are heavily in metals and armaments. Of more recent origin is the firm of Mitsubishi, controlled by the Iwasaki family. Having gained a commanding place in the shipping world through large transport contracts in connection with the Formosan expedition of 1874–75, Mitsubishi today controls a substantial part of Japan's merchant marine and has important shipbuilding as well as a variety of other industrial and commercial interests. Among the "new industrialists," the Nissan interests are outstanding. Based originally on the fortune of Fusanosuke Kuhara, they are directed today by Yoshisuke Aikawa. Nissan's expansion occurred chiefly during the last decade through the preferential position granted it by the Army in the industrial development of Manchuria.

The *Zaibatsu* monopolized iron and steel production, and controlled virtually the entire output of coal, copper, and other minerals. They controlled a large part of the chemical industry and the manufacture of heavy machinery, and had extensive interests in the woolen textile, rayon, and cement industries. Mitsui and Mitsubishi between them controlled the paper industry. Mitsubishi was preëminent in the aircraft, shipbuilding, and shipping industries and had a virtual monopoly on the output of sheet glass, while Sumitomo was supreme in the nonferrous metal industry. In addition, most of the companies founded for the exploitation of raw-material resources in the conquered territories and colonies, in Manchuria, China and the countries of Southeast Asia, were established by the *Zaibatsu* and operated by them or one of their numerous subsidiaries.

Because of their predominant position in banking, industry, and commerce, the *Zaibatsu* were also able to exercise an indirect control over many smaller concerns. The multitude of small producers and merchants in Japan depended on their giant trading companies both for working capital and as a means of distributing their products. Similarly, through their membership in various industrial cartels, the *Zaibatsu* were able to dominate whole industries even when they did not control a major part of the manufacturing capacity. Finally, through their control of the major political parties and through the financial pressure that they could bring to bear on the Government, they were able to control all legislation affecting industry and also to secure substantial subsidies for their enterprises and profitable government contracts.

Thus, despite the fact that at certain points in Japanese history one section of the *Zaibatsu* had differed with the militarists as to the best method of achieving Japanese economic domination over Eastern Asia and the rich colonial resources of the Southwestern Pacific, none of these great monopolies has ever opposed the ultimate aim of Japan's aggressive foreign policy, and they have all profited enormously from equipping Japan's military machine and from exploiting the resources of Formosa, Korea, Manchuria, and other conquered areas. The other important fact to be emphasized about the role of the *Zaibatsu* is that their power derives from an economic system that keeps the great majority of the Japanese people impoverished, and that Japan's limited internal market has constituted one of the major incentives for an aggressive policy of foreign conquest. These two facts should be kept in mind when estimating the probable future policy of a *Zaibatsu*-controlled Japan.

Some commentators tend to minimize the political power of the *Zaibatsu* on the ground that during the war period they were increasingly subjected to State control by the militarists. If this were true, Japanese business and financial interests could be absolved of responsibility for their country's policies in order to build them up as trustworthy candidates for the leadership of postwar Japan. These same commentators contend that the "New Economic Structure" adopted in September 1941 was a plan imposed on the *Zaibatsu* against their will by "extremist" Army leaders determined to bring private industry under their control. This interpretation would be justified if the plan formulated in September 1940 by the Army-dominated Cabinet Planning Board under Naoki Hoshino had gone into effect, since it was designed to effect a drastic State regimentation of industry. But before the Hoshino plan was made public, leading business organizations denounced it as "communistic" and as "denying capital a voice in management." Baron Hiranuma and many conservative Army leaders who had close connections with

Japanese industrial interests hastily registered their opposition to the plan, and Hoshino and other antibusiness elements were dismissed from the Cabinet Planning Board.

In place of the Hoshino Plan, the Cabinet in December 1940 approved a "New Economic Structure" which embodied proposals put forward by the two leading business organizations — the Japanese Economic Federation and the Japan Chamber of Commerce and Industry. This program was put into operation on September 1, 1941 and was taken over without modification by the Tojo Cabinet when it took office on October 18. It stipulated that all war industries would be subject to the control of a series of Control Associations, one for each industry. These Associations, in turn, were to be responsible to the Ministry of Commerce and Industry and were thus technically under government control. As this program was worked out in practice, however, the various Control Associations were made up of the leading firms in each industry and given extensive independent powers. In many cases, moreover, the head of the largest concern in a particular industry became the president of the Control Association for that industry. For example, Hachisaburo Hirao, a Mitsubishi official, was head of both the Iron and Steel Manufacturers Federation and the Iron and Steel Control Association. Similarly, the Coal Control Association was virtually indistinguishable from the Coal Mine Owners Federation, both being headed by Kenjiro Matsumoto, a director of the Mitsui Trust Company.

Thus, though nominally under government control, these Control Associations were actually administered by the *Zaibatsu* and acted entirely independently of the Government as far as questions of labor supply and raw materials were concerned. This naturally made it impossible to enforce an efficient system of priorities, or to compel the *Zaibatsu* to submit to a curtailment of their profits in the interests of increased production. During the first few months of the war, when Japan's armies were piling up rapid victories, this problem was not of primary importance. But when the tide began to turn at the end of 1942, and it became clear that Japan would have to fight a long defensive war, there was an increasing demand for a more effective system for stimulating and controlling industrial production.

This problem was the central issue of debate at three different sessions of the Japanese Diet during 1943. At the regular Diet session that convened late in January 1943, a bitter controversy was precipitated by Premier Tojo's demand for emergency powers to deal with the crisis in economic administration. The net result of this debate was not revealed until March 17, when the text of a new ordinance was made public and the appointment of a Cabinet Advisers Council was announced. Under the new ordinance, the iron and steel, coal, light metals, shipping, and aircraft industries were designated as essential to the war effort, and supreme power for their administration was vested in the Premier. At the same time, however, seven representatives of the *Zaibatsu* were named as a Cabinet Advisers Council with the rank of Ministers of State. Members of this Council were officially empowered to "participate in the Premier's conduct of administrative affairs with regard to the expansion of wartime production and execution of the wartime economy of the nation." It was thus apparent that though Premier Tojo had secured nominal administrative authority over important sections of Japanese industry, the *Zaibatsu's* political power had actually not been diminished. Neither at that time nor at any subsequent stage of the war were they the helpless victims of militarist domination that they subsequently alleged themselves to be.

The next major step was taken in June 1943 when a special session of the Diet passed the Act for the Readjustment of Industrial Enterprises. This Act empowered the Premier to undertake a wholesale conversion of Japan's industrial plant for war purposes, but up to October 1943 there was no evidence that Tojo had used his new powers to reorganize the top administrative system in which representatives of the *Zaibatsu* were firmly entrenched. A wholesale administrative reorganization finally occurred in October 1943, with the centralization of industrial control in a new Ministry of Munitions. Tojo headed this Ministry, but only as a figurehead; executive control over its operation was actually vested in Vice-Minister Kishi, with Ginjiro Fujiwara, who entered the Cabinet in November, as his coadjutor. Fujiwara, a Mitsui official and the actual *Zaibatsu* representative on this issue, took over exclusive control of the Munitions Ministry in July 1944 when the Tojo Cabinet fell. Not only was the executive direction of the Ministry controlled by the *Zaibatsu*, but it functioned under terms laid down in the Munitions Company Control Act. These terms, which left the industrialists undisturbed as managers of their own enterprises and gave additional legal support to the absorption of smaller concerns, were essentially fixed by the *Zaibatsu*. Thus the *Zaibatsu* controlled both the Munitions Ministry and the terms on which that Ministry functioned.

The personnel of the Koiso Cabinet, which held office from July 1944 to April 1945, provides additional evidence that in this continuing struggle for supreme power between the armed forces and the *Zaibatsu*, the latter were increasingly victorious. Not only did Fujiwara become Munitions Minister, but many of the other members of the new Cabinet were connected with either the Mitsui or the Mitsubishi interests. In addition, other Mitsui men were appointed to key positions in the economic and political life of Japan, indicating that the Mitsui interests, at least, had attained a position of full equality with the Army and Navy in determining Japanese policy.[1] This trend was continued in the Suzuki Cabinet, which took office on April 7, 1945, and was composed almost entirely of representatives of the Imperial Household, the Navy, and big business interests. In the new Cabinet the position of Munitions Minister was given to Vice-Admiral Teijiro Toyoda, who in recent years has been president of *Nippon Seitetsu*, Japan's giant semi-official iron and steel trust, as well as of the Iron and Steel Control Association, and whose wife is a member of the Mitsubishi. Other members of the Suzuki Cabinet were also notable for their close connections with the *Zaibatsu* and the Imperial Household, which in itself represents one of the largest business and financial interests in Japan. Fujiwara, though no longer occupying a Cabinet post, was appointed to the new and obviously important position of "Special War Potential Inspector" of Manchukuo.

The increase in the political power of the *Zaibatsu*, despite every effort on the part of the Army and Navy to subject them to militarist control, reflects the greatly increased economic power they had won as a result of the war, and of the industrial policies followed by the Tojo Government. The chief aim of those policies was to consolidate Japanese industry and banking so as to ensure the maximum efficiency in war production. Small business firms were severely penalized and every effort was made to promote their merger with larger enterprises. The *Zaibatsu* were

---

[1] For a detailed analysis of this issue, see T. A. Bisson: "Aspects of Wartime Economic Control in Japan," Ninth Institute of Pacific Relations Conference, January 1945. Secretariat Paper #2, pp. 65–66, 70–74, and 76.

thus able to buy up many smaller firms, and by the terms of the Law Regulating the Application of Capital, passed in October 1943, these firms were compelled to accept payment in shares of the buyer concern rather than in cash. The Adjustment of Enterprises Law, which was passed at the same time, also worked to the benefit of the giant trusts by giving the Government the right to take over all inactive factories, which were then distributed among the essential war industries. As a result of these and other wartime regulations, the *Zaibatsu* increased their already extensive control over the Japanese economy to virtual monopoly proportions. In addition, they profited enormously from being given the juiciest of Japan's spoils of conquest. In all the conquered territories, the best concessions were allotted to the *Zaibatsu* for exploitation. Control of the Laokay phosphate deposits in Indo-China went to the Mitsubishi interests. Philippine resources were parceled out among various companies: Mitsui Products, Mitsui Mining, Ishihara Industries, Mitsubishi Mining, and others; and a similar policy was followed in Malaya and Burma. The 1,100 plantations of Java were first turned over to the Plantation Industry Corporation operated by the Japanese Army, but on May 1, 1944, this policy was reversed and the plantations were divided among 22 private Japanese corporations.

Thus, as in all of Japan's previous wars of conquest, the *Zaibatsu* again joined forces with the militarists in promoting the acquisition of new sources of wealth and profited enormously not only through gaining a lion's share of the spoils in the conquered areas but also by greatly strengthening their domination over all aspects of the Japanese economy. In addition to their support of the policy of expansion abroad, the *Zaibatsu* also cooperated fully in the maintenance of an autocratic political system at home. Throughout the entire war they worked very closely with the militarists, the nobility, and the bureaucracy in promoting the ideology first developed by the rulers of Meiji Japan to ensure the unquestioning obedience of the people to the dictates of the ruling oligarchy, both military and civilian. The main features of this ideology are the system of emperor-worship that requires implicit acceptance of anything done in the Emperor's name, and the doctrine that it is the divinely ordained mission of the Japanese people to unite the world under the rule of the Son of Heaven.

THE POLITICAL FUNCTION OF THE
JAPANESE EMPEROR

THIS RAISES a question that has been the subject of a widespread controversy. Is the Imperial institution in Japan incompatible with the development of a peaceful and democratic Japanese state? There are many who say that it is incompatible on the grounds that it gives whatever group surrounds the throne the powerful weapon of divine sanction for its acts, makes military aggression a religious virtue, demands blind obedience to a divine ruler, and teaches the dangerous doctrine of racial supremacy. On the other hand, as we have seen, there are those who argue that the Emperor could serve a useful purpose, once the militarists have been eliminated, by giving his divine sanction to the policies of a new "moderate" ruling group or even a democratic regime. In view of this sharp disagreement as to the proper attitude toward the Imperial institution in Japan, it is worth while to examine in some detail the political role played by the Japanese Emperor throughout modern Japanese history.

To the architects of the Meiji Restoration must be attributed the responsibility for giving new life to the legend of imperial divinity that had been largely ignored during the long rule of the *Shoguns*. They were quick to see that the protection of a divine monarch would give them the necessary power and prestige not only to subdue the recalcitrant feudal lords, but also to combat the demands of those groups that wished to carry through a genuine democratic revolution. The use of the Imperial Throne to block political progress at a point where all power still remained with the ruling oligarchy was most clearly manifested in the constitution *bestowed* by the Emperor on his people in 1889.

This constitution was skillfully designed to meet the rising demand for a more democratic form of government by granting a representative national assembly, while preserving all the real powers of the ruling oligarchy intact. Its principal author was Prince Ito, who was dispatched on a mission to Europe to study the constitutions of the various European countries. In the course of his investigations, Ito found that the Prussian Constitution preserved the privileges of the Junkers and the military caste, gave the King a position independent of the nobility, and made parliament little more than a façade. He was particularly impressed with the fact that the Prussian Army and Navy were not controlled by Parliament but were subject directly to the Kaiser. In his view, Prussia's semiabsolutist, militarist state was ideally suited to the needs of Japan's ruling caste, and he therefore patterned the new Japanese Constitution on the Prussian model. The phrase, "Japan, the Prussia of the Far East," dates from that period.[1]

After his return to Japan, Ito worked for some years and eventually produced a document that was guaranteed to safeguard Japanese political life from any taint of democracy. In modern Japan, sovereignty does not rest with the people, but is embodied in the person of the Emperor. He is the Supreme Commander of the Army and Navy, appoints all high-ranking officers, the Prime Minister and the Privy Councillors, and approves the Cabinet and foreign and domestic policy. The Cabinet is responsible primarily to the Emperor, and although the consent of the Diet is nominally required for all legislative acts initiated by the Government, it has no independent power of legislation, and in times of "emergency" when the Diet is not in session Imperial Ordinances have the force of law. The Diet is also deprived of the "power of the purse" by the provision that in the event a budget is not passed, the budget of the previous year automatically goes into effect. Finally, though the Lower House of the Diet is now elected by universal manhood suffrage, its Upper House of Peers, whose approval is necessary before any statute becomes law, is composed of all the Princes and higher aristocracy, 125 Imperial appointees, and 65 members selected by the biggest taxpayers. No change in the status of the House of Peers can be made without its consent.

The constitution also established the system of *niju seifu*, or dual government, which gives the armed forces of Japan a pow-

---

[1] See "German-Japanese Relations, Past and Present," by Albert H. Schreiner, *Amerasia*, October 25, 1943, pp. 328–336. Mr. Schreiner comments that "it is interesting to observe in Hitler's Third Reich a reciprocal influence of the Japanese conception of the State. After the collapse of the Hohenzollern monarchy, the spokesmen and theoreticians of German imperialism were in search of a 'profitable' principle of government. The 'Mikado principle,' i.e., the idea of an imperial power transcending all internal political changes, was advocated by General Haushofer and was later adapted for German use as the 'leadership principle' (*Fuehrer-Prinzip*). [General Haushofer, the intellectual leader of German geopolitics, was in Japan as a member of a German military mission before the First World War and subsequently became one of the leading proponents of German-Japanese collaboration.]"

erful and independent status as a *political* force. The Prime Minister and the Cabinet advise the Emperor on all civilian matters, while the Ministers of War and Navy, the Chiefs of Staff, and other high officers advise him on military matters. Neither the Cabinet nor the Diet has any control over the Army and Navy, which are responsible solely to the Emperor and can make or unmake Governments by refusing to nominate officers for the posts of War and Navy Minister. Thus, as an integral part of the ruling system, Japan's militarists have an important stake in preserving Japan's form of monarchist dictatorship. Another important feature of the Japanese political structure is the influential role played by officials of the Imperial Household — the Lord Privy Seal, the Lord Chamberlain, and the Imperial Household Minister. These men are the intimate advisers of the Emperor on all matters of policy, and no audiences with the Emperor can be held without their consent. Yet they have no responsibility whatsoever to the elected parliament.

Having established the principle of an absolute sovereign, ruling by divine right, the ruling oligarchy proceeded to develop a national philosophy based on the institution of emperor-worship and the doctrine of Japan's "divine mission." The Japanese people were taught that blind obedience and devotion to the Emperor were the highest virtues that any Japanese citizen could possess. They were also taught that they themselves were a chosen race, that their Empire was founded on the principle of *Hakko Ichiu,* or "The World as One Family," and that it was the "manifest destiny" of Japan to establish world peace by bringing all nations together under the rule of the Son of Heaven.

This ideology was instilled into the people of Japan by every means at the disposal of the ruling clique. It became a fundamental part of the Japanese state religion — Shintoism — and of the educational system, which was almost entirely State controlled. Every Japanese child was taught the sacred words of Jimmu Tenno, the first Emperor: "We shall build our capital all over the world and make the whole world our dominion." According to the *Army Reader,* which every Japanese soldier must study, this Imperial rescript "has been given to our race and to our troops as an everlasting categorical imperative." Furthermore, the Japanese people were taught that "from the fact of the divine descent of the Japanese people proceeds their immeasurable superiority to the natives of other countries in courage and intelligence." As the chosen race of the gods, Japan must fulfill her destiny by bringing all inferior races under her enlightened rule, and, if these races are so benighted as to resist, they must be forced to submit.

The propagation of this fantastic and highly dangerous philosophy was by no means confined to "fanatical visionaries" within the armed forces. Civilian as well as military leaders of Japan constantly stressed this doctrine, not only as a means of convincing the Japanese people of the righteousness of their "holy war" in Asia, but also to compel their unquestioning acceptance of hardships and privations at home. Thus, former Foreign Minister Matsuoka declared in a recent book: "I firmly believe that the great mission that heaven imposed on Japan is to save humanity. In conformity with the great spirit in which the Emperor Jimmu founded the Empire, Japan should take over the management of the continent on a large scale, propagate *Hakko Ichiu* and the Imperial Way, and extend it all over the world." Similarly, Prince Konoye who is often mentioned as an eminently suitable leader for a "moderate" government in postwar Japan, declared on the occasion of the Tripartite Pact with Germany and Italy: "That the various nations and races of the world should mark out several spheres for mutual existence and common prosperity is inevitable, and that Japan in East Asia and Germany and Italy in Europe should respectively assume leadership in their assigned spheres is equally inevitable from standpoints whether historical, geographical, or economic." On the same occasion, Konoye stated that "to maintain world peace . . . is indeed the immutable national policy of Japan, firmly rooted in the principles on which our nation is founded."

How widely and deeply the fantastic mythology surrounding the person of the Emperor has penetrated every section of Japanese society is nowhere better illustrated than in an article published in the magazine *Chuo Koron* (Central Review) in 1943. This was the most liberal magazine in prewar Japan — so liberal, in fact, that less than a year after this article appeared, *Chuo Koron*, together with another magazine, *Kaizo* (Reconstruction), was compelled to suspend publication. In this article, which concluded with an exhortation to the Japanese people to strengthen their national solidarity around their Emperor as the center of all life, the author, Takao Yamada, wrote in part: "The saying that Japan is the Land of the Gods is, of course, derived from the fact that it was begotten by the two gods, Izanagi and Izanami. It can be considered to be the Land of the Gods by reason of its divine birth. If the parent is a god, then the child also must possess the same divine nature. This means nothing else than that our empire in itself is god. The Emperor who is the direct descendant of the gods holds everlasting sway as ruler, and is the real embodiment of the Land of the Gods itself. Hence the phrase 'the Land of the Gods' is not used in any figurative or metaphorical sense, the actual fact exists in the country; it is the reality. . . . When the time comes for the realization of one body for the true peace of the future world, as the central pivot capable of maintaining that peace, we cannot doubt that, apart from our Imperial Family, there is certainly no other absolute. . . . The impossibility of maintaining peace without a true absolute must be acknowledged by everyone, not only by the Japanese."[1]

These few examples could be multiplied many times, but they are sufficient to indicate the character of the role played by the Imperial institution as the instrument of the ruling oligarchy, both military and civilian. Throughout modern Japanese history, the sanction of Imperial divinity has been repeatedly used to block the development of democratic progress and to safeguard the power of the ruling class. The composition of the groups shielded by the aura of the Throne has shifted repeatedly, but their aims have remained constant: to expand Japan's power abroad and to maintain their autocratic control over her political and economic structure. The Emperor's sacred name has thus been used to justify and strengthen a policy of absolutism and national chauvinism; of militarist aggression abroad and fascist dictatorship at home.

It must be recognized, however, that the doctrine of imperial divinity and the institution of emperor-worship have unquestionably secured a firm hold on the minds of great numbers of Japanese, and that the task of discrediting them presents a very difficult and delicate problem. The reverence with which the average Japanese regards the Imperial Throne is the product of some fifty years of increasingly intensive indoctrination, and there is little evidence that even a disastrous military defeat will under-

---

[1] Takao Yamada: "The Mission of Japan, the Land of the Gods," *Chuo Koron*, Tokyo, September 1943.

mine the belief of the Japanese in their Emperor; such a defeat can easily be attributed to the errors of his military advisers. It is difficult for Western minds to comprehend the attitude of the average Japanese toward the Emperor. He is not only godlike and holy — he is the father of the Japanese people, to be obeyed and venerated. A Japanese professor, lecturing at the "Japan Institute" in Berlin early in 1944, described this fundamental feature of Japanese political thought as follows: "The State concept of the Japanese people is rooted in the belief that rulers and subjects originally derive from the same stock. The Emperor is the head of the State, but at the same time he is the head of the family. The Japanese obey and esteem the Emperor as his subjects and as his children. A successful analysis of Japanese national characteristics cannot be made without the consideration of the Emperor as a 'father.' . . . It is the basis of the peculiar and strength-giving ethics of Japan, which designates that — in the last analysis — devotion and loyalty to the head of the State and love and esteem of parents and family are the same."

There is therefore something to be said for avoiding a frontal attack on the Emperor on the ground that it might arouse fanatical opposition on the part of millions of Japanese and divert their resentment against the militarists into a holy crusade in defense of the Emperor. It may be assumed that our State Department had such considerations in mind when it discouraged public criticism of the Emperor and pictured him as a helpless but unwilling victim of the militarists. But, though there may be reasons for avoiding such a frontal attack, there is no reason for avoiding other measures to discredit the imperial institution, and no excuse for fostering the belief that the Emperor can in future become the instrument of a "moderate" and peace-loving ruling oligarchy. For there is no "liberal element" in Japan's ruling class that is opposed to a powerful autocratic regime or whose economic interests are bound up with political freedom. It seems hardly likely that, so long as the *Zaibatsu* continue to control Japan, the power and influence of the Throne would be exercised in such a way as to diminish the power of the great monopolies. It may be noted in this connection that the Imperial family itself deserves to be included among the *Zaibatsu*, inasmuch as even before the war it owned landed estates and industrial stocks and shares worth more than one billion yen. Those who advocate the retention of the Imperial institution in postwar Japan should be required to state specifically what persons or groups they expect to take the place of the present dictatorship.

One thing is certain and that is that we cannot and should not trust a Japan controlled by the *Zaibatsu* if we do not wish to be confronted with a resurgence of Japanese aggression within a few years' time. However plausibly the representatives of these giant monopolies may plead that they were helpless victims of militarist pressure, their record is clear and unmistakable. In the field of foreign affairs they have aided and abetted the policy of territorial conquest, while in the sphere of domestic policy they have consistently supported measures designed to keep the standards of living of the Japanese people at the lowest possible level and to deny them any real voice in the government of their country.

If we are looking for leaders who will genuinely strive to create a democratic and peaceful Japan, we shall not find them among the men whose power depends upon the maintenance of an autocratic political system and a top-heavy, oppressive economic structure. Instead, we must search for them among those who wish to root out the stifling remnants of feudalism in Japanese society, raise the living standards of the people, and thus remove the fundamental causes of Japan's aggressive policies. We must recognize clearly that no individual who has any ties with the ruling oligarchy and who wishes to preserve his stake in Japan's present economic structure can possibly be a liberal in either the political or the economic sphere. The search for a new "Shidehara" among the civilian members of the ruling class cannot produce a trustworthy leader for postwar Japan.

We may strip Japan of her colonies, disband her armed forces, dismantle her strategic industries, and subject her to a prolonged period of Allied supervision. But if we leave her with an unhealthy economic structure and a leadership that is basically incapable of solving its problems peacefully, that leadership — like the leaders of post-Versailles Germany — will seek out every loophole in the emerging system of world security to rebuild Japan as a military power. Only if we provide opportunities and encouragement for the emergence of a democratically controlled Japan, in which the roots of a feudal economic system have been eliminated and the stranglehold of the great monopolies has been broken, can we hope to see Japan adopt peaceful and coöperative policies and become a trustworthy member of international society. Furthermore, in such a Japan, the power of those groups that have supported the system of emperor-worship for their own aggressive ends will be broken, and the question of the Emperor's future role can be safely left to the Japanese people to decide for themselves.

CHAPTER IX

DEMOCRATIC FORCES IN JAPAN

❀

M UCH OF THE debate over how we should deal with a defeated Japan has been marked by a notable lack of confidence in the ability of the Japanese people themselves to tackle the task of constructing a peaceful and democratic government. The general tenor of most comments on this question has been to the effect that the Japanese people are "sheeplike" in their blind obedience and fanatical devotion to the Emperor and to those who speak in his name; that at best we can expect them to submit docilely to the dictates of their conquerors, but that it is hopeless to count on them to provide effective leadership.

Such a defeatist attitude toward the people of Japan is both dangerous and unjustified. Dangerous, because it provides a plausible argument for doing business with the wartime civilian rulers of Japan on the ground that no other group exists that is capable of assuming the tasks of responsible government. Unjustified, because modern Japanese history proves that the Japanese people have carried on a determined though unsuccessful fight for democratic progress and economic reforms, despite a severity of repression unparalleled in any other country. The drastic methods of police control adopted by successive Japanese Governments from the days of the Meiji era to the present, the brutal suppression of peasant uprisings and industrial strikes, and the continuous persecution of those suspected of harboring "dangerous thoughts" against the regime, are in themselves eloquent proof that the rulers of Japan have gone in constant fear of a popular revolt, and that those popular forces have never been successfully crushed. The hungry, oppressed, and overworked millions in Japan's factories and on her farms constitute a potential democratic force that it would be disastrous to ignore. Admittedly, because of the severity of fifty years of repressive measures, the forces of opposition to the present dictatorial regime are dispersed and poorly organized. But they are by no means nonexistent, even though they may appear so to those whose contacts in Japan did not include these forces.

Although the first industrial strike in Japan occurred in 1886, the real beginnings of organized protest on the part of the Japanese people against their exploitation by the ruling oligarchy may be traced to the decade following the Sino-Japanese War of 1894-95. The expansion of Japanese industry during this period was naturally accompanied by a rapid growth in the number of industrial workers; and these workers, assisted by enlightened intellectuals, began to learn of the activities of organized labor movements in Western countries. The authorities promptly sought to counter this trend by the "Police Law for the Preservation of Public Order and Tranquillity" promulgated in 1900, which provided that political activity against the Government and "recruiting for organizations aimed at collective action on questions relating to working conditions and wages" should be punished by imprisonment with hard labor. A year later the notorious reactionary and chauvinist *Kokuryukai* (Black Dragon Society), devoted to aggression and expansion on the continent and the suppression of popular movements at home, was established with strong connections and protection from the Government. In the same year, 1901, the first Japanese Socialist Party was formed.

The ten years following the Russo-Japanese war witnessed a further expansion of Japanese industry and a corresponding growth in the number of industrial disputes. But it was the economic crisis following the First World War that marked the real beginning of an organized labor movement in Japan, and also a rapid increase in the number of peasant uprisings. Inflation, high prices, profiteering, and intensive exploitation of both peasants and industrial workers combined to cause a widespread movement of popular protest. The number of peasant riots, many of which were suppressed only by the use of troops, increased from 85 in 1917 to 408 in 1920 and 1,255 in 1921. By 1925, they had risen to 2,206 involving more than 100,000 farmers, and the militant Tenant Farmers Union, established in 1922, had grown rapidly into a powerful organization with 350,000 members.

Perhaps the greatest of all peasant uprisings in modern Japan began on August 3, 1918, when fishwives in a tiny village on the Japan Sea protested against the unbearably high price of rice. There soon developed a nationwide series of rice riots, involving workers, farmers, students, clerks, merchants, and unemployed. In Kobe, for example, the rioters attacked rice stores, wrecked homes of officials, set fire to newspaper plants, and even attacked police stations with a variety of home-made weapons. Before the rioters throughout the nation were finally suppressed, some 8,000 were arrested, convicted, and imprisoned. The rapidity and intensity with which the 1918 rice riots spread, provides a suggestive indication of the momentum that a popular movement among the Japanese people may acquire.

Industrial strikes also increased sharply in numbers and scope. From 50 strikes involving fewer than 8,000 workers in 1914, the number rose to 417 strikes involving 66,000 workers in 1918. The Japanese Federation of Labor was formed in 1920; the Japanese Communist Party was organized in 1922 under the leadership of American-educated Sen Katayama; and a Farmer-Labor Party was organized in 1925. In 1926–28 there were 3,484 strikes involving 433,500 workers; in 1929–31 there were 6,165 strikes involving more than 500,000 workers and 7,597 "rice and rent" riots in the rural areas. This growing movement of popular protest against the living and working conditions imposed on the Japanese people by their rulers was countered with every repressive measure at the command of the authorities. The "Peace Preservation Laws" were ruthlessly enforced against every suspected individual and group. The political parties were brought under the control of the great *Zaibatsu* and obediently pursued the policies dictated by their owners. Elections were carefully supervised, and voters were intimidated by the secret societies and terrorist organizations into voting for "orthodox" candidates approved by the authorities.

The rise of popular unrest was a powerful contributing factor in the decision to launch a campaign of military conquest on the continent in 1931. By this means, Japan's rulers planned to allay domestic unrest and transfer the hostility of the people from their own repressive regime to a foreign "enemy." Moreover, by presenting their invasion of Manchuria as a campaign to defend Asia against Chinese and Russian "bolshevism," the Japanese Government acquired a useful tool for suppressing every shade of opposition at home, which was henceforth branded as unpatriotic and "communist." As one observer of Japanese politics during the early thirties pointed out: "A Communist is anyone who seeks to change the Constitution of Japan. So also are all

Koreans and Formosans who seek independence, all labor leaders who stir up strikes, all students who peruse Karl Marx."[1] In 1932 alone, more than 7,000 people were arrested on charges of "Communism," and between 1931 and 1934 more than 24,000 alleged "Communists" were seized and imprisoned. In addition to leaders of trade and peasant unions, these included nurses who had demanded more than 1.20 yen (about 40 cents) for a twelve-hour day; primary school teachers accused of "studying philosophy" and of seeking to give a modern interpretation to the myths that pass for formal history in Japan; and university professors who had contributed funds to help liberal candidates seek election to the Diet.

In addition to their ruthlessly repressive measures against the peasants and workers of Japan, the authorities also endeavored to deprive the people of an educated leadership by instituting an all-pervading system of police spying and "thought control" among university students and teachers. They were particularly alarmed at the rapid spread of "radical" ideas among the children of wealthy and prominent families. Sons and daughters of millionaires, of members of the House of Peers, of college professors, judges, and lawyers, were among those caught in the police dragnet for "radicals."

Despite increasingly severe repression, however, student strikes and demonstrations became increasingly political in character during the early thirties. According to Mr. Wildes, in his book quoted above, "serious student disorders came in 1933, following the dismissal from Kyoto Imperial University Law School of Yokitatsu Takikawa, professor of politics. Takikawa . . . had declared that laws in any country were conditioned by the economic structure of the land. . . . Every law school professor resigned immediately. . . . Kyoto students struck. For the first time in Japan's scholastic history a sympathy strike was begun with the walk-out of six thousand Tokyo Imperial University students. Riots resulted in both Kyoto and Tokyo and half a hundred arrests were made." In that same year, 800 Tokyo students demonstrated in protest against the "imperialist war" on China. In concluding his description of the continued opposition of university students to the repressive measures of the Government and its aggressive foreign policy, Mr. Wildes points out that "to those who know the degree to which success in university

---

[1] Harry Emerson Wildes: *Japan in Crisis* (New York, 1934), p. 99.

life is an essential to adult success in Japan, the phenomena are astonishing . . . [and] a reassuring sign for those who are dismayed by the success of the militarists and reactionaries."

That the Japanese labor movement never attained great numerical strength is not surprising. Trade union leaders not only faced imprisonment and brutal treatment at the hands of the thugs of the secret societies, but also were handicapped in their efforts to secure better wages and working conditions by the fact that the impoverished rural areas could furnish Japanese industrialists with unlimited supplies of cheap labor. During the period 1920–40, membership in Japanese trade unions constituted only about 6% to 7% of the total number of industrial workers, and no industry was fully organized. At their numerical peak, in 1936, organized workers numbered about 420,000 out of a total working force of approximately 6 million.[1] Nevertheless, the antifascist and antimilitarist forces showed their courage and determination during the elections of 1936, when many trade unions came out openly against war. The May Day parade of May 1, 1936 was one of the largest and most militant ever staged in Japan, with workers demanding freedom of political institutions, the nationalization of the monopolies, and the ending of aggression in China. Anti-war leaflets were distributed in the Army, and Japanese arms and ammunition somehow found their way into the hands of the Manchurian guerrillas. In the April 1937 Diet elections, the Social Masses Party, a moderate farmer-labor party supported by the Japanese Federation of Labor, polled 928,000 votes and sent 37 members to the Diet.

The rising movement of popular protest against the recurrent wars and constant exploitation of the Japanese people was intolerable to the ruling oligarchy, who were engaged in preparations for large-scale war on the Asiatic continent. And when they found that the war against China, launched in July 1937, was not going to be the brief "incident" they had expected, they redoubled their efforts to crush all opposition to a totalitarian dictatorship. In December 1937, the National Trade Union Council, the most radical labor federation that had been permitted to

---

[1] The highest percentage (7.8) of organized workers was reached in 1932, with 377,625 organized out of a total of 4,860,276. Numerically, the highest point reached was in 1936, with 420,589 organized out of 6,090,116 for a percentage of 6.9. In 1940, immediately preceding the suppression of trade unions, only 184,000 out of 8,563,000 workers were organized.

exist, was suppressed, together with the Japan Proletariat Party with which it was affiliated. Hundreds of labor leaders were arrested, and the police raided anti-war organizations, trade unions, and peasant leagues. The secret imperialist societies like the "Black Dragon," the "Black Ocean," and other terrorist groups; patriotic leagues like the "Association of Ex-Servicemen" and the "Society of Old Combatants"; and many other chauvinistic organizations were mobilized for the "struggle against bolshevism."

In July 1938, a Government-sponsored "labor front," the *Sangyo Hokoku Kai* (National Industrial Service Association), was initiated and pressure was brought to bear on workers to join. By August 1940 the "labor front" claimed a "membership" of three and a half million workers. The Government then determined to crush the independent unions entirely and to incorporate them into the fascist "New Economic Structure." In November 1940, the Minister of Welfare assumed direct control of the Labor Front, which was henceforth known as the "Patriotic Industrial Society" or *Sampo*. The workers in each plant were ordered to form a "coöperative body" with "the manager of the enterprise as the leader," and the treasuries of the former independent unions had to be surrendered to the Government-controlled *Sampo*.

Despite ruthless suppression, however, the Japanese labor movement gave evidence of continued strength. In April 1941, 100,000 workers in the Kobe war industries waged a five-day strike which affected particularly the Kawasaki dockyard and the Mitsubishi war plants — a strike that was finally smashed by Japanese troops. A second strike, in August 1941, involved some 20,000 workers in the Mitsubishi aircraft plant. This was settled by partial concessions, but extensive arrests followed and many labor leaders were deported for hard labor in Manchuria. The last big strike of 1941 took place in October at one of the heavy industry plants near Tokyo, where 20,000 workers struck. This was also broken by troops. These figures, gathered from a variety of sources, may be high. But even the government admitted that there were 300 strikes involving 14,874 workers in 1941, and 259 strikes involving 13,752 workers in 1942.

These strikes were directed primarily against the intolerable working conditions — the sixteen-hour day, the seven-day week, poor food, low wages, and high accident rate — but in at least two of the strikes the workers also raised anti-war slogans. News of these strikes, eventually gathered from Japanese prisoners in China, was successfully kept from the world for a considerable time, indicating that unrest and popular discontent could be fairly widespread in Japan and yet be concealed by the Japanese authorities. That such unrest and discontent continued and became intensified is suggested by the scanty news items that occasionally leaked through the rigid Japanese censorship, and by the Government's repeated references to the need for "resolute measures" against "persons who disturb the solidarity of the nation." In the spring of 1945, for example, there was abundant evidence that the Japanese Government was deeply disturbed about the problem of "popular morale." The need for "winning popular support," "regaining the people's confidence," and arousing them for an all-out defense effort was being constantly emphasized in official proclamations as well as in the radio and press. Though organized popular opposition to the ruling clique had been largely crushed or driven underground, the fact that Japan's leaders were appealing desperately for the "unification" of the home front in the face of an imminent invasion threat indicated that they were by no means certain of popular support. The organization of a new totalitarian political society — the Greater Japan Political Association — headed by General Jiro Minami of Kwantung Army fame was only one of many measures suggesting the Government's fear of a collapse of the home front in the event of an invasion. Another was the appointment of Genki Abe as Minister of Home Affairs in the Suzuki Cabinet. Abe is known as a professional "Himmlerian" politician who can be relied on to maintain "order" at all costs. As superintendent of the Tokyo Metropolitan Police Board in 1937 and again in 1940, he was officially described as a "courageous" and "efficient" law-enforcement officer. He is also reported to have spent several years in China studying the activities of the Chinese Communists, and is allegedly one of Japan's foremost authorities on this subject.

That this unrest was not confined to industrial workers was indicated by an article published in the October 1943 issue of *Gendai*. In question and answer form, this article presented the usual jingoistic exhortations to the Japanese people, including the assertion that Japan will ultimately triumph, if not in this war, then in the next, even if it takes a hundred years or more. The authors urged that steps should be taken immediately "to prevent our present-day youths from being poisoned intellectually," because "while we must carry through the present war to an effective conclusion, we must continually engage ourselves in preparation for the next war." Their most revealing comments, however, appeared in their criticism of Japan's intellectuals. They suggested that there were a large number of Japanese intellectuals who refused to accept the thesis that this is a holy war to bring the world under the divine rule of the Japanese Emperor, preferring to accept "a European view of the State" as a system to protect the interests and welfare of the individual, instead of recognizing that the individual must be merged with the State. "Ideological warfare in Japan consists in overcoming individualism, and its chief battlefield lies within the country." The article revealed, furthermore, that despite all efforts at censorship, Allied propaganda was reaching the Japanese people to a disturbing extent. "Even now short-wave radio propaganda is being vigorously directed against Japan. . . . There are plenty of receiving and broadcasting stations of an enemy nature within the country. [Here a number of words were expurgated by the censor] . . . Our farmers and laborers have remained unaffected . . . but the intellectual classes are most in need of purification from such tainted views. . . . If such people were in charge of the education of the Army and Navy, we could not make war. The soldier would not give his life peacefully." The authors also reveal that the Japanese Government is rounding up intellectuals considered to be opposed or lukewarm toward the war by their remark that many have been made "scapegoats in connection with the movement to correct erroneous views."[1]

Another indication that prodemocratic forces have not been completely swallowed up in a wave of fanatical patriotism is provided by the story of Yukio Ozaki, one of Japan's most venerable liberal statesmen, who has consistently taken an antimilitarist and prodemocratic stand throughout his sixty years of political life. Elected to the Diet from Miye Prefecture for the first time in 1890, Ozaki was elected to every successive Diet from the same prefecture, and was one of the few political leaders to maintain a critical antimilitarist attitude after December 7, 1941. The greatest test of both his courage and his popularity came during the elections of April 1942 which occurred at the height

---

[1] A discussion by Tsuji Sato, Hinatha Saito, and Tada Saito on "Ideological Warfare in the Present Decisive War Situation," *Gendai*, Tokyo, October 1943.

of Japan's military victories. Japan had not had an election since 1937, and this one was rigorously regulated by the newly formed Imperial Rule Assistance Political Society — parliamentary wing of Japan's new totalitarian party, the Imperial Rule Assistance Association. The chief function of IRAPS was to secure the defeat of liberal candidates like Ozaki, and the Japanese voters were warned to be "careful in their conduct" at the polls.

Despite the repressive political atmosphere, Ozaki was re-elected with a substantial total of 14,525 votes. The Government then determined to silence him by arresting him on charges of lèse majesté for a statement made during one of his campaign speeches, and he was sentenced to eight months' imprisonment. In the spring of 1944, however, the Japanese Supreme Court reversed this decision and acquitted him of the charges. Since the Japanese courts are completely subordinated to the political dictates of the State, this reversal must be considered a reversal of government policy, and an indication that, because of Ozaki's great popularity and the high respect he enjoys among large sections of the people, the Government did not dare to insist on his imprisonment.

Since Ozaki himself is in his eighties, it is improbable that he can be relied on to take an active political role in postwar Japan. What is significant is that by his long career as a fearless critic of militarism and dictatorship, he has won a sufficiently strong popular following to command the fear, if not the respect, of the Japanese Government, and that his supporters were courageous enough to ignore the threats of the authorities at a time when even the most "reliable moderates," deeply impressed by the rapid successes of the militarists, were hastily climbing on the fascist political bandwagon.

No estimate of the potential antimilitarist and prodemocratic forces in Japan would be complete without reference to the work of Japanese antifascists in China, who carried on psychological warfare against Japanese troops and educational work among Japanese prisoners of war. One such group, the Anti-war League (*Hansen Domei*), under the leadership of Wataru Kaji, well-known Japanese revolutionary writer, began working under the auspices of the Chungking Government in 1938. Unfortunately, however, its activities were increasingly circumscribed as a result of the deepening animosity in Chungking against any and all "popular" or "radical" movements. In 1944 this hostility reached such a point that Kaji and his followers were no longer permitted to go to the front lines to broadcast to the Japanese troops, thus depriving China of a weapon of psychological warfare that had admittedly been of great concern to Japanese Army leaders.

Beginning early in 1944, therefore, the principal antimilitarist and prodemocratic activities of the Japanese in China were those carried on by the Japanese People's Emancipation League (*Nippon Jinmin Kaiho Renmei*), which had its headquarters in Yenan. Organized in January 1944 under the leadership of Susumu Okano, prominent Japanese Communist, the aim of the League was to provide antimilitarist leadership to the Japanese people and to win the support of all elements willing to subscribe to its program: the immediate cessation of the war, the withdrawal of Japanese troops from all occupied territories including Manchuria, and the establishment of a democratic form of government in Japan. The program of the League, as outlined in its "Antiwar Call to the Japanese People," emphasized the serious losses suffered by the Japanese people as a result of the war, exposed the false propaganda of the militarists, denounced the giant trusts as profiting from the war jointly with the militarists, and called for the overthrow of the existing regime and the establishment of a representative People's Government that would enact a democratic constitution and also undertake measures to improve the economic position of workers, farmers, and small businessmen.

The life of Susumu Okano, leader of the League, presents an interesting parallel to the political career of Palmiro Togliatti, leader of the Italian Communist Party, who became Minister of State in the Italian Government established after the liberation of Rome. Okano is the most important known member of the seven-man Central Committee of the Japanese Communist Party. His real name is Sanzo Nosaka, which he changed to Okano in 1932 when he was forced to flee from Japan. Born in 1892, his career in the Japanese labor movement dates back to 1912 when he joined the *Yuai Kai* (Fraternal Society), a labor society headed by Bunji Suzuki. Okano is one of the few living Communists that witnessed the inauguration of the Japanese Communist Party in 1922. He became a member of the Central Executive Committee and aided in drafting the "Outline of the Situation in Japan and the Task of the Japanese Communist Party" — a document that set forth two main objectives: resistance to the development of military fascism and the advocacy of basic democratic and antifeudal reforms in Japan. From 1922 to 1932, Okano was active in the labor movement in Japan and in the Workers and Peasants Party (*Rodo Nominto*). He was imprisoned for short periods in 1922 and 1925, and then was arrested in 1928 and sentenced to ten years in jail. Released because of ill health, he fled from Japan and has never returned. In 1935 he was elected a member of the Executive Committee of the Comintern and traveled widely for the next eight years until 1943 when he arrived in Yenan.

In an interview in Yenan in September 1944, during which Okano elaborated on the program of the Emancipation League for postwar Japan, he made the following points: that the power of the Privy Council, the House of Peers, and the Elder Statesmen should be reduced with a view to their eventual elimination from Japan's political structure; that full democratic rights should be given to the people; that full governing power should rest with the Diet, which should be elected by universal suffrage; that all political parties should enjoy legal recognition; and that a new constitution should be enacted on the basis of these points, such a constitution to include the abolition of the special powers and privileges of the militarists.

The economic program of the League, as explained by Okano, advocated government control of large-scale monopoly enterprises, but was opposed to confiscation with the exception of excess profits. Other objectives included the elimination of the armaments industry, the mechanization of agriculture, the eight-hour day, collective bargaining, the right to strike, social insurance, etc. Okano also suggested that as a start toward the elimination of feudalism in landholding, the Government should buy land from absentee landlords and make it available to landless peasants for cultivation. The Government, he repeated, should be a democratic people's government in which all liberal groups should be represented including the Japanese Communists. In Okano's opinion, the greatest obstacle to the peaceful, orderly, and progressive development of Japan would be the undiminished power and influence of the "big capitalists" (*Zaibatsu*). "They must not be left untouched at the end of this war. . . . If their power is not curtailed, they can prevent the democratic, antimilitarist growth of Japan. They can be the major cause of another world war."

One aspect of the program of the Emancipation League which deserves special mention is the fact that it makes no direct reference to the Emperor, placing the entire blame for the war on the militarists and their civilian supporters among the ruling oligarchy. Questioned on this point by American visitors to Yenan, Okano stated explicitly that the League does not demand the abolition of the Imperial institution because, while Japanese Communists are naturally opposed to it, the League is not an exclusively Communist organization. Rather, it welcomes and seeks the support and coöperation of all antiwar Japanese, including those who retain their loyalty to the Emperor. In the opinion of the League, the main task of the Japanese people is to stop the war and throw out the ruling clique. Once the existing regime has been overthrown, leaders of the League believe that the Emperor's future role should be decided by the Japanese people after the introduction of a new and democratic constitution. In their opinion, however, any attempt on the part of the Allies to make use of the Emperor as an instrument of social control would be dangerous, since it might be taken advantage of by groups opposed to a democratic Japan.

Although there were only some 400-odd Japanese members of the Emancipation League working in the Border Regions and guerrilla areas of North China during 1944, the importance of their activities was far greater than their numerical strength. Many of them were serving in the Eighth Route Army as psychological warfare officers, translators, and instructors in Japanese methods of warfare. Others were carrying on highly effective educational work among Japanese prisoners of war. Unlike the Japanese antifascists in the Chungking-controlled areas, the members of the League enjoyed the fullest coöperation from the local authorities in the guerrilla areas, and had the additional advantage of closer proximity to Japan. Since the Eighth Route Army's control extended to the outskirts of Peiping and Tientsin, it was not too difficult to smuggle people and propaganda into and out of Japan.

It is interesting to note in this connection that the views of the Chinese Communist Party regarding the postwar treatment of Japan are very similar to those expressed by Okano. Interviewed on this question by American observers in Yenan, Chinese Communist leaders stated that Japan must be decisively defeated, stripped of her colonies and conquered territories, and disarmed. Following this, everything possible should be done to encourage and strengthen the democratic forces in Japan. "Communism is as impractical in the near future in Japan as it is in China," according to one comment, and therefore the Chinese Communists believe that both countries must progress on the basis of democratic capitalism. They also emphasize, however, that power must not remain centered in the hands of the few big Japanese trusts. Finally, they believe that Japan should be given opportunities for peaceful commercial development, and should be permitted to assist in the industrialization of China.

In concluding this discussion of the Japanese People's Emancipation League, some reference must be made to the Korean People's Emancipation League, organized in Yenan during the latter part of 1944 under the direction of escaped revolutionists from Korea. Inasmuch as Korea has been an integral part of the Japanese Empire for nearly forty years, this Korean people's movement may be considered a part of the prodemocratic and antimilitarist forces in Japan. The Korean League, with some 2,000 members, carried on intensive propaganda work among Koreans in North China, who number about 200,000, and also maintained underground contact with Korean guerrilla bands operating in Korea and Manchuria. (There are almost two million Koreans in Manchuria.) The League's methods were much like those of the Japanese Emancipation League, and it too maintained a workers' and peasants' training school in Yenan. The League was headed by Wu Ting, and the training school by Chin Pai-un.

In April 1945 the Korean Emancipation League issued a manifesto urging that all Koreans in all countries should join to form a united organization based on the principles of democracy and a united front of all parties against the Japanese. The manifesto stated that this united organization should organize armed units to coöperate with the Allies against Japan, declaring that Koreans must prove their right to independence by fighting for their freedom. The common goal of this struggle would be the establishment of a democratic Korean Republic.

When it was first organized, the Korean League had only a one-way contact with the people of Korea through Koreans who had escaped from the country and come to join the League. Early in 1945, however, a movement in the opposite direction had begun, with many Koreans returning to carry on underground activity in Korea in an attempt to organize popular resistance.

Despite severe Japanese repression, Korean guerrilla bands were reported to be becoming more active. One such band, led by Kin Jih-hsing and numbering about 15,000 men, had succeeded in establishing contact with the Eighth Route Army, and was preparing to play an active role in the final defeat of Japan.

In estimating the significance of the activities of such groups as the Emancipation League, the Japanese trade and peasant unions, the followers of liberal political leaders like Ozaki, and the various Korean people's movements, it is important to realize that until the latter part of 1944, the Japanese people's faith in eventual victory had not received any severe jolt. As the inevitability of Japan's defeat was being brought home to them, there is no doubt that the arguments of men like Kaji, Okano, and Ozaki have found an increasing audience among the war-weary Japanese people.

THE TASK BEFORE THE ALLIED POWERS

THIS BRINGS us to the question of how the victorious Allies can use their power to facilitate and encourage the emergence of a trustworthy government in postwar Japan. With the end of the war in Europe, Japan stood alone — her ultimate defeat a certainty. Japanese leaders were unquestionably aware that they could not hope to win the war, but there was every indication that they still hoped to avoid the full consequences of military defeat by preserving intact the political and economic structure that is the basis of their power. This hope rested on several assumptions: first, that the American people, eager for a quick end to the war in Asia, would not support the prolonged supervision of a defeated Japan; second, that there would be a weakening of unity among the major powers on the question of postwar policy in the Pacific; third, that Japan would offer her services as a bulwark against the "menace of Bolshevism"; and fourth, that China would remain weak and disunited.

The personnel of the Suzuki Cabinet, together with the concurrent reorganization of the Japanese high military command, bore out the conclusion that Japan's leaders were planning along these lines. The Cabinet was the result of a skillful interweaving of political forces representing the Imperial Household, big business, the Navy, the bureaucracy, and the Army. It was composed chiefly of "moderate" political leaders, without fanatical "extremists" and enjoying the backing of powerful financial and industrial interests. On the other hand, the military reorganization, which placed supreme control in the hands of rabid die-hards, indicated preparations for a last-ditch defense of the Japanese homeland and Japan's main bases on the continent. In other words, Japan could say to the United States: we have a strong "conservative" government, free from "extremist" elements, which could make a reasonable peace, but if your terms are too severe, we are prepared to compel you to fight a long and costly war in Asia.

Some observers contended that the Suzuki Cabinet was only a "transition" cabinet, and that a "peace-making" government would not take office in Japan until the Japanese militarists were far more convinced than they were at that time that further resistance was useless. But whether or not the Suzuki Government was intended to be the one to sue for peace, its composition was important in that it provided a clue to the methods by which the leaders of Japan hoped to preserve the kind of Japan in which they could continue to enjoy a monopoly of power and thus prevent a democratic revolt against the ruling oligarchy, civilian as well as military.

In the weeks following the Suzuki Cabinet's assumption of office, there were repeated reports of Japanese peace feelers reaching the United States. The general aim of these feelers appeared to be to ascertain whether the Allied Powers would be willing to settle for anything less than invasion and occupation of Japan proper, a fact that bore out the assumption that Japan's leaders were primarily concerned with preserving the internal political and economic structure of Japan. They might well be content with the kind of peace treaty accorded to Germany at Versailles — one that stripped them of their colonies, saddled them with large reparations, and temporarily destroyed their military and naval power, but left them with an army and police force sufficient to maintain "internal law and order," crush all incipient democratic movements, and preserve the basic structure of the prewar regime. That this was clearly in the minds of Japan's leaders was evidenced in the broadcast of an official Japanese message to General MacArthur on August 19, 1945 (well after Japan's acceptance of surrender terms) expressing a desire to maintain their armies "to keep order" in the homeland and even on the continent of Asia.

Unfortunately, the hopes and plans of Japan's rulers were not entirely without foundation. As noted above, influential sections of opinion in both America and Britain had gone on record as favoring the preservation of a politically "reliable" Japan, in preference to the "social upheaval" involved in encouraging the emergence of a genuinely democratic regime. Then too, there had been a marked tendency in both American and British statements concerning Japan to distinguish sharply between the "militarists" and the "moderate" elements in the ruling oligarchy, including the Emperor, when apportioning the blame for Japanese aggression.

This erroneous and confusing approach to the problem of Japan was not entirely corrected or clarified by President Truman's statement of May 8, 1945, appealing to the Japanese people to accept unconditional surrender. Warning the people of Japan that "the striking power and intensity of our blows will steadily increase and bring utter destruction to Japan's industrial war production, to its shipping, and to everything that supports its military activity," President Truman stated that "our blows will not cease until the Japanese military and naval forces lay down their arms in unconditional surrender." He then defined what such a surrender would mean for the Japanese people: "It means the end of the war. It means the termination of the influence of the military leaders who have brought Japan to the brink of disaster. It means provision for the return of soldiers and sailors to their families, their farms, their jobs. It means not prolonging the present agony and suffering of the Japanese in a vain hope of victory. Unconditional surrender does not mean the extermination or enslavement of the Japanese people."

It may be noted that the President's appeal seemingly placed the blame for Japan's plight on the *military* leaders. He also stressed the prospective destruction of Japan's industrial plant. Both statements could be taken to mean that it would be in the interest of Japan's industrial and political leaders to come to terms, provided that they disavowed the militarists. President Truman presumably did not intend his statement to be taken as absolving the non-militarist rulers of Japan from all responsibility for Japanese aggression. However, Captain E. M. Zacharias, U.S.N., former Naval Attaché in Tokyo and one of the Navy's chief Japanese experts, who read the President's statement in a special broadcast to Japan, followed it with a message of his own. And this message made it difficult to place an exact interpretation on the President's statement. Though all students of Japanese affairs are aware that there is as close a relationship between the militarists, the industrialists, and the nobility of Japan as there was between the industrialists and militarists of Nazi Germany, Captain Zacharias apparently went out of his way to placate as many Japanese notables as possible. In one part of his message he addressed himself directly to the various highly-placed personages he had known in Japan, as follows: "Admiral Yonai will recall our many conversations. . . . Admiral Nomura will remember my frank discussions, both in Japan when Admiral Nagano often attended, and on his way to Washington to his last official assignment. Mr. Kurusu will know my regret in the loss of his son, whom as a young boy I often patted on the head. Generals Matsumoto, Teramoto, and Hirota will remember my frequent advice. Likewise Mr. Debuchi, Mr. Wakatsugi, Mr. Horinouchi and the staff of the late Ambassador Saito. Your Premier, Admiral Baron Suzuki, may remember our meetings when he was chief of the naval general staff. My impression of him was fully confirmed by his recent sympathetic statement regarding our loss in the death of Franklin Delano Roosevelt. And, finally, their Imperial Highnesses Prince and Princess Takamatsu will recall when, as their aide-de-camp, I accompanied them during their tour of two months in the United States in 1931." Captain Zacharias concluded his broadcast by telling the people of Japan that they could "choose a peace with honor" — a phrase that must have come as a shock to the veterans of the "Death March" on Bataan.

The concern occasioned by Captain Zacharias's friendly references to Japan's political leaders was heightened by his subsequent broadcast of July 21, in which he promised the enemy that the United States will be a kind victor. He warned that if the Japanese permitted the war to continue, they could not expect very favorable peace terms, for others like "China, Great Britain, Australia, and the Netherlands among them — may acquire a stronger voice if the war drags on and they put more into it, in determining the kind of peace Japan will get." In the same broadcast he said: "In so far as the history of its application is concerned, those Japanese leaders who are sincerely interested in terminating the war with honor would do well to study the American precedents. Historically, the honorable surrender of General Lee to General Grant in 1865 provides a most important example. If Japan should initiate the cessation of hostilities without further delay, it may be assumed that it will be the United States which will enforce the formula and ensure the peace." And finally these words: "At present there are still some influential people in the United States who would not like to see the destruction of Japan. But our patience, too, has its limits, and it is rapidly running out."

Neither in this nor in any of the preceding eleven Zacharias broadcasts was there any mention of Japanese fascism, or any suggestion that the Japanese people be given an opportunity to determine their own future destiny. It was to the representatives of the Imperial Household and of Japanese big business that the official spokesman of the American Government addressed himself, and offered them over and over again what can only be termed a "soft peace."

Fortunately, the terms of the Potsdam ultimatum to Japan, issued on July 26, 1945, did not represent the kind of thinking manifested in the Zacharias broadcasts. Calling on Japan to surrender or face complete destruction at the hands of the Allies, the Potsdam declaration laid down the following terms in the name of the governments of the United States, Great Britain, and China. (The Soviet Government subscribed to the Potsdam terms upon its entry into the war against Japan on August 8.)

There must be eliminated for all time the authority and influence of those who have deceived and misled the people of Japan into embarking on world conquest, for we insist that a new order of peace, security, and justice will be impossible until irresponsible militarism is driven from the world.

Until such a new order is established and until there is convincing proof that Japan's war-making power is destroyed, points in Japanese territory to be designated by the Allies shall be occupied to secure the achievement of the basic objectives we are here setting forth.

The terms of the Cairo declaration shall be carried out and Japanese sovereignty shall be limited to the Islands of Honshu, Hokkaido, Kyushu, Shikoku and such minor islands as we determine.

Japanese military forces after being completely disarmed shall be permitted to return to their homes with the opportunity to lead peaceful and productive lives.

We do not intend that the Japanese shall be enslaved as a race or destroyed as a nation, but stern justice shall be meted out to all war criminals, including those who have visited cruelties upon our prisoners.

The Japanese government shall remove all obstacles to the revival and strengthening of democratic tendencies among the Japanese people. Freedom of speech and religion and of thought, as well as respect for the fundamental human rights, shall be established.

Japan shall be permitted to maintain such industries as will sustain her economy and permit the payment of just reparation in kind, but not those industries which will enable her to rearm for war.

To this end access to, as distinguished from control of, raw materials shall be permitted. Eventual Japanese participation in world trade relations shall be permitted.

The occupying forces of the Allies shall be withdrawn from Japan as soon as these objectives have been accomplished and there has been established in accordance with the freely expressed will of the Japanese people a peacefully inclined and responsible government.

We call upon the government of Japan to proclaim now the unconditional surrender of all Japanese armed forces, and to provide proper and adequate assurances of their good faith in such action. The alternative for Japan is prompt and utter destruction.

Criticism of the terms of the Potsdam ultimatum centered on two points: its failure to mention the future role of the Japanese Emperor, and the failure to state more specifically the means by which the Allied Powers intended to encourage the emergence of a democratic Japan. Then, almost as if in response to both criticisms, Japan's conditional acceptance of the Potsdam offer on the understanding that it did not comprise "any demand which prejudices the prerogatives of His Majesty as a sovereign ruler" elicited the following definition of the Allied attitude toward the Emperor, embodied in a note from Secretary of State Byrnes on behalf of the American, British, Chinese, and Soviet Governments:

Sir:

I have the honor to acknowledge receipt of your note of Aug. 10, and in reply to inform you that the President of the United States has directed me to send to you for transmission by your Government to the Japanese Government the following message on behalf of the Governments of the United States, the United Kingdom, the Union of Soviet Socialist Republics and China:

With regard to the Japanese Government's message accepting the terms of the Potsdam Proclamation but containing the statement, "with the understanding that the said declaration does not comprise any demand which prejudices the prerogatives of His Majesty as a sovereign ruler," our position is as follows:

From the moment of surrender the authority of the Emperor and the

Japanese Government to rule the State shall be subject to the Supreme Commander of the Allied Powers, who will take such steps as he deems proper to effectuate the surrender terms.

The Emperor will be required to authorize and insure the signature by the Government of Japan and the Japanese Imperial General Headquarters of the surrender terms necessary to carry out the provisions of the Potsdam Declaration, and shall issue his commands to all the Japanese military, naval and air authorities and to all of the forces under their control wherever located to cease active operations and to surrender their arms, and to issue such other orders as the Supreme Commander may require to give effect to the surrender terms.

Immediately upon the surrender the Japanese Government shall transport prisoners of war and civilian internees to places of safety, as directed, where they can quickly be placed aboard Allied transports.

The ultimate form of government of Japan shall, in accordance with the Potsdam Declaration, be established — by the freely expressed will of the Japanese people.

The armed forces of the Allied powers will remain in Japan until the purposes set forth in the Potsdam Declaration are achieved.

Accept, sir, the renewed assurances of my highest consideration,

James F. Byrnes, Secretary of State

Confronted with the dual blow of Russia's entry into the war and the use of the atomic bomb by the American Air Force, Japan accepted the Potsdam terms on August 14 and the Second World War came to an official end with the signing of the surrender terms on September 2, 1945.

Amidst the natural rejoicing over the end of the most devastating war in human history, however, students of Japanese affairs still found cause for some concern in the methods used by the Japanese to announce their surrender, particularly in so far as the Emperor was concerned. Though admitting the practical value of using the Emperor to compel the surrender of all Japanese armed forces, they were disturbed at the prospect that the people of Japan would be left with the impression that the Allied Powers had accepted the formula that "the Emperor is sacred." They noted that in Hirohito's precedent-shattering radio rescript of August 14 there was not a word about Japan's surrender, or about the terms of the Potsdam ultimatum. Instead, the whole implication of the Emperor's message to the Japanese people was that he had decided to end the war out of the goodness of his heart — a war moreover which had been waged simply "to insure Japan's self-preservation and the stabilization of East

Asia." Viewed in the light of past Japanese history, it was not difficult to see in this maneuver the first step in a careful plan to preserve the legend of imperial divinity, with all its disastrous implications for the future peace of the world. This conclusion was strengthened when on the following day a Radio Tokyo broadcast stated in part that "we have lost, but this is temporary."

However, the question of whether or not the rulers of Japan will succeed in preserving the basic features of an internal political structure that has bred aggression for fifty years is one that only time can answer. Everything will depend upon the actual policies and practices adopted by the commander-in-chief of the Allied occupation forces to implement the general aims outlined in the Potsdam ultimatum, particularly the statement that the Japanese Government "shall remove all obstacles to the revival and strengthening of democratic tendencies among the Japanese people," and that the ultimate form of government of Japan shall be established in accordance with the freely expressed will of the Japanese people. The leader of the Japanese People's Emancipation League warned the Allies that "the moderates of militarism" in Japan were plotting "to hide and preserve political, economic, and military strength and secretly to prepare for a retaliatory war. This," he said in a broadcast, "is fully disclosed in the Emperor's message. Should the United Nations show the slightest leniency toward moderate elements, the great sacrifices of eight years will have been for nothing."

It is, of course, true that the line of least resistance for the occupation authorities would be to deal with the experienced and powerful representatives of the great business houses and the Imperial Household, who will most willingly oblige with a thoroughgoing "repudiation" of the militarists. But unquestionably such a policy would enable the present rulers of Japan to maintain their monopoly of political and economic power, keep the Japanese people in continued subjection, and set the stage for an eventual resurgence of Japanese aggression.

The alternative is the more difficult task of seeking out and supporting the genuinely antimilitarist and prodemocratic forces in Japan; of finding leaders capable of offering effective resistance to a continuance of the old regime. For one thing, the occupation authorities will have complete control over the radio, the press, and public gatherings. They can see to it that these facilities are open to the spokesmen for the Japanese people, and are denied to all clearly antidemocratic elements. They can secure the release of thousands of political prisoners who have had the courage to express "dangerous thoughts" regarding the present regime. They can assist and encourage the activities of Japanese trade unions and other popular organizations that will certainly reëmerge in an atmosphere of political freedom.

All students of Japan are agreed that the present Japanese Constitution is incompatible with the development of a democratically controlled government, and one of the principal demands of Japanese popular leaders is for the drafting of a new constitution by freely elected representatives of the people. The Allied occupation forces could do much to facilitate such a development by making possible the holding of free elections to a new Diet, which might then serve as a constitutional assembly to determine a form of government that would give the elected representatives of the people real control over the country's domestic and foreign policies.

There is no doubt that such a constitutional assembly would face many difficult problems. The destruction of antidemocratic forces and of the extensive bureaucratic regime whose chief function has been the suppression of all popular demands for a greater voice in the affairs of the nation cannot be accomplished over night. The solution of these problems, however, is more a matter of time than anything else provided that power is firmly vested in a genuinely representative government. Even the delicate question of the Emperor's future role could be safely left to such a representative government. A more difficult and complicated problem would be the question of the future organization and control of Japanese industry.

Obviously, a democratically constituted government could not permit a monopoly of economic power to continue in the hands of a few families. But, for good or for ill, the Japanese economic structure has become perhaps the most centralized and "trustified" in the world, and to attempt to break it up and decentralize it not only would be economically wasteful but would entail insuperable problems of ownership and management. Giant industries are not like large landed estates that can be divided among the cultivators. However, in view of the fact that Japanese industry is not exclusively in the hands of private owners but has always been controlled and regulated to a large extent by the State, the problem of breaking the stranglehold of the

Zaibatsu is not as insuperable as it may appear. Modern industry in Japan was in the first instance entirely State-owned and -operated, and even when large sections of it were handed over to private firms the State retained a large measure of control over all key industries through part ownership and special rights of supervision. Some estimates place the Japanese Government's share in the mammoth monopolies as high as 50%. In addition, there is a close alliance and even family interrelationships between the owners of the industrial and financial combines and the bureaucrats who control and regulate the State's financial and industrial interests. Thus if the Japanese bureaucracy were transformed into a people's government, it would be a relatively easy matter to convert the existing State interest in the giant monopolies into democratic control of at least the basic industries, thereby enabling the people of Japan, through their elected representatives, to shape the policies of these great financial and industrial combines along peaceful and constructive lines.

In addition to the problem of bringing Japanese industrial policy under popular control, the creation of a healthy social and economic structure in Japan would also involve an extensive program of agrarian reform including radical changes in the present systems of land tenure and rural credit. As one leading American student of Japan points out: "The relationship between the poverty-stricken farmers and low-wage industrial workers is a vicious phenomenon directly allied to the ability of the militarists to engross the powers of the State, and in alliance with the landlords and the great *Zaibatsu* magnates, to embark on a mission of world conquest. . . . Improved living conditions for the farmers will force higher wage standards for the industrial workers by removing the inexhaustible reservoir of cheap labor on which the *Zaibatsu* have waxed fat. The resultant increase in purchasing power by the mass of the population will expand Japan's home market and thus reduce the pressure to export; by the same token, the higher cost of labor will diminish the keen edge of Japanese competition which Western merchants have experienced to their distress. An economic margin for these domestic reforms will be provided by the abolition of armament expenditures which have hitherto absorbed such a large proportion of Japan's national income." [1]

---

[1] T. A. Bisson: "The Price of Peace for Japan," *Pacific Affairs*, March 1944, p. 22.

Here again, the transformation of Japan's backward and oppressive agrarian system will take time, but a people's government in which peasant leaders were represented could be relied upon to introduce agrarian reforms that would free the Japanese peasantry from their present crushing burden of extortionate rents and usurious interest charges, break the control of the great landlords, and thereby set the stage for the modernization of Japanese agriculture and a general rise in the living standards of both the farming and the industrial working class.

It is not suggested that the Allied occupation authorities should undertake to enforce such a program of political and economic reform. To be effective and lasting, such reforms must be carried out by the Japanese people themselves. But it will be possible for the Allied authorities to give their support to those forces in Japan that show themselves ready and eager to carry out such a program, and not to lend the weight of their influence to those elements that will seek to reëstablish the old order under a slightly altered guise. The militarists and the *Zaibatsu* have arrested their country's political and economic development at a low level. Through repressive measures, they have stifled the democratic forces that periodically gave signs of rising. The Allied occupation authorities would need only to stand by and protect these democratic forces from suppression, and the pent-up and long-suppressed aspirations of the Japanese people will make themselves felt.

This does not mean that Japan can be quickly transformed into a democratic and nonaggressive state. But the people of Japan have not only been among the worst sufferers from the tyranny of their own rulers, they have also indicated a consistent spirit of rebellion, and there is no reason to doubt that given the opportunity, they would in time seek to change the oppressive political and economic system under which they were compelled to live. There is no question that only a democratically controlled Japan will be a peaceful and trustworthy Japan; that only such a Japan can raise the living standards of her people to the point where they will cease to be a depressing influence on the economies of other Asiatic countries; and that only such a Japan will have no desire to solve her problems by military aggression. The development of democratic institutions in Japan will be the best possible guarantee of the destruction of the independent militarist caste and the cult of emperor-worship which has been used to keep the people in subjection and compel their support of a policy of armed conquest.

As far as Japan's internal structure is concerned, the responsibility of the Allied occupation forces must be limited to giving the democratic forces in Japan a chance to express their wishes freely. It cannot be repeated too often that the task of establishing a democratically controlled government can be accomplished only by the Japanese people themselves. But there is a larger task involved, if we wish to encourage the emergence of a trustworthy Japan — a task that is primarily an Allied responsibility: to establish the kind of world-wide political and economic framework within which a democratic Japan can function. In our resentment at the methods employed by Japan's military-fascist dictatorship, we must not lose sight of the fact that the welfare of the Japanese people depends to a large extent on their economic relations with other countries. Given opportunities for normal economic progress through the expansion of their own domestic market and the development of expanding economies in other countries, the Japanese people could be trusted to follow peaceful and coöperative policies and would be able to make an important contribution to the industrial development of China and other economically backward areas. But, if Japan is denied such opportunities, it will give the aggressive elements an excuse to bring strong pressure to bear on any future Japanese Government to revert to the policy of aggressive expansion.

The failure to realize this basic interrelationship among the countries of Asia, as well as between them and the rest of the world, has been responsible for much loose thinking with regard to the question of how to treat Japan after the war. Americans have become accustomed to the idea that the world is interdependent in the sense that our own welfare is directly affected by what happens in other countries, but we have failed to apply the same reasoning to the problem of Japan. Most American political and business leaders have come to recognize that only in an expanding world economy, in which the weaker and dependent countries are helped to win political and economic freedom and to achieve rising standards of living for their peoples, can the more advanced industrial countries hope to enjoy prosperity and peace. But they have not recognized that this truth does not apply exclusively to the United States.

Given a world in which the standards of living and the purchasing power of the colonial and industrially backward areas were steadily rising, a democratic Japan could find ample room for peaceful economic development, and there would be no need to strip her of all her industrial plant or to keep her under prolonged Allied supervision. But if the postwar world is to be characterized by a continuance of the system of colonial exploitation, by acute rivalries among the industrial powers for control of limited markets, and by reliance on cheap colonial labor and monopoly control of vital raw materials, then no nation depending to a large extent on foreign trade can be trusted to keep the peace.

In such a world of power politics and economics, no amount of Allied supervision, no international police force or arbitration machinery, can prevent a poorly endowed country like Japan from endeavoring to seize a share of the world's colonial resources. If that is the kind of world we intend to establish after the war, the only safe thing to do would be to transform Japan into a weak, impoverished, agricultural nation, even though by so doing we would increase the already too large percentage of the world's population that lives on a bare subsistence level and thus make it all the more difficult for the United States, Britain, and other industrial nations to achieve continued prosperity. The question of our future policy towards Japan cannot be decided in a political vacuum, but is inextricably bound up with our decision as to the character of the international political and economic structure that we intend to establish in the postwar world.

PART FOUR

ON THE INTERNATIONAL FRONT

❀

CHAPTER X

BRITISH IMPERIAL POLICY IN ASIA

❋

I T MAY SEEM obvious to many that the development of free and expanding economies in the backward colonial areas of Asia is essential for a stable and prosperous world economy. It may seem equally obvious that only by aiding these dependent and subject peoples to attain political and economic freedom can we give real meaning to the wartime pledges of the United Nations as the avowed champions of freedom and democracy. But there are powerful forces that see no other way of maintaining their own strength and security than by opposing such an approach to the problems of Asia, and working for a restoration of the prewar colonial system in one form or another.

British imperial policy in Asia, viewed in relationship to the economic needs and interests of Great Britain, is an outstanding case in point. Mr. Churchill's famous declaration that "we mean to hold our own" was not merely an oratorical phrase but was the expression of a profound conviction on the part of the dominant section of British opinion that Britain must retain her colonial empire and a system of imperial preference within the British Commonwealth and Empire if she is to maintain her position as a great industrial and trading nation. This conviction is clearly a serious obstacle to the establishment of a lasting peace in Asia because a retention of the colonial system would inevitably lead to a renewal of power politics and to acute economic rivalries among the major powers competing desperately for a share in a narrow and contracting world market. For this reason, British policy and aims in Asia deserve very careful study both in their historical setting and in relation to the new world situation that is likely to result from the war.

Before the First World War, the countries of Asia were for the most part the objects of imperialist rivalry among the industrial nations of the West. Only Japan had successfully avoided colonial subjection and entered the lists as a competitor in the battle for control of markets and raw materials. Great Britain, Germany, France, Tsarist Russia, Japan, the United States, and the Netherlands were all engaged in the struggle to acquire, or to maintain, or to enlarge their territorial and economic "stakes" in Asia, and the concepts of "power politics" were accepted as the natural and practical basis of international diplomacy. In this "battle for Asia" Britain had been first on the scene and had secured by far the greatest share of the spoils. She held India, Burma, Malaya, and Hong Kong, and a preëminent position in the Far Eastern carrying trade. Her economic stake in China was the greatest of any foreign power, and as a result of her extensive investments in trading, real estate, manufacturing, banking, transport, public utilities, and mining she was able to exert a strong influence on Chinese Government policy. British capital also held a large share of the investment in the rubber, tin, and oil resources of the Netherlands East Indies.

In addition to the substantial profits accruing from the exploitation of these extensive colonial resources, and from shipping, trading, and banking operations throughout colonial Asia, British control over Asiatic sources of such vital industrial raw materials as tin and rubber greatly strengthened her competitive position vis-à-vis her chief commercial rivals, particularly the United States — the great consumer of these two commodities. Malaya, in particular, became known as Britain's "dollar arsenal" because its large favorable trade balance with the United States supplied Britain with huge dollar balances with which to settle its commercial accounts with America.

The two decades following the First World War witnessed a decisive change in the balance of forces in the Far East. The Russian Revolution changed the character of Russia's interests in Asia and removed her as a contestant in the struggle for markets and monopolies. Germany, Britain's other major prewar rival, was also eliminated as a strong political and economic factor. On the other hand, both Japan and the United States had gained enormously in economic strength as a result of the war, and each in its own way was beginning to challenge the traditional aims and methods of British policy in Asia.

American policy in the Far East, for a variety of reasons, had always been more concerned with opportunities for trade than with the protection of colonial possessions and the acquiring of "concessions" in China or elsewhere. The Open Door policy, designed to prevent the complete partition of China into "spheres of interest" monopolized by the various European Powers, was an early expression of this interest in trade as against monopoly control. And during the years following the First World War there were signs of a growing belief that American economic interests in Asia were being hampered rather than benefited by a colonial system that gave America's commercial rivals a monopoly over raw materials essential to American industry and, even more important, left the people of Asia too impoverished to be good customers for American goods.

This was evidenced in our attitude toward our one colonial possession in Asia — the Philippines. It is unquestionably true that the American decision to grant the Philippines their freedom was not a matter of unmixed altruism; that certain powerful American producers — notably the sugar, dairy, and tobacco interests — were very much interested in "freeing" the Philippines so as to deprive Philippine producers of their privileged position in the American market. But this does not detract from the historic significance of the fact that for the first time in the history of the relations between Asia and the West, a controlling power had voluntarily relinquished its hold over a colony and promised an orderly, scheduled evolution along the road to national independence, and by so doing had posed a challenge to the old colonial order of which Britain was the main proponent.

On the other hand, Japan used her newly acquired strength to intensify her program of imperialist aggression on the Asiatic continent and began to threaten British commercial supremacy in China, India, and other Asiatic markets. There was no danger of a Japanese challenge to the colonial system as such, but it was clear that Japan was becoming an increasingly powerful competitor for the role of the dominant power in Eastern Asia. Throughout this period Britain fought a hard though often losing battle to maintain her economic and political position in China, and to stave off a Japanese attack on the heart of her colonial empire in Southeast Asia. The task, however, was a difficult and complicated one. On occasion, Britain was even forced to support Japan as a balancing force, on the one hand against the rising surge of Chinese nationalism and the stimulus that the political, economic, and social achievements of Soviet Siberia had given to the nationalist aspirations of millions of subject peoples in colonial Asia, and on the other, against the growing economic strength and commercial rivalry of the United States.

Only in the light of all these conflicting forces, for example, can we understand Britain's tacit acquiescence in Japan's invasion of Manchuria in 1931. Britain's major concern was to protect something that she deemed vital to her national existence, namely her colonial empire, and she saw no reason to protest against a move that seemed likely to divert Japan's attention from the centers of British power farther south. Moreover, she had a natural sympathy with Japan's imperialist ambitions. Colonel Amery, former Secretary of State for India, expressed this latter attitude perhaps a little too unguardedly when he declared in 1931: "I confess that I see no reason why, whether in act, or in word, or in sympathy, we should go individually or internationally against Japan in this matter. . . . Who is there among us to cast the first stone and to say that Japan ought not to have acted with the object of creating peace and order in Manchuria and defending herself against the continuous aggression of vigorous Chinese nationalism? Our whole policy in India, our whole policy in Egypt, stands condemned if we condemn Japan."

With the spread of the Second World War to the Pacific, and Japan's rapid conquest of the colonial areas of Southeast Asia, it was of course impossible for British statesmen to continue to regard Japan as a trustworthy colleague in maintaining the colonial system in Asia. But nothing occurred during the war years to indicate that the British Government altered its basic belief in the importance of maintaining, or rather restoring, that system in the postwar period. All suggestions that the Atlantic Charter be supplemented by a "Pacific Charter" specifically applying the wartime aims of the United Nations to the colonial peoples of the Pacific have foundered on the rock of British opposition. The Cairo Conference, while pledging the complete military defeat of Japan, was notably lacking in any reference to the future political status of the areas to be "liberated" from Japanese control. This whole matter exploded in the bitter debates on the question of "trusteeship" at the San Francisco Conference in May 1945.

The end of the war has unquestionably made a radical and significant change in the balance of forces in the Far East. Japan will no longer possess a colonial empire. The Soviet Union has never had any interest in the maintenance of that system. The

United States has expressed itself as willing to adopt a policy of aiding in the industrial development of China and would presumably extend that policy to include other backward and dependent areas if the political obstacles to such a program could be removed. Furthermore, there has been a widespread popular feeling in the United States that some new system of international responsibility and control should be established in order to prepare the colonial peoples for full independence and to aid them in the development of more balanced and prosperous economies. Since President Roosevelt's death, however, this aim has been distorted by certain dominant groups in America that are more concerned with obtaining control of "strategic" areas than with urging a general policy of colonial liberation. As a result, American policy on this question has been forced into the false position of supporting what must amount to the retention of unilateral monopoly control of colonial countries.

It is unquestionably clear that Great Britain — supported by her satellites among the imperial powers, such as France and the Netherlands — is determined to restore the old system of imperial control. One of the most explicit statements of this attitude was provided by an editorial in the *Economist* (London) of September 16, 1944, on the subject of Britain's "Far Eastern Stake." The *Economist* pointed out that "for Britain, and in similar measure for France and Holland, the Far East is a necessity of greatness and wealth. . . . The conception of the [Japanese] Co-Prosperity Sphere was an inconvenience to the United States. To Britain, to the Netherlands and to France, it was a death sentence passed on their fundamental way of life." It then went on to state that "the American prejudice against 'imperialism' — British, French, or Dutch — has led many of the post-war planners to assume that the old sovereignties will not be re-established in Southeast Asia and that some form of international control, or the transfer of the imperium to local peoples, will take the place of the old authority exercised by the Western nations. Since this attitude exists and is even backed by some of the most widely distributed American journals and newspapers, it is time that the future intentions of the British, the French, and the Dutch were frankly and fully explained. Since none of them has any intention of abandoning its colonial empire, but on the contrary regards the restoration of Malaya to the British, the East Indies to the Dutch, and French Indo-China to the French as an essential part of the destruction of Japan's Co-Prosperity Sphere, it would be inviting the worst sort of misunderstanding, and even accusations of bad faith, if the three nations allowed any doubt on the matter to continue in the mind of their American ally."

On March 19, 1945, a similar conclusion was expressed officially by Colonel Oliver Stanley, British Colonial Secretary, in a speech to members of the American Outpost in London. Contending that the administration of Britain's colonies was Britain's responsibility, and that she could not share it with others, he said: "We believe that any such division of authority is not only impracticable but wholly against the wishes of the colonial peoples themselves." Colonel Stanley insisted that self-government and not independence is best for colonial territories. "Would it really be an advantage to create another forty independent states, all small?" he asked. "Would the new machinery for world security be made any stronger by the substitution of these forty States for a cohesive empire. Would forty more separate divisions free the flow of world trade?"

The above quotations should be sufficient to dispel any lingering illusions in American minds that Britain accepts the thesis that the "era of imperialism" is ended, or is ready to contemplate anything more than a modernized and more efficient system of colonial administration to remedy some of the abuses and weaknesses which were so glaringly demonstrated during the early days of the war. The Attlee Labor Government's affirmation on August 18, 1945 that the British Government intends to occupy and retain Hong Kong, only adds additional strength to the foregoing conclusion.

The question is why Britain, after a war in which humanity has been bled white in order to destroy the forces of oppression and enslavement, should find herself in the position of being the only major champion of a system that, no matter how much it may be disguised by references to the "ultimate goal" of full self-government and economic freedom, is nevertheless based on oppression and enslavement. This question is all the more difficult for many Americans to answer because so many British statesmen have been emphasizing the need for an expanding world economy—a goal that is obviously incompatible with the preservation of colonial economies in a large part of the world. Clearly, the people of England are not more hard-hearted or more callous to human poverty and subjection than the people of other countries. They do not lack courage or intelligence or ability to meet new and difficult situations. They do not accept the doctrine of inferior and superior peoples, or the "master race" approach to world problems. Why, then, do they feel it necessary to preserve an outmoded system that subjects millions upon millions of people to the autocratic rule of a relative handful of foreign officials? The answer lies in the character of the English economy, the unalterable economic factors with which Britain must contend in her efforts to ensure the welfare of her people.

BRITAIN'S WORLD POSITION

LET US picture Great Britain minus her colonial resources and possessing no preferential position in the markets of the British Dominions. We find a little island country, slightly smaller than the state of Oregon, with a population of approximately 47 million. Britain is rich in coal, has a fair amount of iron, but is totally lacking in most of the other raw materials and minerals necessary to support her industries. She must import all her supplies of petroleum, copper, cotton, manganese, nickel, zinc, antimony, mercury, mica, chromite, and potash, and virtually all her requirements of tin, lead, and tungsten. Before the war she produced about 75% of her normal requirements of iron ore, less than 25% of her consumption of wool, and about 25% of her consumption of phosphates, sulphur, and pyrites. Only in coal and nitrates is she self-sufficient, with a surplus for export.

Furthermore, Britain is normally dependent on imports for nearly 50% of her food supplies. Intensive efforts during the war enabled her to increase her food production to a very considerable extent. R. S. Hudson, British Minister of Agriculture, reported in November 1944 that during the five years Britain had been at war, food production had been increased by 70% in terms of value and by over 120% in terms of shipping space, and the area of land under crops had been increased by about 6 million acres. Spectacular gains had also been made in the production of vegetables and fruits. A further breaking up of large estates and the bringing of new land under cultivation may be expected in the postwar period, as well as intensified efforts to increase dairy farming and the production of vegetables; but Britain does not possess the broad expanses of land required for wheat-growing or cattle- and sheep-raising on a scale sufficient to meet her needs for wool, meat, and dairy products, nor can she undertake cotton-growing to supply her textile industries. In short, of all the so-called Great Powers, Britain is perhaps the most poorly endowed with the economic resources on which industrial and military strength depend.

Under these circumstances, Britain's position as a leading world power has always depended on large-scale imports of food and raw materials, and large-scale exports of manufactured products. In 1937, for example, Britain's per capita imports were by far the largest of any of the leading powers: United Kingdom, $108.20; Germany, $32.50; United States, $25.10; Japan, $15.25; and the U.S.S.R., $1.55. About 60% of the cost of these essential imports was met by exports, while the remainder was paid for with income received from overseas investments, shipping, and financial services. During the three-year period 1936–38, for example, Britain's annual imports averaged £950 million, and her exports averaged £562 million. The difference was met by income from overseas investments, £203 million; net shipping receipts, £105 million; net commissions on banking and insurance, £36 million; and a variety of other smaller sources of "hidden" profits or "invisible" exports.

Foreign trade, and particularly a large volume of exports, is thus of vital importance to the economic welfare of the British people. And to maintain that trade in the face of competition from other countries more richly endowed with raw material and food resources, or with larger internal markets or lower production costs, Britain built up a world-wide mechanism by which she controlled to a varying degree the resources, production, and trade of other countries — the British Dominions and the British colonies. Because of the widely scattered character of this economic empire, it did not give Britain the same degree of economic security as was enjoyed by the United States or the Soviet Union, because the accessibility of these imperial resources to the United Kingdom was subject to control of sea lines of transportation. But apart from this vulnerable aspect, the United Kingdom *with* its empire was very largely self-sufficient in all essential resources and, in addition, exercised a monopoly control over many of the most vital industrial materials.

Even before the present war, however, England's control over her economic empire had weakened, and her preëminent position as the Empire's industrial center and chief source of manufactured goods had been undermined not only by competition rom rival industrial powers but also by the growth of industry n other parts of the Empire. In 1913, for example, the value of British imports was equal to 30% of the British national income, while exports amounted to 24%. By 1937, these percentages had fallen to 19% and 10% respectively. For Britain, this greater fall in the value of exports was more disturbing than the general decline in foreign trade.

As far as the postwar period is concerned, the expansion of Britain's export trade is a more vital necessity than at any previous time in her history. The reason for this is simple. Britain cannot greatly curtail her imports and still maintain the living standards of her people and supply her factories with raw materials. But her prewar ability to meet a normally adverse balance of trade amounting to some £300 million annually will be greatly curtailed as a result of the depletion of her international financial assets and the sharp increase in her external liabilities. During the course of the war, Britain's overseas investments, amounting to roughly £3.9 billion, have been depleted by liquidations and repatriations by approximately £1 billion, and other investments in Europe and the occupied countries of the Far East will certainly not produce their prewar return for a considerable period. These losses are expected to curtail income from foreign investments from a prewar annual average of £203 million to not more than £138 million.

On the other side of the ledger, Britain's external liabilities have been increased by roughly twice this amount, exclusive of any settlement of Lend-Lease obligations, as a result of the huge war debts she has contracted, mainly in the form of sterling balances held chiefly by India, Canada,[1] Eire, Australia, Argentina, Brazil, and Egypt. Britain's external liabilities totaled £2 billion by the end of 1944 and were expected to reach a final total of £3 billion.[2] In current appraisals of Britain's postwar financial position, it is generally assumed that these debts will be converted into long-term obligations at 3% interest. In this event, British payments would amount to some £54 million annually, thus reducing her net investment income to some £84 million, or approximately 41% of the prewar figure. Even if, as appears probable, Britain succeeds in reducing her sterling obligations

---

[1] Canada's claims against the United Kingdom have been converted into an interest-free loan for the duration of the war, totaling £153 million.

[2] A figure confirmed by Lord Keynes on September 19, 1945.

to India by a considerable amount, it is still estimated that she will lose at least half her prewar income from foreign investments. Furthermore, it is generally agreed that Britain's income from shipping and financial services will be substantially reduced, primarily as a result of greatly increased American competition in both these fields. Official estimates state that Britain's income from all these forms of "invisible" exports will be reduced to £150 million or less.

For this reason British officials and business leaders have insisted that British exports must be increased by at least 50% over prewar levels if British standards of living are to be maintained. Just how difficult a task this will be is indicated by the fact that it involves an increase of more than 300% over Britain's 1943 exports, which were valued at only £232 million as compared with £470 million in 1938.[1] It is true that much of this decline was due to wartime restrictions, but even when these restrictions are removed Britain will still face serious difficulties. For one thing, many European countries that will need British goods will have no immediate means of paying for them. The Dominions, India, and certain Latin American countries, on the other hand, can pay out of their sterling balances; but this would not increase Britain's supply of foreign exchange or her ability to import essential food and raw materials. In addition, Britain is confronted with the loss or sharp curtailment of many of her prewar export markets as a result of extensive wartime industrialization in such countries as Canada, Australia, Argentina, and Brazil, plus the fact that in many cases American industry has taken over markets that Britain was unable to supply during the war period. The annual steel production of the Dominions, for example, has more than doubled during the war; both Canada and Australia have enormously increased their production of machinery, machine tools, and other industrial equipment; and Dominion production of such items as cotton and woolen textiles, boots and shoes, and other traditional British exports is reported to be largely adequate for their own needs.

Furthermore, as a result of their wartime industrial development, both Canada and Australia will be seeking export markets

---

[1] According to an official White Paper released on October 20, 1944, British exports during the period 1938–43 declined by 51% in value and by more than 70% in volume, and the figures for 1944 were expected to show a further decline.

for their own manufactures in the postwar period. By 1944, Canada had become the world's third largest trading nation, the largest producer of base metals (copper, nickel, zinc, lead), and the fourth largest producer of war supplies among the United Nations. This great expansion of Canada's industrial plant, power resources, and shipbuilding capacity was accomplished without a single penny of Lend-Lease funds. In addition, Canada had repatriated virtually all the 3 billion dollars' worth of Canadian securities held in Britain before the war, and had established a Mutual Aid Fund that had provided other United Nations with 2 billion dollars' worth of Canadian war materials. At the end of 1944, the Canadian Government was underwriting the export of war supplies at the rate of $100 million a month.

In view of this extensive industrial and commercial development, it was clear that Canada would not resume her former role as a market for British industry and that she would not accept an imperial economic policy designed to meet the needs of the United Kingdom. Canadian leaders had made it clear that Canada intended to stand on her own feet, economically speaking, and to make her own arrangements with other nations in accordance with Canadian needs and interests. In the latter part of 1944, for example, the Canadian Government was considering the desirability of increasing Canada's export credit fund from $400 million to $2 billion in order that Canada "may keep her factories and farms operating at a level which will maintain national income and employment." The Toronto *Financial Post* expressed the general sentiment of Canadian manufacturers when it declared: "During the war, goods are given away with few or no strings attached. For post-war conditions, a new mechanism is required to 'underwrite' foreign 'trade'. This has now been supplied on a modest scale . . . looked at as little more than chicken feed." The Soviet Union had already placed a $25-million order in Canada for heavy electrical equipment and machinery, and Canadian manufacturers were looking forward confidently to postwar trade expansion in the countries of Europe, Asia, and Latin America that would enable Canada to maintain and expand her wartime industrial growth.

The Australian economy, too, changed considerably as a result of the war. Before the war, Australia was largely dependent on the British market for the sale of her major export commodities, particularly wool, wheat, meat, and dairy products. In 1938, more than half of all Australia exports went to the United Kingdom, and seven-tenths went to the British Empire. In return, Australia obtained 42% of her imports from England and another 18% from British Empire countries. The war, coupled with the Lend-Lease program, changed this traditional economic relationship in two important respects: Australia became far more highly industrialized, and she was also drawn into the orbit of the American economy. American exports to Australia increased enormously, and the greater part of these exports consisted of machine tools and industrial equipment. While the war also increased British exports to Australia, not nearly so large a proportion of these exports consisted of production equipment. This was due in part to Britain's own internal needs, but it also reflected the deep-rooted prejudice of British industrialists against Australian industrialization.[1]

Wartime industrial development in Australia merely accelerated a process that was already under way. Before the war, Australia had established a highly efficient, low-cost steel industry. Australian steel production was greatly stimulated by wartime demands, and by 1942, before the beginning of large-scale Lend-Lease, was reported to have risen to nearly three million tons of high-grade steel. On the basis of this industry, and with the extensive aid of Lend-Lease industrial equipment, Australia established modern industrial plants capable of producing all types of manufactured goods, including munitions ranging from 10,000-ton merchant ships to two-engined bombers. By 1944, for example, Australia possessed 100 machine-tool plants as compared with 3 in September 1939; and 190 factories were turning out 25,000 tools and gauges daily, whereas there were only two or three such factories when the war began. Furthermore, since this rapid industrialization had been achieved largely with American machinery and production methods, it was clear that the United States would have an advantage over England in supplying Australia's postwar demands for industrial equipment.

---

[1] An indication of the lack of enthusiasm with which British businessmen regarded the industrialization of Britain's prewar export markets is provided by Mr. Leslie Gamage, president of the Institute of Export, who wrote in the British *Gazette*, April 1943: "It is a tragic coincidence that the difficulties facing export will be immeasurably greater owing mainly to the widespread growth, engendered by the war, of local manufacturing in our overseas markets."

It is true that Australia will continue to need export markets for her agricultural products and that this will tend to preserve close economic relations with the United Kingdom. But the statements of Australian leaders indicate that they are looking forward to more diversified trade relations and the continued industrialization of the Australian economy, which will inevitably lessen Australia's dependence on the British market and British sources of manufactured goods. As the major industrialized country in the Western Pacific, Australia is counting upon the markets of nearby Asia as outlets for her new industries and hopes to play an important part in any plan for aiding in the economic development of these backward areas. This aim was expressed by Dr. Evatt, Australian Minister of External Affairs, in a speech commenting on Article VII of the Master Lend-Lease agreements, which calls for a final adjustment of Lend-Lease agreements in a manner that will promote the expansion of international trade, the reduction of trade barriers, and the elimination of all forms of discriminatory treatment in international commerce. Dr. Evatt declared that "if this objective is honestly pursued, one result for Australia should be expanding markets in the postwar world, not only for our primary industries but for our manufacturing industries as well. North of Australia, in Southeast Asia, and in the Pacific, there are enormous markets virtually untapped. There are millions of people there who must be provided with improved standards of living. . . . I see in it [Article VII] cogent evidence of a more liberal world economic policy in which Australia will, through rapid industrial expansion, help to achieve the great objective of freedom from want, not only in our own country, but especially in those areas which are associated with our defense in time of war, and with our industrial progress in time of peace."[1]

Thus, as far as Canada and Australia and to a lesser extent the other Dominions are concerned, British exporters are not only faced with strong competition from American industry, but must also adjust themselves to the rapidly changing needs of countries that are actively engaged in industrial expansion. The theory of a closed imperial economic bloc, based on a system of preferential treatment for British manufactures in Dominion markets and for Dominion food and raw materials in the United Kingdom market, no longer meets the economic needs and in-

[1] *Sydney Morning Herald*, February 1, 1943.

terests of the Dominions. Even before the war, each of the self-governing members of the Commonwealth had tended increasingly to develop its own policies with reference to its geographic position and economic interests, and the war has greatly strengthened this trend. It is significant, for example, that both Canada and Australia now have their own legations in Washington, Chungking, and Moscow, and no longer rely on Britain to represent them.

In view of Britain's urgent need to expand her export trade, it is natural that her statesmen should think in terms of tightening imperial bonds, assuring British industry a privileged position in empire markets, and giving Britain a powerful voice in the determination of international political and economic arrangements after the war. Lord Halifax, for example, in his speech of January 24, 1944, before the Toronto Board of Trade, called attention to the vast resources and populations of the United States, the Soviet Union, and China, and then put forward the thesis that "not Great Britain alone, but the British Commonwealth and Empire, must be the fourth power in that group on which the peace of the world will henceforth depend." He urged that "in foreign policy, in defense, in economic affairs, and in communications, we should leave nothing undone to bring our people into closer unity of thought and action."

A year later, a similar sentiment was expressed more directly during Lord Keynes' visit to Ottawa. Lord Keynes, it is reported, emphasized very strongly that the United Kingdom intended to protect her commercial interests against such "hard" or dollar currency countries as Canada with every means at her command. She might refuse to purchase Canadian goods rather than accept them on credit. If Canada did not buy British goods and services, the United Kingdom would buy meat and wheat elsewhere.

Canada and Australia, though deeply concerned with the British attitude, have shown no enthusiasm for a policy of imperial integration that would necessitate their acceptance of a "common policy" formulated in London. They are disturbed at the idea of approaching the problems of the postwar world from the standpoint of the rival strength and resources of various "Great Powers," and have no wish to be involved in a system that might compel them to side with Britain against the United States on either political or economic issues. Having no traditions of power and grandeur to maintain, they are chiefly concerned with the establishment of a world system of economic and political relations that will (1) ensure their independence and security, and (2) give them new outlets for their industrial and agricultural production. Hence they are interested primarily in regional security systems as part of a world-wide organization, and in the revival of world trade and the development of the backward areas as markets for their growing industries.

Faced with the prospect of increasing industrial self-sufficiency in the Dominions, British exporters are reported to be counting heavily on an expansion of trade with Latin America. In their opinion, such an expansion will be facilitated by the elimination of Government-subsidized German trade, and also by the likelihood that many American firms will be more concerned with supplying the vast deferred domestic demand in the United States in the immediate postwar period. On the other hand, they face the problem that in many Latin American countries the war stimulated industrial development and thereby reduced the demand for consumer goods formerly purchased from Great Britain. Argentina, for example, has always been a member of the sterling bloc, an important supplier of food and raw materials to Britain, and a large purchaser of British industrial products. In 1943, however, Argentina's industrial output exceeded the value of her agricultural production for the first time, indicating that she is becoming increasingly self-sufficient in many types of manufactured products. Brazil, too, has established many new manufacturing industries, and the character of her import requirements is therefore likely to change considerably in the postwar period. Furthermore, Argentina and other Latin American countries have amassed large sterling balances in London,[1] which means that they can pay for imports from Britain without having to furnish Britain with either foreign exchange or essential raw materials.

In her search for new and expanding markets, therefore, Britain must reckon with the industrialization of former British markets, the existence of a large war debt in the form of sterling balances held by some of her best customers, the loss of overseas investments, and the prospect of increased trade competition

---

[1] Argentina's sterling holdings were estimated as in excess of £50 million at the end of 1943, and Brazil's at more than £30 million. Cf. "Sterling Balances and Britain's External Debt," *Foreign Commerce Weekly*. Nov. 4, 1944, p. 15.

from some of her own Dominions. But, in the eyes of British commercial and financial interests, all these problems are overshadowed by the question of the postwar foreign trade policy of the United States. The British are keenly aware that America has emerged from the war with an enormously increased industrial capacity, and they are fearful that the United States will seek to find new outlets for this enlarged industrial plant by launching a powerful drive for new export markets, based on the footholds already gained by American products and production methods in all parts of the world as a result of the Lend-Lease program. They also fear that the United States will not realize its responsibilities as a powerful creditor nation and the most important single market for many countries.

Discussion of American trade policy in the British press for the most part concentrates on the thesis that America's first responsibility to world prosperity is to expand her domestic market for the products of her own and foreign industries, rather than attempt to flood the world with American goods while maintaining a high tariff against foreign imports. The London *Times*, for example, notes with concern that "American planners, official and unofficial, are eagerly preparing measures to promote a rapidly expanding flow of goods and services from the United States all over the world. But there are few if any signs of preoccupation with measures to provide facilities and opportunities for a corresponding influx of goods into the United States. Yet . . . nothing is more certain to lead to ultimate chaos and calamity on a world-wide scale than a policy which seeks to inflate exports without applying an equal stimulus to imports" (Nov. 15, 1943). The *Statist*, influential British financial journal, takes a similar line, pointing out that "the U.S. will finish this war with the largest potential manufacturing capacity of any country in history, and it is to be feared that their solution to their unemployment problem will be a vigorous drive to employ their people by flooding the world with their exports." Britain is concerned, declares the *Statist*, lest "America escape the much feared breadline by instituting it in these islands." In an editorial of July 29, 1944, on the Bretton Woods Monetary Conference, the London *Economist* contended that the international financial mechanism set up by the conference could work only in a world "in which at least the major countries were successful in avoiding unemployment crises." Maintaining that the chief responsibility for creating such a world lies with the United States, it noted with alarm that America of all countries "is the least persuaded of the necessity of taking positive action to control the economic environment." Finally, the *Economist* asked the question: "What are the prospects of an effective employment policy in the United States?"

Sir George Schuster, M.P. and a director of numerous British banks and industrial enterprises, voiced the same fear in a speech in Parliament on October 19, 1944, in which he suggested that the United States should consider curbing her exports to leave some room for others. Declared Sir George: "There is no more fateful question than this: How will the United States use her surplus capacity after the war? Will she pour it out on the world to find an outlet for goods, or will she concentrate on raising living standards at home and leave some leeway in the export trade for others?" Sir George's speech was only one of numerous assertions, both in Parliament and outside, that the British Government had not been doing enough planning with regard to postwar foreign trade. In response to these criticisms, Harcourt Johnstone, Secretary of the Department of Overseas Trade, assured Parliament that while American efforts to reconvert industry and capture world markets might be more spectacular than those of Great Britain, Britain would not be "left out in the cold." Mr. Johnstone announced that the Government's plan to promote British exports included the appointment of business men resident abroad as marketing officers in the principal countries. Small firms unable to send their own representatives would be represented by group agencies. He added that his Department had made a survey in twenty-six countries outside the battle area of Europe for the "Buy British" drive, and that 140 exporting industries had been organized for the quickest possible trade drive after the war.

There is no doubt that British firms are far from hopelessly beaten in terms of commercial rivalry with the United States. They have had long experience in international commerce and finance, and British quality products can meet any competition. Many people, in fact, contend that Britain is by no means so weak economically as some of her spokesmen imply. They point to the fact that Britain still retains substantial overseas investments, and that she has increased her productive capacity considerably. Both national income and the volume of private savings increased steadily between 1938 and 1943; machine tool production was expanded 70%, and greater technical efficiency was achieved in many export lines. The statement of Lord Catto, governor of the Bank of England, expressing complete confidence in Britain's future, is also cited by those who see no reason for undue concern about Britain's postwar position. Lord Catto declared: "I am fully confident that the country will regain its old financial and industrial leadership in the world. If it was not for the financial miracle of lend-lease and the Canadian war contribution, it might be different. Other countries have debts in the same proportion but without our external financial problems. However, our external obligations should not fill us with dismay. Our national debt is three times that of the last war, but our productive capacity has increased and we have generations of accumulated experience." Finally, it is pointed out by some that the United States, instead of being the world's great creditor nation, is actually a debtor to the amount of some $1.2 billion, as a result of the sharp decline in foreign investment, coupled with a large expansion of foreign assets in this country. This latter argument, however, refers only to a temporary wartime situation which is certain to be quickly reversed in the postwar period when foreign dollar balances are used to pay for American exports or are withdrawn in gold.

But though there is no question that in certain respects Britain may emerge from the war in a stronger position than when she entered it, and that she is far from being a hopeless bankrupt, there is also no doubt that in relation to the United States, she will be decidedly weaker. Nor is there any doubt that a revival of her export trade is of absolutely vital importance to her economic recovery. It is therefore entirely understandable that British business and financial interests should be alarmed at the prospect of the export drive that the United States is capable of launching, particularly as America is in a position to finance such exports with long-term credits, whereas Britain must obtain current receipts to finance essential imports.

Add up all these factors — the loss of overseas investment income, the obstacles to the regaining of prewar markets, the greatly increased importance of export trade, and the fear of American commercial rivalry — and the result equals a desperate British effort to hang on to every possible economic advantage that she possesses, i.e., her colonial empire and, as far as pos-

sible, the system of imperial preference. This latter point was
made unmistakably clear by Prime Minister Churchill in the
House of Commons on April 21, 1944, in a speech winding up a
two-day debate on empire policy. Mr. Churchill informed the
House that it was he who had requested the insertion of the
words: "with due respect for their existing obligations," in the
fourth point of the Atlantic Charter which pledged Britain and
the United States to "further the enjoyment by all States" of
equal access to trade and raw materials. And he stated further
that these words "were inserted for the express purpose of retaining to this House and to the Dominions the fullest possible
rights and liberties over the question of imperial preference."
He also emphasized that he had not agreed to Article VII of the
mutual aid agreement between Britain and the United States
(committing the signatories to a postwar discussion of measures
to promote the expansion of international trade and the elimination of discrimination in international commerce), "without having previously obtained from the President a definite assurance
that we were no more committed to the abolition of imperial
preference than the American Government was committed to
the abolition of their protective tariff walls."

THE INGREDIENTS OF POWER POLITICS
IN THE PACIFIC

As FAR As the preservation of her colonial empire is concerned,
Britain's actions speak louder than her words, but both are unmistakable. There is, first and foremost, convincing evidence
that Britain is determined to retain the advantages she enjoys
by virtue of her power to control Indian economic development;
that she does not intend to encourage Indian industrialization or
allow other countries an equal competitive position in the India
market. British policy toward India, and the reasons why British
interests consider it imperative to maintain India as a colony,
have been discussed in detail in an earlier chapter and need not
be further analyzed here. Another indication of Britain's interest
in the preservation of a colonial system in Asia is provided by
the policy pursued with regard to the reconquest of Burma. Reports from eminently reliable American observers in India state
flatly that the lethargic nature of the British campaign in Burma
during 1943 and 1944 was primarily due to the fact that the
British were not anxious to take Burma back with the aid of the

Americans or the Chinese. If the ultimate purpose was to reëstablish exclusive British control, it obviously served British
interests far better if Burma were retaken by themselves or were
handed back to them at the peace table, without their having
had to enlist the aid of the Americans, the Chinese, or the
Burmans themselves.

It is a notable commentary on the British attitude toward the
colonial question that the United Nations failed to come out with
any program or policy designed to enlist the active support of
the people of Burma or other countries of Southeastern Asia.
In the case of Burma, where a strong nationalist sentiment existed before the war, this failure is particularly serious in view
of the fact that the Japanese assiduously played upon Burmese
nationalist aspirations. It was easy to dismiss the Japanese offer
of "independence" to Burma as meaningless, but the fact remains
that the offer was made, and that it was more than any British
Government in Burma had ever done. The majority of Burmans
became disillusioned with their Japanese "liberators," but this
did not mean that they were enthusiastic over the prospect of a
restoration of British rule.

This serious weakness in Allied political warfare in Asia was
criticized not only by many American observers but also by
British officials with experience in the Far East. An illuminating
comment on British policy in Burma, for example, was made by
Sir Reginald Dorman-Smith, former British Governor in Burma,
in a speech before the East Indian Association in London in
October 1943. Sir Reginald sugar-coated his criticism by first
informing his audience that many Burmans continued to fight
for the Allies, that they were disillusioned with the Japanese,
and that — provided the right approach is made — they will welcome the British back. But he followed these optimistic comments with the blunt warning that "it would be wrong to ignore
the political aspect." Sir Reginald reminded his listeners that the
people of Burma had seen their British rulers "disappear in a
cloud of dust hotly pursued by our victorious enemy" — a sight
not calculated to raise British prestige. He went on to point out
that "politically-minded Burmans will be wondering just what
our intentions towards Burma are. Do we really mean to lead
them on to the goal of full self-government, or have we some
reservations at the back of our minds which will mean that self-
government will always be round the corner and never an ac-

complished fact? . . . I do not pretend to be skilled in Far Eastern affairs . . . but one thing I can say with some surety and that is that neither our word nor our intentions are trusted in that part of the globe. The reason for this is not far to seek. We have fed such countries as Burma on political formulae until they are sick of the very sight and sound of a formula, which has come, as far as my experience shows, to be looked upon as a very British means of avoiding a definite course of action." This criticism might be applied with equal pertinence to India, where British policy has also been notable for its use of political "formulae" and its absence of concrete measures to associate representative Indians with the government of their country, and where it has reaped the same harvest of suspicion and distrust.

But, despite such realistic appraisals of the effects of British policy on the subject peoples of Asia, there is abundant evidence to indicate that the British Government is still unwilling to consider any basic change in the prewar colonial status quo. This evidence is not confined to editorials in the *Economist* and the *Times*. It is to be found in the restrictions imposed on Indian industrial expansion during the war and in the determined effort made to disorganize and weaken the Indian nationalist movement. It is also apparent in the refusal of the British Government even to discuss the possibility of the return of Hong Kong to China. Then, too, certain official British circles have openly expressed the fear that a strong China might become "imperialist"-minded and attempt to extend her influence in Southeastern Asia. They justify such fears on the grounds that there have been Chinese references to the "four southern provinces" of Indo-China, Malaya, Burma, and Siam, but there is reason to believe that the real cause for these alarmist statements is the knowledge that a strong, free, and democratic China would inevitably encourage the nationalist aspirations of the colonial countries. Similarly, some British officials have suggested that one reason why Britain cannot transfer power to an Indian government is that such a government would not be able to prevent the penetration of "foreign" influence into India, and they have supported this argument with suggestive references to the fact that both China and the Soviet Union are close neighbors of India.

Another indication of Britain's desire to bring about a restoration of the prewar political status quo in Asia is, as we have already noted, her attitude on the question of Japan's future form of government; her desire that Japan should remain politically "stable" and "reliable." On this question it is of interest to note the views expressed in a report prepared by a Study Group of Chatham House (the Royal Institute of International Affairs) on the topic, "Japan in Defeat." Though not an official organization, the Royal Institute's studies and reports have won a well-merited reputation as the work of outstanding British experts in foreign affairs, and the report in question may thus be taken as reflecting responsible (if not governmental) British opinion on the question of postwar Japan.

With regard to the imperial institution, the report declares that "the present generation of peasants cannot be expected to understand or support with conviction any other than a monarchical regime. . . . No alternative to a monarchical system, under the present Emperor or some other member of his family, is likely to provide that *focus of stability* which will be essential if the State is not to dissolve into chaos in the impending crisis. Reasons have been given for a belief that, under favorable conditions, the Throne might survive a formal reorientation of its position in popular estimation. One of these conditions would be the emergence of a group of statesmen sufficiently enlightened and influential to create and maintain a constitutional regime. Just as the great upheaval of the Restoration brought to the front an astonishing array of statesmen and administrators, so it is possible that after the war Japan will find hidden resources of reformist ability on which to rely. But unless history repeats itself in this way, it seems probable that the influence of the upper middle-class in the administration will continue; and that constitutional statesmen will be recruited from the bureaucracy, the *zaibatsu*, 'advanced' politicians, 'moderate' generals and admirals, with a sprinkling of liberals."

The British preoccupation with "stability" in postwar Japan is also reflected in the following comments with regard to the postwar role of the Japanese armed forces. Though declaring that "Japanese militarism must be destroyed," and that "an essential preliminary to this destruction will be the relegation of the armed forces to their appropriate influence in the State through constitutional reform," the Chatham House report goes on to emphasize that "notwithstanding the insubordination and terrorism for which military and naval officers were responsible between 1932 and 1936, it remains true that, in internal emergencies, the armed forces have shown themselves to be a *stable element* in the State. Their allegiance is feudal in character and attaches to their military leaders and through them to the Emperor. By contrast, their attitude to representative institutions is one of opposition, and to the civil powers, of aloofness. They regard themselves as the Emperor's forces having their roots in the people, who are his children. Yet, it spite of these limitations, they embody a spirit of discipline. If the Japanese are to remain responsible for their own destinies, in a situation demanding, above all, *maintenance of authority and discipline,* the co-operation of some strong, organized military force will be indispensable."[1] (Author's italics.)

Similar views were expressed by Sir Robert Craigie, British Ambassador to Japan from 1937 to 1941, in an address before the Royal Empire Society on November 10, 1943. It was Sir Robert's opinion, according to the London *Times* report, that "throughout the country, hidden in its shadows, were potentially influential statesmen, politicians, and leaders in the business and professional worlds, who had opposed, and still abhorred, army control of their nation's destinies. When the present tyrannical military regime began to lose its grip, those men were likely to re-emerge and might play an important part in the overthrow of the military domination."

Still further light on British official sentiment toward Japan was provided in the fall of 1944, when a sharp disagreement occurred between the Far Eastern Bureau of the British Ministry of Information in New Delhi and its home office in London, concerning methods to counteract Japanese propaganda in China. The London office forbade the China Section of the New Delhi office to use material which had been prepared for radio and press dissemination to counteract Japanese broadcasts eulogizing the late Wang Ching-wei, Japan's principal puppet, as a true Chinese patriot and follower of Sun Yat-sen. The Canadian, Australian, and New Zealand members of the Far Eastern Bureau were reported to be extremely resentful at this order —a resentment naturally shared by the Chinese on the staff. They attributed it to the fact that the London office was con-

---

[1] *Japan in Defeat.* Report by a Chatham House Study Group. Ninth Institute of Pacific Relations Conference, January 1945. United Kingdom Paper #4, pp. 94–98. Issued by the Royal Institute of International Affairs, London.

trolled by Conservatives who followed a policy of not attacking
Japan too strongly, and who wished to see Britain work closely
with Japan after the war — their aims being: to reëstablish Japan
as a strong counterbalance to the Soviet Union; to prevent China
from becoming strong enough to encourage the nationalist aspirations of Britain's colonies in Asia; and to check the growing
influence of the United States in the Far East.

It must be remembered that Great Britain had been accustomed throughout the duration of the Anglo-Japanese alliance
and even after, to count upon Japan as a balancing force in Asia
— against the spread of Soviet influence, aganst American competition, and against nationalist aspirations in the colonial areas.
It may well be that Captain Lyttelton's remark about the United
States having provoked Japan into war was an unconscious reflection of British disappointment that the war had been permitted to spread to the Pacific and had thus forced the colonial
issue into the foreground and revealed the inherent weakness
of the colonial system. There is no doubt that Britain was thoroughly committed to aiding in Japan's military defeat. Her
prestige as an imperial power was at stake. But this does not mean
that she did not also look forward to an eventual revival of
Japan as a "balancing force" in Asia, on the one hand against
the enormously enhanced power of the United States, and on
the other against the rising demand of the colonies for freedom.

All these factors — the belief that she must retain the colonial
system for her own economic survival, the fear of possible Russian or Chinese influence in the colonial countries, the desire
to muster all available resources to meet the economic competition of the United States — enter into the formulation of British
policy concerning postwar political and economic arrangements.
As we have seen, a dominant concept in that policy is the belief
that Britain, in order to hold her own against America and the
Soviet Union, must be the leader of a group of states far more
closely integrated in their political and economic policies than is
the present British Commonwealth. The ties of sentiment that
now bind the Dominions to Britain must be reinforced by a commercial bond — imperial preference — and also by a financial
bond, i.e., a sterling bloc. Moreover, leading British spokesmen
have urged that in addition to greater imperial centralization,
Britain should further buttress her position by taking the lead

in the establishment of a Western European bloc, pursuing common political and economic aims.

Field Marshal Smuts, for example, in his famous statement of November 1943, contrasted Britain's weakness with the power of the United States and the "Soviet colossus" and urged that the British fortify their position by inviting Scandinavia, the Netherlands, and Belgium into an association with the Empire. Others have followed up this proposal with suggestions that the Western European bloc be widened to include France, Spain, and Portugal as well.

In addition to these proposals for a closer integration of the Empire and the formation of a Western European bloc under British leadership, British financial and industrial interests are exploring other possibilities for strengthening Britain's postwar economic position. Although all these plans stress the necessity for an expansion of Britain's export trade, they appear to be more concerned with securing for Britain a guaranteed share of world markets than with expanding the purchasing power of those markets. In other words, they concentrate on the allocation rather than on the expansion of world trade. One such plan proposes bringing world industry and commerce under the control of a giant system of interlocking cartels, which would determine the output and price of both raw materials and manufactured goods, and would divide world markets among the various industrial nations somewhat along the lines of the system followed during the war. The advocates of this scheme defend private cartels as "essential to keep production equitably allocated between countries and companies," and, though admitting that "it is theoretically possible" that such combinations might devote themselves to "exploiting the consumer instead of using their special efficiency to serve him," they maintain that this tendency could be held in check by "public opinion." British backers of this program hope to enlist the coöperation of American producers, but both sides are reported to be worried by the American antitrust laws and by the fact that the American public is keenly aware of the role that international cartels played in hampering the American war effort. Furthermore, though this program is sugar-coated by references to the need for coöperation with labor, the expansion of purchasing power, and the benefits that will accrue to the consumer as a result of the elimination of wasteful and destructive competition, it is obvious that such a scheme could be put into effect only if conservative governments are established in western Europe, and if the major Western Powers retain complete control of the raw-material-producing countries of Africa, Asia, and Latin America.

The belief that Britain's future economic security could best be secured by a system of cartels was perhaps most clearly expressed at the International Business Conference at Rye, New York, in November 1944, when British delegates openly repudiated the principles of competition and business freedom in favor of monopoly and government control. That these views were not favorably received by American business interests was demonstrated not only by the reaction of the American delegates at Rye, but also by the resolution adopted by the National Association of Manufacturers at their subsequent convention in December, in which the NAM went on record against postwar cartels and "dictated economies." On that occasion, Robert M. Gaylord, retiring head of the NAM, declared that American businessmen were "dismayed by British acceptance of collectivist principles in the name of security." The knowledge that the NAM's reaction did not represent genuine opposition to cartels and monopolies as such, but rather the belief that America's economic strength was now so great that she need not fear completely unrestricted competition in world markets and could therefore afford to ignore the British desire for a guaranteed share in future world commerce, did nothing to mitigate Britain's concern over her economic problems.

Another school of thought in Great Britain, recognizing that a division of world markets and resources among a handful of private cartels would be strongly opposed in the United States, put forward an alternative plan that was discussed in a series of articles in the *Economist* early in 1944, and commented on in some detail in an article in the *New York Times* of March 26, 1944. This program called for a system of State-directed trade within a regional grouping around the sterling bloc. State control of trade within the area would be achieved by preferential tariff agreements, trade quotas, exchange controls, etc. According to the *New York Times* report: "Each member of the group would have to agree to balance accounts within the group; to remove an excess of exports by increasing imports, cancelling debts, or by investing the export surplus in international public works in a member country having a deficit balance; to avoid large-scale depressions within its borders by industrial and monetary policy; to make no exchange control restrictions of purchases of current goods within the group, and to maintain a floor under quantitative restrictions on imports from member countries."

The advocates of this plan frankly admitted that the United States would have a less favored position than members of the sterling bloc, but they hoped to win American approval by "economic concessions and a political arrangement." Furthermore, they contended that, if the United States assented to the formation of such a State-directed, insulated economic region for the immediate postwar period, Britain would agree to work with America for the ultimate restoration of universal, reciprocal trade in the long run, which was considered not so beneficial to Britain as to America. It was also argued that, though the scheme had all the earmarks of protectionism and imperial preference, it would serve to promote trade expansion and economic development within the sterling bloc and thus provide a large market for American goods in spite of their less favored position.

According to the *New York Times* report: "The United Kingdom and the colonial empire would be the founder members of the region under the plan. Australia, New Zealand, South Africa, and India would be drawn in, it is hoped, by the large United Kingdom market and their desire to draw on the huge wartime accumulation of credit in London, which would not be available to them otherwise 'without the complication of a controlled exchange intervening.' If America is 'benevolent,' Holland, Belgium, Denmark, and Norway, and possibly France and Portugal and their dependencies can be induced to join. Canada, Newfoundland and possibly some other areas would remain outside, it is anticipated." Since Britain is the world's largest purchaser of important primary products, and since this is her only remaining advantage in trade competition with the United States, the proponents of this plan argued that she could not be blamed for seeking to make use of it.

Each of these various proposals — for a closer economic integration of the Empire, for a Western European "bloc" under British leadership, for a world-wide "sterling bloc" — had the same general aims: to secure "safe" markets for British goods by bringing an ever larger area of the world into the British financial sphere, to ensure low prices for the industrial raw materials that Britain needs, and to take advantage of the existence of the frozen sterling balances of Britain's creditors to persuade them to buy British. From the political standpoint, these various plans would of course serve to strengthen the colonial system by uniting all the powers that have a stake in its preservation and by setting up what would amount in practice to a federation of colonial empires including the markets and resources of perhaps 60% of the world's population, from which the United States would be excluded except on "terms" dictated by the controlling powers.

Such a program was, of course, diametrically opposed to the American desire for an expansion of international trade on a universal basis. The United States, being far less dependent than Britain on imports of food and raw materials, is primarily concerned with finding new outlets for its surplus capital and production. American industry is ready and able to meet free competition in world markets, if not at home, and therefore opposes the idea of quotas or the allocation of markets. Furthermore, important sections of American business and financial interests are not so much concerned with keeping the price of raw materials low as with raising the purchasing power of the hitherto backward areas, for only in this way can they hope to find expanding outlets for their goods and capital. The economic subjection of colonial areas, with all that it implies in terms of trade restrictions, low purchasing power, and monopoly control of essential raw materials, is unsuited to American economic needs. It is inevitable, therefore, that American opinion in general should be strongly opposed to the idea of strengthening the colonial system through the formation of a federation of colonial-minded powers.

An excellent illustration of the sharp divergence between the British and the American viewpoints on the colonial issue was provided by the case of Thailand. The United States did not declare war on Thailand, but regarded it as enemy-occupied territory. As far as the political future of the country was concerned, the American attitude was defined by Secretary Hull in August 1943, when he wrote that "the efforts of the Government of the United States are and should be limited to assisting the Thai people to restore a native regime capable of discharging its responsibilities and free from foreign control. The final choice of the leaders of such a government is a matter for the Thai people alone to decide." The American Government also continued to recognize the Thai Minister in Washington, who repudiated his Government when it capitulated to the Japanese, as the official representative of Thailand, and took a sympathetic interest in the "Free Thai" movement, which he helped to start. Cordell Hull's position on Thailand was reasserted by Secretary of State James F. Byrnes on August 19, 1945, when the State Department extended a cordial welcome to a Thai declaration that the war against the United States was ended. Revealing that the United States had always felt that the Thai declaration of war was forced by the Japanese and did not represent the sentiments of the people, and that as a result America continued to recognize M. R. Seni Pramoj as the Free Thai Minister to Washington, Secretary Byrnes stated: "Before the war Thailand and the United States had a long history of close friendship. We hope that friendship will be even closer in the future. During the past four years we have regarded Thailand not as an enemy but as a country to be liberated from the enemy. With that liberation now accomplished we look to the resumption by Thailand of its former place in the community of nations as a free, sovereign and independent country."

The official British attitude toward Thailand differed from the American at almost every point. Britain was officially at war with Thailand and considered the country an ally of Japan. With regard to her future political status, the British view was that Thailand's independence should be made contingent on her willingness to meet certain economic and military conditions — the nature of which was not specified. The British also regarded the Government in Bangkok as the responsible authority in Thailand, and gave little or no recognition to the Free Thai movement.

Unofficial British comments regarding Thailand also served to point up the differences between the British and the American attitude. For example, the views expressed by Sir Josiah Crosby, British Minister to Thailand at the time of the Japanese invasion, in a speech at the Royal Institute of International Affairs in London on June 1, 1943, were in decided contrast to the American idea that Thailand should be reëstablished as an independent country with a democratically chosen government.

Sir Josiah declared that "the case of Siam is exceptional in that she alone among the countries of Southeast Asia is at the same time an independent State and an enemy of Great Britain and the United States, upon whom she has formally declared war. When the terms of peace are dictated, she will thus of necessity be liable to punishment, though if the provisions of the Atlantic Charter are observed, her sovereign status and her territorial integrity will remain unimpaired. A consideration of the nature of the sanctions (military, financial, and otherwise) to be imposed on Siam when the time comes would lead me into a premature discussion of details which I wish to avoid. But, both on merits and as a measure of precaution, the establishment of some form of tutelage over Siam for a period following upon the termination of the war is even now sufficiently indicated. If the sovereign status of the country is not to be infringed, the obvious course will in my view lie in a return to the system of foreign advisers, with which the Siamese are already familiar, and which has achieved reasonably satisfactory results hitherto." [1]

In addition, Sir Josiah emphasized that such advisers should be supported by "one of the United Nations" acting as a "quasi-tutelary power, pressure from whom could be forthcoming when required to ensure that their recommendations were carried out." He also gave a revealing picture of the British attitude on the general question of self-government for the peoples of Southeast Asia by remarking that "the attainment by Siam of complete autonomy, as signallized by her signature of fresh treaties with the foreign powers in 1937, cannot be held to have justified itself in practice and the example furnished by her in this regard may be considered typical. Arguing by analogy, I do not think it unfair to conclude that the peoples of the other countries of Southeast Asia, whose political education is even less advanced than that of the Siamese, are no less unfitted for the exercise of completely autonomous government."

The reason for this sharp difference between the British and the American attitude toward Thailand was not difficult to find. Although the first American treaty with a Far Eastern country was made with Siam in 1833, and Americans served as advisers to the Siamese Ministry of Foreign Affairs from 1903 to 1940, the United States had no important strategic or economic interests in the country. American investments were confined chiefly to mis-

---

[1] "Observations on a Post-War Settlement in Southeast Asia," *International Affairs*, London, July 1943, pp. 357–368.

sion property, and American trade with Thailand was negligible. Thus there were no "vested interests" to conflict with the view that a free and democratic Thailand would contribute to peace and stability in the Far East, and also to the emergence of a new political and economic order in place of the old system of Western imperialist control in Southeast Asia.

The British attitude toward Thailand, on the other hand, was a natural reflection of British political and strategic interests in Southeast Asia, and of the British desire to reëstablish control over the rich resources of that area. Though Siam had gained international recognition of her political, financial, and juridical autonomy in the fourteen agreements signed with foreign powers in 1937, she had remained a semicolonial nation in the economic sense, being little more than an economic satellite of the British Empire. The British ports of Hong Kong, Singapore, Penang, and Rangoon were the chief entrepots for Siam's foreign trade, about 70% of which was carried on with the British Empire. The Siamese foreign debt of some £5 million was held in London; an Englishman served as Financial Adviser to the Thai Government; and British capital played a dominant role in the country's economy, controlling the major share of the chief export industries — tin, rubber, and teak. In 1932, the total British investment in Thailand was estimated at £20 million.

Furthermore, Thailand was of great strategic importance to the defense of Malaya and Burma. Long before the Second World War, the growth of Japanese influence in Thailand was viewed with alarm in certain British circles — this alarm being most dramatically manifested in the "Kra Canal issue," which provoked frequent and perturbed discussion in the British press from 1934 onwards. At that time, many observers scoffed at the idea that Japan might attempt to construct a canal across the Kra Isthmus and argued that such a canal would in no way menace Singapore's position as the great trade center of Southeast Asia. The experiences of the war, however, gave the British new cause for concern over the control of this strategic area. Within a week after the outbreak of war in December 1941, Japanese troops had crossed the Kra Isthmus, forced British troops to evacuate southern Burma and then advanced southward along the west coast of the Malay Peninsula to Singapore and northward toward Rangoon. During 1943, furthermore, the Japanese built a railroad connecting Bangkok with Burma and another railroad across the Kra Isthmus to a harbor near Victoria Point — the southern tip of Burma.

It was not surprising, therefore, that British officials should view the question of Thailand's future in terms of the security of the British position in Southeast Asia, and that in consequence they should regard Thailand as a logical component of the political structure which they were seeking to reëstablish in that part of the world. Sir Josiah Crosby's speech was not the only evidence that official British opinion was running along these lines. *The Statesman of India,* for example, in an editorial published on August 18, 1944, pointed out that after the Japanese had been driven out, Thailand would be left "alone in a shaken, devastated and unsettled part of Southeast Asia" and that neither India nor China would be in a position to aid her. The editorial then went on to discuss the long-standing enmity between Burma and Thailand and concluded that "the desirability of breaking it down is another reason why both countries should be in allegiance to and protected by some common authority." Some British officials in India were said to be in favor of transferring the southern Thai province of Pattani to British Malaya; while others believed that the best solution would be for Thailand to join a Southeast Asia Federation, which could then be merged into the British Commonwealth. None of these suggestions had received official recognition or support from the British Government, but they were sufficient to indicate a widespread feeling among British officials on the spot that a fully independent Thailand would not be compatible with the maintenance of British interests in Southeast Asia.

The case of Thailand was merely one illustration of the sharp differences between British and American aims and interests as far as the colonial areas of Asia were concerned. Another evidence that the American Government was disturbed by the prospect of a world-wide alignment of imperial powers and the restoration of the prewar colonial system was the so-called "feud" between President Roosevelt and General De Gaulle, which reached a climax early in 1944 before the Allied invasion of France. At that time, influential circles in the Administration were opposed to the restoration of the prewar colonial system in Southeast Asia, and considered the Philippines an example of

what could be accomplished in the way of progressive development toward self-government and full independence. In general,
they believed that the former colonies should be placed under
international trusteeship, with an administering power governing on behalf of this trusteeship and providing for a steadily increasing measure of native participation in the government. As
the weakest link in the colonial chain, Indo-China appeared the
logical starting point for such a plan. Japan's rapid and bloodless
conquest of the country with the acquiescence of the Vichy Government, coupled with the fact that France itself was still under
Nazi domination, gave added weight to the argument that this
highly strategic area should not be restored to exclusive French
control, but should be administered by France on behalf of an
international trusteeship after the war, thus laying the basis for
the development of a wholly new system of administration for
dependent territories which would be aimed at preparing the
peoples of these areas for full self-government.

That this estimate of the reasons behind the Roosevelt-De
Gaulle "feud" is correct was substantiated by Marquis Childs in
his column of May 8, 1945. There he reported a conversation he
had had with President Roosevelt. Childs wrote: "I have before
me the notes of a conversation I had with the late President a
year ago, in which he talked at some length of his ideal of a trusteeship that would enable colonial peoples to move toward political and economic independence within a fixed number of years.
The President began by talking about the position of the white
man in the Far Pacific. The white man, he pointed out, had
come more and more into disfavor. The quick successes of the
Japs had shaken white prestige that was already badly damaged.
'We are going to have to take some positive steps,' the President
said, 'or find ourselves pushed out completely. Some time ago
I worked out a form of trusteeship for French Indo-China. You
know, that colony was governed very badly. For every dollar the
French put in, they took 10 dollars out. Those little people had
a culture of their own, Cambodia and Cambodian kings. But they
were badly treated. Now my idea is for a trusteeship to admin-
ister Indo-China.' . . . Through a fixed term of years, as the
President outlined it, the Indo-Chinese would work toward political and economic independence. The trustees would guide
that process, with complete freedom as the final goal. At Teheran,

Roosevelt said, he asked Stalin what he thought of the plan. Stalin thought it was 'excellent.' Prime Minister Churchill, however, would have none of it. . . . Churchill was thinking of Burma. He refused to consider such a plan for Burma."

There is good reason to believe that the American Government's reluctance to recognize General De Gaulle's National Committee of Liberation as the government of France was due primarily to the belief that De Gaulle and his supporters were in favor of strengthening rather than weakening France's hold on her prewar empire, and that they would be likely to welcome British proposals for an Anglo-French-Dutch imperial bloc, with the result that American trade would be denied equality of opportunity in large areas of the world. The necessity of maintaining United Nations unity during the war, plus popular pressure in the United States for the recognition of General De Gaulle, rendered it impossible for the American Government to make an open issue of the colonial question at the time. Following the liberation of France, when it became evident that General De Gaulle commanded the loyal support of all sections of the French people, there was no longer any excuse for delaying recognition of his regime as the provisional government of France or for refusing to concur with the British view that France must be restored to her position as a major imperial power. The admission of France to full partnership with Britain, Russia, and the United States in the European Advisory Commission (November 1944) was an indication that henceforth there was to be a "Big Four" instead of a "Big Three" in European affairs.

For the purpose of this study, however, we are concerned with France simply as a potential supporter of British policy with regard to the preservation and strengthening of the colonial system in Asia and Africa. The statements of De Gaulle and other French leaders show that they expect France to regain her colonial empire intact, and that they are primarily interested in tightening the bonds that unite France with her colonies. British arguments in favor of closer "imperial integration" find a sympathetic response in French official circles, where it is clearly recognized that a political unit with a population of 100,000,000 and extensive raw-material resources stands a far better chance of survival in a world of power politics than does a country of 40,000,000 deprived of monoply control over colonial territories. It is significant that responsible official comments on future French colonial policy stress the idea of a French "commonwealth" or "federation" of all territories within the former French Empire, in order that the colonies may be more closely integrated into the political and economic life of France.

It is true that in discussions of this question French officials have made concessions to the American viewpoint by emphasizing that one of the principal objectives of such a federation would be to grant each component the largest possible measure of local autonomy and to increase the participation of the colonial peoples in the government of their own territory. But the emphasis is on local self-government *within* the empire or federation, with no mention of the possibility of complete independence for any of the federating units. Nor is there any indication that French leaders accept the idea of an international trusteeship for dependent areas that would have the right to control the actions of the administering Power. On the occasion of his visit to Washington in July 1944, for example, General De Gaulle declared that "we believe in a federation of all the territories over which the French flag flies. Metropolitan France will be in the federation along with other components. The native peoples in the former colonies are, of course, in various stages of evolution more or less advanced. The policy will be for all the territories to attain a degree of self-government within the federation. This applies in particular to Indo-China." In October 1944, René Pleven, the then French Minister of Colonies, elaborated on this thesis by declaring that French policy aimed at a political and economic integration of all parts of the French Empire into a single federal system, with a view to strengthening the ties between these territories and France. Then, on March 25, 1945, André Giacobbi, the new Minister of Colonies, announced that the French Cabinet had approved a statute by which Indo-China after the war would become the first dominion in the French Union or Commonwealth of Nations. Under the new statute, M. Giacobbi explained, Indo-China will constitute — together with France and other parts of the French Empire — a "French Union" on federal lines with local autonomy. He emphasized that the foreign policy of the Union would be controlled by France. Citizens of Indo-China would also be citizens of the French Union, and would enjoy local autonomy under a federal government headed by a Governor-General and composed of Ministers elected by Indo-Chinese and French residents.

These French proposals bore a significant resemblance to those put forward by the Netherlands Government with regard to the future political organization of the Netherlands Empire. These, too, envisage a "commonwealth" or "federation" in which each unit would enjoy a large measure of local·autonomy. On March 31, 1944, Queen Wilhelmina reiterated her Government's intention to revise the Dutch constitution in order to establish a Netherlands Commonwealth in which all parts of the present Kingdom would have equal status. Autonomy would be complete in internal affairs, with a uniform commonwealth policy for foreign and military affairs. The Dutch authorities also emphasize that they intend to grant the colonial peoples an increasing share in their local governments and a voice in the determination of policies affecting the commonwealth as a whole. In addition, they stress the need for regional security arrangements by which each part of the Dutch Empire would coöperate closely with neighboring states — e.g., the Netherlands with Britain, France, and other Western European countries, the Netherlands East Indies with Australia, etc.

From these various proposals it is clear that French and Dutch officials share the British view that the principles of freedom and self-determination enunciated in the Atlantic Charter do not necessitate the "liquidation" of existing empires or the establishing of international bodies to supervise the administration of colonial territories. They do recognize, however, that the nationalist aspirations of the colonial peoples and the hostility of world opinion toward the prewar colonial system cannot be wholly ignored. Hence they have evolved a program which, on the one hand, assures their continued control over their colonies, and, on the other, is designed to disguise that control by promises of internal "autonomy" in the colonies and by granting the colonial peoples a nominal voice in the determination of empire policy. None of these programs, however, envisages any basic change in the economic relation between the colonies and the mother country. The economic development of the colonies is still to be geared to the needs and interests of French and Dutch industrialists and financiers; they would still serve primarily as sources of raw materials and labor power and as protected markets for the manufactured goods of France and Holland. Furthermore, there is every reason to believe that both Holland and France would be sympathetic to the British idea of an imperial economic bloc embracing British, Dutch, and French colonial territories, since such an arrangement would give them greater security and economic power.

Thus the prevailing British, French, and Dutch attitudes regarding their colonial territories holds out little promise of a postwar expansion of international trade based on the abolition of discriminatory trade practices and monopoly controls, and on the industrialization of formerly backward areas. There is no evidence that Japan's defeat and the "liberation" of Japanese-conquered areas will mark the beginning of a new relationship between those areas and their former rulers except in the case of the Philippines. British interests will control Hong Kong, Burma, Malaya, and India. The Dutch will resume command of the rich resources of the East Indies, and France will regain control of the markets and raw materials of Indo-China. America's economic relations with this vast colonial territory will be on British, Dutch, and French terms. American financial and material aid will undoubtedly be sought for reconstruction purposes, and the American market for tin, rubber, oil, and other raw materials will be assiduously cultivated; but American exports to India and Southeast Asia will be limited not only by the industrial backwardness and poverty of these countries, but also by the preferential treatment accorded to British, French, and Dutch goods in their colonial markets. In short, American hopes for an expanding world market seem likely to founder on the rock of Britain's determination to retain control of her colonial empire and to ensure herself a privileged position with regard to other colonial markets and raw materials.

THE ALTERNATIVES FOR BRITAIN

THE SPOKESMEN for British ruling interests maintain that control of the British empire is essential to maintain the living standards of the British people, who depend so much upon assured access to cheap food and raw materials and "protected" markets for at least a portion of British exports. By implication they deem it just that hundreds of millions of people in Asia and Africa should be kept in colonial subjection to safeguard the wealth and living standards of 47 million people in the British Isles. For the moment let us accept this contention as valid and examine just what it is that is being "protected."

An official White Paper (Cmd. 6520, April 1944) shows that

in 1943 the British national income was distributed as follows:

	Million £	Per Cent
Rent, interest, profits	2,811	34.4
Salaries [1]	1,366	16.8
Wages	2,909	35.5
Pay and allowances to armed forces and auxiliary services	1,086	13.3
Total National Income	8,172	100.0

Thus about 35% of Britain's income went to the class living on interest, rent, and profits, while less than 50% went to wage-earners and men and women in the armed forces. As to the size of this rent-interest-profit group, Daniels and Campion in their study of *The Home Market* give figures showing that 80% of the property in Great Britain is owned by approximately 6% of the population over the age of 25, while more than 77% of the population own less than 5% of the property. They estimate further that there are 66,000 people over 25 who each own property worth more than £25,000 — i.e., three-tenths of one per cent of the British population over 25 own more than two-fifths of the country's total property.[2] It is this group, naturally, that receives the largest share of rent, interest, and profits.

This highly uneven distribution of wealth is further illustrated by the figures for the distribution of private income during 1942–43, as given in the White Paper quoted above:

Size of Income	Number of Incomes
Over £10,000	8,000
£2,000–£10,000	102,000
£1,000–£2,000	295,000
£500–£1,000	1,110,000
£250–£500	5,500,000

[1] The figure for salaries in the above table includes sums paid to directors of companies who, in the majority of cases, are also receivers of income from rent, interest, or profits.

[2] Figures in Daniels and Campion are arrived at by the complicated procedure of dividing ages into ten-year groups; i.e. 25–35, 34–45, etc., and by obtaining property ownership statistics from mortality figures. Since mortality rates under 25 are low and under 15 very low, and property held by those under 25 is mainly inherited, figures for this group are not used to obtain the general conclusions here quoted. It is a certainty that, if these figures were used, the concentration of property ownership would be still greater.

The White Paper does not include figures for those whose incomes were less than £250. However, the total number employed in Britain was 23¾ million in September 1943. Deducting 7 million (the number of incomes covered in the above table), we get 16¾ million, to which must be added the number of those serving in the armed forces and auxiliary services. This gives us a figure of about 23 million people receiving less than £250 a year. Thus, 8,000 people or approximately one-fortieth of one per cent of all income receivers get more than £10,000 a year; while 23 million people or approximately 77 per cent of all income receivers get less than £250; and an additional 5½ million, or 18% of all income receivers, have incomes of between £250 and £500.[1] Or, to put it differently, there are approximately 100,000 people with incomes greater than £2,000 a year, who each own property worth more than £1,000, and 28,000,000 people who each have an income of less than £500 a year and own property worth less than £100. The 100,000 own about four-fifths of the property of Great Britain, while the 28 million own about 5%. This disparity is increasing, since the small wage-earners are compelled to use their entire income for living expenses, whereas the rent-interest-profit group can use part of their income to increase their investments and thereby their control over the country's wealth.

Is this the standard of living that the entire world is called upon to preserve?

The same British spokesmen who speak so feelingly about the necessity of protecting British standards of living are also those who are most vocal in their fear of American industrial competition in world markets. Yet they have so far made no serious efforts to increase the production efficiency and capacity of the British wage-earners. In their anxiety to secure a favored position for British trade in the colonial areas of the world, they tend to ignore the need for increasing British industrial efficiency. Having lived so long within the secure framework of her empire, Britain has allowed her industrial plant to deteriorate and failed to modernize many of her production methods, with the result that her industrial efficiency as measured by production per

---

[1] The earning power of those in the lowest brackets is so low and unemployment is so permanent a feature in peacetime Britain that the return of those in the armed forces to civilian life would not to any appreciable extent modify the statistics here used.

worker is less than half that of the United States. Dr. Leon Rostas, in an article published in the *Economic Journal* (London) for April 1943, concludes that American per capita productivity normally exceeds that of Great Britain by 125%, and the comparison of productivity per man-hour is even less favorable to Britain. The chief cause for this American superiority, in Dr. Rostas's view, is the fact that American industries are far more highly mechanized.

According to an article in the *Economist* (August 19, 1944), Dr. Rostas's conclusion "agrees with other studies on the same subject, and it can be confirmed by the latest figures of national income in the United Kingdom and the United States." The *Economist* points out that "in 1943, when there was full employment in both countries, the output of wealth per head of the population was from 1⅗ to 2½ times as large in America as in Britain (the exact ratio depending on the figure assumed as a fair purchasing power parity between the two currencies). . . . There is little room for doubt that the average American worker produces in an hour from 1½ to 2½ times as much wealth as the average British worker."

Britain's backwardness in many lines of production was brought sharply in focus by the reports submitted by American production experts who visited England in connection with the war effort. Particularly revealing were the reports on textiles, coal-mining, and building. Britain's Cotton Textile Mission itself reported that British per-man-hour production was less than American by from 18 to 49% in spinning, from 80 to 85% in winding, from 79 to 89% in beaming, and from 56 to 67% in weaving. "The average American worker," in the words of the report, "produces from one and a quarter to ten times as much in an hour as the average English worker."' Similar differences exist in the building trades and coal mining. The *Economist* put it clearly when it wrote: "The report on technical methods in the American building industry placed British efficiency in much the same unfavorable light as the textile survey now does for cotton. And a report by American engineers on the technical efficiency of the coal industry is known to be in existence, and is said to be almost equally damning." It is known for example that in the United Kingdom, 700,000 men mine slightly less than 200,000,000 tons of coal annually. In the United States, 550,000 men mine

620,000,000 tons, chiefly because mechanization of mining in America is far more advanced than in Britain.

This weakness in Britain's industrial structure is recognized by many British economists. The *Economist* article of August 19th, for example, deplores the fact that economic postwar planning in Britain appears to be concentrated on attaining (1) full employment — i.e., ensuring that "whatever the size of the national income, its flow is *regular* from year to year," and (2) a more *equitable* distribution of the national income through social security legislation designed to ensure that no citizen shall fall below a minimum standard of welfare. In the *Economist's* opinion, too little attention has been paid to an equally important goal, namely efforts to ensure that the *size* of the national income is increased as much as possible, by increasing the productivity of the British worker.

Similarly, a British economist, E. F. Schumacher, has suggested that technical reorganization in large sections of British industry might increase the supply of goods and services of all kinds by at least 30% or even more, in a fairly short period. Mr. Schumacher raises the question, however, whether British industrialists will be willing to spend enough to effect any such thorough reorganization when capital goods are once more available. He points out that, before the war, many parts of British industry were inadequately equipped with modern machinery and were therefore far less efficient than similar industries in the United States. In 1938, for example, British industrialists spent only $480 million on plant and machinery, of which $400 million went into maintenance and depreciation.

In March 1945, a pamphlet entitled "Tools for the Next Job" was published in London by the Tory Reform Committee. Condemning restrictive agreements and the safety-first attitude of most English business interests, the pamphlet proposed the adoption of a more realistic approach to expansionism. Warning that Britain was in great need of a far-reaching plan for modernizing its industry, the authors called for the expenditure of $32 billion for that purpose in the first six to eight years following the end of the war. But the Tory Reform Committee claimed to have included only one-seventh of the Conservatives in Parliament. One can only conclude that the remaining six sevenths were concerned more with maintaining a controlled profit produced with antiquated equipment than with risking a diminishing accumulation of capital on what they would term a problematical program of modernization.

It is true that the British Government has made some progress toward the goal of a more equitable distribution of national income, although the social-security provisions of the Beveridge Plan have been watered down considerably. There is also no doubt that the goal of full employment is one that any British Government must put foremost in its plans. The Attlee Labor Government is committed to a thoroughgoing program of full employment and extensive social security. But there is as yet no evidence that the majority of Britain's leaders are thinking in terms of expanding their national income both by a thorough modernization of their industrial plant at home and by coöperating actively in the expansion of world economy as a whole. Instead of considering ways and means by which the total volume of world trade could be greatly increased, they appear to be concentrating their efforts on getting as large a share as possible of the trade that can be carried on within the existing world economy.

Britain's control over her empire, and her ability to influence the trade policies of other members of the sterling bloc, unquestionably give her a powerful weapon with which to compete with America in the field of foreign trade, and she would acquire an even stronger weapon if she could place herself at the head of a world-wide imperial bloc embracing the colonial territories of the Netherlands, France, and Belgium. But if she uses that power to restrict American trade within the sterling bloc, and to prevent the colonial territories from developing their own industries so that they may continue to depend on British manufactures, the result will unquestionably be a contraction of the volume of world trade and a correspondingly acute rivalry among the industrial powers. In such a world economy, with the volume of foreign trade curtailed by the continued backwardness and poverty of half the world's population, neither Britain nor America can hope to solve the problem of full employment and rising living standards for its people.

It is understandable that British leaders should fear a powerful American export drive. And it is equally understandable that, in view of Britain's seriously weakened international financial position, she should cling desperately to such short-term advantages as she possesses by virtue of her control over colonial areas. It may be that Britain will choose to use her control over the colonial world as a trade weapon against the United States with all that this involves. But the fact remains that the very power inherent in such control offers Great Britain a more hopeful alternative, one that will not subject the vast majority even of the English people to relative as well as absolute poverty.

This alternative would be to recognize that the colonial areas constitute a potential market that if fully developed would satisfy the export needs of Britain, the United States, and all other industrial powers for many years to come, and that Britain is politically in the best position to take the lead in formulating a program for the development of that market. Instead of dwelling on the alarming possibilities of American trade competition, Britain could invite the United States to coöperate fully in a program designed to raise the living standards of the colonial peoples by a thoroughgoing program of industrial and agricultural development, education, and public health, leading to the attainment of stable, well-rounded economies. Such a program must unquestionably mean the granting of immediate independence to a country like India, and the pledge of ultimate independence to others. In the United States the progressive business and financial interests have sufficient power not only to enlist the full support of the American people for such a program, but also to ensure Great Britain her rightful place in such a world. The best guarantee that such Anglo-American collaboration would prove effective and enduring is that only in such a world can Great Britain and the United States prosper.

CHAPTER XI

THE SOVIET UNION IN THE FAR EAST

❁

No DISCUSSION of the future course of events in Eastern Asia would be complete without some consideration of the policy and interests of the Soviet Union in that part of the world. There is no doubt that the U.S.S.R. must be regarded as a major power in the Pacific as well as in Europe, and that in Asia, as elsewhere, continued Anglo-American-Soviet coöperation would constitute one of the most effective guarantees of lasting peace. A detailed history of Soviet Far Eastern policy would require a volume in itself, but for the purposes of this study we are concerned with Soviet policy only as it relates to the central theme under discussion — i.e., the development of new economic frontiers in the industrially backward countries of Asia, and particularly in China and India. In other words, the question to be considered is whether Soviet policy is likely to be an aid or an obstacle to the development of these potential new frontiers.

In attempting to appraise the probable future course of Soviet policy in Asia, the first and most important fact to be noted is that, unlike the other great industrial powers, the Soviet Union is not faced with the necessity of securing external outlets for surplus capital and production. Because she possesses an economy that is not operated for private profit, the Soviet Union's internal market and standard of living can theoretically develop without periods of recession and depression resulting from the failure of domestic purchasing power to keep pace with increased production. According to Soviet economists, their internal market for goods and capital can never reach a saturation point and therefore they need never seek foreign outlets for capital investment nor attempt to expand their export trade beyond the volume needed to pay for essential imports. The major economic interest of the Soviet Union is not the attainment of new overseas markets, but rather a period of peace and security in which to continue the expansion of her limitless but still largely undeveloped internal market.

There is therefore no need for other powers to fear Soviet economic penetration or commercial rivalry in Eastern Asia; no prospect of Soviet participation in a struggle for markets and investment opportunities. On the other hand, the Soviet Union knows from bitter experience that weak and unbalanced economies are potential war-breeders — a fact conclusively demonstrated by the histories of both China and Japan. It may be assumed, therefore, that the Soviet Government for reasons of national security will take a very keen interest in the types of political and economic systems that emerge in the countries of Eastern Asia so far as they seem likely to contribute to peace or to a renewal of international rivalry and conflict.

The heated debate as to whether or not the Soviet Union should have become an active participant in the war against Japan, a debate that began in 1941 and was intensified after Russia denounced her neutrality pact with Japan on April 5, 1945, caused a great deal of confusion and contributed little to an intelligent understanding of the Soviet Union's role in Far Eastern affairs. There was a widespread feeling that Russia must get into the war against Japan if she expected to have a voice in the Far Eastern peace settlement. Yet, if we had recognized that this was a global war, we should also have recognized that the Soviet Union had done more than its share in achieving victory, and that no form of tortured logic should have deprived her of a voice in the global peace settlement regardless of whether or not her troops had fought on every front. Furthermore, the Soviet Union's role of "armed neutrality" in the Far East was maintained for strictly military reasons that were recognized as sound by all Allied military leaders, and in itself served to immobilize large numbers of Japan's best troops in Manchuria. If Russia had been at war with Japan in 1942, she might well have lost the battle of Stalingrad and with it the war for herself and her allies. Only the Chungking Government was dissatisfied with the well-conceived Allied strategy, and expressed the hope that Russia would attack Japan even while Germany was at the gates first of Moscow and then of Stalingrad. It is significant, however, that by 1944, when there was no longer the slightest prospect of a German victory in Russia, Chinese

Government officials had become fearful of and opposed to Russian participation in the war against Japan, despite their public pronouncements to the contrary.

In marked contrast to the Chinese attitude, both Britain and the United States were eager that the Soviet Union should take an active part in only the final stages of the war in Asia after the defeat of Hitler because they knew that this would shorten the war and save many American and British lives. There was no indication, however, of a willingness on the part of either Britain or America to draw up a Pacific agreement to parallel that reached at Teheran regarding the war in Europe. On the contrary, there was strong evidence that, from the political point of view, the war in Asia was being fought for a return to the pre-war status quo — a reëstablishment of a political and economic system that was the breeding ground for this war and one that cannot but be a breeding ground for the next.

Nevertheless, Soviet Russia acceded to President Truman's request at the Berlin Conference that she join in the war against Japan, and on August 8, 1945 the following announcement was broadcast by Moscow:

After the defeat and capitulation of Hitlerite Germany, Japan became the only great power that still stood for the continuation of the war.

The demand of the three powers, the United States, Great Britain and China, on July 26 for the unconditional surrender of the Japanese armed forces was rejected by Japan, and thus the proposal of the Japanese Government to the Soviet Union on mediation in the war in the Far East loses all basis.

Taking into consideration the refusal of Japan to capitulate, the Allies submitted to the Soviet Government a proposal to join the war against Japanese aggression and thus shorten the duration of the war, reduce the number of victims and facilitate the speedy restoration of universal peace.

Loyal to its Allied duty, the Soviet Government has accepted the proposal of the Allies and has joined in the declaration of the Allied Powers of July 26.

The Soviet Government considers that this policy is the only means able to bring peace nearer, free the people from further sacrifice and suffering and give the Japanese people the possibility of avoiding the dangers and destruction suffered by Germany after her refusal to capitulate unconditionally.

In view of the above, the Soviet Government declares that from tomorrow, that is from August 9, the Soviet Government will consider itself to be at war with Japan.

The almost immediate surrender of Japan gave the anti-Russian cliques in the United States a new opportunity to attack the Soviet Union on the ground that she had joined in the Pacific war at the last minute to share "unjustifiably" in the fruits of victory. This despite of the fact that as far back as Teheran, and again at Yalta, Russia's entry into the war against Japan was reportedly assured. At Yalta, even a time schedule, three months after the defeat of Germany, was set for Russia's attack. That Russia's declaration of war against Japan was the clinching factor in bringing the Pacific war to a rapid end, and thus saved countless American lives, was attested to by Major General Claire Chennault. On August 14 he declared that Russia's entry into the Japanese war was the deciding factor in speeding its end and would have been so even if no atomic bombs had been dropped. General Chennault's comment came as a severe blow to those who endlessly seek an excuse to attack and vilify Russia.

The policy of the Soviet Union toward both China and Japan has been made abundantly clear during the past few years. Beginning in 1937, when Japan launched her drive for the conquest of China, the Soviet Union was one of China's most effective supporters. Not only did Foreign Commissar Litvinov make every effort to secure international support for China, but the material supplies reaching Free China from the U.S.S.R. exceeded those from any other country. In addition, the Soviet Union supplied technical advisers to the Chinese army and air force. At no time since 1937 has Soviet aid gone to the Chinese Communists; all supplies, credits, and technical assistance were given directly and exclusively to the Chungking Government. Following Hitler's invasion of the Soviet Union in June 1941, Russian aid to China was gradually reduced and eventually stopped altogether. This was generally attributed to the fact that Russia needed all her resources for her own struggle against Germany. But it is no longer a secret that the primary reason for this cessation of aid was the political crisis in China, which caused the Soviet Government to fear that Russian supplies might be used by the Chungking regime in civil war rather than against the Japanese.

THE TRUE STORY OF SINKIANG

THERE IS good evidence, however, that the Soviet Union was determined not to intervene in China's internal affairs, and to coöperate with the Chinese Government only if Chungking showed a genuine desire for such coöperation. This attitude was perhaps best exemplified by the remarkable and highly melodramatic events in Sinkiang Province during 1942 and 1943. For centuries, the economic life of Sinkiang, separated from the rest of China by a thousand miles of semidesert, has depended upon trade with Russia. Soviet influence in Sinkiang, however, dated from the early 1930's when Soviet troops assisted the Chinese Governor, Sheng Shih-tsai, to quell a series of internal revolts instigated by the Moslem General Ma Chung-yin. Many commentators have cited this military aid to Sheng Shih-tsai as proof that the Soviet Union was endeavoring to "annex" Sinkiang, but they fail to mention that these disturbances in Sinkiang occurred soon after the Japanese invasion of Manchuria and were, in reality, one move in Japan's campaign to extend her control across North China, Inner Mongolia, and Sinkiang, right up to the Soviet border in Russian Turkestan.

Determined to prevent Japanese infiltration into Sinkiang, the Soviet Union followed up its initial military assistance to Sheng Shih-tsai with economic and technical aid in establishing a number of joint Sino-Soviet industrial enterprises. Commercial agreements involving substantial Russian loans were concluded between the provincial authorities and the Soviet trade agency, Sovsintorg, and Soviet technical advisers were employed in the fields of education, public health, agriculture, transport, and industry. During the ten-year period from 1933 to 1943, Sinkiang became one of the most advanced provinces in China in its economic development and educational system and in the democratic character of its government.

Governor Sheng Shih-tsai retained for himself, as head of the Anti-Imperialist Society, complete control of political propaganda in the province, and the Chinese Communist Party was not permitted to exist as a mass party or to carry on propaganda in Sinkiang. Many important officials in Sinkiang, however, were Communists, including Sheng's brother, General Sheng Shih-chi, commander of the Sinkiang mechanized First Division. Governor Sheng worked in close coöperation with them as with all popular movements that developed in the province. In fact, Governor Sheng Shih-tsai himself applied for admission to the Communist Party, but strangely enough he applied not to the Chinese Communists but to the Russian Communist Party. When he was informed that there was no such membership for other than Soviet citizens and that he must apply to the Communist Party of China, he took no further action.[1]

Throughout this period, the Chinese Government looked with great suspicion on developments in Sinkiang, and brought strong pressure to bear on Sheng Shih-tsai to turn against the Soviet Union. Recognizing that Sinkiang's economic welfare depended on a friendly relationship with Russia, Sheng Shih-tsai ignored these attempts for a considerable period. But in the spring of 1942, when the Nazi armies were driving across Russia toward Stalingrad and many military commentators were predicting the Soviet Union's imminent collapse, Sheng Shih-tsai apparently decided that, in view of the possibility of a Russian defeat, it would be advisable to strengthen his relations with Chungking, and therefore suddenly ordered his brother, General Sheng Shih-chi, to expel the Russian advisers and other Soviet citizens from Sinkiang. His brother refused to obey this order and his refusal was supported by the entire cabinet. It is reliably reported that Governor Sheng Shih-tsai's father-in-law and close adviser then demanded that Sheng Shih-tsai execute his brother. But at a family gathering, Sheng could not bring himself to do the shooting, so his father-in-law followed Sheng Shih-chi into the courtyard and shot him. This was the signal for a violent anti-Soviet campaign in which the assassination was laid at the door of "scheming Soviet citizens." Shortly thereafter, Madame Sheng Shih-chi was executed, after a secret trial, for the killing of her husband. For foreign consumption, Chungking propagandists claimed that Madame Sheng Shih-chi was Russian and the center of a ring of Soviet plotters. In reality, however, she was not Russian but Chinese, and furthermore she was in no way involved in the internal affairs of Sinkiang; she was simply a convenient scapegoat.

---

[1] The facts for this story of events in Sinkiang were gathered from a variety of sources: from Theodore White's reports in *Time* for January 1944; from the unpublished sections of some American correspondents' despatches; from interviews with returned American observers in China; from Chinese newspapers of the period; and from the author's own contacts in China. A more exact description of sources is impossible because of the danger of reprisals against them by the Chinese Government.

There then ensued a remarkable series of journeyings between Chungking and Tihwa, capital of Sinkiang, as the Chungking Government quickly took advantage of the situation to establish its control over Sinkiang. In May 1942, General Chu Shao-liang (Commander-in-Chief of the 8th War Zone, which includes Sinkiang) visited Tihwa to investigate the situation. On July 4, he returned accompanied by a delegation including General Mao Peng-chu, General Ho Ching-wu, and Dr. Weng Wen-hao, Chinese Minister of Economics. This delegation is reported to have accomplished the twofold task of establishing Kuomintang authority in Sinkiang and completely alienating Sheng Shih-tsai from the Soviet Union, although no publicity was given to its activities at the time. At the end of August 1942, another Chungking delegation reached Tihwa with a full fanfare of publicity to confirm and celebrate the entry of Sinkiang into the Kuomintang fold. This second delegation included Madame Chiang Kai-shek; General Chu Shao-liang; General Mao Peng-chu; Liang Han-tsao, the Vice-Minister of the Political Bureau of the Military Affairs Commission; and Chaucer H. Wu, Special Commissioner for Foreign Affairs at Tihwa.

There remained, however, the problem of justifying the sudden anti-Soviet orientation of Sinkiang's policy without admitting that Nazi victories had emboldened the Chinese Government to challenge Russian influence. It is significant that on August 28, 1942, the day before Madame Chiang's arrival, a general arrest of Communist and "Leftist" officials was ordered, and that, after her visit, the records of Madame Sheng Shih-chi's "trial" were sent to Chungking, where it was claimed that these records revealed a "Communist plot" to hand over Sinkiang to the Soviet Union. It may be noted that there was a lapse of at least five months before the news of the "dangerous plot" allegedly discovered at Madame Sheng's trial was passed on to the Chinese Government — a fact which is conclusive evidence that the idea of a "Communist plot" in connection with the assassination of Sheng Shih-chi did not arise until after the visits of the various Chungking delegations. The highly ironic climax to the whole affair was the official account of Sheng Shih-chi's death, published in the Sinkiang Jih Pao on November 15, 1942, which stated that in recognition of General Sheng's meritorious services to his country he had been posthumously promoted to the rank of Lieutenant-General and accorded a public burial.

During the winter and spring of 1943, the Chinese authorities in Sinkiang continued their strongly anti-Russian policy, and in April 1943 Central Government troops from General Hu Tsung-nan's command, together with planes and heavy field guns, were sent into Sinkiang, apparently in the belief that despite the victory of Stalingrad, the Nazis' summer offensive would make it safe for China to indulge in open provocations against the Soviet Union. Incidentally, it is reported that many of the Chinese troops that entered Sinkiang at this time were under the impression that they were going to fight against the Soviet Union.

One reason for telling the story of Sinkiang in some detail is that it illustrates the violently anti-Soviet attitude of the Chung-king regime. But its chief importance lies in its sequel, namely the action taken by the Soviet Union in response to extreme Chinese provocation. If, as so many people insist, the Soviet Government is really interested in interfering in the affairs of other countries, this was certainly an ideal occasion for more than a series of protests against the unwarranted accusations of "a Communist plot against Chinese unity" and the persecution of Soviet citizens in Sinkiang. Actually, however, the Soviet Union took the very opposite stand. Early in May 1943 the Soviet Government notified Chungking of its intention to withdraw not only the small force of Soviet troops stationed at Hami, but also all Soviet experts and advisers, and all Soviet-supported economic enterprise from Sinkiang. *Sovsintorg* was dissolved, every item of Russian industrial equipment was taken back into the Soviet Union, and trade with Russia, on which Sinkiang's economic life had depended for centuries, came to a virtual halt.[1]

Two reasons have been given for Russia's decision to withdraw

[1] An interesting sidelight on the intricacies of Kuomintang politics is provided by the following report from an eminently reliable source: During his visit to Tihwa, Weng Wen-hao was requested by Sheng Shih-tsai to send a group of Chinese technicians to Sinkiang to replace the Soviet technicians who had previously aided in the operation of Sinkiang's industries. Despite the fact that China could ill afford to spare such technically trained men, this request was granted, and a small staff was sent, headed by Lin Chi-yung, an American-educated engineer. Sheng Shih-tsai immediately appointed Lin as Commissioner of Industry, but in 1943 Lin and his entire staff were arrested and were not released until January 1945 when Lin was appointed Commissioner of Foreign Affairs of Sinkiang. These arrests were reported to have been carried out by the secret police of the "CC" clique, which leaves no stone unturned to preserve its control of the Kuomintang Party, and which has always feared the influence of the Political Science group of which Weng Wen-hao is a member.

from Sinkiang: first, the fact that there was no longer any danger of Japanese infiltration, and second, the desire to demonstrate conclusively that the Soviet Union had no territorial designs on China. It seems certain, however, that the Soviet Government would not have taken the drastic step of severing all economic relations with Sinkiang if it had not been made to feel that this was the only way to avoid open conflict with the Chungking regime. Thus, though the matter was settled peacefully, it also demonstrated the inability of the Chungking Government to deal constructively with its great neighbor, to the detriment of the economic welfare of Sinkiang.

In concluding the story of Sinkiang, some reference must be made to the affair of the Kazakhs in the Altai region of Sinkiang. Late in 1943, some Kazakhs fled from Sinkiang across the border into Outer Mongolia in protest against an attempt by the Chinese authorities to evacuate them to southern Sinkiang. Chinese troops pursued the Kazakhs across the border and Chinese planes strafed Outer Mongolian villages. The Soviet Union protested, and the incident was seized upon in many quarters as proof that the Soviet Union still harbored designs on Sinkiang and was supporting the Kazakhs against the lawful Chinese authorities. In reality, the Kazakh revolt was merely an extension of the peasant rebellion in Kansu Province, described previously as a revolt directed solely against the Chinese officials for their brutal methods of conscription and taxation. It represented only the most recent phases of a long-standing antagonism between the Chinese and the Mohammedan nomads of the Northwest, whose grazing land was being continually appropriated for the use of Chinese farmers.

During Sheng Shih-tsai's regime, there was comparatively little racial antagonism in Sinkiang, where only about 10% of the population are Chinese or Chinese-speaking and the majority are closely related to the Kirghiz, Kazakhs, Uigurs, Uzbeks, and other Mohammedan peoples of Soviet Central Asia. When the Chungking Government assumed control in Sinkiang, however, many of the educational and social policies developed during the preceding decade were abandoned or reversed, and the old antagonisms immediately reappeared. The Kazakhs rebelled against the Chinese plan to evacuate them from their fertile grazing lands in the North to the arid southern districts of the province, which are virtually starvation areas, and some took refuge across the border in Outer Mongolia. Others continued their rebellion within the province, and in December 1944 it was reported from Sinkiang that the Kazakhs had captured the Chinese airfield at Ining and blocked the motor road from Alma-Ata to Tihwa at Erhtai, and later captured Ili. By May 1945 the situation in Sinkiang was "very serious." Thus, despite all efforts to present the border incident of 1943 as a Soviet plot, it is clear that it reflected only the inability of the Chinese Government to deal constructively with its problem of racial minorities.

The Soviet Union's determination not to interfere in Chinese affairs was reasserted by Foreign Commissar Molotov in an interview with Donald Nelson on August 31, 1944, when the latter was in Moscow en route to Chungking. Mr. Molotov recalled how the Soviet Union, through its famous Tass release of December 1936, had helped to save Chiang Kai-shek's life when he was kidnaped by Chang Hsueh-liang at Sian by denouncing the kidnaping as a pro-Japanese move and as a move that would be disastrous for Chinese unity. He stressed this incident as proof that, as far back as 1936, the Soviet Union was primarily concerned with the preservation of Chinese unity under Chiang Kai-shek. He added that, despite every effort on the part of the Soviet Union, the Chinese Government had shown no interest in strengthening relations between the two countries, which had in reality deteriorated in recent years. Molotov also stressed the fact that the Soviet Union cannot be held responsible for any internal developments in China. In concluding the interview, he stated that the Soviet Union would be glad to see the United States take a lead economically, politically, and militarily in Chinese affairs, and added that until Chiang Kai-shek and the Chungking Government showed by changes in their policies that they desired to improve Sino-Soviet relations, the Soviet Government did not intend to take the first step.

At the end of 1943, when the defeat of Nazi Germany and Japan seemed assured, the Chungking Government belatedly attempted to appear friendly to the Soviet Union. On October 10th, an article by Chaucer H. Wu, entitled "A Survey of Future Sino-Soviet Relations," was published in the *Sinkiang Jih Pao*. In this article, Mr. Wu dwelt at length on China's and Russia's joint responsibility for the "surveillance" of Japan and maintenance of peace in the Far East, the long common boundary between the two countries, and the strong economic ties, and concluded with a plea for the "development of still more intimate friendship."

In Chungking, too, there appeared press comments friendly to the Soviet Union. On September 19, in the Chinese language daily, *China Times*, and on September 22 in the English language daily, *National Herald*, editorials were published stressing the need for closer Sino-Soviet coöperation and even expressing the belief that Soviet participation in the Pacific war is essential in order to ensure the complete destruction of Japan's military power. (The *National Herald* is owned and controlled by the Ministry of Foreign Affairs and edited by Percy Chen, and the *China Times* is owned by H. H. Kung.) For the next year and a half there appeared a steady stream of editorial comments in the Kuomintang press expressing friendship for the Soviet Union. The Chungking press, however, is well known for its ability to publish editorial pronouncements that have no basis in actual government policy. In reality, there were no changes in Chinese policy that indicated any desire to improve Sino-Soviet relations.

Yet despite Russia's awareness of Chungking's basic animosity toward her, a Sino-Soviet treaty of friendship and alliance was signed on August 14, 1945. The main terms of this thirty-year treaty were as follows: (1) joint action against a resurgent Japan; (2) non-interference in the internal affairs of the two respective countries; and (3) mutual economic assistance in the postwar period. Five supplementary agreements, designed to implement the general pact, embodied the following provisions: The Chinese Eastern and South Manchuria railways are to be operated jointly. The Manchurian harbor city of Port Arthur is to be used jointly as a naval base. The Manchurian city of Dairen is to be established as a free port open to all nations but administered by China. The Soviet Union reaffirms Chinese sovereignty in Manchuria and stipulates withdrawal of Soviet forces within three months. China recognizes the independence of the Outer Mongolian Republic, to be determined by plebiscite. The Soviet Union reaffirms Chinese sovereignty in Sinkiang Province. The Soviet Union pledges moral and military assistance to the National Government of China. The moderation of these terms, which came as a surprise to certain sections of foreign opinion, was merely added proof that it was not the Soviet Union that was responsible for the lack of amity between Chungking and

Moscow. That the treaty, however, did not mark any alteration in the Russian attitude toward China's internal problems was indicated by an editorial in *Red Star* on August 29, 1945, which stated: "The treaty concluded between China and the USSR is of tremendous importance. . . . China can no longer be a backward, semi-feudal country. . . . Any attempt to lead China along a path of reaction will be opposed by the democratic forces of China. The only path for her is progressive democratic development in close coöperation with other great democratic powers."

SOVIET POLICY TOWARD JAPAN

As FAR AS Japan is concerned, there can be no question that the Soviet Union has bitter memories of Japanese aggression, dating back to the Russo-Japanese war of 1904–5 and more particularly to the brutal character of Japanese intervention in Siberia following the Russian Revolution. Nor was there any doubt that, despite the Russian-Japanese neutrality pact signed in April 1941, the two countries were aligned on opposite sides of the world struggle, a fact conclusively proved in the Soviet Union's statement notifying Japan of its denunciation of the pact, and again in her war declaration of August 8, 1945. Innumerable Soviet newspaper comments and official statements gave concrete evidence that Russia regarded Japan as an aggressor nation and looked forward to her decisive defeat as part of the common triumph of the United Nations. As early as December 1941, only a few months after the signing of the Soviet-Japanese neutrality pact, Ambassador Litvinov did not hesitate to describe Japan as one of the "Axis gangsters" and "the common enemy." The relations of the U.S.S.R. to Japan, he declared, would depend on the common need. "I am sure that complete understanding exists among the three Allies as to which of them should concentrate its greatest efforts on which sector. . . . We are all in the same war."

Despite the strict diplomatic neutrality maintained by the Soviet Union toward Japan from 1941 to 1945, the history of Soviet-Japanese relations since 1931 reveals clearly that the Soviet Union has been a determined opponent of Japanese aggression on the mainland of Asia. The Soviet press has never hesitated to recall Japanese aggression against Russia in 1904–5, in 1918–25, and from 1931 to 1939 when on at least two occasions the "border incidents" between the two countries threatened to develop into large-scale warfare. According to all Soviet writings on the subject, aggressor nations must be so handled as to prevent any recurrence of their aggression, and thus it may be assumed that the Soviet policy regarding the question of the postwar treatment of Japan will have as its primary objective the creating of a peaceful Japan that will once and for all relinquish its predatory designs on Russia's Far Eastern territories.

It may also be assumed that the Soviet Union is not concerned with the type of government that is established in Japan so long as it is not reactionary and aggressive. As was pointed out in an earlier chapter, Susumu Okano, who heads the Japanese People's Emancipation League at Yenan, was for many years an important member of the Communist International. Certainly, if the pathological haters of the Soviet Union were correct in their contentions concerning the Soviet Union's designs to "bolshevize" Asia, Okano would be a highly useful tool for Moscow to use in an attempt to promote a revolutionary or Communist Japan. But, as Okano's program for postwar Japan reveals, the aims of the Emancipation League are confined to the establishment of a genuinely democratic government, and its economic program stops far short of any socialization of industry or agriculture.

As in the case of China, so with reference to Japan, Soviet policy indicates that the primary aim of the U.S.S.R. is that her neighbors be peaceful, stable, and democratically controlled, in order that they may not again serve as breeding grounds for international conflict. It seems obvious that the interests of the Soviet Union in Asia would be best satisfied by the emergence of a united China engaged in building an expanding economy and strong enough to prevent even the subtlest forms of foreign domination; a democratic Japan enjoying opportunities for peaceful participation in the economic development of Eastern Asia; an expanding world economy and a series of international agreements that would permit both England and the United States to maintain and raise the living standards of their people without resorting to cut-throat commercial competition, colonial monopolies, and the maneuvers of power politics. It may be assumed that the weight of Soviet influence will be exerted in support of the emergence of this type of international order in Eastern Asia in the future, since under these circumstances the Soviet Union would not have to fear the development of an anti-Soviet coalition and could proceed in peace and security with the task of developing her own resources and raising the living standards of her people.

At the present writing, however, there is clearly no assurance that this type of international order will, in fact, emerge in the Far East. China, though theoretically free, may remain weak and disunited, with a government that retains a strongly anti-Soviet bias, in which event she would not only be subject to economic domination by foreign powers but would also constitute a potential source of danger to the U.S.S.R. Then too, as we have seen, there is the possibility that Japan may be left under the control of an expansionist-minded ruling class whose primary aim will be to rebuild Japanese strength for a renewed attempt at foreign conquest, particularly if Western colonial monopolies continue to block normal economic development for Japan and if a weak China presents itself as a constant temptation to Japan's rulers. Finally, there is certainly a strong likelihood that international economic relations in Asia will continue to be characterized by the existence of a large, impoverished colonial population and by acute commercial rivalries among the great powers, with political stability and security complicated further by increasingly powerful revolutionary movements in the colonial countries. Under such conditions, it is safe to assume that the Soviet Union would retain a high degree of armed strength in Asia, and would itself join in the game of power politics to prevent the thing it most fears — the development of an anti-Soviet coalition among those powers that are determined to suppress the development of popular democratic forces in the areas under their control. Those who are seeking to restore the prewar balance of power in Asia because they fear the rise of a strong and influential Russia would do well to remember that two can play at power politics, and that the Soviet Union has shown itself to be nothing if not realistic when it comes to a question of protecting its national security.

ANGLO-AMERICAN-SOVIET COÖPERATION

ANY OBJECTIVE analysis of Soviet aims and interests leads to the conclusion that there is ample ground for close and continued American-Soviet coöperation in Asia. Both countries stand to benefit from the emergence of a strong, united, and economically prosperous China and a peaceful, democratically-controlled Japan. Both stand to lose if China remains weak and backward, and if Japan retains an autocratic and aggressive government coupled with an oppressive and top-heavy economic structure. Similarly, both Russia and the United States, for different reasons, stand to gain from a program designed to aid the colonial territories in attaining economic and political freedom, and, conversely, both stand to lose from the retention of the colonial system, with its depressing effect on world economy and its tendency to breed internal dissension and international conflict.

This does not mean, of course, that it will be easy for America and the Soviet Union to reach an agreement with regard to postwar policy in Eastern Asia. There are still serious obstacles of mutual suspicion and distrust to overcome. But it does mean that, to answer the question raised at the beginning of this chapter, Russian policy is likely to be an aid rather than an obstacle to the development of the formerly backward countries of Asia as new economic frontiers for the industrial nations of the world for two reasons: first, because the security of the Soviet Union is bound up with the attainment of world-wide peace and prosperity; and second, because she has no stake in the preservation of these countries in their former impoverished and dependent status.

The greatest single obstacle to coöperation among the "Big Three" in any program for political and economic progress in postwar Asia seems likely to be Britain's attitude on the colonial question, for it is at this point that the aims and interests of the three powers are most widely divergent. It is with regard to the colonial areas that, on the one hand, Anglo-American trade competition is likely to assume its most acute form, and, on the other hand, fear of the influence of Russian revolutionary thought will be most pronounced. It is certain, therefore, that the maintenance of Anglo-American-Soviet coöperation in the postwar period will involve far more complex and difficult problems in Asia than in Europe. The continued existence of an imperialist system that does not serve the best interests of the United States and the Soviet Union, and that seems likely to prevent the attainment of security and economic welfare for themselves and the rest of the world, must of necessity create obstacles to effective coöperation among the three great powers.

The key to a successful solution of this problem lies in China. It is more than a political platitude to say that a strong, united, and economically progressive China is essential for the future peace and prosperity of the Far East. If America, Russia, and such a China could coöperate in the development of the Chinese economy to the point where China can provide not only for the welfare of her own people but also a large and expanding market for the goods of all industrial nations, this would do more than any form of treaty or agreement to convince Britain that it was both feasible and desirable to abandon the old-style system of colonial exploitation and would thus remove a major barrier to effective Anglo-American-Soviet collaboration in the building of a new and enduring structure of world peace and security.

MEETING THE CHALLENGE

✾

THERE CAN BE no permanent peace unless the emerging international political structure is supported by a world economic system better than that which produced widespread poverty and political enslavement, a continuous series of revolutions, and two World Wars within a single generation, the second far more devastating than the first. The United Nations Charter and Bretton Woods constitute absolutely essential first steps toward the setting up of a framework on which to build continued international coöperation. But by themselves they are not sufficient to establish the basis for a lasting peace. Economic obstacles can too easily obstruct political collaboration. It is not enough to create the machinery for joint action against aggression and for patching up the broken-down parts of the existing world economic structure, without doing anything to remove the potential sources of international conflict. No matter how many arrangements are made to regulate the existing volume of world trade, to rehabilitate the shattered economies of liberated countries, or to allocate markets and investment opportunities among the various powers in order to avoid commercial conflict, the fact remains that a *deliberately restricted* world economy in which half the world's population is compelled to live at a bare subsistence level will inevitably breed future strife.

Both the United States and Great Britain are seeking ways and means to achieve full employment and enhance the economic and social welfare of their people. But by and large neither American nor British leaders have shown a willingness to recognize that these goals cannot be attained within the existing narrow world economic structure. Temporary American financial assistance to Great Britain and other industrialized countries in order that they may rebuild their weakened economies is unquestionably important. But it cannot serve as a substitute for a program designed to increase the total volume of the world's wealth and thus provide all nations with expanding opportunities for production and trade.

The aim of this study has been to indicate that the only way to create an expanding world economy that can satisfy the needs of America, Britain, and other industrial nations is by large-scale development programs in the hitherto backward and impoverished areas of the world, particularly India and China. Only in this way can we hope to bring about an increase in world purchasing power on a scale sufficient to keep the world's productive facilities fully employed and provide profitable outlets for capital investment.

For India and China, and the other backward areas, such a program would mean rising standards of living for their people, an escape from the oppressive fetters of feudal and semifeudal land systems, and an opportunity to build a strong economic foundation for political democracy and national independence. For the United States, such a program holds out the only long-term hope for the maintenance of full employment and a high level of national income. The enormous financial and industrial resources with which this country has emerged from the war must be put to productive use if we are to avoid a catastrophic depression that will affect not only ourselves but all countries that depend on a prosperous American market. By a long-range program designed to develop the resources and raise the living standards of the Indian, Chinese, and other impoverished peoples, we can create a new and expanding demand for our goods and capital that can never be achieved solely by internal "pump-priming." Similarly, the development of such new and expanding markets holds out by far the best hope for a solution of Britain's serious economic problems. Only an expanding world economy can enable her to achieve the substantial increase in her export trade that is imperative if British standards of living are not to suffer a serious decline. The Soviet Union's interest in such a program is less direct, since she does not depend upon an expanding foreign trade or on foreign capital investment for the prosperity and expansion of her internal economy. But, so far as she is vitally concerned with the maintenance of peace and stability in the world as a whole, Russia too stands to benefit immeasurably from the development of prosperous and expanding economies in the hitherto backward and dependent areas, and the consequent elimination of a major source of international conflict.

Thus the development of "new economic frontiers" in Asia would serve to satisfy the varying needs and desires not only of China and India, but also of America, Britain, the Soviet Union, and all other industrialized nations. It would provide a sound economic basis for the international political agreements that are in the making. Above all, it would remove the threat of disastrous economic rivalry among the major powers, particularly Great Britain and the United States. There is no denying that the achieving of these highly desirable goals constitutes an extremely difficult problem in that it requires a complete break with former political and economic policies toward backward and dependent areas. But fortunately there are available two keys to the solution of this problem: one American, and the other British.

Because of its enormous resources in investment funds and capital goods, the United States is in a position to take the lead in formulating a program for the constructive economic development of the backward areas. It is essential, however, that the future trade and investment policies of the United States be shaped with an eye to the needs of the world as a whole, and not designed merely to protect the short-term interests of individual American business concerns. For, unless American policy on this question is designed primarily with a view to benefiting the peoples of the backward areas, and not to securing special advantages for American trade, there will be no chance of achieving the long-term goal of an expanding world economy. Furthermore, the way in which America fulfills her responsibilities as the major foreign market for many countries — her willingness to absorb increased imports and her ability to maintain a high level of domestic purchasing power — will obviously have an important bearing on whether or not this goal can be attained.

The other key rests in British hands, for Great Britain is in political control of by far the largest colonial area possessed by any country, and there is little doubt that the other imperial powers such as France and the Netherlands will follow the British lead on matters of colonial policy. Britain therefore has it in her power to determine whether the half of the world's population which now lives in colonial subjection shall have a chance to advance to economic and political independence; whether the rich resources of the colonial areas are to be developed for the benefit of the people of those areas, or for a handful of "vested interests" in the mother countries. She, and she alone, can say whether the prewar colonial status quo is to be restored intact, or whether there shall be a genuine "new order" in Asia under which the old ideas of imperialist exploitation will be replaced by new concepts of political and economic progress.

Neither of these two keys can be used separately. Without the assurance of continued American coöperation, Britain cannot be expected to abandon the advantages of imperial control. Without British coöperation, the United States cannot hope to participate in the creation of expanding economies in the colonial areas, since American trade and investment in a colonial world must of necessity be subject to terms laid down by the controlling imperial powers. Used together, however, these two keys could unlock the doors to future world peace and prosperity. Failure to use them will inevitably result in a restoration of the prewar status quo in Asia, and set the stage for intensive commercial rivalries among the major industrial powers competing for a share in a narrow and contracting world market. It will stimulate a revival of the aggressive designs of the less amply endowed nations. It will condemn hundreds of millions of people to a life of poverty and repression. It will produce unemployment and social unrest in both America and Britain. And, finally, it may well start the world on the disastrous downward path toward a third great war.

The world faces the choice between progress and reaction, and the two powers mainly responsible for making that choice are Great Britain and the United States. Will they choose the adventurous path of constructive economic collaboration for developing the backward areas of the world? Or will they turn back once more to the old, well-worn paths of economic nationalism, commercial rivalry, and the struggle for larger and larger shares of trade in an ever-contracting world economy?

As far as the American people are concerned, they have proved that they can meet the challenge of aggression with courage, ability, and determination. They have also learned that in war they need the help and coöperation of the people of other nations to ensure their own national security. Will they meet the challenge of maintaining peace in the same way and with the same understanding? Admittedly, the obstacles are many and serious, but they are not insuperable. Perhaps the greatest single obstacle lies in our anxiety to put the hardships and difficulties of the war years behind us, and to grasp at all opportunities for immediate prosperity regardless of the effects of our actions on the people of other countries. There is danger that the American people as a whole may forget too easily the lessons learned during the war. If they succumb to this temptation, the direction of America's future policy will be left in the hands of those who cherish the illusion that the United States can and should play a lone hand. This group includes the "expansionists," who are out to grab as big a share as possible of the world's commerce for the United States, and also the "economic nationalists," who believe that American prosperity can be attained by purely domestic measures and does not depend on the prosperity of other parts of the world. Either of these policies, or a combination of the two, would lead us backward to disaster, and would also confirm the British view that it is impossible to rely on American coöperation and that therefore the only alternative is to create the strongest possible imperial bloc with which to compete economically with the United States.

If they are successfully to meet the challenge of maintaining peace, the American people must not be deluded into believing that with the end of the military phase of the war their problems are solved. They must become a strong and active democratic force in their own country. They must make their wishes heard against the powerful voices of both the "American Century" variety of expansionists and the "isolationists" in whatever form they may appear. To safeguard their future welfare and security, they must insist that their government coöperate with other nations, not only in setting up machinery to prevent aggression, but also in building the kind of world economic structure that will give to all peoples of the world a chance for peaceful progress.

INDEX

❄